D0208933

Gender and Global Restructuring

How does gender affect global restructuring and vice versa? What are the gendered effects of globalization on women's and men's lives in different parts of the world? What are the connections among various forms of women's resistance to global restructuring? These and many other questions are thoroughly analyzed in this pioneering collection.

Taking us beyond the narrow limits of conventional approaches to globalization, this book reveals the complexities and contradictions inherent in ongoing global restructuring. Gender analysis reveals the simultaneous restructuring of states, markets, civil society, households, and gender identities in differing national and regional contexts – changes which profoundly affect the daily lives of women and men.

What sets this volume apart from a growing literature on gender and globalization is that it extends and complicates how we think, what we look for, and what we do in relation to global restructuring by highlighting the interactions among the material, ideological, and subjective dimensions of global restructuring. It also foregrounds women's agency in terms of reinterpreting, resisting, and redirecting restructuring.

Marianne H. Marchand is Senior Lecturer in the department of Political Science and a member of both the Research Centre for International Political Economy and the Belle van Zuylen Institute for Comparative Gender and Multicultural Studies at the University of Amsterdam. She is the co-editor of *Feminism/Postmodernism/Development*, also published by Routledge, and of the Routledge/RIPE Studies in Global Political Economy.

Anne Sisson Runyan is Director of the Women's Studies Program and Associate Professor in the department of Political Science at Wright State University, USA. She is the co-author of the first and second editions of *Global Gender Issues*, and on the editorial boards of *International Politics* and the Rowman and Littlefield New Millennium Book series.

Both editors are on the editorial board of the *International Journal of Feminist Politics*, also published by Routledge.

Routledge/RIPE Studies in Global Political Economy

Series editors: Otto Holman, Marianne H. Marchand and Henk Overbeek

Research Centre for International Political Economy, University of Amsterdam

This series, published in association with the *Review of International Political Economy*, provides a forum for current debates in international political economy. The series aims to cover all the central topics in IPE and to present innovative analyses of emerging topics. The titles in the series seek to transcend a state-centred discourse and focus on three broad themes:

- the nature of the forces driving globalisation forward
- resistance to globalisation
- the transformation of world order.

The series comprises two strands:

Routledge/RIPE Studies in Global Political Economy is a forum for innovative new research intended for a high-level specialist readership, and the titles will be available in hardback only. Titles include:

1 Globalization and Governance
Edited by Aseem Prakash and Jeffrey A. Hart

2 Nation-states and Money
The past, present and future of national currencies
Edited by Emily Gilbert and Eric Helleiner

The *RIPE Series in Global Political Economy* aims to address the needs of students and teachers, and the titles will be published in hardback and paperback. Titles include:

Transnational Classes and International Relations
Kees van der Pijl

Gender and Global Restructuring
Sightings, sites and resistances
Edited by Marianne H. Marchand and Anne Sisson Runyan

Gender and Global Restructuring

Sightings, sites and resistances

305.42
628 m
2000

Edited by
**Marianne H. Marchand
and Anne Sisson Runyan**

London and New York

First published 2000
by Routledge
11 New Fetter Lane, London EC4P 4EE

Simultaneously published in the USA and Canada
by Routledge
29 West 35th Street, New York, NY 10001

Routledge is an imprint of the Taylor & Francis Group

Selection and editorial matter © 2000 Marianne H. Marchand and
Anne Sisson Runyan. Individual chapters © the contributors.

Typeset in Baskerville by Taylor & Francis Books Ltd
Printed and bound in Great Britain by Biddles Ltd, Guildford and King's
Lynn

All rights reserved. No part of this book may be reprinted or
reproduced or utilised in any form or by any electronic,
mechanical, or other means, now known or hereafter
invented, including photocopying and recording, or in any
information storage or retrieval system, without permission in
writing from the publishers.

British Library Cataloguing in Publication Data
A catalogue record for this book is available from the British Library

Library of Congress Cataloging in Publication Data
Gender and global restructuring : sightings, sites and resistances /
edited by Marianne H. Marchand and Anne Sisson Runyan.
(Routledge/RIPE studies in global political economy)
Includes bibliographical references and index.
1. Women–Social conditions–Case studies. 2. International economic
relations. I. Marchand, Marianne H. II. Runyan, Anne Sisson.
III. Series: RIPE series in global political economy
HQ1161.G46 2000
305.42–dc21   99–41531

ISBN 0–415–22174–9 (hbk)
ISBN 0–415–22175–7 (pbk)

For all those who resist inequality and social injustice

Contents

Illustrations

Figures

Tables

Contributors

Julie A. Beck is a doctoral student at the University of California at Santa Cruz, USA. Her research focuses on the moral discourses that shroud US social welfare and criminal policy and state transition. She has taught critical criminology at the University of California and conducted research in Prague on the impact of the transition from communism on Czech women and Gypsies.

Kimberly A. Chang is Associate Professor of Social and Political Psychology at Hampshire College, USA. Her research focuses on dilemmas of identity, place and belonging for women, migrants, expatriates and others who live across borders and between worlds. She has lived and worked in Hong Kong and China for nearly a decade.

Charlotte Hooper completed her doctoral studies in international politics at the University of Bristol, UK and her dissertation, 'Manly states: masculinities, international relations (IR) and gender politics', is under review for publication. She has taught gender politics, gender and social policy, international relations, and international political economy at the University of the West of England and the University of Bristol.

Azza M. Karam is an Egyptian national and a member of the Board of the International Dialogue's Foundation in The Hague. She has set up the Gender and Arab World Programmes at the International Institute of Democracy and Electoral Assistance (International IDEA) in Stockholm, Sweden, and is now lecturing in politics at Queens University, Belfast, Northern Ireland. Her latest publications include: *Women, Islamism and the State* (1997), *Women in Parliament: Beyond Numbers* (1998), and *Transnational Political Islam* (forthcoming).

Eleonore Kofman is Professor of Human Geography at Nottingham Trent University, UK. She has published extensively on migrant women and exclusion in the European Union. She has co-edited *Globalization: Theory and Practice* (Pinter 1996) and is co-authoring *Gender and International Migration in Europe* (Routledge, forthcoming).

Mayke Kromhout is a sociologist and former lecturer at the University of Suriname. At present she is doing PhD research on the socioeconomic effects of the current economic crisis in Suriname on gender relations within households. Her main fields of interest are gender, household relations and bargaining power. She has published *Vrouwen en Economische Crisis* (Women and Economic Crisis) (Leo Victor, 1995) and 'Women and social networking activities' in the *Journal of Social Science Studies* (1995).

Amy Lind is Assistant Professor of Women's Studies at Arizona State University, USA. She is currently completing her manuscript on women's movements and the cultural politics of 'development' in Latin America.

L.H.M. Ling is Senior Lecturer in International Studies at the Institute of Social Studies (ISS), The Netherlands. Her book, *Conquest and Desire: Postcolonial Learning between Asia and the West*, is forthcoming from Macmillan in London and St. Martin's Press in New York.

Marianne H. Marchand is Senior Lecturer in the Department of Political Science and a member of both the Research Center for International Political Economy and the Belle van Zuylen Institute for Comparative Gender and Multicultural Studies at the University of Amsterdam. Her research interests focus on feminist theory and international relations/international political economy as well as the political economy of development (especially Latin America). She has published widely in these areas, including *Feminism/Postmodernism/Development* (with Jane L. Parpart). In addition, she is the co-editor of the RIPE Series in Global Political Economy (Routledge).

Yumiko Mikanagi is Associate Professor in the Division of Social Sciences at the International Christian University, Japan. She is the author of *Japan's Trade Policy: Action or Reaction?* (Routledge, 1996); 'Japan's gender-biased social security system' (*Japan Forum* 1998) and 'Gender and Public Policy', in *Political Psychology in Japan* (Nova Science Publishers, 1999). She is currently working on a book entitled *Josei to Seiji* (*Women and Politics*) (Shin Hyōron).

Valentine M. Moghadam is Director of Women's Studies and Associate Professor of Sociology at Illinois State University, USA. She was previously a senior researcher with the United Nations University. Born in Iran, she has published extensively on women, work, and social change in the Middle East, North Africa and Afghanistan. Her current research interests include globalization and transnational feminism.

Anne Sisson Runyan is Director of Women's Studies and Associate Professor of Political Science at Wright State University, USA. She is the co-author (with V. Spike Peterson) of the first and second editions of *Global Gender Issues* (Westview Press, 1993 and 1999) and has been published widely in world politics and women's studies books and journals on gender/feminism and IR theory, transnational social movements, global governance and global restructuring. Her current interests include shifts in feminist theorizing in the context of global restructuring.

Deborah Stienstra teaches International Relations and Women's Studies at the University of Winnipeg. She has published two books, including *Women's Movements and International Organizations* (Macmillan, 1994). She has also published articles on gender and foreign policy, the Internet, prostitution and disability, and international relations.

Jacqui True is a doctoral candidate in the Department of Political Science, York University, Canada. She is currently writing a dissertation entitled 'Engendering transformations: re-constructing states and civil societies in post-socialist Europe' on the role of gender in the systemic changes in East-Central Europe. She has published several articles and chapters in, for example, the *Review of International Political Economy* and *Theories of International Relations* (2000, 2nd edn).

Gillian Youngs is an international political economist lecturing at the Centre for Mass Communication Research at the University of Leicester, UK. Her research areas include feminist perspectives on globalization and changing state/market relations. She was based in Hong Kong between 1995 and 1997 when she conducted research on the political economy its transition to Chinese sovereignty. She is co-editor with Eleonore Kofman of *Globalization: Theory and Practice* (Pinter, 1996). Her other publications include *International Relations in Global Age: A Conceptual Challenge* (Polity Press, 1999) and an edited collection, *Political Economy, Power and the Body: Global Perspectives* (Macmillan, 1999).

Series editors' preface

The international political economy is commonly studied through the lens of the states/markets dichotomy. When approached from this perspective, IPE is about the joining together of two distinct universes, that of the market and that of the state. The state remains in essence the state as it is conceptualized in the traditional paradigm in International Relations Theory, i.e. the rational actor faced with the anarchy pertaining in the interstate system. The market is something essentially external to the state, imposing certain constraints, object of attempts at control by states.

Critical approaches to IPE have done much to correct this image. Historical studies show how markets and states have mutually determined each other, and Marxist analyses have defined globalization as the expanding discipline of capital. The restructuring of markets (commodities, finance, labor), the redefinition of the boundaries between 'market' and 'state' (through privatization and liberalization), the neoliberal restructuring and internationalization of the state, the emergence of transnational elites, the resulting processes of social marginalization transnationally, nationally and regionally, these have all received ample attention in critical analyses of the global political economy.

Postmodern writers have argued that critical theory has failed to truly transcend the parameters of the existing world. What these analyses of global restructuring fail to recognize, they argue, is that globalization in fact represents an epochal shift: the transition from the Modern Age to the Global Age, which fundamentally transforms the understanding of our world.

A feminist theory of IPE, argue the authors in *Gender and Global Restructuring*, is uniquely equipped to bridge the divide between critical and postmodern understandings of globalization. The contributions to this volume do this in three distinct ways. Firstly, and most familiarly, they expose and analyze the gendered dimensions of market, state and civil society. They analyze how restructuring processes have affected and continue to affect men and women very unequally, economically and politically as well as culturally. Secondly, several contributors extend this analysis beyond the confines of the more familiar terrain to the symbolisms and metaphors that define masculinity and femininity. Globalization produces new gendered identities through a redefinition of the conditions of exploitation of (especially female) labor. Finally, all contributions are concerned with understanding the ways in which global restructuring implies recasting the boundaries between the public and the private, the state and the market, and many pursue the ways in which gender, class and ethnicity come together in this process to pose new questions about identity and citizenship in the global system.

Beyond these obvious strengths, however, this book's most original contribution is the combination of high level theoretical refinement with a ceaseless search for the sites of resistance which even the most penetrating forms of globalization fail to neutralize, or which are created precisely by the contradictions of the restructuring process itself.

We are convinced that *Gender and Global Restructuring* will stand out as one of the few available studies in IPE of high quality and originality which take gender seriously.

Otto Holman
Henk Overbeek
Amsterdam, September 1999

Acknowledgements

This volume arose out of an international and interdisciplinary conference on 'Gender and global restructuring: shifting sites and sightings', which we co-organized at the University of Amsterdam in May 1995 under the auspices of the Belle van Zuylen Institute for comparative and multicultural gender studies and the Research Center for International Political Economy (RECIPE). We are grateful to the generous funders of that conference, in particular the Belle van Zuylen Institute, the Faculty of Social Sciences at the University of Amsterdam and the Nederlandse Organisatie voor Wetenschappelijk Onderzoek (NWO – The Dutch Organization for Scientific Research), for making the beginnings of this volume possible. In addition, we wish to thank Barbara van Balen, Sarah Richardson and all the Dutch and international students (in particular, the members of the FAIR group) who helped us to organize the conference.

Since that conference, we have had the opportunity to share thoughts and ideas from the evolving manuscript with colleagues in academic and NGO settings (in Bad Böl, New York, San Diego, Vienna, Kansas and back in Amsterdam) and with our students, who have over the years participated in our research seminars. The critical and constructive input of all these friends, colleagues and students has sharpened our analysis and enabled us to develop our ideas more fully. For this support and input, we are very grateful.

Several of the contributors participated in the May 1995 Conference and the rest joined in the project as the volume took shape. Our greatest thanks go to the contributors for their insights, patience, and ongoing support for the project. We also wish to thank V. Spike Peterson, Christine Chin, Henk Overbeek and Otto Holman for their very thoughtful and helpful reviews of the manuscript as well as Vicki Smith, Craig Fowlie, Fintan Power, Eve Daintith and other Routledge staff in London for their assistance in bringing this volume to fruition.

We are particularly indebted to people who were vital to the production of the manuscript at our respective institutions: Marianne Franklin, editorial assistant for the *RIPE Series in Global Political Economy*, kept the project on track with Routledge, and at Wright State University, Connie Jacobs, administrative assistant to the Women's Studies Program, and work-study student Heidi Gerstenberger deserve tremendous credit for their extraordinary clerical support, without which we would have been hard-pressed to compile the manuscript. A faculty development grant from the College of Liberal Arts at Wright State also helped to defray manuscript production costs.

On more personal notes, we owe our deepest gratitude to our partners, Steven Stusek and Albert Adrian Kanters, and our families for all their emotional support. We also thank and celebrate each other for so joyfully engaging in this transcontinental collaboration, building a friendship in the process, and so diligently bringing the work to its conclusion. We can only hope that it will do justice to the many women and men who are progressively resisting and redirecting global restructuring, for whom it was written.

Abbreviations

Alt-WID	Alternatives for Women in Development
CAORC	Council of American Overseas Research Centers
CRIAW	Canadian Research Institute for the Advancement of Women
DAWN	Development Alternatives with Women for a New Era
DINAMU	National Women's Bureau (Ecuador)
EEOL	Equal Employment Opportunity Law (Japan)
ESCWA	UN Economic and Social Commission for West Asia
EU	European Union
EURPS	Employment, Unemployment, Returnees and Poverty Survey (Jordan)
FDI	foreign direct investment
FHH	female-headed household
FISE	Emergency Social Investment Fund (Ecuador)
GI	Global Restructuring I
GII	Global Restructuring II
GBS	General Bureau of Statistics (Suriname)
GDP	gross domestic product
GNP	gross national product
ICHR	International Covenant on Human Rights
ICPD	International Conference on Population and Development
ICT	information and communication technology
IGO	intergovernmental organization
ILO	International Labor Organization
IMF	International Monetary Fund
IPE	International Political Economy
IR	international relations
JEDCO	Jordan Export Development Corporation and Trade Centers
JIT	just-in-time
JNCW	Jordanian National Committee for Women
LDP	Liberal Democratic Party (Japan)
OECD	Organization for Economic Cooperation and Development
M&A	Mergers and Acquisitions
MHH	male-headed household

MOL	Ministry of Labor (Japan)
NAC	National Action Committee on the Status of Women (Canada)
NAFTA	North American Free Trade Agreement
NPS	National Pension System (Japan)
NGO	non-governmental organization
NWA	New Woman Association (Egypt)
RLI	regime of labor intimacy
SAP	structural adjustment policy (Latin America)
TMC	techno-muscular capitalism
TNC	transnational corporation
UK	United Kingdom
UN	United Nations
UNCED	United Nations Conference on Environment and Development
UNCTAD	United Nations Conference on Trade and Development
UNDP	United Nations Development Programme
UNIFEM	United Nations Development Fund for Women
US	United States
USAID	United States Agency for International Development
WASP	White, Anglo-Saxon, Protestant
WIDE	Women in Development Europe
WEDO	Women's Environment and Development Organization (United States)
WTO	World Trade Organization

Introduction

Feminist sightings of global restructuring: conceptualizations and reconceptualizations

Marianne H. Marchand and Anne Sisson Runyan

'Young ladies don't understand political economy, you know', said Mr Brooke, smiling towards Mr Casaubon. 'I remember when we were all reading Adam Smith. *There* is a book now.'

(George Eliot, *Middlemarch*)[1]

Introduction

In this citation from Eliot's influential work, the underlying assumption is that "young ladies" don't understand political economy because they don't have anything to do with it: the world of political economy is far removed from the experiential world and daily lives of young, middle-class women in nineteenth-century Britain. Moreover, as Eliot's character reveals, the dominant view in nineteenth-century Britain was that "young ladies" were too emotionally inclined to be able to discuss matters of political economy rationally.

Times have certainly changed since George Eliot wrote these lines. It is nowadays increasingly recognized that the "world of political economy" and the daily lives of women are no longer (and never have been) two separate worlds. Moreover, about a century after her book was first published, (young) women not only understand, discuss, and analyze political economy, but feminist and gender analyses of international political and economic issues are becoming increasingly prominent as well. The objective of this collection is to continue this tradition by analyzing how globalization, one of the central themes of contemporary international political economy, and gender, as a relation of inequality based on social constructions of masculinity and femininity, are intricately connected.[2]

More specifically, this volume sets out to go beyond conventional representations and interpretations of globalization. Such interpretations tend either to be too narrowly economistic or to focus primarily on changes in the nature of and relationships between the market and the state. In so doing, they pay little attention to attendant global/local restructurings of social, cultural, racial, ethnic, gender, national, and familial identities, roles, and relations. However, as the chapters in this collection illustrate, gender analysis (in its several variations) is particularly well-equipped for developing a better understanding of globalization's multidimensionality.

In its endeavor to reveal the comprehensive and complex nature of globalization through a series of gender analyses, the present collection will focus in particular on three interrelated issues and concerns. First, it intends to develop conceptualizations of globalization or global restructuring (the latter being our preferred term) through applying a gender lens. This includes raising such questions as: What are the gendered constructions of the new global political economy? How can we reconceptualize global space from a gender perspective? These questions imply that global restructuring represents nothing less than the construction, reconstruction, and transformation of categories of knowing, which tend to produce new gender biases as well as reifying others.

The focus of our second concern is on the concrete sites or spaces of global restructuring, such as the state, global city, economy, household, and civil society, in which actors operate and various transformative processes are being articulated. One of the important themes here is that various processes of global restructuring are not occurring in isolation but are connected. Moreover, the articulation of global restructuring processes leads to new forms of inclusion and exclusion, while often exacerbating existing inequalities.

The third concern guiding this research deals specifically with the responses and forms of resistance which global restructuring has evoked. These responses and resistances include a range of activities and strategies as well as oppositional voices, from women's groups and labor and environmental movements. In contrast to the more inclusive transformative agendas of these groups, there is also a more exclusionary, sometimes even violent, resistance mounted against global restructuring. This resistance is most often articulated through ethnic conflict, emerging nationalisms, and religious fundamentalisms. Similar to the questions raised with respect to the other two concerns, the underlying question is what insights does gender analysis provide to make sense of a wide variety of dispersed, isolated responses and resistance practices? Additionally, does gender analysis enable us to formulate, and even advocate, varying kinds of resistance strategies which make sense from a feminist perspective?

In the remainder of this introduction we will further explore these issues and concerns. These same issues will also provide the basis for the organization of the entire collection. As there is still no comprehensive gender analysis of global restructuring or globalization available, this introduction will try to partially fill this gap in the literature by outlining the major elements such an analysis should include. To do so we will first briefly discuss the main issues concerning globalization/global restructuring raised by scholars of international political economy (IPE). The subsequent section will embark upon a gender analysis of global restructuring. Finally, the section on sightings, sites, and resistances will provide more concrete discussions on the connections among these three instances of global restructuring.

Globalization versus global restructuring

Globalization appears to be the buzzword of the 1990s. Over the last few years the number of books and articles on globalization has grown exponentially. Such is its attraction that it is now a research topic in many academic fields, including sociology, international relations, economics, anthropology, geography, and even cultural studies. In addition, globalization has garnered the attention of the media and those involved in policy making.

It is not our intention to provide a full overview of the current state of globalization discussions – the mere scope of the issues raised and the controversial nature of globalization make such a task a daunting, if not impossible, prospect. Instead we intend to outline some of the major issues as well as developments and dispel some of the myths connected to globalization. This will provide a stepping stone for raising gender issues in the context of globalization.

A closer look at the globalization literature reveals a plethora of views and ways of categorizing them. First, it is possible to roughly distinguish two broad traditions or categories which are closely related to various social science disciplines. One tends to focus on the economic (and secondarily, political) aspects of globalization, while the other deals with the cultural and sociological aspects of globalization, such as the purported emergence of a "global village" and the "McDonaldization" of culture.

For a second type of classification it is necessary to peel off the first layer of these broad political-economy and cultural categories; doing so will reveal that each one of them encompasses different positions toward and understandings of globalization. Within the political economy tradition to globalization, for instance, we find various contending discourses. Jan Aart Scholte identifies at least five different positions, including the denial by realist scholars that globalization is occurring, the advocacy of globalization processes by both neoliberals and their reformist counterparts, and the questioning stance of critical poststructuralist and historical materialist scholars (Scholte 1996: 49–53). Within the broad cultural and sociological tradition toward globalization it is possible to distinguish between so-called *homogenizers* and *heterogenizers*. According to Featherstone and Lash:

> The *homogenizers* tend, ideal-typically, to subscribe to some sort of notion of world system. They look primarily at the presence of the universal in the particular, whether as commodification or as time–space distanciation. They would at least implicitly invoke a scenario of convergent development. *Heterogenizers* would tend to dispute that a system existed, will disclaim the distinction of the universal and particular, and see the dominance of the West over the "rest" as that of simply one particular over others.
>
> (Featherstone and Lash 1995: 4)

A third classification is introduced by Kimberly Chang and L.H.M. Ling (see Chapter 1, this volume). While only distinguishing between liberals or advocates and critics of globalization, they try to bridge the gap between the broad polit-ical economy and cultural categories by extending their discussion beyond a narrow IPE interpretation and including questions of global culture and issues of representation in their discussion.

Despite the multiple classifications and perspectives among the representa-tives of various approaches to globalization, there still appears to be a basic agreement on what the important actors, processes, debates, and issues are. The first question concerns the nature of globalization and the extent to which glob-alization is a new phenomenon to be distinguished from previous periods of economic internationalization.

Students of IPE generally agree that (late modern) capitalism is the defining feature of and driving force behind current globalization processes. Peter Dicken, for instance, refers to globalization as "a more advanced and complex form of internationalization which implies a degree of functional integration between internationally dispersed economic activities" (Dicken 1992: 1). David Harvey (1989), in turn, focuses on the time–space compression, which was brought about by the transition to flexible accumulation and for which the mate-rial basis was formed by new information and communications technology. James Mittelman provides one of the most comprehensive definitions of global-ization:

> The manifestations of globalization … include the spatial reorganization of production, the interpenetration of industries across borders, the spread of financial markets, the diffusion of identical consumer goods to distant coun-tries, massive transfers of population within the South as well as from the South and the East to the West, resultant conflicts between immigrant and established communities in formerly tight-knit neighborhoods, and emerging world-wide preference for democracy. A rubric for varied phenomena, the concept of globalization interrelates multiple levels of anal-ysis: economics, politics, culture and ideology.
>
> (Mittelman 1996: 2)

Defining the extent and novelty of globalization depends largely on one's interpretation of its nature and the driving forces behind it. Although there is still some disagreement as to whether globalization represents a new phenomenon, most IPE scholars agree that a significant economic and political transformation has been occurring since the early 1970s.

Second, most analysts agree that firms or transnational corporations (TNCs), states, and financial institutions and actors (i.e. banks, institutional investors, speculators, etc.) constitute the main driving forces behind globalization. Partly in response to the perceived profit squeeze of the 1970s, firms have been searching to improve their competitiveness and expand their reach in terms of market share. They have done so by introducing flexible production methods, integrating their production into global commodity and production chains, transforming their sourcing and location strategies as well as embarking upon strategic alliances with other firms (Ohmae 1990; Dicken 1992; Barnet and Cavanagh 1994; Berger 1996). Likewise, financial markets have undergone a major shift since the 1970s due to the fall of the Bretton Woods system, rapid deregulation of international capital flows, and the introduction of new information and communication technologies (ICTs), which enabled the creation of an integrated global financial system. These developments have raised serious concerns about the stability and soundness of the global financial system, so much so that it is now often likened to a casino (Strange 1986 and 1998). The transformations in both the productive and financial spheres of the economy have significantly undermined the role of the state in economic and monetary policy making ("Sovereignty at Bay" 1991: 189–307; Barnet and Cavanagh 1994; Strange 1996; Germain 1997).

The undermining of state sovereignty is nowadays seen as one of the most significant aspects of globalization. As several IPE scholars (Cox 1994; Helleiner 1994; Gill 1995c; Cerny 1995; Hirst and Thompson 1996; Mittelman 1997) have pointed out, the reduced role of the state in economic matters raises questions concerning democracy and accountability: How democratic are firms and financial institutions? To whom are these actors accountable? How can an increasingly globalized economy be regulated? For Paul Hirst and Grahame Thompson (1996) globalization primarily invokes a (global) governance dilemma. Although they oppose the current hype about globalization and reject the notion that a truly global economy has emerged, Hirst and Thompson assert that economic globalization will have profound consequences for regulatory practices:

> Global socially decontextualised markets would be difficult to regulate, even supposing effective cooperation by the regulators and a coincidence of their interests. The principal difficulty is to construct both effective and integrated patterns of national and international public policy to cope with global market forces.
>
> (Hirst and Thompson 1996: 10)

Stephen Gill (1995c), in turn, focuses on the question of global governance as well. According to him the problem is not so much a lack of governance, but rather the emergence of non-democratic and unaccountable global governance or "new constitutionalism," which must be countered by a cross-conditionality according to which representatives of global civil society provide democratic oversight for international organizations (Gill 1995c 1: 39–42).

Third, it is increasingly recognized that technology, and in particular ICT, has been an enabling and contributing factor to globalization processes: without the advent of computers and other new means of communication, financial markets would, for instance, never have been able to integrate into one global financial market. Likewise, firms' integrated production networks and strategies of just-in-time (JIT) delivery would have been impossible without computers. This has led Manuel Castells, among others, to conclude that a new technological revolution is under way, which is making information (and the processing of information) the product of the production process (1998a: Chapters 1–2, in particular p. 67). This technological revolution is also bringing about fundamental social transformation, creating in Castells' terms, a knowledge-driven network society:

> [which] is made up of networks of production, power and experience, which construct a culture of virtuality in the global flows that transcend time and space. Not all dimensions and institutions of society follow the logic of the network society, in the same way that industrial societies included for a long time many preindustrial forms of human existence.
>
> (Castells 1998c: 350)

Fourth, quite a few scholars emphasize the influence of neoliberal ideology in determining the direction of globalization. In particular the disciplinary nature of neoliberalism is a focal point of attention (Cox 1994; Gill 1995c). According to neo-Gramscians, neoliberal ideology has provided the direction for global transformation processes since the 1970s, leading states to introduce deregulatory policies, liberalize domestic markets, and privatize state enterprises as well as a host of social services (Cox 1994; Gill 1994). Moreover, as neo-Gramscians assert, a transnational class of political, economic, and intellectual elites has been rather effective in spreading neoliberal thought through both intergovernmental institutions like the International Monetary Fund (IMF), the World Bank and the Organization of Economic Cooperation and Development (OECD), and such non-governmental forums as the Trilateral Commission and the Davos World Economic Forum (Cox 1994; Gill 1995c; van der Pijl 1998)

Finally, there is the question of whether globalization leads to a homogenization or universalizing of culture. Most analysts agree that globalization is transforming the familiar organizational structures of society, although there is less agreement on what these changes entail. On the one hand, it is suggested that the extreme concentration of the mass media, the film industry and publishing into the hands of a few companies and individuals is leading to a homogeneous global mass culture (Castells 1998a; Barber 1996; Featherstone 1990; Waters 1995). This is either heralded as the emergence of a so-called "global village" or bemoaned as a thorough-going "global pillage" (see Brecher and Costello 1994). Moreover, global firms are also critical in the further commodification (and homogenizing) of various social and cultural practices as well as in promoting their products globally through clever marketing and advertising strategies (Gill 1995c; van der Pijl 1998). These homogenizing tendencies in the context of larger processes of globalization are fundamentally restructuring society and the ways in which individuals relate the changing meaning structures. On the one hand this leads to the emergence of a network society (Castells 1996), dominated by cosmopolitans (Friedman 1997). On the other hand, there is the suggestion that late modern (or postmodern) capitalism is also accompanied by increased fragmentation, in the form of (radical) individualism (Giddens 1991; Melucci 1997), identity politics (Castells 1997), and various forms of Balkanization or fundamentalism (Friedman 1997; Barber 1996; for further discussion of some of these issues see Chang and Ling, Chapter 1, this volume).

Together, the arguments outlined above are part of a second or critical wave of literature on globalization which is rejecting the narrow economistic and often unquestioning literature of the first wave (Kofman and Youngs 1996: 1). This critical literature is trying to dispel the most prevalent and tenacious myths about globalization which are being produced and reproduced by orthodox (liberal) explanations as well as popularized accounts in the business press. At least four such myths can be distinguished: (1) Globalization is first and foremost an economic process; (2) Globalization is a process generated outside our own (immediate) environment and hence we are unable to influence it; (3) Globalization is a universalizing process and involves a predetermined logic;[3] (4) Globalization is not a new phenomenon.[4]

In particular, the second and third myths, about the structural nature of globalization as well as its universalizing and predetermined logic, send a powerful message: not only is globalization "larger than us," but it cannot be resisted because the outcome has already been determined. In other words, orthodox discursive practices on globalization leave very little room for agency and lead to a feeling of disempowerment as well as alienation.

The second wave of critical approaches toward globalization makes an important contribution to our understanding of globalization first by challenging some of the prevalent myths about it and, second, in emphasizing the role of human agency in producing and resisting it. This critical scrutiny moreover reveals that globalization is a problematic term that has become very fashionable, but obfuscates more than it illuminates and has become associated with a certain (pro-free market) ideology. As Marianne Marchand has argued elsewhere, it is therefore preferable to use the term "global restructuring" over "globalization" since the former term "explicitly refers to a process of (partially) breaking down an old order and attempting to construct a new one" (Marchand 1996: 577). This construction is not necessarily based on some teleological notion of what this new order may entail – the direction and form of the new order under construction are open (Marchand 1996: 577). However, the term global restructuring reflects the notion that we are dealing with a set of multidimensional, multispeed, and disjuncted processes. In the remainder of this introduction we will use the term global restructuring because it also allows us to analyze how the market, state, and civil society are embedded in and (re)constructed through these processes.

Gender and global restructuring

By dispensing with dominant globalization myths and raising the issue of human agency, critical approaches provide an opening for developing critical feminist or gender analyses of globalization, according to Sandra Whitworth (1994a, b) and Jill Steans (1998). However, the problem Whitworth and Steans signal is that most critical IPE authors tend to ignore these openings and thereby forgo the opportunity to enrich and improve their analyses by engaging in a serious dialogue with critical feminist and gender analyses of international political economy. This collection of chapters is part of the effort to foster such a dialogue by specifically showing the multiple ways in which gender plays a role in global restructuring.

Feminist scholars have repeatedly shown that gender operates at various levels at which it intersects with class, ethnicity, race, nationality, and sexuality to produce and reproduce an intricate web of inequalities between and among men and women. In other words, gender can be defined as "socially learned behavior and expectations that distinguish between masculinity and femininity" (Peterson and Runyan 1999: 5). Gender operates in at least three distinct, yet interconnected, ways: (1) ideologically, especially in terms of gendered representations and valorizations of social processes and practices; (2) at the level of social relations; and (3) physically through the social construction of male and female bodies. In other words, developing a gender analysis of global restructuring requires more than inserting "women" into already existing IPE analyses. It involves going beyond a narrow materialist understanding of global restructuring. As various authors (Whitworth 1994a, b; Steans 1998) have revealed, one of the problems with critical IPE is precisely its materialist underpinnings. Despite, for instance, neo-Gramscian attempts to recognize the role of ideas in their formulation of hegemony, they still privilege its materialist foundations by asserting the centrality of production (Cox 1987: 2–9; Cox 1993: *passim*; Ling 1996b; Whitworth 1994a, b). Moreover, neo-Gramscian IPE has been challenged because of its strong preoccupation with the activities of elites, which tends to marginalize the potential for counter-hegemonic forces at the grassroots (Drainville 1994).

In order to move beyond a narrow materialist analysis of global restructuring it is important to address its ideational dimensions as well. Such an analysis is in step with the recent turn in IPE/IR theory toward developing a better understanding of the roles played by ideas, identities and culture in international affairs (see Lapid and Kratochwil 1997). As the contributions to this anthology will reveal, feminist IPE/IR is in a very good position to bridge the divide between a predominantly materialist IPE analysis and a critical analysis of the ideational/cultural underpinnings of global restructuring. First, within feminist theory there exists a strong research tradition concerning questions of identity construction and issues of representation. Second, there is a well-developed feminist literature on issues such as development, labor market structures, export processing zones, structural adjustment programs, and free trade issues, which are pertinent to the field of IPE. Together, these two strong traditions within feminist scholarship provide an excellent starting point for developing a more inclusive interpretation of global restructuring.

According to Spike Peterson, understanding and interpreting global restructuring, and indeed social reality more generally, involves relational thinking which brings together three distinct dimensions: "[t]his involves understanding the world 'out there' (practices, institutions, structures of social re/production), how we think (meaning systems, ideologies, paradigms), and who we are (subjectivity, agency, self and collective identities) as interacting dimensions of social reality" (Peterson 1997: 185). In other words, relational thinking allows us to introduce subjects and subjectivity into an otherwise rather abstract discussion about processes, structures, markets, and states. Second, it sensitizes us to the specifically gendered representations and valorizations of global restructuring. For instance, are certain sectors of the market becoming increasingly masculinized, that is, spaces where "masculine" behavior is being rewarded and which will consequently attract more men than women? Alternatively, are parts of (civil) society and the state becoming feminized? If so, what are the consequences of this? Third, relational thinking reveals the gendered power dimensions of global restructuring. How and to what extent is global restructuring embedded in and exacerbating unequal power relations? How are processes of inclusion and exclusion being mediated through gender, race, ethnicity, and class?

The conceptual richness of relational thinking can be illustrated through the analysis of an advertisement by the AFL-CIO, which appeared in the *New York Times*, 8 October 1997 (see Figure 0.1). This ad is interesting and powerful in many respects. It is clearly designed to influence the United States Congress to vote against the Clinton Administration's quest to negotiate free trade agreements under fast-track rules. Yet the significance of this ad extends beyond its immediate objective, as its text and images inform us about US labor's views on global restructuring or globalization.

From organized labor's perspective, global restructuring is pitting "working families" against "corporate interests" and will take away US jobs, worsen living standards and working conditions, lead to environmental degradation, and subject Americans to new (and alien) sources of food poisoning. This overt message is accompanied by the more covert use of a gendered and racialized image to influence public opinion. The ad not only features a picture of a young, Caucasian woman with blond hair (who is suggestive of a working mother), but also carries the banner: "In a **fast-track** world, she gets **left behind**" (emphasis in the original). The messages evoked by this picture and headline are complex and contradictory. First, the ad informs us about the world "out there". As a result the US labor force has significantly changed over the years and now includes many working women who do their share to keep the economy in shape. Moreover, the ad stipulates that women are not working just to earn a little money on the side, but are significant contributors to household incomes as well. In other words, they are helping to prevent America's families from (even further) disintegrating. This particular script of the ad clearly targets working women who fear that they may lose their jobs. It also emphasizes the importance of their productive and reproductive roles for the US economy and American families, respectively.

However, this is not the only script informing the ad. According to the second script, dealing with the ideological and representational dimensions of social reality, the hardworking young woman in the ad is a (passive) victim of

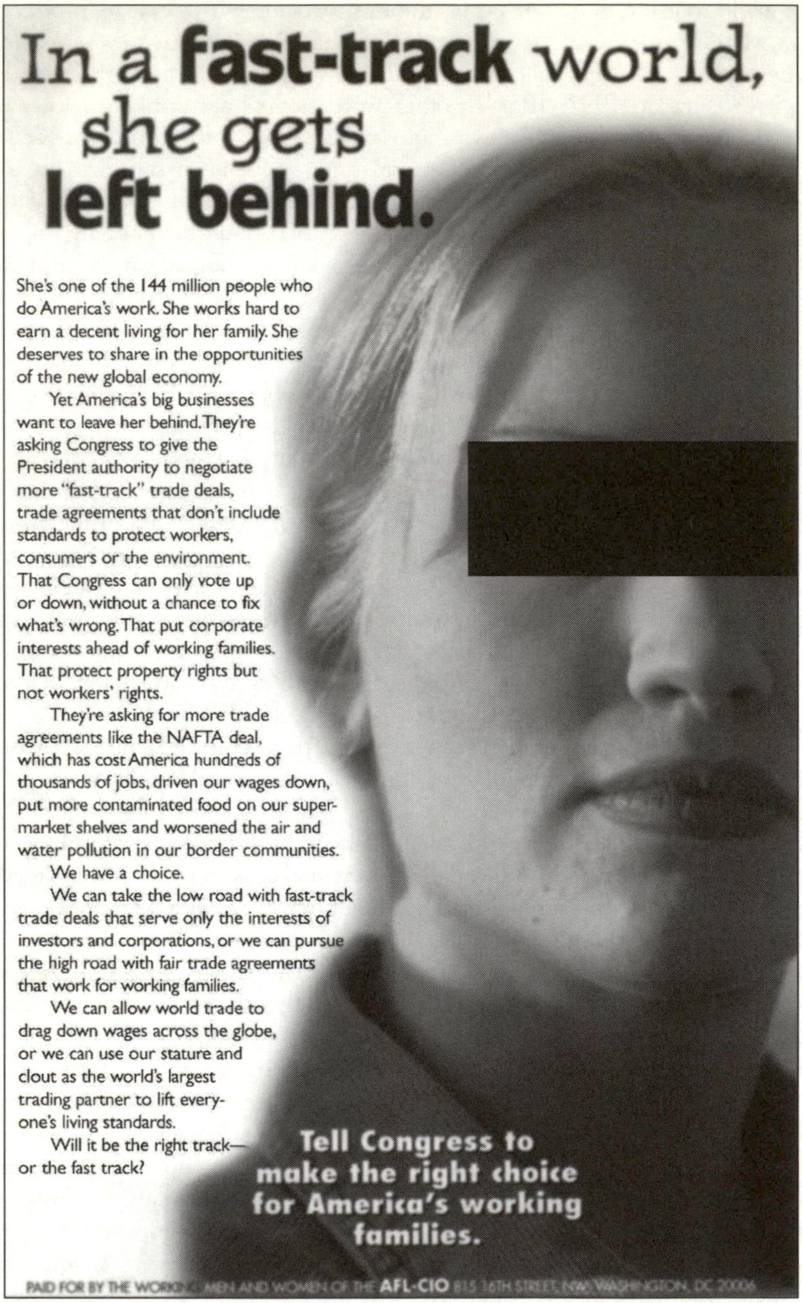

In a **fast-track** world, she gets **left behind.**

She's one of the 144 million people who do America's work. She works hard to earn a decent living for her family. She deserves to share in the opportunities of the new global economy.

Yet America's big businesses want to leave her behind. They're asking Congress to give the President authority to negotiate more "fast-track" trade deals, trade agreements that don't include standards to protect workers, consumers or the environment. That Congress can only vote up or down, without a chance to fix what's wrong. That put corporate interests ahead of working families. That protect property rights but not workers' rights.

They're asking for more trade agreements like the NAFTA deal, which has cost America hundreds of thousands of jobs, driven our wages down, put more contaminated food on our supermarket shelves and worsened the air and water pollution in our border communities.

We have a choice.

We can take the low road with fast-track trade deals that serve only the interests of investors and corporations, or we can pursue the high road with fair trade agreements that work for working families.

We can allow world trade to drag down wages across the globe, or we can use our stature and clout as the world's largest trading partner to lift everyone's living standards.

Will it be the right track—or the fast track?

Tell Congress to make the right choice for America's working families.

PAID FOR BY THE WORKING MEN AND WOMEN OF THE **AFL-CIO** 815 16TH STREET, NW, WASHINGTON, DC 20006

Figure 0.1   Advertisement, *New York Times*, 8 October 1997

Source: Courtesy of AFL-CIO, Washington, DC. (The face in the original advertisement has been disguised.)

globalization. Tellingly, the ad objectifies the woman by referring to her in the third person: she is not allowed to speak for herself or stand up for her own rights; instead she is portrayed as someone in need of protection from the woes of the global economy and deserving her fair share of the opportunities created by that same global economy. This image seems to convey that the fast-track world of globalization is highly masculinized and not a place to which women can easily gain access. With this second script the ad calls upon the readership to take on the traditional masculine role of protecting women and families by demanding that Congress reject the fast-track legislation.

There is also a third script operating in the ad which is the most invisible and which deals with the question of who we (that is, US labor) are. Choosing a young Caucasian woman as the symbol to be protected from fast-track trade agreements, the ad makes invisible the diverse nature of America's working class, which includes members of several minority groups. The message appears to be that White women deserve more protection than other working people. Moreover, the fact that the ad appeared in the *New York Times*, whose readership tends to be liberal and well-educated, seems to suggest that it is not just working-class families who will suffer from the fast-track trade deals but White middle-class families as well.

Together these three scripts create a complex and contradictory picture of globalization's gendered implications. Whereas the contributions of working women to the US economy and American families are placed in a positive light, these same women are denied agency in choosing their own or their country's future. Instead they are portrayed as the helpless victims of fast-track globalization who are in need of protection. At the same time it is significant that the woman to be protected is Caucasian and that the ad appeared in the *New York Times*, not the newspaper one expects to find on the coffee-tables of America's working class. What our discussion of this ad illustrates is that globalization is a set of complex, contradictory processes in which gender, race, ethnicity, and class play an important role. It is precisely this notion of global restructuring which constitutes the central theme of this book. Although the mainstream and critical literature often overlook or silence the gendered dimensions of global restructuring, the AFL-CIO ad clearly illustrates that gender figures prominently in the globalization problématique: not only because global restructuring tends to reinforce and exacerbate existing gender inequalities, but also because it is embedded in highly gendered discourse. The contributors to this volume touch upon various aspects of the material, ideological and discursive dimensions of global restructuring. Although the contributors address different issues and write from various perspectives, they share the notion that a gender analysis of global restructuring involves more than a discussion about the latter's differential impact on women and men.

Sightings, sites, and resistances

In the final section of this introduction we will further develop a gender analysis of global restructuring which is informed by relational thinking. The question of how feminists think about global restructuring is specifically captured by the part entitled "sightings,"[5] while the discussion on "sites" is concerned with the material structures and practices of global restructuring in specific places. Finally, "resistances" not only deal with concrete strategies and instances of opposition but also with the identities and subjectivities of those involved. Bringing these three elements – sightings, sites, and resistances – together will show how (gendered) changes in production, labor organization, and household structures are intricately connected to transformations in the role (and policies) of the state and the rearticulation of society. There are, for instance, clear signs of multiple globalizations (or global restructurings), reformulations of gender relations, and the emergence of new forms of organizing to counteract the negative impact of political/economic/cultural restructuring worldwide. In the remainder of this section we will take a closer look at some of these gendered "unsettlings."

Feminist sightings: critiques of the gendered discourses of restructuring

As we have indicated, gender operates at the level of ideology by valorizing certain social institutions, actors, practices, and processes that are associated with men and masculinity at the expense of others that are associated with women and femininity. Feminist theorizing is centrally concerned with breaking down or deconstructing this hierarchical dualism of masculinity/femininity, which constitutes an ordering system that determines what is deemed to be of value and what is not. Moreover, Western feminist theorizing, in particular, is concerned with the distinction between public and private spheres and the relegation of the latter to the former (see Peterson and Runyan 1999).

Feminist observers of global restructuring have pointed out that discourses of globalization[6] are highly gendered and that the relations of domination entailed in global restructuring could not be sustained without gendered symbolism and metaphors, which serve to "naturalize" hierarchies. Such symbolism and metaphors act to ward off resistance by variously valorizing globalization, making it appear natural and inevitable, and dampening debate about its effects and alternative social, political, and economic arrangements. For example, as Julie Graham and Katharine Gibson (1996: Chapter 6) have argued, globalization narratives of neoliberals and even some critical theorists read like "rape scripts," which are based on the assumption that men and women play out fixed gender roles of aggressors (whose behavior cannot be controlled) and victims (who are too weak to actually stop the violence). The invocation of (masculine) "capitalist penetration" into presumably weaker non-capitalist economic systems has also been noted by Charlotte Hooper (see Chapter 3, this volume). She finds that *The Economist* sometimes actually uses the metaphor of rape in article headings to promote the entry of transnational capital into "underdeveloped" economies.

Thus, part of critiquing global restructuring requires countering such narratives, whether from the right or left, which project globalization as an "irresistible" (masculine) force. This countering can be assisted by deconstructing dominant constructions of, in particular, emerging Anglo-American hegemonic masculinity under global restructuring and revealing how many men (e.g. as workers) are also being subordinated by these constructions. Interestingly, this newly emergent Anglo-American hegemonic masculinity reveals certain dualistic tendencies. On the one hand, it maintains the image of aggressive frontier masculinity. On the other, there are also seemingly more benign images of the same captains of global capital, which herald feminized skills of non-hierarchical management associated with networking, teamwork, and flexibility (see Hooper, Chapter 3, this volume and also Chang and Ling, Chapter 1, this volume). This multi-tasked feminized management style is juxtaposed in globalization scripts with labor, which is portrayed as anachronistically needful of hierarchical rules and structures, and, thus, poorly suited for the brave new world of flexibility that global capital demands (see Hooper, Chapter 3, this volume and True, Chapter 4, this volume).

It is the use of above-described gendered constructs and symbolisms that provides the legitimation and rationalization for neoliberal economic policies. This is particularly evident with respect to development and structural adjustment policies promoted by economists from international financial institutions, donor countries, and international donor agencies. The irony behind these narratives is that while these technical experts are prescribing export-oriented (agricultural and industrial) development policies to Southern states, the Organization for Economic Cooperation and Development (OECD) countries are phasing out much of their own manufacturing sector and moving toward a high-tech information and finance-based service economy (see, for example, Sassen 1991; Runyan 1996). This is the new "taut and terrific body economic" (Gibson-Graham 1996: 107) of the "new man." The "old man" of industrial production is increasingly beleaguered and marginalized as indicated by an article in the *Financial Times* (by John Thornhill, 25 November 1997: 35) entitled "Ivan the Terribly Lost." In this piece, the once proud symbol of Soviet manhood, the industrial worker or "Homo Sovieticus," has fallen prey to high "mortality, unemployment, alcohol abuse, and suicide" as the liberalization of the Russian economy passes him by.

Feminists have also noted how gendered metaphors and symbolism in globalization discourses act to privilege particular agents and sectors over others, such as finance capital over manufacturing, finance ministries over social welfare ministries, the market over the state, the global over the local, and consumers over citizens. In each of these cases, the latter is constructed as "feminized" in relation to the former, which is often depicted as masculine space (see, for example, Marchand 2000a). Although other critical theorists have observed these hierarchizations in the context of global restructuring, they have failed to connect them to gendering processes, including shifting meanings of public and private (Brodie 1994).

A well-established tradition of Western feminist scholarship has revealed that women's subordination stems from men's assignment to and control over the public realm of the state and the market and women's consignment to the private realm of the home and family (see, for example, Okin 1979; Elshtain 1981; Hartsock 1985; Tong 1989; Coole 1993). Neoliberal discourse, however, constructs the market as the private sector in contradistinction to the state as the public sector and either totally disregards the private realm of the household/family or lumps it into a very broad conception of (private) civil society that includes market actors and which is also counter-posed to the (public) state.

In neoliberal discourse on globalization, the state is typically "feminized" in relation to the more robust market by being represented as a drag on the global economy that must be subordinated and minimized. As critics have noted, however, the state also paradoxically takes on a new role by becoming more akin to the private sector (and thus remasculinized) as it is internationalized to assist global capital and as its coercive and surveillance capacities are being enhanced.

To make feminist sense of these conflicting engenderings of the state, it is first necessary to note that not all states have similar capacities to participate in the global economy. While OECD states are in a position to "male-bond" with global capital and thus partially retain or recapture their masculine status, Southern (and other subordinated) states are forced to accept a more feminized status. Second, it is important to recognize that the state is not a homogeneous entity. Within states (Central and East European, OECD as well as Southern), there are sectors that remain "domesticated" even as other sectors are internationalized. For example, ministries that focus on domestic health, education, and social welfare are becoming increasingly disadvantaged or "feminized" in relation to ministries of finance and economic affairs that are directly related to the global economy and, thus, invested with masculine authority. Such ministries are also displacing the power of elected officials as democratic processes are increasingly viewed as too cumbersome for the fast-track world of global economics. The restructuring which has so privileged these (masculinized) sectors, coupled with the still considerable coercive apparatuses of states, makes (parts of) the state complicit in restructuring processes rather than obsolete.

In this context it is important to note that Western feminist theorizing about the public and private in relation to the state has been challenged by non-Western feminists. For instance, in the case of the modernizing state the private becomes a space of contestation and redefinition as modernizing elites seek to "suppress" the private as a source of social and economic traditional values and "colonize" it with public statist values in order to undermine inward-looking, patriarchal family values (Kandiyoti 1991: 435). Fundamentalist revolutions and resistances to this represent a masculinist reclaiming of private patriarchal space. Writing from the perspective of migrant women, Annanya Bhattacharjee challenges Western feminist assumptions about the home as an essentially private space by arguing that "home" for these women has far more "public" dimensions. For them, not only does home refer to "the (conventional) domestic sphere of the heterosexual and patriarchal family," but it also entails "an extended ethnic community" and "nations of origin," which shape their identities and roles (Bhattacharjee 1997: 313–14).

Finally, Western feminist theorizing about public and private is also being challenged by women in the "transitional" or post-communist states of Eastern Europe and the former Soviet Union. Historically, the communist state sought also to obliterate private space in terms of capitalism, autonomous civil society organizations, and household privacy. Communist ideology purported to solve "the woman question" by enjoining unprecedented numbers of women to enter the formal workforce, and to some degree governance, by providing free access to child care, health care, and abortion as well as paid maternity leaves. Women living through post-communist transitions in this period of global restructuring are turning Western feminist theorizing on its head as they question any value in seeking traditionally public roles in government given their deep suspicion of the state as a site of liberation. Instead, those who are positioned to afford it are experiencing more senses of freedom through the private market, which is giving them their first taste of entrepreneurial careers, consumerism, and individual expression. Accompanying this is a sense of the private realm of home and family as a larger space for agency than the public realm of the state, since under communist regimes this area was the least likely to be effectively kept under surveillance (see True (Chapter 4) and Beck (Chapter 10), this volume).

Even as the private sector is valorized over the public sector more generally, the private realm is hyperfeminized in relation to not only the state and the market, but also civil society in which it is rendered either invisible or highly subordinated. Ironically, however, the private realm has become highly politicized as a site of and for restructuring processes. As feminists have observed, the global economy demands that women simultaneously step up both their productive and reproductive labor are met by contradictory rhetoric and public policies. For instance, in the US women are caught between neoliberal rhetoric which casts women as the "new entrepreneurs" by devaluing women's traditional family roles and neoconservative views which emphasize "family values" and cast women as selfish and irresponsible if they do not fulfill their mothering roles. The contradictory nature of both processes and rhetoric, requiring women to be simultaneously in the workforce, sustain family income and take on additional caring responsibilities, is leading to "a crisis in social reproduction" (Brodie 1994: 58).

These and other shifts in the meanings and designations of public and private as both a form and result of global restructuring are also challenging and prompting reworkings of feminist theory. As the public arena itself is being redefined and subordinated to private capital, women are even further distanced from power even as they become workers and elected officials because the nature of work is being degraded and the powers of legislatures are being diminished. The locus of power is shifting from the public world of politics to the privatizing, and thus, depoliticizing, world of economics. However the latter is, in turn, repoliticized by labor, environmental, and women's activists (among others) who are increasingly demanding more accountability and transparency from firms and international financial institutions.

Feminist sites: critiques of the market, the state, and civil society

There is a wealth of feminist research on the gendered impacts of economic development and global restructuring processes. These investigations of the relationship between gender and global restructuring tend to focus largely on the materialist or economic dimensions of restructuring and tend to reduce gender analysis of restructuring to the differential effects it has on women and men in the workplace and the home. Nevertheless, they have been instrumental in exposing the vast underside of restructuring and thus have acted to significantly counter neoliberal advocacy of globalization. The contributions in Part II of this volume draw upon this body of work, but further complicate these feminist analyses of the material consequences of global restructuring and the nature of the market, state, and civil society.

Feminist critiques of the global capitalist market have primarily focused on gendered divisions of labor in which men's work is privileged over women's work in terms of status, pay, and working conditions. Feminists have long pointed to the gender inequalities arising from the split between productive labor associated with men's paid work outside the home and reproductive labor associated with women's unpaid labor inside the home which was solidified by the rise of industrial capitalism in the West (see, for example, Rowbotham 1974; Eisenstein 1979). Such inequalities were (re)produced through early colonization practices and later post-World War II economic development strategies imposed on the South by the North (see, for example, Boserup 1970; Charlton 1984; Mies 1986; Sen and Grown 1987). More recently, feminists have observed that these inequalities are being both exacerbated and complicated with the advent of post-industrial capitalism (see, for example, Mitter 1986; Joekes 1987; Ward 1990; Vickers 1991; Bakker 1994; Joekes and Weston 1994; Marchand and Parpart 1995; Kofman and Youngs 1996; Moghadam 1998).

Women have become preferred candidates for certain kinds of jobs needed in a global economy organized around services and JIT production processes. The main reasons for this are that women remain associated with unremunerated and service-oriented reproductive labor and are often seen as physically better suited to perform tedious repetitive tasks as well as more docile and, therefore, less likely to organize than men (see, for example, Fernandez-Kelly 1983). The jobs women now perform range from light assembly work in export processing or free trade zones and subcontracted sweatshop/homework labor to clerical and domestic work and sex tourism (see, for example, Enloe 1989; Peterson and Runyan 1993, 1999; Boris and Prugl 1996; Pettman 1996a, b). Poor, working-class, Third-World, minority, and migrant women, as the cheapest and most vulnerable sources of labor, are most sought for such jobs which are characterized by low wages, few benefits, little union representation, and minimal regulation and tend to be part-time, temporary, and highly insecure in nature (see, for example, Aslanbeigui *et al.* 1994; Bullock 1994; Rowbotham and Mitter 1994; Alexander and Mohanty 1997). Thus, what feminists call the "feminization of labor" in the context of global restructuring refers not only to the unprecedented increase in the numbers of women workers in the formal (and informal) labor force to service the global economy, but also to the "flexibiliza-tion" and "casualization" of (especially women's) labor to keep labor costs down and productivity up in the name of free trade, global competitiveness, and economic efficiency.

Another feature of the economic impact of global restructuring on women is the unprecedented rise in the migration of women (especially, but not solely, poor and working-class ones from Third-World states) across borders to earn incomes and provide foreign exchange for their governments. Numerous feminist scholars have documented the rise in the international "maid trade," interna-tional sex trafficking and tourism, and other service labor women immigrants/migrants provide to elites in "global cities" (or world financial centers) (see, for example, Enloe 1989; Pettman 1996a, b; Peterson and Runyan 1999; and Kofman, Chapter 7, this volume).

As we have noted, feminists have also called attention to cutbacks in social services provided by the state – a process which particularly disadvantages women as the major recipients and providers of such services (see for example, Harrington 1992; Dahlerup 1994; WIDE (Women in Development Europe) *et al.* 1994; Sen 1997). Such cutbacks were initially instituted during the 1980s through structural adjustment programs (SAPs) imposed on debt-ridden nations in the South by the International Monetary Fund (IMF) and World Bank. In addition to stepping up export production (for which women's labor is needed), SAPs require developing countries to reduce state expenditures particularly in the area of social welfare. As structural adjustment has become more globalized, welfare states in the North have subjected themselves to similar austerity measures involving significant reductions in public funding and the increasing privatization of social welfare programs. Post-Communist states (and most recently the so-called Asian Tigers), too, have fallen under the rigors of SAPs, drastically cutting and/or privatizing formerly free state services upon which women had depended for health, child, and elder care. Thus, privatization processes are essentially reprivatizing reproductive labor – that is, shifting public responsibility for social welfare back to the private realm of the home where women must pick up the slack. As we noted earlier, many women must now simultaneously be in the workforce and at home to serve the global economy, make up for shortfalls in working-class men's declining wages and jobs in indus-trial sectors, earn money to pay for privatized social services, and provide the reproductive services for which the state is abandoning responsibility. This is prompting various kinds of renegotiations of gender relations in households, as Moghadam and Kromhout point out in Chapters 5 and 8 of this volume, respectively.

Feminist analyses of the economic effects of restructuring on women have been increasingly accompanied by analyses of the consequences for women of the political effects of restructuring on the state and civil society. Economic privatization is producing political privatization which takes several forms (see Eisenstein 1996). As Anne Sisson Runyan has described this elsewhere:

> One form is the oft-cited erosion of the state as it is internationalized or made more beholden and accountable to global capital than to citizens. In this process, the state is depoliticized through the reduction of all political issues to matters of economic efficiency. This, in turn, leads to another form of political privatization – the reduction of "public citizens" to "private consumers."
>
> (Runyan 1997: 26)

This process derails traditional feminist demands on the state to provide full citizenship, human, equality, and social welfare rights for women (see Mikanagi, Chapter 6, this volume). Further undercutting the basis for state-centered feminist organizing is the rise of neoconservative political forces which blame "both the welfare state and feminism for the breakdown in the social and moral fabric" and see "the family as the fundamental building block in the new order, asserting that families should look after their own, and that state policies should act to make sure they do" (Brodie 1994: 57). Fundamentalist religious and nationalist forces in civil society that are fostered by and provide support for neoconservative policies which focus on controlling women's lives and bodies represent the most reactionary responses to global restructuring (see Grewal and Kaplan 1994). As we have argued, these ideological shifts have led feminists to probe beyond the material economic and political effects of global restructuring on women and focus on how gender operates at the symbolic, ideational, and cultural level to produce and direct global restructuring in particular ways and to reduce resistance to it. These processes have also led them to search for alternative conceptions of resistance which highlight women's agency not just in large-scale economic (labor) movements, but also in cultural and political struggles at all levels from the household to the transnational arena.

Feminist resistances: local/national/global struggles, hybrid spaces, and multiple strategies[7]

The previous discussions on sightings and sites reveal global restructuring as a process that constitutes and is constituted by a myriad of unsettlings and renegotiations of boundaries and identities. Moreover, gender as a significant boundary ma(r)ker and identity producer, is a focal point both of and for restructuring. On the one hand, restructuring depends heavily on gendered discourse and gender ideology for its own construction because they make it appear natural and inevitable. On the other hand, restructuring entails reworkings of the boundaries between and meanings of femininity and masculinity, which are intimately related to the shifting boundaries and meanings of private and public, domestic and international, and local and global. In this last part of the introduction, we will explore how global restructuring is constructing hybrid spaces and identities and thus new spaces for (feminist) resistance, even as it is reproducing and intensifying relations of domination.

The question of resistance has always received scant attention from International Relations (IR) and IPE scholars, especially those working within the (neo)realist tradition. And when attention has been paid, it has tended to concentrate mostly on forms of resistance that involve large-scale, organized, mass mobilizations such as international labor, guerrilla and independence movements. Following this same pattern, it is only recently that IR/IPE scholars have started to look at globalization and the politics of resistance (see, for example, "Globalisation and the Politics of Resistance" 1997). One explanation for this relative lack of attention toward resistance in the context of globalization has been discussed earlier: the dominant portrayal of globalization as inevitable and a 'bigger-than-thou' phenomenon has led to feelings of disempowerment (and thus eroding the basis for resistance). However, breaking through the various globalization myths, critical IPE scholars have started to explore and analyze possible counter-hegemonic forces and attempts to resist, reduce, and channel the negative implications of globalization. Yet, the issue of resistance still remains under-theorized. Moreover, existing analyses are not only gender-blind (Marchand 2000b), but also employ rather narrow interpretive frames which tend to prioritize large-scale (sometimes violent) counter-movements and overlook, for instance, more localized practices of resistance.

Developing a feminist analysis of and perspective on resistance involves, first of all, a recognition of the contextual nature of resistance. Resistance, in other words, is embedded in, structured by as well as structuring global restructuring. As global restructuring involves not only transformations of the state, the market, and civil society, but also the reworkings of masculinity and femininity as well as gender relations, it tends to problematize such oppositional categories as private/public, home/work, domestic/international, and local/global by placing women (and men) simultaneously in these various realms. This recognition of the complexities surrounding the politics of resistance in an era of globalization, in turn, opens up the possibility to identify multiple forms of resistance and sites of intervention. In other words, resistance needs to be reconceptualized in order to go beyond a narrow interpretation of resistance which would only consider a contemporary variation of the international working-class struggle worthy of attention. As Chin and Mittelman (1997) suggest, such a (more inclusive) reconceptualization of resistance would involve the charting of various dimensions of resistance, including its various sites, strategies, forms, and objectives. In addition, it is important to consider the (re)articulation of collective identities as an integral part of the politics of resistance (see Castells 1997). As the contributions in the Part III, the final section of this volume reveal, resistance can take on diverse forms and strategies, ranging from survival or coping strategies to (more or less) organized resistance and transnational organizing, all of which entail cultural (not just economic) struggles and the development of new identities and subjectivities (see Chapters 9 (Lind), 10 (Beck), and 11 (Karam), this volume). These various strategies not only bring the local/global nexus into play, but are also located at the interstices of private/public, home/work, masculine/feminine and involve a renegotiation of the boundaries of the market/state/civil society.

A second area for feminist theorizing (and activism) is the shift in the balance of power within states which tilts power in favor of ministries of finance and economic affairs. Traditionally, such ministries have been relatively insulated from direct political accountability toward the public (except for business lobby groups) and have had few, if any, interactions with representatives of women's groups. For NGOs (non-governmental organizations) involved in lobbying activities the major challenge of the 1990s is to raise the level of gender awareness and sensitivity at these ministries. The feeling which still pervades many of these bureaucracies is that gender issues, finance, and the (global) economy are totally unrelated.

Finally, processes of global restructuring have also had their impact on civil society and brought about increased social activism beyond national borders (see Keck and Sikkink 1998; Stienstra, Chapter 12, this volume). This phenomenon is often referred to as the emergence of a so-called global civil society. Here it is important to stress that this would not have happened without, on the one hand, the emergence of new communication technologies, such as the fax and computer, and, on the other, the United Nations which has played an important enabling role by providing a meeting place for NGOs. Clearly, civil society is one of the most familiar grounds for feminist activists and women NGOs. Strengthening civil society is often seen as an important tool and objective in the struggle for democracy and in the fight to improve women's/human rights. It is also seen, from critical perspectives, as the place to start counteracting the negative impact of SAPs and trade liberalization. However, as noted earlier, civil society is also the terrain on which religious and nationalist fundamentalist groups, business networks, and other groups with "less-than-progressive" agendas are active. Moreover, it is important to keep in mind that a strengthened civil society is also on the neoliberal agenda. However, the elements of civil society neoliberals wish to privilege over the state are precisely those which will broaden and deepen relations of domination in the absence of any recourse to democratic governance at local, national, or global levels.[8]

These developments require feminist scholars to revisit their implicit and explicit assumptions about civil society and the formulation of more nuanced ideas about and understandings of civil society's power dimensions. For instance, one issue which deserves attention is how women's networks and NGOs can or are trying to take advantage of the more diffuse power structures within civil society to keep gender on the political agenda. Early indications are that the use of new technologies will become very important in this struggle as they may well structure the ways in which women's groups and other alternative networks relate to each other, to the state and to the market (see Castells 1998b). From a feminist activist point of view, women's networks and NGOs should not only insist on making new technologies easily accessible, but they should also explore them to their fullest potential in terms of information-sharing and networking-supporting capacities.

Concluding comments

In this introduction we have shown how processes of global restructuring involve simultaneous transformations of the state, civil society, and the market. We have also given some examples of how women (and men) in various parts of the world are involved in and affected by these processes. An important starting point for feminist academics, women's networks, and NGOs to counteract this (neoliberal and patriarchal) global restructuring is to reveal how all these processes are gendered. This can be done by employing relational thinking through "bringing people" (as highly diverse "women" and "men") into the analysis of global restructuring and by focusing on its gendered representations. In trying to counteract the negative impact of global restructuring, NGOs and grassroots organizations need to be aware of how their local concerns are related to larger processes of global restructuring and reflect upon how their activities may affect or influence these processes (and vice versa).

The chapters that follow contribute to ongoing feminist debates about and approaches to global restructuring by further extending and complicating how we think (Part 1 – Sightings), what we look for (Part II – Sites), and what we do (Part III – Resistances) in relation to global restructuring. Although each contribution contains analyses of all three, we have grouped chapters according to which of these three aspects they most emphasize. Each part is preceded by an introduction which highlights and summarizes the arguments in and commonalities among the contributions included in that section. In the first part dominant constructions of globalization are being challenged by highlighting its cosmopolitan, masculinized character and its silencing of public–private renegotiations as well as the underlying restructuring of gender relations. The second part addresses the more material structures and practices of global restructuring by focusing on specific places, spaces, and processes such as states, global cities, the labor force, migrations, and households. These contributions not only pay attention to economic forces but also draw attention to cultural, political and familial dimensions. Finally, in the Conclusion to this volume, the contributors further develop feminist understandings of resistance. The concluding chapter speaks to the importance of these contributions and the value of feminist approaches more generally in terms of increasing our understanding of global restructuring and resistances to it and will raise some points for further research.

Notes

1   G. Eliot, *Middlemarch*, London,Wordsworth Classics,1994 edn, p. 14 (emphasis in the original).
2   For a definition of gender, gender analysis and feminist theory, see below.
3   James Mittelman critiques this teleological dimension in much of the globalization literature in the following way:

> it embodies a teleology, or a predetermined logic with an imputed final state of affairs – a global village, a worldwide economy, a world government, and so on. On the contrary, even if globalization involves a set of deep historical structures,

and since history has no end, its course must be resolved through the intervention of human agency. It is a mistake to rigidify the structures of globalization
and transform them into a form of structuralism, which banishes agency and
severs historical moorings.

(Mittelman 1996: 232)

4   The first three myths are discussed in detail in Marchand 1997: 25–28 and Marchand
    2000a.
5   The term feminism is being used here to denote a broad view or orientation which
    sees gender as an important ordering device in today's world. As such feminism
    embraces many perspectives. Thus, feminists are those who hold such a broad orien-
    tation (see Peterson and Runyan 1999: 256).
6   In the remainder of this chapter, the term globalization script or discourse is being
    used critically to reflect: (a) the views of those who advocate globalization; or (b) its
    ideological connotation and dimension. Global restructuring will be used consistently
    to indicate material and ideational processes of transformation.
7   Parts of this section draw upon the discussion in Marchand 1997.
8   We wish to thank Valentine Moghadam for pointing this out to us.

Part I

Sightings

How does a gender lens alter our vision of conventional accounts of "globalization" and move us to more complex understandings of global restructuring? How does gender affect global restructuring and how does global restructuring affect gender? These are some of the questions that are addressed in this first set of contributions by Kimberly Chang and L.H.M. Ling (Chapter 1), Gillian Youngs (Chapter 2), Charlotte Hooper (Chapter 3) , and Jacqui True (Chapter 4), all of which reconceptualize global restructuring through gender analysis. These new "sightings" of the relationship(s) between gender and global restructuring both problematize and complicate the meanings, structures, and agencies typically associated with both global restructuring and gender.

In Chapter 1, Chang and Ling contest the universality of features usually ascribed to globalization in neoliberal and some structuralist accounts. These include the total integration of high technology, finance, and production, the complete "hollowing out" of states, the full embrace of liberal capitalism, and the omnipresence of postmodern individualism. They argue that these features are representative only of certain male-dominated sectors of the global political economy and the Western masculinist ideologies and identities that both arise from and create them. They go on to reveal that this dominant masculinist construction of globalization, depicted as a thorough-going process that is variously cosmopolitan, postmodern, or "freeing" in nature (and which they label "Global Restructuring I" or "GI"), not only hides, but also rests upon another kind of globalization. What they label "Global Restructuring II" or "GII" is the low-wage and highly sexualized and racialized labor done by largely Third-World women workers which serves the cosmopolitanites of G1 and is enforced by still quite potent modernist and traditional forces of the state, culture, religion, and family. We can see this underside of global restructuring only when we adopt a gender lens and look at the lives of diverse women in the global political economy. In Chang and Ling's case, it is the lives of Filipina maids in Hong Kong that inform this very different picture of global restructuring. Although these women have crossed borders to work, they are still entrapped in old and new webs of oppression and exploitation which demand that they conform to traditional gender roles and identities and limit their agency. Nonetheless, Chang and Ling do provide some examples of their resistance. However, they argue that

some of these women's attempts, for example, to refashion their sexuality constitute coping strategies that offer only momentary escapes from, on the one hand,
the relentless messages from their home country for them to chastely serve God,
country, and family and, on the other, the expectations of wealthy employers in
the host country for them to be subservient, but also sexually available. Thus,
viewed from and through GII, global restructuring is far from "freeing" for most
(especially most women of color). Nor does it represent a significant dissolution
of modern hierarchies and boundaries or traditional structures and ideologies.
Rather, it often exacerbates them.

Dominant GI discourses within the study of international political economy
(IPE) also act as a "patriarchal prism" through which changes in the relationship
between states and the market are reflected to the exclusion of attention to
spatial reorganizations of civil society, according to Youngs in Chapter 2.
Although critical IPE focuses on the enlargement of the private sector at the
expense of the public sector through the process of privatization of state institutions, there is little analysis of the changing power relationships between what
feminists have long identified as the public realm (of both the state and market)
and the private realm (of the household/family). Moreover, there is little attention paid to how conceptions of public and private *spaces* and the ways in which
people occupy and act in them are being altered. To explore these lacunas in
conventional accounts, Youngs also takes her cue from observations of Filipina
maids in Hong Kong. What she finds is that: (1) the so-called public/global
realm of the global political economy is manifested in private/local space in the
case of the "hidden" work of migrant domestic workers in foreign households;
and (2) the so-called private realm to which domestic workers are confined
cannot contain them all the time. On weekends, in the case of Hong Kong, they
congregate in the central business district plaza (private sector/global space) in
very visible ways and thereby locally create a public space and constitute a
"public force." Thus, these women workers are renegotiating the boundaries of
public/private and local/global in ways that reveal these supposed oppositions as
complexly and contradictorily interconnected.

Hooper in Chapter 3 draws our attention to another kind of renegotiation of
boundaries. Her examination of the rise of a new hegemonic masculinity in the
context of global restructuring, as it is exemplified in the pages of *The Economist*,
also finds that hierarchies are not dissolving, but does show that ideologies and
identities are shifting at the top of the gender hierarchy. The "new man" is the
jet-setting, post-industrial, postmodern global executive who is privileged in
accounts of GI. He subordinates "industrial man" who is dismissed as too rigid
and unimaginative to be successful in the bold new world of high technology
and finance. Aggression, risk, adventure, and conquest are still features of hegemonic masculinity but capital and information technology, not arms and
machines, constitute the weapons and corporate takeovers and global reach, not
country takeovers and national control, constitute the goals. But the new man
must also incorporate some "feminine" attributes into his identity and management style in order to successfully "network" and negotiate. Thus, although

femininity remains subordinated as do women more generally in the global corporate world, the new hegemonic masculinity blurs the boundaries and softens the oppositions somewhat between masculinity and femininity in the body and identity of the new man.

These boundaries and oppositions, however, are intensified (albeit in some new ways) in so-called transitional states and economies in Eastern Europe, as True in Chapter 4 on the case of the Czech Republic reveals. Her chapter, which completes this section on "sightings," challenges both conventional and Western feminist interpretations of post-Communist economic, political, and social transitions associated with global restructuring. Her treatment shows that the "winners" and "losers" in transition processes (which vary in terms of each country and do not necessarily lead in the same direction as presupposed by neoliberals) cannot be determined along gender lines. Although it is the case that the job market (in terms of both positions and wages) has become bifurcated according to gender and that women have in general lost many public positions and services, many men, too, have been displaced. "Homo Sovieticus," the socialist version of "industrial man," has lost out in the face of massive deindustrialization and become subordinated to the domestic and foreign entrepreneurs who now dominate economic life in the Czech Republic. This masculine identity crisis, along with the preference for women to perform service work for domestic and especially foreign firms, has created crises both in social reproduction and in the gender order at the household level. The question remains where these disruptions and new contradictions may lead.

Thus, taken as a whole, the contributions in this part of the book cause us to rethink a variety of conventional assumptions about global restructuring and about gender. They also show that the relationship between these two processes is quite complex and dynamic, and, thus, offer new avenues for thinking about openings for resistance.

1 Globalization and its intimate other

Filipina domestic workers in Hong Kong

Kimberly A. Chang and L.H.M. Ling

Introduction

At least two processes of globalization or global restructuring operate in the world political economy today. One reflects a glitzy, Internet-surfing, structurally integrated world of global finance, production, trade, and telecommunications. Populated primarily by men at its top rungs of decision making, this global restructuring valorizes all those norms and practices usually associated with Western capitalist masculinity – "deregulation," "privatization," "strategic alliances," "core regions," "deadlands" – but masked as global or universal. Like the colonial rhetoric of old, it claims to subsume all local cultures under a global umbrella of aggressive market competition – only now with technology driving the latest stage of capitalism. We refer to this global restructuring as "techno-muscular" capitalism (TMC).[1]

There is a second process of global restructuring. It is more explicitly sexualized, racialized, and class-based than TMC and concentrates on low-wage, low-skilled menial service provided by mostly female migrant workers. They perform intimate, household services: e.g., caring for the young and elderly, cleaning house, washing clothes, preparing food, and generally providing domestic comfort and care. This service economy involves other intimacies as well: leaving home, living among strangers, facing sexual harassment and abuse, making moral choices. We refer to this second global restructuring as a regime of labor intimacy. It is, in every sense, an intimate other to TMC.

Filipina migrant workers in Hong Kong stand at the nexus of these two globalization processes.[2] They inhabit the regime of labor intimacy needed and created by TMC. These women work at low-wage, low to semi-skilled jobs as nannies, nurses, maids, entertainers, and/or hostesses to the upwardly mobile, technically linked, high-salaried cosmopolitans of TMC. While they can earn up to six times what they would make at home, Filipina domestic workers often find themselves incarcerated within this regime of "labor intimacy." Sending and receiving states promise them wealth and mobility through domestic work but deliver instead a sentence of sexualized, racialized service. In this way, the twin processes of globalization exacerbate a growing gap between cosmopolitans and those who toil in the intimacy of their homes.

In this chapter, we ask: Why are certain segments of the world population geared towards the high-tech, high-wage world of TMC, while others are assigned to a low-tech, low-wage regime of labor intimacy? How do these different positionings within a globalized political economy affect subjectivity in general, and that of the subaltern woman, in particular? And what implications can we draw about the nature of global restructuring as it polarizes TMC from labor intimacy even while sustaining both?

We rely on ethnographic fieldwork conducted by Chang and Groves (forthcoming) on Filipina domestic workers in Hong Kong from 1992 to 1997. Their research includes various media sources on the Filipina migrant community from both the Hong Kong press and Filipino publications. One such source, *Tinig Filipino*, is published by and for the Filipino migrant community overseas. We conclude with the implications of both global restructuring processes for understanding our contemporary world order.

Global restructuring I: techno-muscular capitalism (TMC)

Studies of global restructuring typically reflect two normative stances: a liberal internationalism that accepts "globalization" as a contemporary, market response to "internationalized" consumer and producer demands, and a critical reassessment of global restructuring as historically continuous, ideologically hegemonic, and materially impoverishing for the majority of the world. Liberals cite the canons of *laissez-faire* neo-classical economics to promote global restructuring and generally focus on policy prescriptions to adjust to newfound opportunities (e.g. capital gains) as well as challenges (e.g. unemployment). Critics of global restructuring reflect a more varied theoretical background, e.g. Gramscian international political economy, world system theory, classical Marxism, regulation theory. They focus primarily on the structural inequities and/or inherent instabilities that arise from global restructuring such as the emergence of global elites, a capitalist "world-hegemony," and regressive structural adjustment policies. Instead of public policy, critics assess the nature of our global political economy and its future scenarios. For example, they speculate on the outbreak of counter-hegemonic movements at various localities (Gramscian globalists), systemic consequences to deepening inequalities in center/periphery relations (world system theorists), capitalism's "internal contradictions" (classical Marxists), or alternative "regimes of accumulation" to latemodern capitalism (regulation theorists).

Despite these differences, both liberals and critics agree on the subject matter itself, i.e. "globalization's" characteristics, impact, ideology, and culture.

Identifying features of global restructuring

"Globalization" studies conventionally refer to unprecedented levels of integration in finance, production, trade, telecommunications, and the media on a world-wide scale.[3] As such, "globalization" differs from "internationalization" which suggests only "the geographic spread of economic activities across national boundaries" (Dicken 1992: 1). Some authors date the rise of global restructuring to the heyday of "casino capitalism" (Strange 1986) or "hyperliberalism" (Cox 1987) in the 1980s when the Reagan–Thatcher–Kohl triad of industrialized economies deregulated capital and taxation. Others trace it to the 1970s when world capital markets broke from the nation-based Bretton Woods system (Kapstein 1996). Whatever the periodization, global restructuring signals an era of extraordinary collaboration across states, between firms, and also between states and firms (Dicken 1994). Integrated media and marketing networks also globalize the production of images, ideas, and consumption patterns (Leslie 1995). Some find a structural convergence across multinational (or better, transnational) corporations that transcend traditional boundaries in production, finance, and distribution (Reich 1992; Berger 1996). These circuits of capital and institutions contribute to the rise of "core regions" in a new post-Cold War geopolitical order (Agnew and Corbridge 1995). "Global cities" (Sassen 1991) like New York, London, Tokyo, and Hong Kong, among others, now have more in common with one another than with their respective local municipalities. Similarly, "deadlands" of economic development afflict regions located in the First World as much as they do in the former Second or Third Worlds. This new, transnationalized geopolitical order supersedes and obsolesces the state-led, territory-bound one of Cold War politics and superpower rivalry (Agnew and Corbridge 1995).

The role of the state

Liberals and critics alike view global restructuring as a fundamental challenge to the traditional functions, if not viability, of the state.[4] Some liberals argue that states must accept their reduced role under the new reality of global competition. The state's sole responsibility is to educate the consuming public with better information. Even the liberal capitalist state in the West, caution democratic theorists, needs to revise its understanding of sovereignty, democracy, and political community to survive under global restructuring (Barber 1996; Held and McGrew 1993). Otherwise, a crisis of politics and economics may emerge, stoked by post-Cold War nationalism in face of the coming century's new "world empires" – multinational corporations (Barnet and Cavanagh 1994) – and their dire consequences for unemployment/underemployment (Kapstein 1996).

Critics of global restructuring admit that the state is "hollowing-out" in a distinctive way, e.g. it is becoming increasingly obsolete as "more and more economic, social, and cultural activity is going to take place across (rather than within) national frontiers" (Thrift 1992: 6). Gramscian globalists label this process an "internationalizing of the state." That is, states turn inside-out to accommodate the external exigencies of globalized production (Cox 1987). According to some, this will lead to greater instability between a territorially based interstate system and a global economy that daily undermines it (Gill 1992).

A transnationalized ideology of liberal capitalism

Liberal capitalism, almost all agree, is spreading to both the "heartland" and "outposts" of the world economy. Liberal internationalists laud globalization as a triumph of self-interest matched with rationality. Fukuyama (1989) remains the most blatant advocate of this perspective.

Critics, especially Gramscian globalists, castigate Western liberal capitalism as oppressive, invidious, and hegemonic. Not only does it ensure the dominance of certain capitalist production processes and relations, it also perpetuates a world-order ideology that validates the supremacy of leading states and their dominant social classes (Gill 1995a; Cox 1987). With its seductive profits and privileges, the world-hegemony of liberal capitalism sets up specific relations of production. Many fear that this increasing interconnectedness among global elites may widen gaps between the rich and the poor, thereby further destabilizing the global political economy (Marshall 1996; Agnew and Corbridge 1995; Dicken 1992). For this reason, Gramscian globalists forecast the possibility of multiple counter-hegemonic movements. These will lay the foundation, they believe, for a new, emancipatory transnational historic bloc that will transform the capitalist world-hegemony.

Global society / culture / persons

All agree also that globalization transforms familiar forms of social organization and cultural meaning. Liberals emphasize the "bridging mechanisms" of a new revolutionary class emerging under globalization – culture-straddling, globe-spanning cosmopolitans. Hannerz (1990: 239) defines cosmopolitanism as "an orientation, a willingness to engage with the Other. It is an intellectual and aesthetic stance of openness toward divergent cultural experiences, a search for contrasts rather than uniformity." For this reason, Hannerz disqualifies expatriates and migrants as cosmopolitan for, he explains, they retain an indigenous cultural identity even while living/working overseas.

Critics, in contrast, view these late/postmodern cosmopolitans as another in a long line of capitalist elites. Gramscian globalists theorize that cosmopolitans operate as a "global historic bloc." They form cross-national, cross-cultural "global classes" which uphold "mutual interests and ideological perspectives" that institutionalize a "common criteria of interpretation ... and common goals anchored in the idea of an open world economy" (Cox 1993: 254). This global historic bloc includes the "affluent minorities in the OECD and ... the urban elites and new middle classes in the Third World" (Gill 1995a: 405).

Subjectivity under late modernity

Given their concern with elites, both liberals and critics view global restructuring in terms of the cosmopolitan and his subjectivity. Lash and Urry (1994) extend liberal optimism to the latemodern subject by characterizing it as "reflexive individualism." The latemodern subject, they write, "deepens" by "open(ing) up many positive possibilities for social relations – for intimate relations, for friendship, for work relations, for leisure and for consumption" (Lash and Urry 1994: 31). Global restructuring, they claim, produces not only *objects* but also *signs* that traverse rapidly and easily across communication networks (Lash and Urry 1994: 5).

Harvey (1989) voices concern rather than celebration for the latemodern subject. He identifies a latemodern "fragmentation" due to time/space compression under globalized, flexible production methods. This modern treatment of time and space as coherent and linear – e.g. "annihilation of space by time (Becoming)" – now faces obsolescence from a postmodern sensibility where time and space are simultaneous, disjointed, and multiple, e.g. "spatialization of time (Being)" (Harvey 1989: 261). This induces a postmodern response, according to Harvey (1989: 350), of withdrawal "into a kind of shell-shocked, blasé, or exhausted silence" that convinces the latemodern subject "to bow down before the overwhelming sense of how vast, intractable, and outside any individual or even collective control everything is."

Globalization as colonial rhetoric

These renditions of global restructuring, while informative and important, exhibit what Spurr (1993) calls the "rhetoric of empire." By this, he means a discursive pattern of image-making, referencing, cataloguing, and general reality framing that stems from the Western colonial enterprise originating from the sixteenth century and lasting to the present.

Both liberals and critics of global restructuring partake in this colonizing rhetoric. To begin with, they survey the world with a god's-eye-view. Buttressed with scientific objectivity and rational argumentation, they ascertain for the rest of us what global restructuring is, who it affects, where it is going, and why. This perspective, more likely than not, reflects a common configuration of race/gender/class/age/location, e.g. older white masculinized cosmopolitans working in or near global cities. One may protest: the nature of the subject – global restructuring – requires a god's-eye-view! But what Spurr critiques – and what ails "globalization" studies – is that the colonial gaze unreflexively focuses on only a small segment of the world at the expense of its vast majority.

Take, for example, how "globalization" studies cast the relationship between global and local forces. Liberals outrightly embrace one-way penetration of the local by the global. Not only does the global provide greater "modernity," "progress," "democracy" (even "history"!), they assert, but that is what the global *should* do to the local. Critics disagree, at least theoretically. Gramscian globalists, for example, may recognize that "different master (global) narratives" may fuse with "local vernaculars (e.g. separatism, folklorism, local sacred beliefs)" to produce a heterogeneous "global culture" (Editors, *Review of International Political Economy*, 1994: 4.) In the end, we learn little of how a transnationalized ideology like liberal capitalism *interacts* with and subsequently *constructs* a local ideological context and its subject. What Gramscian globalists tell us instead is how liberal capitalism triumphs over and annihilates the local (Ling 1996b).

This one-sided rendition of global restructuring reflects an underlying classification scheme: e.g. history-making capitalist economies vs. history-lagging non-capitalist ones; wealthy centers vs. exploited peripheries; transnational firms vs. territorially bound states; globe-straddling cosmopolitans vs. locally bound parochials. Thus, the world divides into dichotomous categories that reproduce the West/rest, self/other rationales of an older colonial tradition. Additionally, the global and the local are placed in irreconcilable oppositions, thereby compelling a (false) choice between one or the other. This distracts attention from those processes of interaction, appropriation, synthesis, hybridity, and transformation that course through global and local forces. Some coin a trendy phrase, "glocalization" (see Karam, Chapter 11, this volume), to refer to this phenomenon, but it remains (as yet) undertheorized and underspecified.

"Globalization" studies also train our intellectual sights onto macro-corporate entities such as finance, production, trade, telecommunications, media, drug cartels, and the Mafia. Liberals and critics alike fixate on their "structural integration," "corporate strategies," "logic of collective action," and "economic vs. state power." Those who populate this global economy become abstracted into consumers, producers, citizens, elites, or cosmopolitans. These same liberals and critics presume that "categories of capitalism" and their *laissez-faire* principles apply universally across culture, race, or gender. In so doing, they mask normative and ideological presuppositions regarding "who is 'wealthy' and who is 'poor,' who is 'advanced' and who is 'behind,' who is 'rational' and who is 'irrational,' who is 'peaceful' and who is 'violent'" (Murphy and Rojas de Ferro 1995: 63). What results is an unreflexive reproduction of the values, norms, institutions, and practices of those who have always been on top.

Not surprisingly, the few probes that we have on subjectivity under late-modern capitalism are idealized also. As we have already mentioned, the "globalization" literature privileges one type of subjectivity – Westernized, masculinized, and industrialized – over other possible configurations. In both liberal and critical scenarios, the latemodern subject confronts a high-tech, postmodern world in which traditional forms of social organization (e.g. the nation-state) no longer hold.

This presumption stems from the literature's constant affirmation of liberal capitalism as globalization's defining ideology. Whether celebrating or castigating it, the literature sets liberal capitalism – which essentially upholds Western-style capitalism – as the organizing rationale behind the world political economy. In so doing, "globalization" studies implicitly place the industrialized West at the geopolitical–economic center of the world, with "the rest" as its reactionary appendage.[5]

Such discursive moves eradicate the subaltern.[6] Though subalterns may constitute the majority of the world's population, its labor force, and consumption market, they are omitted from consideration when surveyed from a god's-eye-view. It discounts, in short, all those who are not westernized, capitalized, and masculinized living in global cities as consumers, producers, citizens, elites, or cosmopolitans. At the same time, we lose sight of what it means to live, work, play, and die in a globalized but varied economy – and how all these may differ for different groups. Here, Spivak (1988) rightly charges, the subaltern woman suffers especially. She is "invisibilized" and silenced by two crushing discourses: a masculinist discourse of imperialism and an equally masculinist reactionary anti-imperialism. Consequently, the subaltern woman and other feminized subjects have no language, rhetoric, discourse, or even voice to express their subjectivities. As we will demonstrate in the remainder of this chapter, they are perhaps the most globalized subjects of all.

A growing body of feminist scholarship aims to "re-visibilize" and re-articulate women under various processes of global change (Safa 1981; Nash and Fernandez-Kelly 1983; Sen and Grown 1987; Ward 1990; Marchand 1996). Though primarily concerned with global restructuring rather than "globalization," this literature explicitly recognizes gender as a fundamental dimension along which all social processes and practices are organized, experienced, and rendered meaningful. Thus, the subjects of these studies are not disembodied persons who transverse across time and space, but corporeal women and men whose choices and movements reflect their gendered, racialized, and class-based identities in the worlds they inhabit.

Throughout, feminist analyses of "everyday resistance" recurs, returning both the subject and agency to our understanding of global restructuring. In underscoring women's responses, though, many such studies underestimate the impact of macro-structures in limiting women's choices. This tendency to "romanticise resistance" (Abu-Lughod 1990: 42) ignores the complex structures of power in which acts of resistance are embedded. Not only is this historically inaccurate but it obscures the very problem that initially motivated these studies.

Global restructuring II: a regime of labor intimacy (RLI)

In this chapter, we seek to learn from these insights while redressing their weaknesses. To *de-colonize* global restructuring, we retain the focus on corporeal agency found in feminist literature. This requires viewing global restructuring from below, in person, and located at a specific geopolitical–cultural site. We also look at non-corporate, though no less organized, forms of working and living in the global political economy. This "re-sighting" helps us examine the full complement of global life from its macro-structural aspects (like the gendered, racialized state) to its micro-subjective impact (such as on the subaltern woman). At the same time, we aim to avoid romanticizing or individualizing subjectivity by placing it within larger structures that operate in the global political economy. Through ethnographic research, we decipher what Murphy and Rojas de Ferro (1995) refer to as the "circulation of meanings" or "regimes of representation" that shape history and embed structures of power. This means redefining what constitutes global culture/society/persons. It also requires taking seriously how corporeal subjects themselves make sense of their globalizing world. From this basis, we may trace how contending ideologies may intertwine or co-exist in a latemodern subjectivity, thereby extending a different definition to cosmopolitanism and cosmopolitans.

More specifically, we examine global restructuring from a gendered and racialized perspective. By this, we refer to the recognition that all social processes, practices, meaning-structures, and institutions (like the state) assign and reflect historically constructed notions of "masculinity" and "femininity" that are also class-based, racially specific, and culturally defined. Typically, this gendering process reflects a patriarchal power structure that glorifies men, masculinity, and manhood and denigrates women, femininity, and womanhood. These constructions of gender differences entail more than biological differences. They may apply to whole groups of people regardless of sex. Both male and female cosmopolitans of TMC, for example, take on "masculinized" traits of high-tech mobility, autonomy, and challenging opportunities in comparison to their "feminized" counterparts in the regime of labor intimacy who must contend with low-wage menial labor, enforced intimacy, and incarcerating daily routines. As a case in point, we focus on Filipina domestic workers in Hong Kong.

A globalized service economy

TMC's "structural adjustment" policies of the 1970s–80s account for today's "global feminization" of labor intimacy.[7] These policies forced governmental retrenchments into anti-unionism, subcontracting, and resort to temporary or contract workers. This led to development of three major categories of workers in the Philippines: women, overseas contract workers, and child workers.[8] Women were more cost-effective to hire but they also became the first ones fired. A worldwide "skill polarization" emerged with some workers representing "an elite of technically skilled, high-status specialist workers possessing higher-level institutional qualifications" (such as financial analysts) while others constituted "a larger mass of technically semi-skilled production and subsidiary workers requiring minor training" such as assembly line workers (Standing 1989: 1079). As states further deregulated labor to enhance flexible accumulation under global restructuring,[9] many workers saw overseas employment as their only hope. In 1992, 2.5 million people or 8 per cent of the Filipino workforce sought contract work overseas (*FEER* 2 April 1992: 22).

These economic forces combined with a historical racialization and sexualization of work channeled massive numbers of Filipinos to venture overseas for income in the regime of labor intimacy. In the mid-1980s, nearly half of Filipino contract workers overseas were women (Eviota 1992). First, they worked as "medical workers, secretaries, clerks, and teachers, then eventually as domestic help and sex workers" (Rosca 1995: 526). In 1984, 84 per cent of Filipina migrants went to the Middle East; by 1987, they started to shift to the capital-surplus countries of East Asia such as Hong Kong, Singapore, and Japan (Heyzer 1989: 1116).[10]

Filipina migrants are usually the sole supporters of landless parents and/or unemployed husbands, as well as children. A large proportion are college-educated but were unable to find work at home in the fields for which they were trained. Migrant workers from the Philippines average 6.9 years of work abroad; 18 per cent have had some college education and 36.8 per cent have earned a college degree (*FEER* 8 March 1990: 32–3). Domestic work overseas can bring Filipinas six times what they earned in the Philippines (Eviota 1992).

While overseas pay may be high, Filipina migrants often find themselves incarcerated within a regime of labor intimacy. They discover that the larger community often links their domestic work with sexualized service (Chang and Groves, forthcoming). Pseudo-employment agencies and other illegal under-ground networks recruit an undetermined number of Filipinas under the guise of domestic service or "entertainment jobs" only to put them to work as prosti-tutes in bars or brothels (*FEER* 14 October 1993: 38–9; Eviota 1992). Still other women turn to prostitution when domestic contracts are prematurely terminated and/or crippling debts are owed to recruitment agencies in the Philippines. Indeed, the governments of both the Philippines and receiving countries – particularly in Asia where the sex trade is most rampant – are complicit in promoting such forms of sexual exploitation, particularly with their failure to regulate recruitment agencies or enact legislation to protect (rather than limit) the rights of domestic workers.

The complicit, patriarchal state

The state may be "hollowing-out" under TMC, but it enjoys a renewed vigor in the regime of labor intimacy. The state actively structures, facilitates, and sustains a globalized service economy. The Philippines government, for example, supervises, regulates, transports, and taxes its overseas contract workers with various state agencies organized under the Department of Labor. In the 1970s, the Marcos government initiated overseas contract work as a developmental strategy to enhance economic competitiveness. A decade later, it utilized overseas employment to manage a spiraling external debt (Jose 1991; Standing 1989).[11] The state initially decreed that all migrant workers must remit at least half of their monthly salary through authorized government channels. But a grassroots organization of migrant workers, United Filipinos Against Forced Remittance, defeated this legislation in 1984.[12] Now, the government seeks to charge migrant workers for "health care" (Rosca 1995).

Despite recent protests over the treatment of Filipina domestic workers over-seas, the state continues to market overseas contract work as part of a national development policy. President Fidel Ramos refers to Filipina migrant workers as "a vital export commodity (for) the Philippines' own economic strategy" (Rosca 1995: 524). In 1991, remittances to the Philippines from overseas contract workers amounted to approximately 12 per cent of its gross national product (GNP) (*FEER* 22 August 1991: 56). In 1992, overseas remittances accounted for 25 per cent of the country's foreign-exchange earnings (*FEER* 2 April 1992: 22).

Reliance on overseas remittances is complemented by the Philippine government's development policy at home. This development policy for the next century, *Philippines 2000*, centers on efforts to woo foreign investors with attractive deals – which often include women – at the expense of social, economic, and environmental deterioration within the country (Eviota 1992). Increasingly, "development" and "sex tourism" have become mutually reinforcing sources of hard currency. Even with the closure of US military bases, "bikini bars" remain a lucrative feature of the tourism and business landscape in the Philippines. In addition, with the growth of the bride trade and the exportation of female "entertainers" to Japan and other Asian countries, the "services" of Filipinas are increasingly available abroad.[13]

Receiving states are equally complicit. In Hong Kong, immigration policies subject Filipina domestic workers to effective indentured servitude by legally binding them to full-time, live-in work for one employer without specifying the conditions of their service. Authorities in both Singapore and Hong Kong restrict Filipinas from changing employers, type of employment, and even having the right to terminate their jobs for two years (Heyzer 1989: 1116). In Singapore, maids must undergo a mandatory six-month pregnancy check to determine their "employability" (Heyzer 1989: 1116). State authorities in Japan often turn a blind eye to the illegal but lucrative recruitment of Filipinas to serve as its "hostesses" and "entertainers" (*FEER* 14 October 1993: 39).

The state's complicity in this regime of labor intimacy is not a recent adaptation to globalizing trends. It reflects a long-standing ideology of sexualized, racialized service for certain sectors and members of the world political economy.

Transnational ideology of racialized, sexualized service

As TMC spouts the transnational ideology of universalism and liberalism to promote capital mobility, technological development, and flexible production, the regime of labor intimacy operates on a symbiotic ideology of racism/sexism to institutionalize its globalized service economy. The de-territorialization of capital under TMC helps to mystify both transnational ideologies of liberalism and sexualized, racialized service. The former becomes a shining standard bearer to all that is possible while the latter remains hidden and illegitimate despite the virtual incarceration of, in particular, female migrants into sexualized service with all its abuses, exploitation, and possibility of life-threatening disease.[14]

Indeed, the global economy casts Filipinas and other Asian women as the very embodiment of "service" (Ling 1996a, 1997). The stereotype of the Filipina as sexually subservient is rooted in a history of colonialism, sexism, and poverty. As already mentioned, "sex tourism" has underwritten the Philippines' debt-ridden economy for decades. Exceptionally, the Aquino government sought to clean up this "service economy" – especially its offshoot into sex tourism – as part of a larger campaign to restore national dignity. But such efforts failed because it ignored the entrenchment of this service economy in an international political economy that limits options for Filipinas and which provides wealthy Western, and increasingly Asian, businessmen with the economic power to purchase and trade women as sexual commodities (Enloe 1989). Commodification of Filipinas now takes on the form of a "maid trade" (Chang and Groves, forthcoming).

In Hong Kong, as the Filipina community has grown and become more visible, their presence has created a public debate about domestic workers that has been framed largely in terms of the women's sexuality (Chang and Groves, forthcoming). Complaints about their occupation of public space, neglect of duties, or illegal activities condemn this all-female community in moral terms. The Filipinas, many imply, offer more than domestic services in exchange for money. Filipinas are held as "morally suspect" (Constable 1996) by many local residents and employers, who presume that the women have an ulterior motive in going abroad: "to find a man and obtain financial security" (Constable 1996: 466). Such debates often take place in newspaper editorials where Filipina domestic workers are accused of neglecting children, seducing husbands, and moonlighting as prostitutes. Indeed, the media are full of such allusions to the women's sexuality and its economic significance, from suggestive newspaper headlines such as "Maids too much of a distraction for employers" (*Hong Kong Standard* 12 May 1997) to more sensationalist captions such as "Maid turned to prostitution" (*South China Morning Post* 12 May 1983). This sexualized image of the Filipina pervades public discourse in Hong Kong, casting domestic workers into the morally dubious category of laborers associated with the sex industry. Filipina domestics are thus judged and held accountable, not for the "intimate labor" that they provide for the families of Hong Kong, but as women who leave their own families to sell their services abroad for economic gain.

The image of the Filipina woman as "prostitute" is also highly racialized in Hong Kong. One local writer, for example, devoted a whole chapter in his book, *The Great Hong Kong Sex Novel*, to the sexual escapades of Filipina domestic workers as seen through the eyes of two Western businessmen. Entitled "Filipina Mon Amour," this chapter depicts Filipina women as "little brown Eskimos" (Adams 1993: 73) who perform sex with great "tropical ardor" (p. 83). Such images hark back to the days of sex tourism in the Philippines yet are revived in Hong Kong, which is still marketed as one of Asia's ports of "entertainment" for foreign enlisted – and increasingly business – men. In one newspaper editorial, an employer complained that his maid entertained foreign men in his house while he was away and frequented bars in the red-light district of Hong Kong:

> The main reason why Chinese employers do not like their maid staying away overnight is because they know all too well how it is being spent! Just drop by any Wanchai bar and you will see Filipinas walking off arm in arm with sailors. Many of them don't even bother to get into the bars but wait outside to be picked up.
>
> (W.C.Lau, "Sensible to pay return air fare to Philippines," letter to the editor, *South China Morning Post* 24 June 1985: 22)

As this quotation suggests, the mere association with a foreign man is enough to impose upon a Filipina woman the label of "prostitute."

At the same time, migrant workers themselves succumb to the honeyed rhetoric of transnational liberalism. Many see overseas employment as a means of bootstrapping from intimate labor to TMC: "A lowly job overseas with good pay is better than working as a professional with a low salary in the Philippines" (*FEER* 8 March 1990: 32). Once abroad, however, they find a very different outcome:

> In the Philippines, it's really difficult for even university graduates to get work, and even then the pay is bad. I thought that if I worked here for one or two years, I could save enough to go home and start business. But by the time I pay my debts here (in Japan), I will have saved almost nothing.
>
> (*FEER* 14 October 1993: 9)

In response to liberalism's empty promises, Filipina domestic workers often retrench into a romanticized conservatism of God, family, and country.

Cultural reification: God, family, and country[15]

In Hong Kong, many Filipina domestic workers resist their racialization and sexualization by redefining service in terms of devotion to God, family, and country. They regularly center social activities around religious organizations (usually affiliated with the local Catholic Church) which enforce extensive rules, both formal and informal, on where to go, what to do, when to do it, and with whom. Penalties for breaking the rules include fines, ostracism, and even expulsion from the group. These organizations emphasize religious or cultural activities such as singing church hymns or Filipino folk dances to ward off society's association of Filipinas with prostitution: e.g. singing Karaoke songs, disco dancing in places of ill repute. In the process of redefining service, many Filipinas mythologize a "traditional culture" that does not necessarily reflect life as it is in the Philippines (Chang and Groves, forthcoming).

Some Filipinas draw upon their religious faith to define themselves as servants of the Lord rather than the physical world of men. They describe this service to God and the Church as cleansing, filling them with a sense of "righteousness" and "completeness" that comes only once a week on Sundays. Articles in *Tinig Filipino* speak directly to the women's faith as a means of redefining sexual service. In one issue, the editor imagined a "love letter" written by God to Filipina overseas contract workers, who are described as the "Chosen People to be Helpers of the World" (L.R. Layosa "Into Thy Hands," *Tinig Filipino* April 1994: 6). In this letter, God urges Filipina domestic workers to embrace their work as servants, bringing to it their "true Christian values, your resilient, cheerful, persevering and helpful qualities" and "humble ways." As one woman put it: "I am not only here to earn money, I am here used by God as an instrument to show special light to my employers." In this way, the notion of service is cleansed of its sexual overtones and becomes an almost sacred activity, giving the women a sense of moral identity and purpose (Chang and Groves, forthcoming).

Many Filipinas also embrace their identities as wives, mothers, and daughters to counter the sexualized image of the service provider. They invoke their marital or family status to ward off sexual advances from male employers: e.g., they are "not available" because they must "sacrifice for the family first." Public events also advance this theme of sacrifice for and devotion to migrant families. Articles in *Tinig Filipino* frequently flag traditional family values as a means of resisting the temptations of Hong Kong – e.g. illegal part-time work, "loan sharks," spending on oneself instead of sending remittances back home, extra-marital or illicit affairs, and so on. For example, one article emphasizes various kinds of "patience," including "patience with desire" such as "buying a house, saving money, marrying, etc." (M.E. Loria "Adjustments to the local situation," *Tinig Filipino* April 1994: 25) as a way of serving one's family rather than oneself.

Finally, some maids seek refuge in a refurbished national identity. Articles in *Tinig Filipino* repeatedly remind the women of their role as "economic heroes" of the Philippines:

> Through your good works in those places where you are temporarily working, you will become instruments in the economic improvement or progress of your "sick" nation through the dollars you send back home. In the future, through your perseverance and hard work, your children and your children's children will be the ones to benefit from your nation's progress.
>
> (L.R. Layosa "Into Thy Hands," *Tinig Filipino* April 1994: 6)

Such articles portray the women as active participants in the economic destiny of the Philippines, as opposed to sexual commodities. Other articles redefine Filipinas as "helpers of the world" rather than the "world's cleaners" (M. de Torres "The Filipino: world class," *Tinig Filipino* March 1994: 15). Service, in this sense, takes on a strong nationalistic overtone. For example, in the letter from God, the editor urges maids not only to educate their employers' children, but to "Filipinize" them (L.R. Layosa "Into Thy Hands," *Tinig Filipino* April 1994: 6).

While this retrenchment into God, family, and country provides a moral identity, it also creates painful moral dilemmas for Filipinas. Cultural and religious values offer a haven from the transnational ideology of sexualized, racialized service. But they also become controlling and oppressive, depriving the Filipina woman of the autonomy and independence that liberal capitalism insists is hers. Yet, if she fails to live up to the moral standards of her community, she risks being labeled as loose or promiscuous. Thus the two processes of global restructuring – TMC and labor intimacy – catch the Filipina migrant worker in between: tradition or modernity, virtue or independence, sainthood or sin. Recognizing the impossibility of such choices ("I'm no saint! You have to be naughty sometimes!"), some women choose to loosen or even break their ties with their community – often at great personal cost. Still others choose another alternative: "tomboyism."

Sexual alternative: tomboyism

Given such intense scrutiny on their sexuality by their immediate environment as well as the global economy at large, some Filipina migrant workers opt out through a homosexual identity they call "tomboyism."[16] Tomboys wear men's clothing, have short hair, behave in a conventionally masculine manner, and have liaisons or affairs with other Filipinas. Some claim that outfitting as a tomboy allows them to avoid being perceived as "cheap." It also saves them from sexual harassment from men while offering some protection themselves to other Filipinas. As one woman put it: "Any friend can protect you, but the protection of a tomboy is different." A tomboy, for example, replaced the former president of the Filipina shelter in Hong Kong when the latter was caught having an affair with her male employer. Indeed, many tomboys hold positions of power and responsibility within the Filipino community, where their image as "strong" and "faithful" women challenges the stereotype of Filipinas as sexually subservient or promiscuous.

The migrant community tolerates tomboyism, despite the Catholic Church's injunction against homosexuality, precisely because it relieves Filipinas from their intense sexualization while overseas. Some women even speak of lesbianism as a show of devotion to their families. Tomboys are seen to offer a "safe outlet" for women: a means of enjoying the romance and intimacy of a relationship while at the same time preserving marital vows. The women thus construct lesbianism as a form of fidelity rather than promiscuity. Most importantly, a relationship with a tomboy would not disrupt family life since there is no risk of pregnancy. One article in *Tinig Filipino*, for example, describes tomboys as "gorgeous, faithful, sympathetic," etc. These are words from women who are too afraid of flushing their fetus in the toilet: "With a lesbian, I'm safe" (L. Eronico "The Modern Romeos in the Making," *Tinig Filipino* March 1994: 10).

Conclusion

The moral dilemmas of Filipina domestic workers in Hong Kong stem from their placement between two processes of global restructuring: labor intimacy and TMC. An examination of their internal dialectics provides a more comprehensive understanding of our latemodern global economy (see Table 1.1):

Table 1.1 Schematic representation of techno-muscular capitalism (TMC) and regime of labor intimacy (RLI)

Category	TMC	RLI
Identifying features	Integration of technology, trade, production, and communications facilitated by globalized financial networks	Exportation of low-wage, low-to-medium skilled workers to service "intimate" jobs in cosmopolitan homes
The role of the state	Internationalized or "hollowed out"	Complicit, patriarchal, vigorous
Transnationalized ideology	Liberal capitalism	Sexualized, racialized service
Nature of global society, culture, persons	Global elites, or cosmopolitans, postmodern individualism, or "shell-shocked" withdrawal	Cultural reification: God, family, and country, crossing sexual boundaries, moral dilemmas

1   Labor intimacy results from and sustains TMC. Gross wage inequities increasingly casualize and informalize labor so that some workers have more means to hire others who need more economic compensation. Migrant workers toiling in the household also release cosmopolitans from time-consuming, mind-numbing, non-rewarding chores so that they may pursue their "casino capitalism," "technology districts," "strategic alliances," "global cities," and "trilateral economies." Thus, the cycle of wage inflation and labor domestication continues.

2   The state may be released from traditional duties of sovereignty or community to further the "flexible production" or "mobile capital" of TMC. But this reserves the state's resources to continue its historical institutionalization of racist, sexist, and classist policies in the regime of labor intimacy.[17] As migration within East Asia shows, such state power parallels that of firms in its global reach.

3   A transnational ideology of sexualized, racialized service privatizes and mutes the contradictions of transnational liberalism. In this way, liberal internationalists may promote the public rhetoric of wealth, opportunity, and mobility even as a majority of the world's population struggles in poverty, exploitation, and structural incarceration. As demonstrated by Filipina domestic workers in Hong Kong, sometimes local resistance to global restructuring takes on the form of reifying those very pillars of society and state that are most conservative, patriarchal, and hegemonic.

4   The cultural retrenchment and paralyzing moral dilemmas found in the regime of labor intimacy provides a stable pool of labor for the latemodern cosmopolitans of TMC to experiment with their time–space compression and/or reflexive individualism. Little chance exists, then, of local counter-

hegemonies overhauling the capitalist world-hegemony. Most likely, systemic changes or transformations will arise from the interstices of local–global interaction and the constituent-specific negotiations that they reflect.

This case study on Filipina migrant workers in Hong Kong broadens our understanding of subjectivity and cosmopolitanism under latemodern capitalism. It demonstrates that geographical mobility does not necessarily translate into a psychological or emotional detachment. Indeed, our case study underscores that recourse to "reflexive individualism" or "blasé withdrawal" highly correlates with relative power disparities in the global political economy. A middle-aged, middle-income, masculinized professional without household duties may feel free to "reinvent" himself or herself to "join new communities." But the scope of such choice for a middle-aged, low-income feminized domestic worker facing a barrage of sexual and racial discrimination is much smaller. Though choices do exist, they take very different and unanticipated forms. Some migrant workers choose to reify their indigenous culture; others seek subterfuge in an alternative sexuality.

In shifting from a (neo)colonial, masculinist god's-eye-view to the perspective of a subaltern woman from a specific location, we change also our notion of what constitutes the global and globalism. Hannerz's high-style multiculturalism still applies, but another kind of cosmopolitanism/globalism comes into sight as well. It also requires competence, mastery, autonomy, self-made-ness, and intellectual acumen. But it has less to do with abstract, evaluative qualities like intellectualism or aesthetics than with a pragmatic outlook that aims to engage with, fit in, sort through, and negotiate across differences. Less idealized, it is instead embodied in the daily demands of global life: caring for young and elderly people who are not from one's own culture or country, cleaning their houses, washing their clothes, preparing their food, living a life where local knowledge, tastes, habits, and customs blur ceaselessly with global ones. This "pragmatic globalism" recognizes contending ideologies (sometimes incommensurate ontologies) where they exist (e.g., work vs. family, devotion vs. service, saint vs. whore, Catholicism vs. homosexuality, Tagalog vs. English) but ultimately seeks to work them out such that they emerge as reformed, transmuted parts of oneself, not a quaint custom or exotic locale that can be "exited" at will. Thus, pragmatic globalism does not force a selection between false choices: modernity vs. tradition, contrast vs. uniformity, globalism vs. localism, reflexivity vs. withdrawal. Rather, it aspires for an overall sanity that endures through all the conflicts and contradictions that beset our daily, global life.

Notes

1   We borrow the description, "techno-muscular," from Elaine Boose's (1993: 67–106) identification of American self-perceptions during the Vietnam War.
2   Since the mid-1980s, Hong Kong has become the second largest destination (next to the Middle East) for Filipina migrant workers. From 1975 to 1991, the number of Filipina domestic workers in Hong Kong jumped from 1,000 to nearly 66,000 (*Asia-*

Pacific Mission for Migrant Filipinos 1991). At present, new arrivals estimate at a rate of eighty per day, bringing the Filipina population to over 130,000, making it the largest non-Chinese community in Hong Kong (Constable 1997).

3   Welfens (1989: 273) notes, for example, that "85 percent of international trade in technology is concentrated among companies from just ten market-economy, industrial countries – and that these are all among the top fifteen countries for direct investment."

4   A caveat: debates about the demise of the state under global restructuring are far from settled. Krasner (1994), for instance, reiterates that states remain what they have always been: rational, self-interested, unitary, and the most important actor in international relations. Thus a state-centric analysis still offers the most parsimonious elegance for predictive theory while, at the same time, explaining radical changes in the world political economy. *The Economist* (7 October 1995: 15–16) agrees that the powerless state is a "myth." For evidence, it refers to continued high levels of public spending in states that are supposed to be the most globalized. For a critique of this line of reasoning, see Strange 1994.

5   This literature identifies Japan as an industrialized economy but not a member of the geopolitical club.

6   The concept of subalternity builds on earlier notions of the comprador: that is, a class or grouping of people structurally placed to serve the governing needs of another. But where comprador connotes a commercial relationship, subaltern suggests a political one.

7   Here, "feminization" refers to a process of physical embodiment as well as social construction. That is, more women are working in certain sectors of the global economy. These are usually low-wage, low-skilled, and low-mobility workers. At the same time, the global economy assigns to both women and men who work on its lower rungs traits historically identified as "feminine": e.g. backwardness, irrationality, passivity, and victimhood.

8   In 1985, there were 5–7 million Filipino working children within the 5–14 year age group, mostly in rural areas (Ofreneo 1993: 255).

9   For example, the Philippines government in the 1980s removed most enterprises from coverage by various labor laws to reduce production costs for multinational corporations (Standing 1989).

10 Surveys on Filipina migrant workers indicate the following figures: 20,000 in Greece; 40,000 in England; 50,000–100,000 in Hong Kong; 60,000 in Spain; 75,000 in Singapore; 80,000 in Italy; and 750,000 in the Middle East (Rosca 1995; *Asia-Pacific Mission for Migrant Filipinos* 1991).

11 In 1974, the Philippines' external debt amounted to $3.75 billion; by 1990, it had risen to $28 billion with a 8.6 per cent unemployment rate (*FEER* 8 March 1990: 32–3).

12 In 1990, for instance, overseas contract workers remitted $856 million through official channels and another $3 billion through private channels (*FEER* 8 March 1990: 32–3).

13 Rosca (1995: 524) reports that over 75,000 Filipinas work in the Japanese sex industry.

14 According to Rosca (1995: 524), between 30,000 and 50,000 Filipinos around the US bases in the Philippines have contracted the HIV virus.

15 This portion of the chapter draws directly from Chang and Groves (forthcoming).

16 "Coming out" is common for migrants who may cross sexual borders along with national ones (Espin 1994).

17 This dual strategy is apparent in the US Congress, for example, where many conservatives call for less governmental regulation of the "private," corporate sector while advocating more for the "public," civic sector such as immigration, welfare, education, and reproductive rights for women.

2 Breaking patriarchal bonds

Demythologizing the public/private

Gillian Youngs

Global restructuring and the processes of globalization which effect it are disrupting traditional conceptualizations of political and economic space (Harvey 1989; Bird *et al.* 1993; Agnew and Corbridge 1995; Featherstone *et al.* 1995). In broad terms, globalization can be understood as "the emergence and spread of a supraterritorial dimension of social relations" (Scholte 1996: 46). Restructuring concerns among other things "the mobility of capital vs. the fixedness of the state as a territorial unit" (Runyan 1996: 238; see also the Introduction to this volume). Analysts are being pressed towards increasingly integrated understandings of the old state/market configuration in order not only to map the changing patterns of transnational production and consumption but to explore the political economic dynamics characteristic of them. Female labor is central to restructuring as a major feature of the cheaper resources of the South (compared to the North) sought out by transnational corporations, and as mobile labor to service various forms of economic transition in home and host states. Hence the recent growth of global flows of domestic workers, the subject of this chapter (see also Pettman 1998).

Differentiated hierarchies of globally and locally defined spaces have begun to steer perceptions of the world economy and its key networks and interconnections. The growing linkages between global cities reflect a highly technologized concentration of wealth and consumption (Sassen 1991; Lash and Urry 1994), which is the antithesis of the "deadlands" of economically drained sectors of industrialized economies and even more so of the poorest regions of the world (Agnew and Corbridge 1995: 206). State boundaries are no longer sufficient *containers* for recognizing global divisions between rich and poor which are growing in scale within as well as across nations.[1]

Adequate spatial conceptualizations of states and markets as interactive phenomena are now being sought but the in-built limitations of the patriarchal bonds which have constrained them in the past make this endeavor highly problematic. The purpose of this chapter is to set out the nature of this problem and to explain how the developed sensitivity of gender critiques to public/private boundaries, and their fundamental relevance to our understanding of social relations of power as spatially constructed, in theoretical as well as other practices, are central to its solution.

The first section examines the nature of the patriarchal "prism,"[2] through which political and economic space has been predominantly viewed, and the ways in which it obscures the deep operations of power relations through its abstraction of the public from the private and the prioritization of the former over the latter.

The second section explains how gender critiques of public/private dynamics break apart this prism and provide access to an understanding of the world economy which is meaningful in both local and global terms. The arguments direct our attention to the relevance of public/private questions for consideration of structure/agency interactions in an era of globalization.

The final section illustrates why this is important in relation to issues of empowerment as well as oppression through a discussion of the mass utilization of public space in the center of Hong Kong on Sundays by the overseas domestic workforce, which for the working week is largely confined to the domestic private space of homes in the city.

The nature of the patriarchal "prism"

Patriarchy has traditionally been most closely associated with the structures of state, family, and household and the gender inequalities expressed and maintained by them. The focus in such contexts is primarily on public and private political power. The political-economy approach to patriarchy explored here emphasizes rather the interactive nature of households and the economy at large: "[c]apitalism and patriarchy are viewed as two systems of social relations that interact in every domain of social life" (Gibson-Graham 1996: 64). But achieving such a perspective is far from straightforward because of the patriarchal and "capitalocentric" (Ibid.: 6) nature of mainstream economic discourse. The notion of the patriarchal prism assists in the problematization of this discourse. It facilitates both thinking about the distortions of the dominant patriarchal economic viewpoint and the interrogation of them.

The patriarchal prism through which political economy has traditionally been interpreted is based on a prioritization of public sphere activities over the private realm on the basis of a power relationship between the two. The public sphere of states and markets is defined primarily in terms of their major players, governments and transnational corporations as well as the influential international entities involving and/or affecting both, such as the European Union (EU), the North American Free Trade Agreement (NAFTA), the United Nations (UN), the International Monetary Fund (IMF), and the World Trade Organization (WTO).

The statistics which are utilized to describe the power and division of wealth across the world economy reflect this framing of it in terms of these major players but they also reflect associated narrowly defined interpretations of production and consumption at state and market levels. These are related to the elevation of the public over the private as determinant of international reality, a process which in theory and practice works to obscure various aspects of social reproduction in the private realm, that is the home and the family (Peterson 1992b; Whitworth 1994b).

Extensive gender analysis of this situation has demonstrated that the historically established dominance of men in the public sphere and the restriction of women's identity, roles, and prime social influence to the private sphere are fundamental to the construction of gendered identities and the perpetuation of unequal power relations.[3] Global restructuring is bringing increasing numbers of women into the workplace, and feminist analysis stresses that these changes must be understood against the historical background of established gender inequalities. Thus, women are often entering the market place to meet demands for cheap, docile labor and to fill semi-skilled and low-level tasks in production processes and the expanding service sectors (Runyan 1996). An increasing number of women across the world are adding wage-earning to domestic and family functions and suffering from their socially unequal status in both public and private arenas (Walby 1990; Tickner 1991; Aslanbeigui *et al.* 1994; Elson 1995).

These are among the developments which highlight the renewed importance of a better understanding of public/private dynamics in relation to globalization. They indicate that the participation of women in the global economy is intrinsic to its processes of transformation. But the patriarchal prism works to keep the full nature of these processes hidden from the analytical gaze in theoretical as well as other forms of practice.

It does so through an essentially abstract approach to political and economic space which has gained powerful "common-sense" status.[4] Political space is aligned with the category of the state in a particularistic vein which is both reductive and disempowering for our assessment of relations of inequality within and across state boundaries. Not only is the state identified via the prism as the prime and, in any powerful sense, exclusive political category, but it is represented as a unified entity.[5] Its personification as *key actor* symbolically assigns agency to it, and this is supported by the ideas of *legitimate* internal and external power contained in the crucial concept of sovereignty (Ashley and Walker 1990; Ashley 1988).

Two points can be stressed here. The first is that this perspective depoliticizes notions of the state. It removes any need to think of the state as a political *space* within which power struggles take place and thus to *map* those struggles, including within and across public/private divides. Such questions are locked within the notion of the state as actor, as agent. Interest is located primarily in its capacity to act or not in particular circumstances, and internal factors are explored in relation to that. Second, while territoriality is claimed to be central to the concept of the state as a unified entity, its socially constructed meanings are not opened up for exploration.

It is no accident that critiques of state-centrism have focused analytically on the "inside/outside" (Walker 1993) definitive power of state boundaries because that is largely what state-centrism has reduced understandings of territoriality to (Agnew and Corbridge 1995: 78–100). Political boundaries, if they have mattered at all, have been largely delimited as state boundaries, those which oppose the claimed *ordered* interior of the state to the claimed *disorder* of the external world. The full social and material qualities of these boundaries are taken too much for granted. The abstract nature of the state-centric patriarchal prism prioritizes rather their symbolic qualities portrayed by the sense of security and permanence attached to sovereign power.[6] Socially and spatially constructed boundaries within and across states, affecting race and class as well as gender, in this context, are depoliticized too, because they are not identified as aspects of the dynamics of power relations and struggle.

Analytical endeavors to reclaim concepts of space and boundary as sites of struggle are crucial to our understanding of processes of global restructuring because these concern the interactivity of political and economic factors inside as well as outside state boundaries, and, in transnational and global senses, across them (Youngs 1996a).

However, significantly due to the reasons outlined above, spatiality remains a problematic concept and fundamental to continued efforts to integrate the study of politics and, economics (Ashley 1987; Rosow *et al.* 1994; Youngs 1999). For if politics has largely been aligned with abstract concepts of the state, economics has tended to be similarly aligned with abstract constructions of the market. The counterparts of states as unified *actors* in this context are the powerful transnational corporations increasingly understood to both transcend and utilize state boundaries in their efforts to mold the global economy in their interests, seeking out cheap sources of labor and new consumer markets and restructuring their operations accordingly.

The globalized scope of much economic activity is undoubtedly uneven and reveals an increasing concentration of wealth in individuals, businesses, and nationally defined economies of the powerful centers of the developed world: the US, Europe, and Japan.[7] But the key role of developing economies, notably in East Asia,[8] affirms that the varieties of political, economic, and cultural conditions within which processes of global restructuring are taking place are expanding. Studies of globalization have prompted interest, for example, in the changing political role, internally and externally, of individual states in relation to market forces (Cerny 1995; Hutton 1996), but mainstream neglect of public/private perspectives on the construction of social space stops analysis of spatiality short, leaving the patriarchal prism intact, and reconceptualizing local/global relations within its undynamic parameters.

Space and power: gender and public/private divides

Space and power, or rather the specificities of space and power, have always been central to gender analysis. Feminists have long illustrated how men and women, male and female as categories, have been socially produced and reproduced in relation to the divisions between the public and private.[9] As processes of struggle and emancipation, as well as oppression, grow in complexity, the value of greater precision in our understanding of the nature of public and private increases too. One of the strengths of the feminist public/private critique is that it overtly associates power relations with particular definitions of social spaces and activities. As a strategy, it encourages attention to the primary locations of social existence and the ways in which social meanings are generated and maintained in definitions of that existence. It seeks to break into the patriarchal forces which work towards the representation of society as unified, and actively undermines the hierarchical opposition of public over private which abstracts the former from the latter. In order to understand gender inequalities and gendered identities, it is essential to investigate how they are constructed *across* public/private divides, and to recognize that these divides are not fixed but themselves transform according to wider political economic processes.

The orientation of feminist critique, in exposing the dynamics of public/private power relations, in disrupting the *presence* of the public based on an *absence* of the private,[10] aims towards a new spatial ontology in social analysis, explicitly locating the relationship of politics and economics in the context of the socially and spatially constructed relationships between public and private. Ontology operates at the most fundamental level conceptually; it shapes the parameters of potential insight and analysis (Youngs 1996b). With regard to dominant ontological standpoints, this involves assumptions which have been legitimized *over time* to the point where they become *hidden* or gain an apparently non-negotiable status. The crystallized overtones of the prism are helpful for capturing the nature of patriarchal perspectives, suggesting rigidity of viewpoint as well as an indication of this having hardened over time into "common sense."

Feminist frameworks offer the conceptual tools to shatter the patriarchal prism but we need to take due account of the obstacles to this possibility. There may be a well-established tradition of feminist theorizing about the public/private, but because this form of theorizing has always been, in important respects, marginal, it remains largely invisible and ineffective; it lacks historical force in the context of mainstream patriarchal discourses of politics and political economy. As Spike Peterson (1996: 18) has put it: "masculinist ways of knowing marginalize women as agents and gender as an analytic category." This is illustrated by the *absence* of feminist insights even in important new work on spatiality and international political economy. It is significant that this work overtly addresses the *local* in a range of ways but still views it through the patriarchal prism with its spatial constraints basically intact as far as the public/private is concerned. This is an important limitation when capitalistic forms of work for women have been increasing both in and outside the home. The patriarchal prism simply obscures the complexities of these processes of feminization. This is a static and abstracted view of the local complemented by a similarly static and abstracted view of the global. We are dealing here with *a gender-neutral sense of spatiality*. Neutral because questions of power related to gender and spatiality are evaded by means of patriarchal assumptions about what counts (the public) and what does not count (the private) in assessments of political economy.[11]

As Sylvia Walby's (1990) assessment of "private to public patriarchy" indicates, we need to have regard to both historical and spatial factors, and the integrated influence of political, economic and cultural forces, to arrive at dynamic understandings of patriarchal structures in local and global contexts. The nature of women's work, paid and unpaid, inside and outside the home, and its varied roles and lowly status, can only be fully analyzed on such bases. Private/public linkages are key in this regard.

> The main basis of the tension between capitalism and patriarchy is over the exploitation of women's labor. On the one hand, capitalists have interests in the recruitment and exploitation of female labor, which is cheaper than that of men because of patriarchal structures. On the other, there is resistance to this by that patriarchal strategy which seeks to maintain the exploitation of women in the household.
>
> (Walby 1990: 185)

The "strategy" of "allowing women into paid employment, but segregating them from men and paying them less" (Walby 1990: 185) has continued to grow in significance in terms of the kinds of employment involved, the geographical globalization of the economy and its recent processes of restructuring (Sassen 1991; Aslanbeigui *et al.* 1994; Runyan 1996; United Nations Development Programme (UNDP) 1997). A growing number of women around the world are experiencing dual forms of interrelated public and private oppression which can be fully understood only when informed by a range of historical *and* spatial considerations.[12] If anything, the intricacies of public/private formulations as they have become historically embedded in the global political economy are producing increased conceptual challenges. When we think about integrating them into our approach to power and globalization, we must be aware that the construction of *public* and *private* is *fundamental* to our understanding even of what politics (Peterson 1995) and political economy (Whitworth 1994b) are understood to represent.

I would go so far as to argue that the progress of new and more meaningful spatial ontologies is substantially dependent on negotiation of public/private constructions, and I argue elsewhere (Youngs 1999) that this is especially so with regard to our renegotiation of the *local*, which is becoming such a familiar spatial motif in new forms of global analysis. Here we are dealing specifically with historico-spatial questions. The history of public/private constructions of space is as old as politics and political economy themselves, and as the discourses associated with these processes (as feminist analysis has revealed). The discourses which have asserted the dominant meanings of politics and political economy are inherently spatial, especially as they designate which relations of power are of prime relevance or interest, that is those in the *public* sphere, and which can just be taken for granted, that is those confined to the *private*. Essential to considerations of local/global relations/dynamics (as I will illustrate further below in relation to migrant domestic workers) is overt exploration of public/private relations/dynamics: the recognition of the interactivity between the so-called private (household) sphere and the wider political economy. The work (paid and unpaid) which women (including migrant women) do inside, as well as outside, the home is part of the explanation of global/local linkages. But this is a perspective the patriarchal prism obscures.

For these reasons, a substantial part of feminist analysis has been preoccupied with pressing for redefinitions of politics and political economy as domains understood to incorporate not only *private* as well as *public* relations of power, but equally importantly the dependencies and interactions across them.[13] When we do so in global as well as national contexts, we are reminded that there are multi-plicitous formulations of public and private space associated with specific forms of institutionalized social practices. These practices in part at least demonstrate how states and markets interact, how political, economic, and cultural hierar-chical forces situate and work to maintain individuals and social groupings within specific relations of power.

In tracing patterns and effects of global restructuring, it is adjustments and transformations in these interactions and forces that we are mapping. It is helpful to think in terms of mapping because we are dealing with a global market which is expanding in geographical scope and complexity, involving a growing number of states and societies, developing the transnational characteristics of states them-selves, not just as major economic players internally and externally, and collectively through regional entities such as NAFTA, the EU and the Asia Pacific Economic Co-operation Forum, and influential institutions such as the IMF and World Bank, but also as bargaining partners with transnational capital.[14]

We can still retain a strong sense of the uneven nature of globalization while recognizing that the overlapping economic, political, and cultural spaces societies occupy are subject to various transnational influences mediated by state and market forces. The growing importance of migrant workforces, ranging from the least to the most skilled, is driving home also that social groups and individuals operating in one geographical location are linked in a web of formal and informal relations of state and market whose origins and spheres of operation may be variously located.[15] Deeply embedded within those relations is a range of historically constructed and newly created connections among private spheres and among public spheres which are separated geographically, as well as across the public/private. Jan Jindy Pettman's (1996a, b) identification of an "interna-tional political economy of sex" based on the range of servicing roles provided by women is illuminating in this respect, reminding us that processes of global-ization and global restructuring are linked to long-term divisions between the public and private and fresh manipulations of them.

This is clearly indicative of the new approaches to structure/agency issues which are required. Chang and Ling's chapter in this collection highlights the shadow role of "servicing" as the dark structural side of globalization, underpin-ning and making possible the glossy images of the service sector in finance and communications. Social constructions of public and private and the inferior roles of women associated with them are being, in certain respects, globalized, or at least transnationalized, and interconnected. Hence our study of structural forces must increasingly take account of mutual reinforcements or contradictions across them.

The introduction to a collection of essays on women in Hong Kong, for example, argues that "any explanation of gender inequality in Hong Kong in terms of traditional Chinese patriarchy has to address the issue of how patriarchy complements, or has been modified by, Hong Kong's brand of industrial capitalism" (Pearson and Leung 1995a: 5–6). This kind of perspective enables us to think through patriarchy in a disaggregated social fashion, that is to consider how patriarchal structures operate across public and private spheres in political, economic and cultural senses. But it goes further in addressing globalization directly, recognizing that patriarchal influences with starkly different histories and locations are merging and creating, through dynamic processes of political economy, restructured patriarchal forms.

Globalized and spatially gendered structures of oppression require such understanding, and they also prompt us to reframe our thinking about agency and structure/agency interactions. We know from feminist analysis that one of the major challenges in the social sciences is the expansion of the structure/agency debate to take full account of feminist critiques of public/private constructions in theoretical and other forms of practice. This would allow gender to be "conceptualized in terms of an interweaving of, and recursive relationships between, personal life and conscious human action, on the one hand, and social structures or constraints, on the other" (Bondi 1994: 194). Such analysis is rooted in an awareness of diverse facets of gendered spatiality which can be understood predominantly in terms of public/private, but which associate structure and agency, spatiality, identity and consciousness, thus asserting that "gender exists both as an aspect of individual, subjective identity and as an external, social construct that constrains the behavior of women and men" (Bondi 1994: 194).

In taking such an approach forward in the context of globalization and global restructuring, the key challenge is the spatially dynamic quality of multiple linkages among public and private spheres operating frequently across state boundaries and associating patterns of oppression of different social groupings which might superficially be regarded as *separate* on nationality, race, and class bases. To put it simply, the global economy, traditionally interpreted as public space, can overtly be demonstrated, for example in the case of migrant service workforces, as *privatized*. Furthermore, these workers from less developed or developing economies become an explicit as well as implicit *public* force in relation to their input to both their host and home economies. The boundaries between public and private as captured by the patriarchal prism are transgressed. In the following discussion I want to reflect on spatial issues related to the overseas domestic workforce in Hong Kong.

From the private to the public: agency and spatiality

There can be few instances where a predominantly female social group has made such a successful and dramatic claim to high-profile public space as have domestic workers in Hong Kong. These workers, mainly from the Philippines, play an increasingly important part in their host and home economies,[16] with close involvement of both their governments in their operation and control as a migrant workforce, as Chang and Ling detail in Chapter 1, this volume. A Hong Kong government survey showed the number of households employing these workers had nearly doubled between 1988 and 1993. The workforce totaled 150,000 in 1996 with estimates that it could rise to 200,000 by the end the century. As well as making a vital contribution to keeping the Hong Kong economy running smoothly by supporting working households, including care of children, elderly relatives, and expectant mothers, these employees have been estimated to send 75 per cent of their earnings back to their home countries.

This migrant workforce has played a dual integral role in the development of the Hong Kong and Philippine economies. In Hong Kong, as in Western economies generally, the participation of women in the labor force has been a growing structural element of both the economy's growth and its transformation to a service orientation (Leung 1995; Wong 1995). The importance of the family in Chinese society has given the public/private tensions in this respect a high priority in terms of maintaining the *feminized* domestic care role (Ng 1995). The migrant workforce has been crucial as a major *external* solution to this *internal* problem, but the associated public and private connections between Hong Kong and the Philippines are equally important. The migrant domestic workers are key economic agents for their families at home,[17] regularly sending back goods as well as money, facilitated by their relatively high earning power in the context of their home economy, despite their significantly low status in terms of the Hong Kong economy.[18]

It is fascinating, however, to pay close attention to the *hidden* nature of these workers as an economic force. In the working week they are predominantly confined to the "private" domestic space, and their restricted living conditions, whether in their employer's home or otherwise, generally reflect the high premium on space (real estate) in Hong Kong. In terms of their home economies, they are *absent*, returning only as holidays and their visas allow and require, often largely cut off from experiencing their own children growing up. Thus their *absence* can be understood in both public and private contexts as pervasive.

On Sundays in Hong Kong, the confinement of these workers to the private sphere is starkly contrasted by their gatherings in the heart of Hong Kong's government and business world (see Figures 2.1 and 2.2). With the Legislative Council building as a backdrop, hundreds of small groups settle in the Statue Square and Chater Gardens areas, more recently spreading further east into Admiralty Gardens. The vast paved area beneath the dominant Hong Kong and Shanghai Banking Corporation building is covered with picnickers. Large amounts of plastic taping, especially around the Exchange Square financial center, indicate the efforts to control the geographic spread of the gatherings. Groups are increasingly extending along the walkway past Exchange Square towards Sheung Wan.

If the presence of this section of Hong Kong's community is largely unfelt

Figure 2.1 Domestic workers in Hong Kong Central: Throngs in Chater Road, the focus
of activity on Sundays. The trees in Statue Square screen the arches of the
Legislative Council Building.

Source: Copyright Gillian Youngs

during the week, it has become one of the most prominent features of the
weekend, dominating Central on Sundays, including pavement areas around the
world-famous Mandarin Hotel. The vast amount of newsprint devoted to the
situation and conflicting views of it over recent years indicate the degree to
which these high-profile spatial claims on an unswervingly regular, weekly, year-
round basis have made a political statement and impact. Efforts to establish
centers in the suburbs as alternative meeting places to Central indicate that the
presence, the *public* visibility, of this gathering is discomforting for officialdom
("Maids' Centres to Ease Pressure on Public Places," *South China Morning Post* 15
November 1994: 9; and "Maids' Centre Hits Right Note," *South China Morning
Post* 5 December 1994: 2).

Further international political dimensions of this group of workers' visibility
were also evident in their public protests over the execution of Flor
Contemplacion in Singapore, and outrage over the case was linked directly to
their own rights campaigns and their assertions of their contributions to home
and host countries ("Maids Vow To Follow 1997 Closely," *Eastern Express*, 27
March 1995: 3; "40,000 Attend Maid's Funeral," *South China Morning Post* 27
March 1995: 2; Asian Domestic Workers Union 1995). Despite these important
factors, it would be reductive to view the nature of the spatial claims being made
as primarily political.

Figure 2.2   Domestic workers in Hong Kong Central: Picnickers line the pavements of
Chater Road. The road is closed to traffic on Sundays so that the Statue
Square area is available for public leisure events.

Source: Copyright Gillian Youngs

What is most striking about the weekend phenomenon is the diversity of
activities it incorporates: religious, social, personal, economic, and political.
Various group and individual elements of religious celebration and study are
prominent. Personal, social, and cultural aspects combine in activities such as
singing and dance. Demonstrations that have taken place have involved issues of
personal, political, and economic rights. The occupation of this public space
represents a disruption of public/private divides directly related to the transnational characteristics of this workforce and its participation in the host and home
economies, including via its own formal and informal economic networks
(*Window* 17 May 1996). This is evidenced by the transactions in goods and
services common to the Sunday gathering, including portrait photography and
hairdressing.

The reader can understand through these descriptions the complexity and
intense personal and social atmosphere generated by the gathering. This
demonstrates the severe restriction on private *and* public space suffered by this

migrant work force in its general living and working conditions. The limitations on private space and personal and social privacy are influential. The Sunday occupation of public space is intrinsically multipurpose in private and public senses and these overlap in the condensed space/time framework of the weekly day off.

A particular kind of continuum relating to individual, social, and cultural identity is achieved via this means from week to week, year to year. The focal activity is the sharing of meals picnic-style on covers on the ground usually in groups of between eight and fifteen or so but sometimes in twos or fours. Surrounding this are a host of activities, from reading and writing letters, examining and discussing documents, looking at photographs, to reading books and individual and group prayer or bible-reading sessions. Manicures and pedicures are quite common and symbolic of the highly personalized level of activities. And what is notable is the manner in which the different activities intermingle in a fairly seamless way. Interesting also is the response of local large-scale as well as small-scale economic actors. Communications giants have installed special permanent and mobile telephone units to take advantage in a competitive fashion of the huge demand for overseas calls from the gathering in Central on Sundays. Queues have formed into the evening at these facilities.

Conclusions: an atypical case points the way

The case of Hong Kong's overseas domestic workers demonstrates the complexities of public and private social and spatial linkages characteristic of global restructuring. These workers associate the private spheres of Hong Kong and the Philippines through their domestic and familial roles in both countries and the impact of their displacement. They have been instrumental in easing the public/private tensions resulting from the increasing involvement of Chinese women in Hong Kong's labor force. This is a key role in terms of the centrality of the patriarchal family structure in Chinese society and its heavy dependence on *feminized* domestic and caring roles. The overseas domestic workers have been a largely *hidden* force in the continuing development and success of Hong Kong's economy. At the same time they have been an important source of external revenue for their home economy.

Their status as a large migrant workforce is fundamental to their manipulation of public space in Hong Kong for public and private purposes. There is no doubt that the use of their free time in this specific fashion on a regular basis is essential to our reflections on their interaction as agents with their overall structural conditions. The collective nature of the Central gathering and its shared and regularly repeated rituals of more and less formal quality represent a created social space which, in its personal, communal, economic, and cultural attachments, is truly transnational in character. This one-day phenomenon is a powerful counterpoint to the dominance of the working week and establishes its own form of "time–space compression" and continuum.[19]

The public/private spatial engagements of this workforce are essential to a comprehensive perspective on structure/agency considerations. We can note these workers' distinctive situation and still draw conclusions of general assistance in our analysis of global restructuring. These direct our attention to the inner dynamics of so-called local/global connections; dynamics inherently based on assertions, transformations, and challenges to gendered spatiality, and the various public/private boundaries associated with it and instituted through social practices. Such practices can relate distant, including inter-state, locations.

I conclude from the theoretical and substantive arguments above, and from my wider considerations of globalization, that it may be necessary to study particular agents and processes of agency closely in order to gain a fuller picture of structural forces and points of structure/agency interaction. Many of these points have become deeply obscured by the public over private abstractions which characterize dominant conceptualizations of social, political, and economic space. I have outlined the Hong Kong case partly to illustrate the conceptual blindness that these entail. Extensive and sophisticated feminist attacks on such theoretical blindness continue to suffer from marginalization, largely because theory does not operate in exclusion from other kinds of practice. This chapter has set out ways in which patriarchal forces are overlapping and interacting in transnationalized circumstances through global restructuring. The implication is that new and even more complex patriarchal structures are developing. These require us to adopt multi-locational perspectives on patriarchal forces in terms of state and market, to recognize that public/private social and spatial constructions are, in certain senses, mobilized and reconfigured in the globalizing world.

Notes

1   UNDP (1996: 2, 13) charts widening disparities in global economic performance "creating two worlds – ever more polarized" reflecting growing gulfs between both rich and poor countries and sectors within countries. Between 1960 and 1991 the share of the richest 20 per cent of the world's people rose from 70 per cent of global income to 85 per cent – while that of the poorest 20 per cent declined from 2.3 per cent to 1.4 per cent – a ratio change in the shares of richest and poorest from 30:1 to 61:1.

2   I am using a term here which Richard Ashley (1984) has applied to the restrictions of neorealism's state-centric perspective. It is helpful because it can allow us to think in terms of a fusion of patriarchal influences in theoretical and other political economic practices. For discussions of patriarchy see Pateman (1988) and Walby (1990). It is important to note that through the concept of patriarchy we can address gender inequalities at large, affecting the differentiated positions of men and women within and across different societies.

3   For discussions of associated issues see, for example, Millett (1977), Weedon (1987), and Peterson and Runyan (1993, 1999).

4   Murphy and Tooze's (1991a) discussion of "common sense" helps us to understand the tendency of assumptions of dominant theoretical perspectives to go unquestioned.

5   For critical discussions of this position, see, in particular, Peterson (1992a), Ashley (1984, 1988), and Walker (1993).

6 Walker's (1993: 159–83) discussion of "sovereign identities and the politics of forget-ting" is helpful in setting out the theory/practice problematic.

7 Foreign direct investment (FDI) levels indicate concentrations of wealth underpinning processes of globalization. The United Nations Conference on Trade and Development (UNCTAD) (1996) reported that corporations headquartered in the US, Germany, the UK, Japan, and France accounted for two-thirds of total global FDI outflows in 1995. US corporations as a group were the largest foreign investors, and the US was the largest single host country for FDI. Overall, FDI into and out of developed countries rose 53 and 42 per cent, respectively. In comparison, total FDI into developing countries rose 15 per cent, with China alone taking more than a third of the total. The top 100 transnational corporations accounting for about one-third of total FDI stock are all headquartered in developed countries. Mergers and acquisi-tions (M&A) have come to dominate the FDI picture.

8 Almost two-thirds of all FDI into developing countries in 1995 went to Asia, with China the major recipient (UNCTAD 1996).

9 Within feminist debates, the whole question of how we should address public/private divides and definitions in reclaiming politics has been a key area of contestation. See, for example, Phillips (1991). In the historical context see also Wollstonecraft (1985 (1792)). Critical work related to gender in geography and development studies has been instrumental in furthering understanding of gendered and spatial divisions of labor on localized and internationalized scales. See, for example, Mies (1986), Massey (1995), Spain (1992), Harcourt (1994), and Kobayashi (1994). See also Massey (1994).

10 I have borrowed the use of presence and absence from Ashley's (1988) discussion of sovereignty.

11 Agnew and Corbridge (1995) and Lash and Urry (1994) are two notable examples in this respect. In different ways their analyses open up the category of spatiality, in the first case in relation to hegemony and international political economy, and in the second around issues of production and consumption. While they are definitely chal-lenging certain parameters of patriarchal viewpoints, they are not fundamentally disrupting them as gender critiques do.

12 Thus questions of equality between women on the basis of class and race as well as gender are gaining more attention. These assist also in focusing attention on areas such as *militarization* and their differentiated impact on societies of the developed and less developed countries. See Ashworth (1995) and Enloe (1993).

13 See, for example, Millett (1977), Elshtain (1981), Tickner (1992), and Whitworth (1994a).

14 Stephen Gill's (1995b) discussion of recent "Social Darwinist" characteristics of the global political economy is interesting in this respect.

15 I have found Pellerin's (1996) assessment of state-capital interrelationships in global restructuring and the changing characteristics of international migration especially helpful. See also Pettman (1998).

16 On the following points see "Having a nanny no longer limited to the super rich," *South China Morning Post* 11 December 1994: 4; "Retailers seek out Filipinos," *South China Morning Post* 6 February 1995: 3; and "Central bazaar," *Window* 17 May 1996: 32–7. On political economy and gender in the Philippines see, for example, Eviota (1992). The research for this section of the chapter was conducted in Hong Kong between 1995 and 1997.

17 "migrants, individually and collectively, are agents participating in structural change as well as subjects of dynamics they do not control" (Pellerin 1996: 83).

18 What is often overlooked is that these workers may be highly qualified, for example as teachers, but they can earn far more in domestic service in Hong Kong than in their profession at home (Eviota 1992).

19 "Time–space compression" (Harvey 1989) is more generally applied to considerations of the technologized processes of modern communications which have collapsed time–space relations. I am using the term here to indicate its broad application to our thinking about agency in contemporary conditions.

3 Masculinities in transition

The case of globalization[1]

Charlotte Hooper

Introduction

While the majority of contributions to a feminist book on "Gender and Global Restructuring" rightly concentrate on what is happening to those who are marginalized by mainstream analysis, this chapter is slightly different. It is also important to "know thine enemy." So at the risk of giving even more attention to the powerful and privileged than they already get, this chapter sets out to map some of the gendered struggles which are taking place at the top, amongst the increasingly integrated global elites of (largely) White male professionals and businessmen.

In the final quarter of the twentieth century, the world economy has been transformed from an international economy into a global one. In the postwar period the capitalist international economy was characterized by a stable currency regime (Bretton Woods), the predominance of Keynesian economic management and welfare systems, and the operation of multinationals in segregated primary and secondary markets. Now the world is virtually a single integrated market. Multinational production has gone global and is being constantly relocated in the search for skills and cheaper labor, while capital flows freely and instantaneously and foreign direct investment has replaced a large proportion of international trade (Gill and Law 1988; Dunning 1988). The initial impetus for this transformation of the world economy can be traced back to 1973, with the collapse of the Bretton Woods currency system, the OPEC oil crisis, and the growth of Eurocurrency markets as a source of finance (Harvey 1989; McDowell 1991). Developments were then accelerated by the financial "big bangs" of the 1980s, which produced unprecedented capital mobility and have been further enhanced by the collapse of Soviet Communism. By the 1990s, global economic restructuring had touched almost every part of the world.[2]

This large-scale economic restructuring has been accompanied by a complex set of political, institutional, and social changes in which increasing cross-border linkages combined with ever more instantaneous communications have reconstituted the world as a single social space, shrinking time and space (Giddens 1990). These changes have been linked to psychological and aesthetic developments associated with the "condition of postmodernity" (Harvey 1989). Gender relations are also being transformed as an integral part of this restructuring. In political economy terms, it has heralded a casualization and feminization of the workforce; the erosion of welfare provision; the collapse of the family wage system; an increase in female-headed households; expanded opportunities for women at the professional level; and a feminization of poverty. It has also undermined men's personal authority in the family, brought blue-collar unemployment, and is reducing the value of so-called masculine attributes in the labor market (McDowell 1991; Runyan 1996). Linda McDowell suggests that gender is being used to divide women's and men's interests in the labor market in such a way that both sexes – at least among the majority of the population – are losing out (McDowell 1991: 401). Global restructuring clearly presents a major challenge to the existing gender order, with varied effects with regard to the position of different groups of men and women.

However, rather than examining gender and global restructuring in terms of material causes and practical effects, this chapter will look at the gendered political processes involved – that is the "thick" interconnecting web of ongoing political struggles, processes, and decisions in many diverse arenas of life and in many geographical locations. Seeing globalization at least in part as a broadly political process allows one to examine these integral struggles over the direction, nature, and scope of developments. Such politicized struggles include power struggles between different gendered interests. An upheaval of this magnitude clearly de-naturalizes existing patterns of gender divisions, and therefore opens up the space for an intensification of "interpretive wars" over the way in which gender differences are constructed and articulated. Indeed, the discourse of globalization itself becomes one site amongst many for such gendered interpretive struggles, as the meaning of globalization is contested. In the process, different "elements" or ingredients of masculinity and femininity are co-opted in new or old configurations to serve particular interests, and particular gendered (and other) identities are consolidated and legitimated or downgraded and devalued. This involves gendered power struggles not only between men and women, but also between different groups of men as they jostle for position and control; articulating and re-articulating the relationship between masculinity and power as they go.[3] It is important to examine such struggles not least because they help to "steer" and influence more traditionally studied economic, institutional, and "political" developments in particular directions. No comprehensive study of what globalization means to IPE should ignore this political and subjective aspect.[4]

Conceptual tools which can map such processes need to be alert to the way in which different gender interests are mobilized and how such interests intersect with class, race, and other social cleavages in different situations.[5] The challenge of mapping the complex gendered politics of globalization necessitates moving beyond a standard analysis of masculinism and its focus on the admittedly powerful masculine/feminine dichotomies which construct and naturalize gender differences and inequalities (see, for example, Harding 1986). In order to understand how gendered struggles and changing relationships vary between different groups of women and men, we need to see femininities and masculinities as both multiple and fluid over time and space.[6] From a feminist perspective, this is a risky project. If the postmodern emphasis on difference is already threatening to undermine the feminist project by dissolving the category of women as an oppressed group,[7] then to expand this to include an examination of the differences between men threatens to dissolve, or at least obscure, our view of the oppressor.[8] This problem is not insurmountable, however, given a theoretical framework which combines sensitivity to change and contextualized multiplicity with a clear recognition of the operation of power and collective inequalities between men and women.

Below is an outline of a theoretical perspective which goes some way towards fulfilling such criteria, a perspective adapted from the theory of hegemonic and subordinate masculinities, and subordinated femininities (Connell 1987), which I elaborate upon later. Using this perspective, there follows a short analysis of the changing representations of hegemonic masculinity and their relationship to global restructuring as constructed in the pages of *The Economist*, which identifies itself as a weekly "newspaper" (although it is published in a magazine format). *The Economist* is a periodical which is largely aimed at and read by an international readership of elite businessmen, professionals and academics. As will be argued in more detail, it presents itself as a booster of capitalist restructuring and globalization. It is in a prominent position to help construct the dominant symbolic imagery of the new globalized political economy, including the gendered imagery of masculinity associated with the interlocking elites who form a global ruling class. An analysis of the periodical reveals how the gendered power-moves of elite and would-be elite groups of men are articulated through particular masculine identifications and associations with globalization.

Multiple masculinities

Historical narratives contradict the apparent timeless stability of "masculinity," which is naturalized by the masculine/feminine dichotomy. In the light of recent historical research the term "masculinities" now seems more appropriate than does the concept of "masculinity" in the singular.[9] A useful way of understanding the relationship between such "masculinities" is proposed by Harry Brod, who applies Wittgenstein's philosophical concept of "family resemblances": just as members of a family may be said to resemble each other without necessarily all having any single feature in common, so masculinities may form common patterns without sharing any single universal characteristic (Brod 1987: 275–6).

Masculinities need have no ultimate common basis. By sharing some common characteristics with a number of other masculinities, each variety remains recognizably masculine. New elements can be introduced to accommodate change, and no two images or manifestations of masculinity need be exactly alike, but there is generally enough overlap and intertextuality between individual representations to mask the instability of the term "masculinity," so that the masculine/feminine dichotomy remains apparently unchallenged (Hooper 1998).

While masculinism produces and reinforces the links between power, masculinity and men, what counts as masculine may itself be subject to change according to the requirements of power in different circumstances. Strategies of masculinization and feminization are likely to play an important part in the direction and consolidation of such changes, by upgrading or downgrading various activities, practices, and groups of people in the struggle for recognition and power. In this context, the interpretation or reinterpretation of a quality, an activity or a person as "masculine" (revalued) or "feminine" (devalued) is a profoundly political act (Hooper 1998). Often similar activities are labeled "masculine" or "feminine" depending on context or even the choice of descriptive words, so that in employment, for example, what counts as acquired skills (culture) in men, gets described as mere natural ability (nature) in women, with reduced pay and status to follow (McDowell 1991). In addition, once masculinity is seen as an attribute of power rather than as an attribute of men, it becomes clear that while all men gain to some extent from the associations between masculinity and power, not all men have equal access to these associations. Strategies of feminization can be used to marginalize groups of men as well as women (Hooper 1998).

Bob Connell's notion of "hegemonic" and "subordinate" masculinities usefully encapsulates men's differential access to the power associated with their gender (Connell 1987: 183–8).[10] There is a hierarchy of masculinities, in which gender intersects with other factors such as class, race, and sexuality. While there may be many masculinities and femininities in existence at the same time, hegemonic patterns of masculinity operate at the level of the whole society, shoring up male power and advantage. Hegemonic masculinity may be articulated differently at different times, but it is always constructed in opposition to a range of subordinate masculinities (as well as femininities). In Connell's view there can be no equivalent hegemonic femininity, because while there may be prevailing constructions of femininity, and some women may be more privileged than others, all femininities are subordinate to hegemonic masculinity. Of course, this does not mean that women are entirely unable to re-construct femininity in an empowering way, and indeed overturning this inequality in the power to define gender identities remains a central goal of feminism.[11] Hegemonic masculinity is constitutive of and embodied in numerous institutional practices, such as enforced competitive sport for schoolboys. Individual men are therefore forced to negotiate their identities in relation to practices and relationships informed by hegemonic masculinity. If they publicly identify with it, or otherwise collaborate with such public images, they help to boost their own position, although any degree of compliance, however grudging or unconscious, will help to shore up existing inequalities (Hooper 1998).

Anglo-American hegemonic masculinity

Contemporary Anglo-American hegemonic masculinity is almost always constructed as heterosexual, White and, drawing on the history of imperialism, naturally superior (Mohanty 1991b). In one particular inflection, influential since the late nineteenth century, it has become associated with an anti-domestic expansionism. This is bound up with the ideology of "frontier" culture (in the American case), and with imperial foreign adventures (in the British case), both positioned far from the domestic hearth of femininity, women, and children (Mangan and Walvin 1987; Roper and Tosh 1991). However, its various representations also draw on elements from a much longer cultural history, and are constructed from at least four different "ideal types," which have been historically overlaid on each other. These are the Greek citizen/warrior, which combined militarism with rationalism (Stearns 1979; Elshtain 1981); the Judaeo/Christian patriarch, a more domesticated masculinity emphasizing responsibility, ownership of property, and paternal authority (Cocks 1989; Connell 1993); an honor/patronage model based on aristocratic ideals of male bonding, military heroism, and risk taking (Morgan 1992) and a bourgeois rational masculinity, idealizing competitive individualism, calculative rationality, self-denial, and emotional self-control (Cocks 1989; Seidler 1989). The honor/patronage and patriarchal codes are now fairly muted. Patriarchal forms of masculine domination have gradually been eroded in favor of technical/rational forms (Cocks 1989).

In the aftermath of two world wars, the honor/patronage code and the dominance of martial masculinities had largely been broken, although vestiges and symbolic echoes remain. In the Bretton Woods period, Anglo-American hegemonic masculinity was loosely organized around technical rationality and calculation sustained by a hypermasculine myth of toughness, power, and strength. This obscured an underlying conflict between the declining masculinity of patriarchal domination and the more "modern" bourgeois rational one based on expertise (Connell 1993). Hegemonic masculinity was defined against a range of subordinated masculinities – "oversexed" Blacks (Segal 1990), "untrustworthy" "Orientals" (Campbell 1992), and "sick" homosexuals. Indeed in the USA every upright man had to gain "maturity" and guard against "latent homosexuality" through marriage and bread winning, an ideology which depended on women's domesticity (Ehrenreich 1983). For "The Man in the Grey Flannel Suit" (1950s book title) and his ilk, personal flamboyance was frowned upon – hegemonic masculinity was associated with performance, rationality, paternalism, and self-control (Seidler 1989).

However, since the onset of global restructuring in the early 1970s, a number of commentators have noted a softening of this image. Activities and qualities which were previously defined as feminine or effeminate are being increasingly integrated into hegemonic masculinity. For example, men in the developed world are now routinely positioned as consumers, a traditionally feminine role (Chapman and Rutherford 1988); Anglo-American mainstream culture is becoming increasingly, if subtly, homo-erotic as exemplified by the increasingly sensual and narcissistic display of male bodies in advertising imagery aimed at men (Simpson 1994); and business and managerial strategies are changing to emphasize the formerly feminine qualities of flexibility, interpersonal skills, and team-working (Connell 1993). This reconstitution of hegemonic masculinity might on the face of it offer improved career prospects for professional women, but it has been suggested that hegemonic masculinity is being redefined so that professional men can stay ahead of the employment game, albeit under less secure conditions. For example, the techniques of alternative therapy forged in the 1960s counterculture, which were originally used by anti-sexist men and feminist sympathizers to discover their so-called "feminine" side, are now widely used in management training seminars designed to cultivate interpersonal skills and group work, and in mythopoetic men's movement workshops, which claim to develop the emotional "wild man" within. Such activities are not only social-izing White middle-class men into feminized working practices but are crucially redefining these practices as masculine. As Connell argues, "The larger conse-quence of the popular forms of masculinity therapy is an adaptation of patriarchal structures through the modernization of masculinity" (Connell 1995: 211). The "New Man" is very much a middle-class, middle-management image, not so much defined against femininity or effeminacy, as against a pathologized version of 1950s tough-guy masculinity, now projected on to less privileged groups of men, such as working-class men and Latinos, who may in practice lead more egalitarian family lives (Hondagneau-Sotelo and Messner 1994; Ehrenreich 1983). But what about the men at the very top? And what is the rela-tionship between the new man image and the entrenched symbolism of masculine power? And how does the new man image relate to the discourse of globalization and global restructuring itself? The discussion below attempts to shed light on these questions.

Globalization and hegemonic masculinity in *The Economist*

The Economist is a fruitful site to observe how the various ingredients of hege-monic masculinity get played and replayed in different combinations, and in particular to map in more detail how changing constructions of hegemonic masculinity are being articulated in relation to global restructuring. Founded in 1843 as an arm of the City of London financial press, it is a weekly international news and business paper, with a readership largely made up of elite men.[12] Its circulation rose rapidly after the financial "big bangs" of the 1980s, and it is now one of a handful of papers which serve the global financial markets (Thrift 1994). Unsurprisingly, it is an enthusiastic booster of globalization. It is also widely read in academic and professional IR and IPE circles, as witnessed by the regular stream of job advertisements for the UN, NGOs, and academics in the field. With its terse, "cocksure" house style (*The Economist* 22 December 1990: 34) and its upmarket advertising aimed at businessmen, it is saturated with the imagery of hegemonic masculinity and elitism with which the reader is invited to identify. The following discussion tracks developments in the period 1990–6.

In keeping with the cultural history of businessmen, for whom in the nineteenth century "war and the Darwinian jungle were the moral analogues of modern business" (Stearns 1979: 83), the business world portrayed in *The Economist* is an evolutionary one of Darwinistic struggle, where the market place ensures the survival of the fittest. What counts as fittest is not necessarily force, strength, or size but rather a wide range of traits – never stable but always changing to whatever the market requires at any given moment. At the heart of survival, therefore, are intelligence and strategy. In this atmosphere of relentless competition, styles of masculinity become grist for the mill of business success.

"Globalization" is presented as a glamorous process at the cutting edge of progressive capitalist development, which is "enforcing a kind of natural selection between those cultures which rise to the challenge and those which do not" (*The Economist* 9 November 1996: 30). It is seen as wholly beneficial, with multinational companies now welcomed by developing countries as "the embodiment of modernity and the prospect of wealth: full of technology, rich in capital, replete with skilled jobs" (*The Economist* 27 March 1993: survey, 5). Meanwhile in developed countries, restructuring problems will be ironed out by the promise of new markets and the workings of comparative advantage. *The Economist* is resolutely upbeat in its assessment of globalization, arguing that "for the rich world, almost as much as for today's poor countries, the next twenty-five years will be a time of unprecedented opportunity" (1 October 1994: survey, 3). It is seen to be sweeping away paternalistic and patriarchal forms of business management:

> the old view was that strategy should be set by a tiny elite at the top … now the men at corporate headquarters realize that decisions are often best taken by those who spend their lives developing products or dealing with customers.
>
> (*The Economist* 24 June 1995: survey, 5)

In place of paternalism from headquarters, corporate strategy now includes regional decentralization. There is also an ongoing rivalry between competitive individualism and a more "feminized" cooperative style of management, the outcome of which, in terms of business success, is yet to be determined. This rivalry is often articulated within a discourse of competition and cross-fertilization between Western and Asian business practices in corporate culture. For example, in 1991, *The Economist* argued that to keep up with the pace of change, Western businesses need to adopt cooperative joint ventures; "flatter" companies with less hierarchy; more part-time and temporary workers; cross-disciplinary and team-work approaches; and a change in corporate culture as ethics and environmentalism emerge as a new set of "soft" issues. Note the "feminized" language: soft to touch, hard to grasp. The toughest challenge facing senior managers (and the business schools charged with nurturing them) could come from a hard-to-define set of "soft" problems (2 March 1991: survey, 8).

Japan was the model for American corporate change. Japanese managers' success was apparently due to on the job training, job rotation, vague job descriptions, group learning, and knowledge sharing. On the other hand, it appeared that the Japanese now had a need for a new "entrepreneur type" of manager who was more innovative and creative. The solution would be a "marriage" where Japanese MBA students would learn Western analytical skills but with the aggressiveness "mellowed down," while Western students were taught to "open their minds" and have competitiveness discouraged or even penalized in favor of "team learning" (*The Economist* 2 March 1991: survey, 24–6).

By 1992, Japanese capitalism was being defended against American critics who saw it as unfair and ruthlessly "predatory" (*The Economist* 4 April 1992: 19–24). Meanwhile, Japan's "greying corporate warriors" were being replaced by a younger generation who were more competitive, less consensual, and keener on leisure (*The Economist* 2 May 1992: 99). By 1994, the desirability of Far-Eastern economies copying the West was hotly contested in the debate over "Asian values," with *The Economist* arguing that "Asian" values are in fact universal ones (28 May 1994: 14 and 77–8). In 1995, Japan was exporting a distinctive, Far-Eastern variety of "non-capitalist market economy" (*The Economist* 14 January 1995: 20). Meanwhile Japanese multinationals themselves were continuing to "look West" (24 June 1995: survey, 20). Finally, in 1996 *The Economist* endorsed the view of an UNCTAD world investment report, which argued that the collision between cultures had produced successful hybrid management systems (16 March 1996: review, 9).

This "cross-fertilization" discourse has been accompanied by a marked decline in patriarchal and paternalistic imagery and a general increase in informality in advertising. In 1990, for example, it was still common for banking and financial advertisements in *The Economist* to feature sober pictures of their chairmen or founders, and extracts from chairmen's statements.[13] One particularly memorable one (that of J.P. Morgan) featured a picture of an upright, sober and elderly former chairman taken in the pre-World War II era, together with a boast of 150 years of experience and "sound analysis" (*The Economist* 3 November 1990: 2–3). These images deliberately invoked the patriarchal hierarchies and solidly bourgeois credentials of a bygone era. As such, they represent the last gasp of the old order of "gentlemanly" codes of dress and behavior, which was broken by the globalization of finance (Thrift 1994), and a nostalgic invocation of stability in a world of change. By 1996, however, company presidents were more likely to be depicted out fishing in casual clothes; managing directors wore casual leather jackets; suits were being replaced by jeans and denim shirts; and offices by living rooms, with the AMP man now telecommuting from home in an open-neck check shirt, accompanied by his daughter and teddy (*The Economist* 12 October 1996: 41; 108; 87 and 93). Informality in these advertisements has been constituted as a desirable and "cool" masculine trait.

All this is in line with increasingly informal management styles associated with the introduction of computers, which would at first sight appear to be in the interests of gender equality. The standard feminist critique of masculinist working practices contrasts masculine management styles which are defined as autocratic, overly hierarchical, rational, and focused on efficiency and task orientation with feminine management styles, which are seen as based on relationships, consensus, collaboration, teamwork, and cooperation (Court 1994). These "feminine" management styles are now being introduced on a widespread scale, and are associated with informality. However as this new informality is predominantly being constituted as masculine, it doesn't necessarily do much for women. Informal working practices can be sex discriminating – as formal promotion procedures are often replaced by a "laddish" social network, which grooms young men to rise up the ladder. Women and those men who do not fit the "lad" culture are excluded from this important source of advice, support, and visibility, and are consequently regularly overlooked. Meanwhile, old-fashioned patriarchal hierarchies are themselves being increasingly feminized, with "girls" and "wimps" being seen as more comfortable with rules and hierarchy, and less able to deal with flexibility (Tierney, 1995).[14]

While all this softening and informality may be less progressive for women than it first appears, and only a few advertisers have taken the opportunity to break the masculinist mold altogether,[15] it is not the only, nor even the dominant, masculine imagery associated with globalization in the paper. Perhaps the most powerful construction of globalization in *The Economist* is through imagery which integrates science, technology, business, and images of globalization into a kind of entrepreneurial frontier masculinity, in which capitalism meets science fiction. This futuristic vision, in which science and business mix to solve all our problems (including environmental ones), is played out through special surveys with titles such as: "Defence in the 21st Century: Breaking Free"; "The Frontiers of Finance"; "The Future of Medicine – peering into 2010"; "The Global Economy: War of the Worlds"; and "The World Economy: The Hitchhiker's Guide to Cybernomics"; accompanied by a liberal use of science fiction imagery on the covers (*The Economist* 5 September 1992; 9 October 1993; 19 March 1994; 1 October 1994; and 28 September 1996). At the same time, in corporate advertisements "global" has become a buzzword and images of "spaceship earth" have become ubiquitous, as in the following illustrative examples taken from the two world-economy surveys: a Bank of New York advertisement features a picture of the globe from space and mentions the word "global" three times; ABB deploys similar imagery, with a large photograph of the globe, and several instances of the words "world" and "global;" Singapore Telecom shows a photo of the world taken from the moon, and talks about its "mission" to be at the forefront of technology; and Ernst and Young feature the globe from space with a satellite in the foreground, while claiming to operate in the "dynamic global marketplace" (*The Economist* 1 October 1994, survey, 17 and 24–5; 27 March 1993: survey, 8 and 15).

This imagery positions globalization firmly in the glamorous masculine conceptual space of the "international," as far from the feminized world of domestic life as possible. While "spaceship earth" images reinforce the view of the world as a single locality, "the global village," making it appear easily accessible in its entirety (Giddens 1990), at the same time globalization is also positioned as "out there" by the space mission analogy, so that globalization becomes "the final frontier." It is "out there" in the international arena where only intrepid businessmen fear to tread, as opposed to "in here" in the domestic space of businessmen's homes where global restructuring has directed a tide of often illegal and under-age female migrants as domestic servants.[16] It is largely presented as a grand top-down ideology which suits expansive business interests, rather than as an everyday phenomenon touching our domestic lives. It "belongs to" an elite internationalist cosmopolitan culture of males, whom the reader is invited to join, at least in spirit. The world has become the adventure playground of the new global business elite.[17]

In addition, there is a steady stream of aggressive and sporting imagery in computer advertisements, including a coal miner with phallic drill; men's athletics; a fast car; a weight-lifter; a shot-putter; a power drill; and a flexed biceps (*The Economist* 5 November 1994: 114–15, 93 and 90; 3 June 1995: 103; 13 May 1995: 90; 29 April 1995: 94; 11 February 1995: 57). In financial services this has been combined with the language of "risk." Indeed, after an attack of "risk" anxiety in late 1994,[18] a hardening of images of masculinity in banking generally took place through 1995 and 1996, and "risk" became more associated with virility. In one example, The Union Bank of Switzerland deployed a series of images from formula one racing, with the slogan "Master the detail, manage the risk" (*The Economist* 7 October 1995: 108–9). The word "risk" was repeated no less than five times in an advertisement which boasted that:

> our clients expect fast reactions, technical skill and total attention to detail, continuously, not just for an hour or two. And though the dangers are not physical, they are nevertheless very real…at UBS Global Risk Management, we combine constant attention to detail with coolness under pressure, to help drive your business forward.
>
> (*The Economist* 7 October 1995: 109)

This upbeat approach to "risk" aggressively remasculinizes financial services. Together with male-oriented sports imagery, it can be partly attributed to the Americanization of both financial masculinities and the general imagery of *The Economist* itself.[19] However, when also combined with technocratic globalization imagery, it can also be interpreted as a way of re-staking a claim to non-domestic masculinity in arenas where women are now encroaching.

As if to underline the association of globalization with an aggressive (and heterosexual) masculinity, *The Economist* lapsed into the worst kind of sexual metaphor in its 1994 article on Myanmar, entitled "Ripe for Rape":

> Asia's businessmen have had their eyes on Myanmar's rich resources for a while. Unlike most of its neighbors, it still has teak forests to be felled and its

gem deposits are barely exploited. Its natural beauties and its aston-
ishing Buddhist architecture make it potentially irresistible to tourists....
Businessmen are beginning to take the first steps towards exploiting this
undeveloped land.

(*The Economist* 15 January 1994: 65)

Meanwhile, the government is "increasingly welcoming" to foreign businessmen. The reader is metaphorically invited to identify with the foreign
(Western) businessmen hoping to rape this pubescent girl with her unexploited
gems and irresistible natural beauties. This imagery draws directly on racist and
sexist colonial discourse about White male exploration and adventure in "virgin
territories." Its continuing real-life salience can be seen when one remembers
that Myanmar is next to Thailand, where the internationalization of the
economy has led to one of the biggest sexploitation industries in the world
(Enloe 1989). No doubt Myanmar would be "ripe" for the same experience. This
rhetoric clearly signals a tacit acceptance, promotion even, of international sex
tourism which involves forced prostitution, rape (often of minors), and even
slavery in some cases, as *The Economist* itself admits only too readily (31 August
1996: 15 and 35; 21 September 1996: 73).[20]

So the shiny new discourse of globalization draws strength from the old
formulas of racism, masculinism, and imperialism. *The Economist*'s treatment of
women does little to mitigate against this tendency. Nominally of liberal feminist persuasion,[21] and while occasionally incorporating stories on topics such as
women's employment (e.g. 30 June 1990: 21–4), women's education (21
September 1991: 18), feminism (12 August 1995: 34–5), and the glass ceiling
(10 August 1996: 61), men are generally assumed to be the norm, with terms
such as "men" and "workers" being used interchangeably (e.g. 1 October
1994: survey 16–21). Individual stateswomen, such as Mrs. Thatcher, tend to
be treated as "one of the boys" (e.g. 3 November 1990: 17), and where women
depart from the bounds of "normal" politics and economics, they tend to get
reported in humorous "boxed" anecdotes, such as one on the "log cabinet"
where the Swedish minister telecommutes from home while changing her
baby's nappies (25 February 1995: 52). The occasional in-depth report on the
progress of women in public life plus use of humorous anecdotes can give the
paper a false sense of gender "balance," whilst at the same time legitimizing
the main masculinist message of the paper by implying that men get on with
the serious and important business of life, and women provide the embellish-
ment.

In its boosting of the brave new world of globalization, and its belief that
technological innovation will solve all our problems, *The Economist* is guilty of
what Beverley Burris describes as "technological hubris" (Burris 1989: 458).
Technocratic ideology is based on the authority of experts, the legitimacy of
science, and the mystique of advanced technology, where the political and social
choices of elite male decision makers are masked by an allegedly neutral system
of technical imperatives and interests. In Burris's analysis, it is associated with

the development of technocracy as a form of organizational control. In technocratic organizations, the workforce is divided into "experts" and "non-experts."
Technical complexity replaces organizational complexity in a culture that values
"conspicuous expertise" as "in technocratic organizations who you know
becomes less important than how knowledgeable you can appear" (Burris 1989:
458). Rigid rules and hierarchies are replaced by flexible, collegiate, collaborative
working styles and enhanced communication for largely male "experts."
Meanwhile for the rest, the "non-experts" and "para-professionals," work
becomes increasingly routinized and regimented under computer control,
geographically isolated, and feminized (done by women). The fact that both
experts and non-experts use the same technology, namely computers, masks the
very different ways in which their work is organized.

In the light of this analysis, both the aggressive frontier masculinity of globalization and the softer, more informal imagery associated with economic
restructuring are being mobilized in the service of technocracy and an international technocratic elite. What is almost entirely missing from *The Economist* is a
conservative backlash masculinity which would restore patriarchal privilege.[22]
This is in keeping with its extreme economic and political liberalism. However,
in 1996 there have been increasingly overt displays of gender anxiety, both in
semi-spoof editorial discussions on the current state of masculinity, such as "The
Male Dodo/Are men necessary?" and "[Men], tomorrow's second sex" (*The
Economist* 23 December 1995: 121–3; and 28 September 1996: 20–5); and in
advertisements such as NCR's "big consumer is watching you" which depicts a
huge woman peering through a glass wall of an office, and towering over the
workers (12 October 1996: 116–17). Globalization in these cases is not so much
a boy's game as a very feminine threat. The triumph of a masculine technocracy
is not yet complete.

Conclusions

The perspective outlined here suggests that as well as divisions between men and
women, the relationships between different masculinities also play a part in the
gender order. While in hierarchies of masculinities and competition between
different masculinist interests, gender is unlikely to be the only or even the most
salient division, it is worth examining because it allow us to think more clearly
about the complex gendered relationships between differently positioned women
and different groups of men. It also underlines the pervasiveness of masculinist
strategies and gendered metaphors in struggles for power.

The brief analysis of changes in the imagery of Anglo-American hegemonic
masculinity in *The Economist* suggests that hegemonic masculinity is being reconfigured in the image of a less formal, less patriarchal but more technocratic
masculine elite with the whole globe as its playground. This emerging hegemonic masculinity contains elements of continuity with earlier forms, as well as
change. The aggressive deployment of "frontier masculinity" (now tied to
contemporary globalization) provides a link to the past, as does the use of impe-

rialist imagery. The need for softer, more informal qualities in business, previously associated with "femininity," is not matched by demands for increased women's status, but rather is associated with Japanese business masculinity.[23] Whether Japanese and other Far-Eastern businessmen are really being invited to share in the new globalized hegemonic masculinity of technocracy is less clear. Given the persistence of racist and colonial metaphors in the paper, and the West's history of absorbing useful traits from other cultures, it would seem unlikely, in spite of the paper's liberal, race-blind editorial stand.[24]

But the news is not all bad from a feminist point of view. Even in *The Economist*, which serves and reflects the interests of Anglo-American hegemonic masculinity, the masculinist sci-fi discourse of globalization is regularly disrupted. It is undermined by its own internal contradictions, as it attempts to both feminize and remasculinize hegemonic masculinity at the same time. It is disrupted by the attacks of gender anxiety which this uncertainty about the content of masculinity provokes. It is disrupted by the increasing visibility of professional women and of feminist and gender issues which have to be reported if *The Economist* wishes to keep its reputation for progressive liberalism.

Feminists can exploit these vulnerabilities. The association of globalization with elite masculinity and frontier culture can be countered by alternative accounts of its spatialization which incorporate the personal and the domestic. In particular the contradictions between "softer" and "harder" constructions of this emerging hegemonic masculinity can be exploited to contest the new coding of flexibility, informality, and team work as "masculine" and hierarchy and rule-following as "feminine." Perhaps alliances can be forged with subordinate groups of men in countering negative gender constructions. But above all it is worth nurturing all the alternative relations, identities and narratives with which diverse groups of women attempt to construct empowering relationships between themselves and globalization.

Notes

1 I would like to thank the Economic and Social Science Research Council for their support during this research. The arguments about theorizing masculinity have been developed more fully in my PhD thesis "Manly states: masculinities, international relations and gender politics," which also contains a more extensive case study of the gendered imagery of *The Economist* and its relationship to IR and IPE. The study covers the period 1988–96 and consisted of a manual search through and textual analysis of all the issues produced in these years. Examples of advertisements and articles referred to were generally representative unless otherwise stated. No contact was made with the editor or staff of the paper and neither was their sexual composition nor their views on gender taken into consideration when analyzing the gendered meanings embedded in the text.

2 A number of explanations have been provided for this global restructuring. It is variously due to the policies of a dominant USA (Gilpin 1987; Strange 1990); developments within capitalism itself (Harvey 1989); or technological progress (Rosenau 1990).

3 Of course, groups of women, too, may compete for position, although the language of masculinity and power is less accessible to them.

4   Globalization is more often than not viewed in largely material terms, at least in non-feminist IR and IPE analysis. Even where political "causes" are invoked, as in Gilpin (1987), the focus is on the high politics of state, rather than the low politics of everyday struggle.

5   While recent feminist scholarship has been very attentive to differences between women, so that in the best feminist scholarship, categories of "women" and "femininity" are now rarely used as a blanket term, but have been replaced by carefully situated analyses (see Mohanty *et al.* 1991), there has perhaps been less sensitivity to differences between men.

6   This recognition of "fluidity" does not mean to imply that gender identities can be worn or discarded at will, as we are clearly forced to negotiate our identities in relation to powerful social and structural constraints. Multiplicity and fluidity, therefore, always need to be carefully specified in context.

7   The question of whether postmodern feminism does indeed threaten the feminist project in this way is discussed in Nicholson 1990.

8   Susan Bordo (1990: 149) warns that "there are dangers in too wholesale a commitment to either dual or multiple grids."

9   Examples of such research include: Roper and Tosh 1991; Mangan and Walvin 1987; Stearns 1979; Connell 1993; Brittan 1989; Ehrenreich 1983; Segal 1990.

10 Although this interpretation has shed much of the structural theory which originally accompanied it.

11 For example, ecofeminists have appropriated and renegotiated qualities such as "nurturing" and women's connection to nature to challenge unsustainable development (Mies and Shiva 1993). In contrast cyberfeminists have embraced the new technologies in an attempt to forge a new relationship between "femininity" and technology (Haraway 1991).

12 It has a circulation of over 500,000. Eighty-one per cent of subscribers are from outside the UK, and 89 per cent are male. They have an average personal income of $107,600, household income of $155,800 and net worth of $1,152,600. Ninety per cent are graduates, and 49 per cent have postgraduate qualifications. Thirty-seven per cent hold board directorships, 45 per cent have given a speech or addressed a public meeting, and 23 per cent have been interviewed by the media in the last year. All figures are for 1990 and are taken from *The Economist*'s "World Profile," an in-house promotional brochure.

13 For example, banking and financial advertisements featuring pictures of chairmen include: J.P. Morgan and First Chicago (*The Economist* 3 November 1990: 2–3; 10 November 1990: 128). Even the conglomerate ABB capitalized on this trend with a picture of its chairman: "Bill Coleman [the] Banker" (*The Economist* 28 April 1990: 60–1). Meanwhile extracts from chairman's statements proved popular, appearing, for example, in advertisements from General Accident, Sun Alliance, and J.F. Fledgling (*The Economist* 28 April 1990: 91; 28 April 1990: 114–15; 15 December 1990: 26).

14 This is ironic given that women are in fact the most flexibilized workers (Runyan 1996).

15 A prominent exception is a series of Citibank advertisements featuring a range of bankers and clients presented as business couples engaging in friendly and animated discussion. Altogether these advertisements cover virtually every racial and gender permutation. Meanwhile the copy stresses "relationships," "partners," "commitment," and "understanding" (*The Economist* 5 October 1996: back cover; 17 February 1996: back cover; 8 June 1996: 149; 9 March 1996: back cover).

16 See Chang and Ling, Chapter 1, this volume.

17 Recently even the globe itself seems too restrictive a playground in the science-fiction-alized world of globalization. For example, France Telecom has cyclists racing between planets in outer space with the slogan "global networking partnerships to

keep you in the lead virtually anywhere," while Inmarsat shows a Mars-like planetary landscape with the slogan "communicate with travelers in space and time" and the copy "long-distance truck drivers can find themselves in places so far beyond the reach of conventional communications, they might as well be on another planet" (*The Economist* 16 December 1995: back cover; 21 September 1996: 32–3).

18 Financial risk anxiety was variously presented as a threatening volcanic eruption; the cause of a potential nervous breakdown; a rickety rope bridge about to snap; or a piece of suit cloth caught on a barbed wire fence (*The Economist* 19 November 1994: 32–3, 57–9, 86; 22 October 1994: 4).

19 WASP (White, Anglo-Saxon, Protestant) masculinity has always been less secure than that of the "English Gentleman" and has historically been more much concerned with physical fitness and the cult of youthfulness.

20 While the Myanmar quote may have been an extreme and particularly nasty example of the use of the rape metaphor (possibly related to the fact that *The Economist* was banned from the country at the time), it is by no means the only one. Only the following week another reference was made to rape, this time in the title of an article on wind farms in Wales: "A new way to rape the countryside" (22 January 1994: 26). This time it is the "masculine" rape of "feminine" nature ironically effected by misguided environmentalists. In the context of such overt references to rape, numerous seemingly innocent phrases such as the suggestion (in the same issue) that changes are "forcing open the over-protected economy" of Israel, begin to carry aggressive sexual overtones (22 January 1994: survey, 4).

21 *The Economist's* own track record on the employment of women is not bad. The chief executive of *The Economist* group from 1992 to 1996 was a woman, Marjorie Scardino, who as chief executive of Pearson (1996–), became the first female chief executive of a FT-SE 100 company. Several women have also held senior journalistic positions with the paper, including those of economics editor, diplomatic editor, and environmental editor during the period under investigation.

22 This is the conservative masculinity of the "angry white males" who have disciplined Bill Clinton, forcing him to reinvent himself as an "all American man's man" (*Independent on Sunday*, 12 February 1995).

23 Japanese business practices, for all their "softness," are not noted for their sympathetic treatment of women's employment aspirations, as discussed by Mikanagi, Chapter 6, this volume.

24 Of course, liberal universalism itself is implicated in racism as it erases difference. Coding Japanese business culture as "soft" or "feminine" may also be interpreted as a new twist on the existing racist stereotype of the "effeminate oriental" who is "mute, passive, charming, inscrutable" (Mercer and Julien 1988: 108).

4 Gendering post-socialist transitions[1]

Jacqui True

It is an obvious absurdity, but one rarely noticed, that most social science research on the transformations in Central and Eastern Europe fails to consider what is happening in post-socialist societies, what is changing and what is staying the same, and in what direction they are heading. The transitology paradigm, writes Akos Rona-Tas (1998), assumes the answers to the most intriguing questions before they can even be posed. Eastern European transformations are seen as leading inexorably to the consolidation of liberal democracy and capitalism. Post-socialist societies are consequently categorized as "in transition". *Transition* is the orthodox term drawn from 1970s and 1980s experiences of transition from authoritarianism to democracy in Latin America and Southern Europe.[2] As such, it tends to conceive systemic change in a narrow, teleological fashion, presupposing "a fundamental political and economic distinction between what was and what is to come" (Kennedy 1994: 2).[3] Dissenting from this view are sociologists who suggest that East European transitions are path-dependent or *sui generis* given their recent socialist past. They study the post-socialist emergence of new and hybrid institutional forms that are distinct from Western markets and polities (Stark and Bruszt 1997; Burawoy and Krotov 1992). Very few scholars however, have analyzed the so-termed *transitions* as a comprehensive societal transformation that is shifting the very boundaries of state and civil society, public and private, national and international.

In this chapter, by examining the changes and continuities in gender I seek to address the lack of scholarly attention to the social and political dimensions of transition. Systemic economic reform aims at permanently changing class relations, but it has also had the effect of altering gender relations. Privatization and liberalization have redefined and created new gendered as well as class divisions of labor, resources, and power. Radical structural change has reconstituted group identities and interests. Thus, the transitions in Central and Eastern Europe are a strategic site for analysing simultaneous transformations in the global political economy and in gender relations. Post-socialist societies are a rich source for the study of the interplay between gender and the emergence of markets; in particular for exploring how external regional and global market forces interact with local identities such as gender (Molyneux 1995). This chapter is in two parts. First, I situate *gender in transition* in the global context of state restructuring and capitalist integration. Second, I analyze the re-siting of gender relationships in post-socialism as the market economy extends its dominance.

While many new forms of gendering have emerged or become visible in the Czech market transition, it can be argued that they are path-dependent upon prior structural inequalities; in particular, gender segregation in the socialist labor force and latent gender stereotypes and discrimination in state and society (Heinen 1990). Here my argument is similar in nature to Carole Pateman's (1988) thesis about the way in which patriarchal relationships facilitate and underpin modern transitions. Pateman has argued that the nineteenth-century transition to liberalism instituted a "social contract" between the individual and the state, which was preceded by a repressed "sexual contract" among men as a fraternal group. In her analysis, the statist transition from absolutism to liberalism was a transition from patriarchalism to fraternal patriarchalism: the social formation of contractual individualism was dependent upon women's subordination in patriarchal families. However, the problem of patriarchal relations within the family–household is repressed in liberalism because the separation of public and private is "re-established as a division within civil society itself, within the world of men" (Pateman 1989: 122). In the East–Central European context, historically embedded gendered relationships have more recently played important roles in facilitating and legitimizing transitions *to* and *from* socialism. In their early days, Stalinist regimes sought to collapse utterly the dichotomy between public and private spheres. In practice, though, state socialism delineated public and private work and intervened in the constitution and character of family life in ways that bear a striking resemblance to patriarchal regulation in capitalist states (see Havelkova 1993). Qualities associated with patriarchal capitalism such as possessive individualism, utilitarianism, commodity fetishism, and a stark distinction between public and private "were significantly furthered by the policies of the socialist state" (Lampland 1995: 5). Thus, post-socialist transitions *ostensibly* to liberal capitalism and democracy have been able to rely on prior gendered social arrangements in the family and at the heart of civil society. Post-socialist state restructuring in a globalizing political economy represents "a struggle over the appropriate boundaries of the public and the private and the constitution of gendered subjects within these spheres" (Brodie 1994: 52).

Gender in the global political economy

Feminist scholarship on global restructuring has analyzed how the processes of global economic integration are also processes of gendering. Research in the 1970s on the role of women in international economic development first identified the gender dynamics of capitalist expansion in the south. This scholarship revealed how Western gender divisions of labor were created in modernizing societies when men's labor was extracted for capitalist, cash-cropping production and women were left in charge of subsistence production. In the 1980s, feminist scholars analyzed how the incorporation of Third-World women into wage labor through immigration and offshore production has been linked to state strategies for economic development through export-oriented trade, to the rise of multinational firms as powerful actors, and thus, to the competitive globalization of production (Sassen-Koob 1984; Sassen 1998). Guy Standing (1989) further argued that the global spread of flexible forms of labor was encouraging the growth of female employment worldwide and that the absorption of women into mainstream labor markets was in turn encouraging this global process of *flexibilization*. Together, these scholars documented the *feminization* of the international division of labor, but they also observed a dialectic process of *housewifization* at work. Housewifization described the process, where as a result of global restructuring, men increasingly found themselves in the situation of housewives, in low-paid, insecure, unprotected, and atomised employment (Mies 1986).

More recently, feminist researchers have considered how these global capitalist processes shape women's subjectivities and transform local gender relations (Ong 1987, 1991; Kabeer 1994; Sassen 1998). In contrast to feminist scholars who analyze globalization one-dimensionally as a structurally determining process that reinforces patriarchal relationships,[4] these researchers highlight subtle forms of empowerment and cultural change in the lives of differently located women. Gender regimes are undergoing change in the course of global restructuring and women are not only victims in this process, in many cases they are empowered by it. Naila Kabeer (1991), for example, has investigated how changing material incentives provided by the re-siting of transnational corporations' garment production, opened up possibilities for Bangladeshi poor women to make a better living and at the same time to challenge patriarchal gender arrangements. A similar case of global restructuring disrupting local gender arrangements has been observed along the US–Mexico border. There, in the *maquiladora* factories, women are the favored employees while men, now the majority of the unemployed, are supported by the wages of their wives and daughters (Nash and Fernandez-Kelly 1983). Globalization does not always restructure gender relations and empower women at the expense of men, however. The spread of consumption, cultural production, and information in the global political economy can enable women to create new identities as individuals and citizens. Their increased agency may have implications for the ungendering of divisions of labor and power but global marketing creates new gender-specific desires and needs in order to expand markets and profit margins. On a world scale these processes can have the effect of destroying traditional spaces of women's power, in the family, kin-community, and local social networks.

The dual transformations in political economy and gender in post-socialist societies are also complex, socially mediated processes. As in previous extensions of the global market, they are bringing both new forms of exploitation and empowerment to women in Central and Eastern Europe. However, all too often feminist scholarship has emphasized the victimization of women, rather than their increased differentiation and opportunity in post-socialist transitions. Barbara Einhorn (1993), Chris Corrin (1992), Val Moghadam (1993a), Peggy Watson (1993b) and others in collected volumes (Funk and Mueller 1993;

Rueschemeyer 1994; Mies and Shiva 1993) have analyzed the differential consequences of the economic and political changes for women and men in several
post-socialist countries. In their view, state restructuring and the rescinding of
former socialist rights to employment, living wages, child care and other public
services disproportionately affect women. As well, they have observed that the
diffusion of Western democracy across Central and Eastern Europe has
produced a masculine public sphere and representative institutions inhabited
almost exclusively by men (Heinen 1992; Waylen 1994; Eisenstein 1994; Hunt
1997). In addition to observing women's absence from politics, feminist scholars
point out that there are no strong women's or feminist movements in post-
socialist countries. Women participate in professional, humanitarian, ecological,
motherhood, and traditional (often formerly communist) women's associations,
but these are analyzed as conservative and/or anti-feminist. Overall, most feminist interpretations shed doubt on the assumption made by transitologists that
market capitalism and democratic rights have been expanded for all post-
socialist citizens. Nonetheless, like mainstream scholars, feminists have
approached the study of post-socialism from a teleological rather than a
gendered perspective. They have by and large focused exclusively on women as
the *losers* of the transitions. In so doing, they have created the category of the
victimized "Eastern European woman," not unlike the "Third-World woman"
that Chandra Mohanty (1991b) has located and criticized in Western feminist
scholarship (see also Jung 1994).

Winners or losers in post-socialist transitions?

During my fieldwork in the Czech Republic, I found that many women there
resent the assumption that they are, or will be, the new victims of global capitalism. They are victims only if you view *socialism* as having liberated women and
post-socialism as reversing the gains of this former system. Eradicating the so-
termed material causes of women's oppression by nationalizing private property
and integrating women into the wage labor force hardly transformed gender
inequalities in socialist states (Engels 1992). Women did not consider themselves
to be *liberated*, but *overworked* by state socialism. If we take into account that in
former socialist countries women have endured a double burden of work at
home and in the labor force for more than two generations, then the recent
creation of a market in labor may or may not constitute greater exploitation.
Indeed, new idioms of emancipation have emerged in post-socialism: They
include a cult of domesticity and the celebration of femininity. Women express
their freedom in being able to choose traditional female roles and dispositions
over state-dictated laboring ones. Women (and men) can choose not to "work"
but to devote themselves to their families and communities. At the same time, the
influx of foreign capital and spread of markets since 1989 has opened up new
employment opportunities, especially for well-educated women. Overall, the
gender effects of market reform in this region have yet to be systematically anal-
ysed. But rising female unemployment, household poverty, reductions in state

social support, the privatization of child care and reproductive medical services, and dramatically declining marriage and birth rates all suggest that women are indeed facing significantly new economic difficulties and opportunity costs as the marketized order takes root. None the less, in this chapter I argue in contrast to existing feminist interpretations, that women are as prominent among the winners as they are among the losers of post-socialist transitions.

Post-socialist transformations have been driven by the goal of reintegrating with the global economy and by the ideology of neoliberalism. Scholars of global political economy have unmasked the social and class forces associated with the emergence of neoliberal reform across states, in particular the structural power of transnational capital (Gill 1993). Similarly, feminist theorists have argued that neoliberalism is premised on a masculine concept of agency and is dependent on gendered social arrangements that underpin (global and local) markets (Bakker 1994, 1997). Neoliberal theory and policy maintain that post-socialist states must create an appropriate business environment for transnational investment and trade in order to resume their economic growth and benefit nationally from global market integration. Thus, neoliberal reforms restructure post-socialist states and societies by introducing private property rights and the price mechanism, and by radically reducing state intervention and redistribution. Until recently, the Czech Republic was hailed as a model of transformation through neoliberal "shock therapy." This ostensibly technical, macroeconomic integration process has not been neutral in its implications or effects, however.

The past decade of state restructuring in the Czech Republic has introduced socioeconomic and identity differentiation into what was a comparatively egalitarian and homogeneous society (Večerník *et al.* 1997). This has brought both increased opportunities and difficulties for women in particular. As a result, individual women have had to develop new strategies to help them adapt to uncertain political, economic, and ideological terrain. In the sections that follow, I consider how gender is being restructured and re-sited in post-socialist transitions. I contest some of the common assumptions about women's victimization, qualify the existing research on gender in transition, and further investigate the relationship between gender and markets in the post-socialist context. This analysis suggests that women and men in the Czech Republic are engaged with their societies' transformation, albeit in ways that conventional analysis has not expected.

Re-siting gender in post-socialism

Researchers studying gender relations in post-socialism have variously pointed out that women bear a disproportionate burden of the economic transition. Nanette Funk (1993) states in her introduction to the volume, *Gender Politics and Post-Communism*, (Funk and Mueller 1993) that "women's interests are being sacrificed to the transformation." In her book, *Cinderella Goes to Market*, Barbara Einhorn (1993: 67–8) stresses women's loss of significant rights to work, child care and social welfare as neoliberal austerity causes the retreat of the socialist state. In addition to these trends, Peggy Watson (1993b) argues that the new market democracies are immersed in a "cult of domesticity." Chris Corrin (1992) also analyses women's "double-day" burnout and their retreat to the home. Elzbieta Matynia (1995: 386, also 390) writes that "in Czechoslovakia one of the most puzzling trends ... post-1989, has been the expressed desire of women to withdraw from the world of work into the world of the household, domesticity, and the family." Valentine Moghadam (1992, 1993a) documents the marginalization of women on the nascent labor market as a result of restructuring and privatization. Women workers are made redundant or become unemployed at greater rates than men in nearly all the countries in the region. They face employment discrimination as employers perceive them to be more expensive and unreliable as workers than men, given their likelihood of becoming pregnant and taking parental leave. On this basis, Moghadam suggests that female labor will play an essentially more important role in the restructuring of post-socialist labor markets: "The global integration of Central and Eastern Europe will in effect reduce female employment just as the peripheral integration of third world economies has increased the employment of women workers on the global assembly line" (Moghadam 1992: 62–3; also Einhorn 1995: 221). In contrast, Susan Gal (1997: 39) argues that women's double workday, which was a constant burden under socialism, is a model of flexibility in post-socialism. In her view the post-socialist female subject is ideally suited to the new flexible specialization of the post-Fordist labor market. There is some truth in all of these observations, but when scrutinized in the Czech context, they reveal only part of the picture of the transformation, and lack much country-specific detail of the processes of gendered restructuring. These early analyses of gender in transition require further study to specify how gender is being restructured in a complex process of social change that includes the effects of political and economic liberalization, and the powerful influence of domestic as well as global, supranational forces (Molyneux 1994, 1995). While the initial reforms in 1990–2 have had path-dependent effects, nearly a decade of restructuring allows us to examine the strategic and the idiosyncratic ways that gender has shaped and been shaped by post-socialist transitions.

The creation of a bifurcated market in labor

The adoption of a neoliberal reform program one year after the communist government fell in the former Czechoslovakia has served to redefine gender relations, and they have, in turn, structured the nascent market society. Since 1989 a dual labor market or two-tiered society has gradually emerged (see Cox 1993: 261; Sassen 1998). This dualism is, moreover, characterized by a gender hierarchy. The Czechs have seen the most rapid rise in wage inequality in the region since 1989 (Kapoor 1996/7). As a result, two tiers of workers have developed in post-socialism; an upper tier akin to a *labor aristocracy* of skilled and professional workers who command high salaries and secure jobs with fringe benefits and the possibility of promotion, and a lower tier made up of those workers whose employment is insecure, low-paid, and unskilled or manual labor. Women are increasingly among those in the upper tier as well as very often the majority of those workers/unemployed in the lower tier. This dual labor market also involves a growing distinction between the former socialist *public* sector and the new *private* sector. In the Czech Republic this public–private differentiation is further overlaid by the emergence of a division between *domestic* firms producing mostly for the national market and *foreign* firms that are net exporters (of approximately 20 per cent of Czech exports).[5] *Business Central Europe*, the regional journal of the London-based *Economist*, considers the Czech and Hungarian economies to be "split down the middle," with foreign-owned companies making high-value-added products for export and attracting the most productive labor and locally owned companies starved of investment and equipment, and competing solely on the basis of low wages (Nicholls 1999; see also the article by J. Komínek "Czechs falling behind in R&D spending" *The Prague Post*, 15–22 July 1998).

A two-tiered economy?

What is most staggering in the growth of the private sector, though, is its overwhelming masculinization. Many more men have shifted their labor to the private sector, accounting for 83.5 per cent in 1990, 64 per cent in 1992, and 62 per cent in 1994 of private sector employees (Český statistický úřad 1995), and there are relatively few female entrepreneurs and employers. More often than managers in Poland, Hungary, and Slovakia, Czech managers admitted that they used gender as a high criterion (second only to low productivity) for laying off employees in the restructuring and privatization of state firms (Paukert 1995a, b based on a 1993 ILO regional survey). Unions too, have accepted redundancies in "feminized" sectors that are female-labor-intensive as a legacy of gender segregation in the planned economy. According to Peter Rutland (1993: 125), when approving female redundancies Czech union officials volunteered comments such as: "a lot of these girls were not really productive workers anyway." The male-dominated engineering industry is considered "the mother of Czech industry" that must not be lost.[6] Organized labor's adaptation to neoliberal policies has thus occurred along gender lines. Consequently, the public sector (education, health, social and civil services) is even more feminized than during communism, with women constituting approximately 60 per cent of Czech public employees (Paukert 1995b).[7] This outcome is due to the combined effects of the socialist occupational structure of female employment, private firms' gender bias in recruitment, women's greater sense of security in public sector employment and their lack of time for re-training due to family responsibilities.

A 1995 ILO study notes that "the pattern of employment shifts from the public to the private sector has been detrimental to women in all countries of the Central European region, in an alarmingly similar way" (Paukert 1995a: 15). Many women experience the negative outcomes of rapid privatization because as primary caregivers they are usually more reliant than men on public provision for non-market social reproduction and as workers, on public sector employment. Wages are also much higher (and come with many more benefits) in the private sector than in the public sector. Thus, Czech women are doubly disadvantaged by their gender segregation in the latter sector (Bednácek and Zemplínerová 1997). Indeed, Csilla Kollonay (forthcoming) argues that gender segregation in the public sector (e.g. education, health and social welfare) versus the private sector (financial services, business entrepreneurship) represents a form of "disguised discrimination" considering that there are over three times more women employed in the former areas, where working conditions are substandard and wages are consistently below the average. Moreover, despite the strong association between labor and the core male-dominated industries, it is these non-core (women) workers in highly feminized sectors such as education and health, that have engaged in labor militancy and strike action in the Czech Republic. This is not surprising given the declining, below-average wages in those sectors and the underfunded, impoverished state of hospitals and schools – both legacies of communist priorities which privileged industrial production. The Czech government has reinforced this preference for the industrial sector in the transition by deliberately sustaining the status quo. Labor costs in the Czech Republic are among the lowest in the Central European region.[8] By negotiating a low wage, low unemployment compact with the male-dominated unions, the Czech government has maintained the pre-existing occupational wage structure that places education and health workers amongst the lowest-paid public employees. In spite of already falling state expenditures during the transition, the austerity *baličky* (little packages) in the summer of 1997 cut education and health budgets by an additional 10 per cent.

Foreign enclaves

The two-tiered structure of foreign and domestic sectors in the Czech Republic is, to a greater extent than even public and private sectors, characterized by gender division.[9] Foreign direct investment has so far concentrated in capital-intensive areas such as automobiles, rubber and plastics, printing and publishing, chemicals, and telecommunications and less so in female labor-intensive industries (e.g. light industries such as foodstuffs, glass and ceramics, textiles and garment manufacturing). In the former industries, the vast majority of employees tend to be men (Bednáček and Zemplínerová 1997), although the only export-processing zone established in the post-socialist Czech Republic is the textile manufacturing industry on the Western Bohemian border with Germany, where unsurprisingly most of the workers are women (S. Murray, "In Czech Republic's move to capitalism, high unemployment is notably absent," *The Wall Street Journal* 24 August 1995). The average wages in foreign companies are 50 per cent greater than the average wage in the female-dominated public sector.[10] The wage differential between workers and managers, the lowest and highest paid, is also far bigger in foreign firms, disproportionately affecting women who are generally at the low end of these corporate hierarchies.[11]

Furthermore, human resources firms testify to the explicit preference of many foreign firms for male managers and staff, who frequently give the reason that women employees are less productive and cost more since they take between two and four years of maternity leave (E. McClune, "So, how far have you really come baby?" *The Prague Tribune* March 1998). As such, gender-neutral English and German job descriptions are converted into Czech gender-specific forms. Advertising preferences for male or female employees are usually also within a certain age range (Jedličková 1996: 30; *Ekonom* 1998).[12] Local Czech and foreign executive search and personnel services reproduce this discriminatory environment on behalf of their clients. When asked if foreign firms discriminate against Czech employees, Petra Vanková of the Commercial Union responded that most people prefer men of a certain age group as executives or managers (*Ekonom* 1998: 34). Young educated women with foreign language competency are an exception. Western companies needing local managers and expertise often find them appealing because they can be rapidly socialised into Western corporate culture; they are even more appealing as trophy secretaries (see Dvořák and Solčová 1998). Petr Zahradník comments that Czech women who are secretaries or assistants to foreign managers are expected to work overtime and respond to their requests beyond the workday. Little consideration is apparently given to the fact that these women employees may have small children and family responsibilities (*Ekonom* 1998: 34). Nonetheless, personnel firms openly acknowledge the corporate preference for young male managers. For their part, young men are attracted by the masculine, slick image of Western corporations, regardless of whether this involves marketing Coca-Cola or feminine sanitary products (Ascoly 1994; K. Wheatly, "Overpaid, oversexed, and all-over Prague," *The Times* 11 April 1992; Brdečková 1994).[13] Curiously, *foreign* women working in the Czech Republic have remarked that they have achieved greater experience, more prestigious positions, and are treated with more respect as managers and executives than would be the case in North America or Western Europe. They are taken seriously on account of being *foreigners* with so-called "expertise." Czech women managers, however, are often not taken seriously on account of their gender (R. Orol, "Foreign women enjoy advantage," *The Prague Post* 18–24 March 1998: A8).

Stereotypical perceptions and prejudices against women in the foreign and multinational sector have strategic implications for the gendered restructuring of the entire labor market in the Czech Republic. Economists generally hold foreign firms to be key actors in the diffusion of innovative knowledge, management, and technology to domestic public and private industries in transition countries. Their "best practices" in the region are thought to strategically raise the standards of local firms through competition and demonstration effect (e.g. resulting in institutional isomorphism with the West (see Eichengreen and Kohl 1998)). However, what if foreign firms in the Czech Republic are routinely practicing gender discrimination in their recruitment and employment policies, consciously preferring men over women and restructuring the labor market in explicitly gendered ways? What may be diffused to domestic firms in this case are not "best practices" but idiosyncratic, discriminatory practices that are generally illegal in the home countries of multinationals. Gender and age discrimination though may be perfectly legal in the host country due to vague laws, poor enforcement of labor codes, and a society that unconsciously has turned a blind eye to such practices during communism. The Czech Republic, for example, has yet to pass a law to explicitly prevent gender-based employment discrimination and to ensure equal employment opportunities for men and women (Karat Coalition 1999). The requirement that applicant countries to the European Union harmonise their legislation with European law in the pre-accession process, including the body of European equal opportunities legislation and policy by April 1999, makes this lack of action viable only in the short term, however.

Cushioning the transition – women go home!

A common assumption of the mainstream as well as the feminist literature on the Czech transition is that there was a massive withdrawal of women from the labor force after 1989 (for example, see Matynia 1995; S. Murray, "In Czech Republic's move to capitalism, high unemployment is notably absent," *The Wall Street Journal* 24 August 1995). Mitchell Orenstein (1996: 210) claims that 10 per cent of working-age women dropped out of the Czechoslovak labor force between 1989 and 1992. Indeed, an article in *The Economist* entitled "The Czech Republic, the New Bohemians" (22 October 1994: 23–7) argues that this phenomenon explains the Czech success in keeping unemployment down until recently. These assertions are based on government policy in 1990 to reduce the size of the labor force and prevent anticipated unemployment in this way. During communism, the private sphere of family, informal friendship networks, and household production and consumption was highly valued as a place of freedom from state domination. It was also a place embedded in deep-seated notions of gender difference that preserved conventional roles for men and women (Einhorn 1993). Family and private life thus became potent resources for post-communist neoliberals who wanted to rewrite the collectivist social contract in 1990–1 (Klaus 1991; Goven 1993). At that time, the social policy group in the Civic Forum (the first post-socialist government) believed that increasing mater-nity leave and other social welfare incentives would encourage women, especially of child-rearing age, to exit the labor force.[14] Their initial manifesto on social policy read as follows: "A differentiation of incomes will gradually help to reduce the disproportionate economic activity of women, a rehabilitation of the family and the creation of better conditions for raising children" (see Castle 1990). Moreover, in a 1990 interview, a senior aide to the Czech Finance Minister (Václav Klaus) criticized the "overemployment" of women and said:

> The Ministry of Labour and Social Affairs is preparing a program for young women so they can afford to stay home with small children, and we

will aid them with social support. This policy in the end will save money because when women work they need state-supported care.[15]

Sharon Wolchik (1994) cites public opinion polls that suggest there was a widespread belief in 1991 that women's employment was too high.

As they reduce social expenditures and begin to privatize the public sector, state elites often seek to transfer the burden of social reproduction to the family and to rely upon the continuity of gendered notions of women's place. The non-commodified private sphere distinct from the market and the state is crucial to them both economically and in producing their meanings. As long as women are carrying caring values as individuals and in the family–household for society, "they do not have to be put into operation socially" (Williamson 1986: 110). In 1995 then, Václav Klaus's neoliberal coalition government changed the Czech Labour Code to extend legal *maternity* leave to men, and increase this parental leave from three to four years – now the longest in the world (International Labor Organization (ILO) 1997). Exceedingly few fathers, though, have put this parental provision into practice. Despite its gender-neutrality, this policy change was implicitly designed to encourage women to stay out of the labor force. Prior to it, child care and abortion facilities were privatized and have operated on a largely user-pays basis since 1991. This shift from state to market provision has primarily affected women (Cook 1993; Reuters, "Facing a rush from Poland, Czechs limit abortion rights," *New York Times* 14 April 1993). The financial austerity package introduced in April and May of 1997, following the collapse of the Czech currency, further included progressive cuts to child care, health care, and infrastructure provision, and eliminated inflation-adjustments to social security benefits (Pehe 1997).

However, irrespective of the intentions and decisions of state policy makers to entice women to leave the workforce in the transition, working-age women's labor-force participation has hardly been reduced. Although the total labor force was massively reduced by 10 per cent in 1989–91, the labor market activity of this group of women decreased by only about 2–3 per cent between 1989 and 1994 (Paukert 1995a; Čermáková 1996).[16] Liba Paukert's ILO study concludes that during the early phase of transition *age*, rather than *gender*, was the determinant factor for labor-force reduction, although some gender differences were noted (Paukert 1995b: 4). Women are 51.5 per cent of the Czech population and still 47.6 per cent of the labor force (Research Institute for Labour and Social Affairs 1998). Hungary is probably the only post-socialist country that has seen a drop of 10 per cent or more in the labor-force participation of women in this age group (ILO, forthcoming). But there has been a noticeable decrease in the participation of Czech women compared with Czech men of post-retirement age. The withdrawal of women over the age of 53–57 years has been very large, constituting the majority of the reduction in women's economic activity as a result of opportunities for early retirement immediately following the "velvet" revolution (Paukert 1995a: 18). Among working-age women though, the striking development has not been their retreat into the home and family and exit from the nascent labor market, but precisely the opposite. In this respect, the continuity with women's near full employment for at least two generations during socialism is what is most noteworthy; claims that women have "returned home" since the fall of communist regimes are pure myth.

Fertility strike!

Since 1991 Czech society has seen a dramatic and unprecedented decline in fertility and marriage rates, implying a spontaneous strike on the home front by young women.[17] Moreover, although the maternity leave has been extended to four years, the average leave is only twenty-four months (Research Institute for Labour and Social Affairs 1998). Robert Chase (1997a) argues that the sudden contraction in fertility in the Czech Republic cannot be explained by conventional factors like alignment with Western reproductive behavior, increases in women's labor-force participation and changes in family support policies. This phenomenon can only be explained by changes in economic conditions and expectations such as anticipated unemployment, declining wages, and high inflation, which increase the costs of marriage and child-rearing and counter pronatalist state policy (Heitlinger 1993). While Chase (1997b) assesses the impact of economic transition on the reproductive system, his evidence also suggests an inverse causal relation: changes in family forms as a result of economic uncertainty and insecurity affect the process of economic transition itself. Indeed, the Czech sociologist Ivo Možný (1994: 62) argues that the breakdown of the informal family insurance system, which compensated for the failing paternalistic state, actually precipitated the Czechoslovak velvet revolution. Tensions and difficulties in the family substantially contributed to the widespread feeling that it was no longer possible to maintain a socialist system.[18]

Deferring family formation is explicable given the economic transition and protracted depression in the Czech Republic. Neoliberal reforms have made the situation of women, in particular, more difficult by removing socialized child care and public services and at the same time relying on their unpaid household labor as a transitional coping mechanism. Their choices are stark in the new market society; combining family and employment increasingly involves discrimination, career interruption, or marginalization, and the physical exhaustion of a "double day": being a full-time mother usually involves dependence on a male breadwinner or a targeted state benefit and typically economic difficulty. Instead, the "fertility strike" by young women has externalized the burden of this masculinist trade-off in the form of a negative population growth rate. This rapid demographic change will likely have serious consequences for economic growth and structural adjustment in the Czech Republic. Differences in family forms may account for important differences in the relative success of economic transitions. The family facilitates economic transformation in two ways, for example: (1) it serves to cushion the transformation by redistributing resources and providing for needs in the case of both government and market failure; and (2) it assists structural adjustment by re-allocating labor (often women's labor) in the most efficient way and/or deferring gratification, even biological reproduction to ensure adequate social reproduction. Kazimierz Poznanski (1998: 198) suggests that "the striking contrast between China and Russia's growth pattern has much to do with the different state of their family structures." Collectivization in Russia turned family members into independent wage workers, while in China, parental authority and family distribution was largely preserved and has been able to revive agricultural production and economic growth.

In sum, although neoliberal reforms appear to be gender-neutral, they generate conflict in the gender order and threaten the system of social organization. The full extension of the market mechanism, for instance, encourages women like men to participate fully in the paid labor force and thus partly or completely to relinquish their traditional roles as biological and social reproducers of labor in the family household. This has resulted not only in what the Pope has called a "demographic winter" descending on East Central Europe but in a "crisis of social reproduction," which is reflected in the declining general health and well-being of the population (Pearson 1997). Moreover, where state actors in the Czech Republic have resorted to conservative and discriminatory policies to re-establish the traditional gender regime in the marketplace and in the family, their efforts have had unanticipated, and entirely opposite, effects.

Men of steel? Preserving male industries in the transition

It is not only women who are being affected by the Czech transformation through neoliberal "shock therapy." Men are also experiencing labor-market insecurities and a loss in personal status (e.g. as the main household earner), albeit in different ways than women. While women have for the most part had to face such insecurities for generations, in the transition to capitalism, many more men are being exposed to them. Traditional labor, as represented by mainly male core workers in strategic industries, has lost the privileged place it obtained under state socialism. The social and structural effects of post-socialist transitions thus raise *gender* issues, not issues merely concerning women. Feminist research on the East European transitions, however, has not explored or adequately analyzed gender *relations*. This research has been focused almost solely on the situation of women without attending to the relational aspects of gender; that is, to simultaneous transformations in the position of men and women and in social constructions of masculinity and femininity. "Men are among the losers in Eastern Europe" as are women (Molyneux 1995). In Peggy Watson's words (1994) "there is a male identity crisis, a product of a widespread masculine anomie, reflected in the rising male suicide and mortality rates," alcohol abuse, unemployment, and crime rates as well in the former Eastern bloc (see also John Thornhill "Ivan the Terribly Lost," *The Financial Times*, London, 29 November 1997: 35).

In the past, *Homo Sovieticus*, the man of steel, was lauded as the emblem and agent of communism. Since its fall though, individualised subjects of competitive capitalism, such as the entrepreneur and the consumer, have gradually replaced the laboring man. Workers in mining, steel and other major heavy industries in Eastern Europe have been made redundant with restructuring and privatization. This is only now occurring in the Czech Republic. The Czech government managed to forestall this restructuring by focusing on privatization first and maintaining a low-wage, low-unemployment economic policy between 1990 and 1996. Male-dominant industries were largely protected and losses/debt written off by the government in the initial "shock therapy" phase of the transition. Industrial production output fell by 30 per cent between 1990 and 1994 while employment fell only 20 per cent. Employment in the female-dominated textile industry though, was reduced by half, from 155,000 workers in 1990 to 86,000 in 1995 (K. Cohen 1997). In the female labor-intensive glass and ceramic industry, employment fell from 69,000 to 34,000 with near-complete privatization (*Czech Business and Trade Journal* 1998). In contrast to Hungary, where nearly 60,000 steel workers were sacked, leaving only a rump industry employing 17,000, the Czech steel industry still employs 60,000 workers (Kapoor 1996/7). The Czech government has been reluctant to privatize major steel works, such as Nová Hut' and Vitkovice in Ostrava, for fear of mass redundancies, although several foreign investors, including the International Finance Corporation of the World Bank, have offered considerable capital in return for a joint venture stake (Cook 1996). However, the Poldní Kládno steel mill was sold (and went bankrupt in 1998), while some brown coal mines have been closed in Northern Bohemia for environmental reasons and others are now in the process of being privatized.

The auto industry, the lynchpin of which is Škoda, is a source of national pride, but it has been a virtual foreign enclave since Volkswagen became its main manager and owner in 1991. Lately, the Czech government has been spending billions to renationalize strategic industries on the verge of bankruptcy (*The Economist* "Czech renationalisation," 6 February 1999: 65–6). Unemployment is the highest in the former socialist industrial regions; for example, in Ostrava, an industrial city in northern Moravia, it is predicted to be 18.5 per cent in 1999. Still, more women than men will be unemployed even in those heavily industrialized regions worst hit by downsizing. ILO study findings that Czech managers prefer to lay off women before men workers partly explain this gendered outcome. At the same time, Western industrial firms that have located in the Czech Republic have often capitalized on cheap female manual labor. The French-owned TRW Automotive bought out a failing Czech electronics firms to cut costs and has transformed it into a manufacturing supplier for French automakers like Citroen and Peugeot. At the Benešov plant, the factory's managing director, Jan Gregor, has his largely young and female workforce on 12-hour shifts (Knight 1994).

Industrial sector wages are barely at the levels they were in 1989, when they were among the highest in Czechoslovakia. As a result, many Czech men are facing so-called *housewifization*. They are experiencing wage depreciation, job insecurity, and unemployment without the support of strong unions as women have done for generations. The dominant forms of regulation have changed from being pro-collective, protective, statutory regulations to pro-individualistic, market-oriented, and fiscal regulations. The labor market has not been deregulated, but rather, has given rise to more statutory regulation of economic and social behavior. Tax and social benefit systems have been transformed into mechanisms to control behavior through targeting and incentives structures (see Standing 1998b). Unemployment benefits in the Czech Republic are only available for six months, three months at 50 per cent of the average wage and three months at 40 per cent. In many ways these neoliberal reforms have destroyed the security and privilege that socialism conferred on the working man. They seek to produce flexible subjects for regional and global markets without regard for gender differences.

One of the reasons why Russian men have been more vulnerable to death, suicide, and illness in the transition, Guy Standing (1998a: 33) suggests, is that "women were made more resilient by their need to adjust to difficulties in the Soviet era, [whereas] men were accustomed to a rather passive role in that period." Their job security and status as head of household were basically ensured under communism. In Hungary, the sociologist Julia Szalai (1997) also contends that men have experienced greater stress and difficulty in adjusting to the new economic system than women. Unlike in Russia, however, the Czech male mortality rate has not drastically increased, nor as in Hungary has their rate of unemployment been above 10 per cent or greater than women's. Yet, many of those I interviewed in the Czech Republic expressed similar concerns about men. Czech psychologist Helena Klímová linked men's anxiety or "crisis of masculinity" in the current economic transition to the rapid social change women experienced during the Stalinist drive in Czechoslovakia to integrate them into the labor force:

> What happened in the 1950s and 1960s was a massive change in the lives of women but compared with this, the changes in the 1990s are influencing mainly men. I would say the communists did some of the dirty work and as a result, women became very independent. In the 1980s, we did not feel any oppression by men, as *women*. We were oppressed by the regime, not especially as women, but together with men. When we entered the 1990s new values spread, I mean the values of the free market economy, of career and money. All this has had a much greater influence on men. This phenomenon, I think, is somehow connected with the fate of women in the 1950s and 1960s. It seems that we underwent something that men are only now undergoing. When I work with patients and clients, I see that indeed it is men who are subject to greater change; they are living through these social changes more intensely than women I would say.
>
> (Klímová, interview, August 1996)

Men, of course, were also exploited in various ways during communism but unlike women, the experience of balancing job and family and working a double shift, of being laid off and demoted is relatively new to them. Feminist scholars of state socialism also suggest that women's identities during communism rested less on laboring than did men's, and as much on their private family and domestic roles. These roles gained importance and power during the most repressive and harsh times, and may have helped women to adapt psychologically and practically in today's transition from socialism.

Structural disequilibrium: transitional gains for post-socialist women?

Women's inequality with men has intensified with the creation of a market in labor, although their participation in the workforce has not been greatly altered by the transition. Women are currently more than 60 per cent of unemployed persons in the Czech Republic (approximately 8–9 per cent of women were unemployed at the end of 1998). At the same time, the demand for labor in the service sector, especially in finance, tourism, information, and administrative services, has grown steadily over the last decade, and women are expected to benefit from this trend (Szalai 1997).[19] However, as Paukert's study (1995b: 11–12) notes, newly privatized trading and retail businesses are largely registered in the names of men and have resulted in mass unemployment for women who formerly worked in the state retail sector. Further, the greater demand for male labor in the private sector, in banking among other areas, has resulted in a greater increase in their share of employment in services (Shen 1994).

Sixty-two per cent of female labor is now in the tertiary sector in the Czech Republic, however (including public sector education and health services). The knowledge capital that women acquired during socialism, including their higher education, foreign language competency and experience in service-related areas such as banking and finance, is being re-valued in post-socialism. Analysts such as Eva Fodor (forthcoming; see also Fong and Paull 1993) argue that women are advantaged in the post-socialist labor markets, ironically because of their segregation in the service sector before 1989. Market transitions amplify and accelerate the changes that have been occurring in the larger global political economy, i.e. the rise in the service sector and concomitant demise of the manufacturing sector, especially heavy industry. These rapid transformations have the potential to improve women's structural position in the labor market and counter any effects of gender discrimination (Fodor forthcoming). Jaroslava Šťatsná (1995) emphasizes these new opportunities for Czech women in the emerging service economy. She points to the growth of private tertiary sector employment in the Czech Republic that she argues has effectively closed the wage-gap between men and women by several percent since 1989: women's average wages have risen slightly to 78 per cent of men's (Čermáková 1996).

Shifts in the relative structural power of men and women are not altogether uncommon in radical upheavals of a political and economic system. Aili Tripp

(1997) for instance has studied the transitional gains Tanzanian women experienced in the liberalization of their political and economic system. Under socialism, women in Tanzania were exempt from most state employment and developed informal market initiatives to supplement family income. When market liberalization was introduced, as a result of their adaptation to socialist structures, these women were in a position to formalize their informal cross-ethnic networks and skills in profitable market exchange. Women rapidly became the major income earners in a transformed Tanzania, and this had significant effects on their social status within the family and broader society. The sustainability of what is effectively a situation of "structural disequilibrium" in Tanzania, however, is uncertain and is highly dependent on institutional reinforcement of women's new-found power. Such a situation appears to have parallels in post-socialist East Central Europe.

Unfortunately, there is no substantial evidence in the Czech transition for the structural transformation of gender inequality. The gender gap in wages may be less than during communism but it is still remarkably persistent under capitalism (Lidové Noviny 1998). Women constitute less than 40 per cent of private sector employment and so are not receiving the same gains as men from privatization. Returns to education have increased substantially more for men than for women in the course of the market transition (Chase 1997c). Indeed, there are fewer women engineers and technicians since 1989, while the numbers of female university graduates in law and business in relation to men has actually suffered a recent drop. In 1997 over 91,000 men graduated in these fields compared with only 16,000 women (McClune 1998). These responses of various groups of women in the Czech Republic to restructuring, however, do not suggest their victimization, but rather reveal the resistance to gender equality in the market and the state. Women's continuing strong labor-force participation and personal preferences show that they value both paid employment and their roles in the family–household. In fact, the majority of post-socialist societies, including the Czech Republic, approve both of self-regulating market principles and a strong state sector that supports women's workforce participation, as Julie Beck also argues in Chapter 10, this volume.

Since 1989 changes in social policy in the Czech Republic have often been makeshift. Although the pensionable age has been raised, universal family benefits have been withdrawn and private health insurance funds have been introduced, the comprehensive privatization of health, education, housing, and welfare sectors has been strongly resisted. Social policy in the Czech transition has been designed in compromising ways to cushion the social effects of macro-economic adjustment, against a background of microeconomic reform that has maximized incentives for the emerging private sector and entrepreneurial class. However, as Mitchell Orenstein (1998: 48) has observed, once the Czech government moved away from the social liberal policies of 1990–2 to neoliberal ones in 1993–6, their popularity quickly waned. In 1997, the right-of-center government led by Václav Klaus fell from power and was replaced in 1998 by a Social Democratic, Left coalition government. No longer the showcase of neoliberalism, the Czechs may have proved the limits of global economic theory applied to post-socialist transitions.

Conclusion: between the market and the state

Unlike the macroeconomists who stated that the Czech transformation was over in 1994 or those feminists who claimed early on that women were the losers in the transition, I do not want to foreclose discussion of what are essentially multi-dimensional and open-ended processes of change. Rather, in this chapter I have considered the various ways in which the global economic integration of the Czech Republic is taking place on gendered terrain. I have argued that gender relations, not merely the situation of women, are being transformed in post-socialism. Women and men are among the winners and the losers in the Czech transitions. The creation of a labor market and the restructuring of the state has altered the prior socialist gender regime in striking ways, but there is much greater continuity with past practices and divisions than is generally understood or acknowledged. Incorporation into the gendered global division of labor as well as patterns of gender segregation under socialism have shaped the emergence of markets in the Czech Republic. Concepts of gender have also shaped neoliberal reform programs. Privatization and liberalization, for example, are associated with the construction of a specifically masculine form of political and economic agency that is represented discursively as universal and gender-neutral. State downsizing and replacement by an almost religious faith in the market mechanism have created and reinforced gender inequalities. At the same time, the family is hailed by the Czech government and the majority of political parties as the fundamental unit of the new market economy.

As in other world regions, women have generally been more disadvantaged than men by these structural changes. Privatizing the state and its provision of universal benefits and services has removed support for women in their roles as mothers and spouses as well as workers. Focusing on the family has restored patriarchal assumptions about women's primary care-giving role and shifted the burden of social reproduction onto women in place of the state. Commodifying labor in an unfettered market has promoted gender discrimination in the hiring, firing and employment of women on the basis of spurious stereotypes and socialist norms that privilege men. So far, the Czech state has failed to develop the institutional mechanisms or show the political will with which to challenge this pervasive gender bias in the nascent labor market. Given the penetration of Western investment capital and imports in Central and Eastern Europe, however, the saturation of marketing, media and new forms of legal and property rights may be more important than questions of labor or employment/unemployment in conceptualizing gender dynamics and global transformations (Gill and True 1997). I take up this argument elsewhere, in an exploration of gender and the expansion of commodification and consumer markets in post-socialist Europe (True 1999).

This chapter has explored the uneven and complex impact that locally mediated global restructuring has had on gender relations in the Czech Republic. It has analyzed globalization as a process that is sociocultural as well as economic, that has repressive as well as empowering effects in the post-socialist context. In this regard, the experiences of women and men as they shape their own gendered transitions offer important lessons for rethinking restructuring. By focusing on gender in transition we can see global restructuring for what it is in Central and Eastern Europe: a major societal transformation perhaps only rivaled by that earlier post-war social transformation in this region.

Notes

1   In addition to the sources cited, the research in this chapter is based on thirty-five personal interviews in the Czech Republic, 1996–8.
2   For an introduction to the scholarly literature on transitions from authoritarianism to democracy in Latin America and Southern Europe applied to the post-socialist transitions in Central and Eastern Europe, see O'Donnell *et al.* 1986; Schmitter and Karl 1991; and Linz and Stepan 1996.
3   The orthodox literature tends to present general, mechanistic models to explain communism's collapse and macroeconomic, technical solutions to the "problem of transition" to democracy and capitalism (see Sachs 1994).
4   Feminists have often viewed "globalization" only in terms of its negative effects; as a homogenizing, structurally determining process that "will almost certainly shrink the public space available for women to exercise their democratic rights as voters, citizens and workers ... and will reinforce patriarchal rights" (see Menon 1996: 15).
5   Foreign investors also own approximately 50 per cent of the state assets sold by the Ministry of Privatization and National Property Fund under their large-scale privatization program (distinct from those former state assets diffused through voucher privatization). The proceeds from these sales amounted to a total of US$4.6 billion (Zemplínerová 1997: 19).
6   Senator Richard Falbr, President of the Czech and Moravian Combined Trade Unions, is cited by *Business Central Europe* here (see Cook 1996).
7   For example, in the education and health sectors, which are traditionally public goods provided by the public sector, women are 76 per cent and 81 per cent of the employees, respectively.
8   At the end of 1996, average unit labor costs compared at purchasing power parity in the Czech Republic amounted to only 28 per cent of the Austrian level; in Slovenia they were 60 per cent (Lyons 1996). For much of the decade Czech labor costs were as much as 50 per cent lower than in Poland and Hungary (Rutland 1993). In western Germany the average male worker earns $33.21 an hour, in Poland $2.36, and in the Czech Republic $1.76.
9   Foreign firms employ about 10 per cent of the workforce in the Czech Republic.
10   These higher wages currently exceed public sector wages by an average of 50 per cent, and this gap is increasing. They are paid in spite of punitive government tax, designed to keep wages down, incurred by companies that pay wages above the state-mandated ceiling. In 1997 the Czech Ministry of Industry and Trade reported that the average wage in the public sector was 9,913 Czech crowns (ČZK), in the private sector 10,962 ČZK and in foreign firms 14,704 ČZK. Foreign organizations also reported the greatest increase in wages. The lowest wages were reported in the female labor-intensive clothing industry; the highest wages were reported in the banking, insurance, real estate, and research and development sectors.
11   Coopers & Lybrand's half-year study of employee wages in foreign companies in the Czech Republic showed that in 1998 a joint venture director earned ČZK 171,000 or

approximately $5,000 per month while the most highly qualified worker at the same firm earned ČZK 13,214.

12 The Czech Helsinki Foundation in Prague has compiled a file of discriminatory job advertisements according to job titles, the specified age and sex required for the position.

13 Looking good is believed to be essential to gaining employment in Western corporations (where particular personal features are often a job specification), and being successful generally. A recent *Wall Street Journal* article reports the increase in plastic surgery and personal makeovers in the Czech Republic. The owner of a Medical Cosmetics Institute in Prague commented: "It's good to look young, to look successful, to look active. Companies want that image. They want young people. A man or woman who enters here can leave after a couple of days, completely new" (B. Newman, "Dip and snip: Czechs take to the waters, go under the knife: new post-communist values include health and beauty: radon baths, face lifts," *The Wall Street Journal* 20 March 1995).

14 Former Charter 77 signatory Jiřina Šiklová commented in 1990 that most of the Civic Forum leaders – all but one of whom are male – basically agreed on the benefit of women returning to the home. "They see it not only as a wise way of dealing with the potential high unemployment but also as the natural order of things" (cited in Rosen 1990: 12; also in a personal interview with Šiklová, August 1996).

15 When the official was asked whether this meant some decline in the role of women, the answer was: "'No, no. Women especially don't consider it a decline in their role. Their role is in the family and in the education of children. This is their natural and primary role'" (quoted in Moghadam 1990: 27). Orenstein (1996) also discusses the role of incentives to encourage women to retreat to the home in the active labor market strategy of the first democratic government. In May 1998 when I asked two prominent sociologists involved in those initial discussions in the Civic Forum about this strategy, they denied ever pursuing it. Now that the Czech Republic must approximate European Union standards of equal opportunities it is certainly not *comme il faut* to admit to this earlier discriminatory thinking.

16 Housewives represent only 9 per cent of the "non-active" female population in the Czech Republic (Paukert 1995b: 6).

17 During the six years between 1990 and 1996, marriages fell by 41 per cent while registered births dropped by almost a third. In 1990, there were 90,953 recorded marriages, a figure slightly higher than the year before, but by 1996 this level had fallen to 53,896. The average age of marriage has also risen, in the direction of that in Western countries. Similarly, births registered in 1990 were 130,564 while six years later the number was just 90,446 (Open Media Research Institute 1997).

18 Difficulties and tensions could be observed in the family system of social capital, Možný (1991, 1994) argues, as divorce and spatial mobility increased and the younger generation began to react against its parents' norms (or *normalization*) in the 1970s and 1980s. Conflicts between men and women over the expectations of gender roles were no doubt also present. The socialist system was too reliant on social capital, which was context bound, uncertain, and becoming difficult to transfer from generation to generation. The transition to capitalism allowed this social capital to be partly converted into economic capital, which has the qualities necessary for a rapidly changing society.

19 The Czech Republic has fostered a strong service sector more quickly than other countries in the region. They have been helped by booming tourism, small privatization (22,000 shops and other state-owned services were sold to private owners in 1991–3), financial sector employment rising from 5,000–55,000, and simply by living in a small country bordering rich Austria and Germany (Kapoor 1996/7).

Part II

Sites

In the previous section we have seen how "bringing gender in" leads to theoretical reformulations and new understandings of global restructuring, steering it away from abstract accounts towards analyses which are grounded in the daily lives and experiences of women and men. This section moves us even further along this trajectory by addressing such questions as: What are the gendered effects of particular aspects of global restructuring on women's lives in particular "sites" or locales in the global political economy? How are gender ideologies and relations changing (or not) in different national and regional contexts? What roles do not only global economic, but also political, cultural, and social forces at all levels play in restructuring?

The aspects of global restructuring explored in these contributions by Valentine Moghadam, Yumiko Mikanagi, Eleonore Kofman, and Mayke Kromhout go beyond consideration of global economic forces by focusing attention on the roles of particular state policies, migration patterns, and household arrangements. Moreover, the gendered effects they document are not confined to economic impacts on women in the formal workplace. They extend to effects on the gender policies of states, gender patterns in migration, and gender arrangements in the household. These more extensive and often contradictory effects that vary in terms of national and regional contexts challenge assumptions about the homogenizing nature of global restructuring and claims that women are only victimized by it. They also provide glimpses of new and potential "sites" of and for resistance.

A focus on the Middle East is rare in studies of global restructuring, in part because the features associated with it in Orientalist discourse (such as aristocratic rule, Islam, patriarchalism, anti-Westernism, and reliance on natural resources rather than high-tech industries) are seen as antithetical to globalization. Moghadam's chapter, however, reveals that although there is less foreign direct investment in the Middle East than in Asia and Latin America, the end of the oil boom is leading to the liberalization and privatization of economies in the Middle East, and particularly in Jordan. The increasing poverty that now characterizes Jordan is creating a feminization of both labor participation and unemployment. Poor and working-class women are entering the formal and informal labor force as well as seeking employment at unprecedented rates. The economic necessity for women to work is eroding to some degree the "patriarchal gender contract" in Jordan that has kept women from working outside of the home. However, patriarchy still slots them into service work and light industry work (to replace migrant labor), denies them education and skills, and prefers male labor over female labor in higher-wage formal occupations in the private sector. Moghadam concludes that liberalization, although loosening patriarchal relations and structures, will not "free" women. Only active women's organizations, which address the difficulties women face when joining the labor force as well as the contradictions between women's need for work and high rates of unemployment, can do so.

In contrast to countries in the Middle East, Japan is typically considered to be a major site of global capitalism, with all the GI trappings of cosmopolitanism and liberal democracy. As Mikanagi in Chapter 6 illustrates, however, Japan has been particularly adept at appearing to be a modern, Westernized state, which upholds liberal values while, in fact, undermining equal opportunity legislation for women. It has done so by posing as a good global citizen who signs off on UN conventions against discrimination and then enacts them. What it enacts, however, has no teeth. In her case study of the recent rise and fall of equal opportunity legislation for women in Japan, Mikanagi finds that there were political forces at work which sought to deny women workers equal wages and greater benefits. The lack of truly diverse public representation in the study groups that drafted the legislation, the weakness of labor unions (and their insensitivity to women's interests), and the inattention of the ruling party to a growing gender gap in voting patterns led most directly to a "toothless" law. Such a study enables us to better determine where and how political interventions can be made in state policy making to produce different outcomes.

Kofman in Chapter 7 takes us to other sites associated with the world of GI – global cities in Europe – through an examination of female labor migration to these places. Until recently the field of IPE has shown keener interest in the movement of capital and production than in the movement of people. Serious interest in labor migration only emerged in the context of the post-Fordist onslaught on the welfare state and increasingly restrictive policies in OECD states toward labor migration. Both critical and feminist accounts of labor migration have focused on the experiences of poor and working-class migrants who constitute the world of GII, particularly in global cities. Kofman argues, however, that this important but too singular focus prevents us from examining other experiences of migration, particularly among women. Many migrant or transient women in Europe are well-educated, skilled professionals who do not fit the image of the unskilled migrant worker highlighted in global city literature. However, because their professional qualities are not always recognized, they often are compelled to find employment in the sector where there exists a high demand for female labor, i.e. the domestic service sector. This of course leads to serious deskilling and "brain waste" of the women in question (and the labor force in general). Whereas many women immigrants, regardless of their level of education and skills, are likely to end up in the GII sphere, or underside of globalization, there are also women who are able to pursue professional careers, and thus operate in the realm of GI. Yet, as Kofman suggests, the experiences of these female expatriates tend to differ from their male counterparts. This can be due to the unwillingness of large companies to send female managers abroad or the segmentation of the local labor market for (female) professionals from ethnic minorities. Further complicating the situation for female professional migrants are their family responsibilities. As Kofman notes, because these migrants have been understudied, it is unclear what negotiations at the household level are occurring and how these affect gender relations and gender roles in families of migrating female professionals.

How migration affects household arrangements and gender relations in families is the subject of Kromhout's study on Surinamese women's social networks and household survival strategies. As she argues in the final chapter of Part II, the economic crisis in Suriname has made it increasingly difficult for urban families to survive. They have had to rely increasingly on remittances from family members who have migrated to The Netherlands to work. Thus, migration is one of the survival strategies used by households, but additional forms of coping include increased labor force participation by women in formal and informal sectors and the re-emergence of extended families to pool incomes and/or provide child care for working women. However, the pursuit of these strategies varies by household make-up (i.e. female-headed vs. male-headed households) and ethno-cultural factors (i.e. whether the families are Creole, Hindustani, or Javanese) which can limit or facilitate women's access to financial and other resources. Kromhout finds that household survival is improved and women's intra-household bargaining positions in these varying contexts are strengthened to the degree that women are able to earn their own incomes *and* exact financial and service obligations from migrant relatives and extended family members through social networking.

We learn from all of these contributions that global restructuring does cause a renegotiation of boundaries that actually or potentially challenges existing gender contracts across public and private realms. However, it is unclear whether in each case this entails only a temporary suspension of the old gender contract, which will be reinstated and reinforced if and when a situation of "normalcy" returns. What is clear, however, from this section and the previous one is that women can and do pursue multiple objectives and strategies in all sorts of sites to increase their opportunities and improve their conditions in the global political economy.

5 Economic restructuring and the gender contract

A case study of Jordan

Valentine M. Moghadam

Like other regions in the world economy, the Middle East is undergoing a restructuring of its political economy. During the oil-boom era of the 1960s and 1970s, "petrodollars" were put to use toward a state-directed and largely inward-looking strategy of economic development in which the government was the largest owner and employer. Foreign investments were limited but imports of Western technology and especially weaponry were massive. The oil-rich countries imported labor from the non-oil Arab states, creating what some have termed a regional oil economy. In Middle Eastern countries, the social and economic infrastructure was largely owned by the state, and government agencies administered subsidies, price controls, and trade regulations.

Today the region is shifting to a more market- and export-oriented system of growth in which investment, prices, and trade are liberalized. This shift is a response to the imperatives of globalization, the current stage of international capitalism. In its economic manifestation, globalization is characterized by new forms of competition, technological progress in transportation and communications, flexibilization of labor markets, and international production by transnational corporations (TNCs). Outside of North America, Europe, and Japan, where the bulk of foreign direct investment (FDI) flows, TNCs are especially active in Latin America and in East and Southeast Asia, and China has been receiving a very large share of total investments in developing countries. But FDI flows and TNC investments are much smaller in the Middle East. This is partly a legacy of the oil wealth of the past, and partly the result of political instabilities in the region. In the post-oil boom era, Middle Eastern states are actively trying to attract foreign investment and are implementing export-led industrial growth strategies (Economic and Social Commission for West Asia (ESCWA) 1995c: 99).

Economic restructuring is not a gender-neutral process; gender definitions influence the shaping of policy, and policy choices and outcomes affect men and women differently (see Moghadam 1995b, 1995c). The impact of restructuring on women as a group is mediated by such factors as class and ethnicity, while individual women are affected according to their educational attainment, work experience, and sectoral or occupational location. For the region of the Middle East, an additional factor needs to be taken into account, namely that economic restructuring has been occurring against the backdrop of Islamic fundamentalism. Islamist political and cultural influence exacerbates the vulnerable legal and social positions of women and impedes progress toward gender equality.

Gender relations and the position of women in the Middle East have been characterized by (a) relatively low rates of female labor-force participation and involvement in the formal sectors of the economy; and (b) conservative traditions, Islamist movements, and family laws which favor men. In light of this, the changing political economy in an era of globalization raises at least three questions. How will economic restructuring affect women's economic participation and employment prospects? How will gender relations and the legal status of women be affected? How are women responding to the changing political economy? This chapter examines the gender implications of economic restructuring in the Middle East, with a focus on Jordan, a culturally conservative country where women have thus far played a very limited role in the economy, in the employment structure, and in formal politics. In particular, I explore the ways in which the long-standing "patriarchal gender contract" could be affected by the changing political economy.[1]

Liberalizing economies and working women

Before focusing attention on Jordan, it may be useful to elaborate on the process of economic restructuring in the Middle East region, of which Jordan is a part. Beginning in the mid-1980s Middle Eastern countries experienced a recession, caused in part by the deterioration of terms of trade, the drop in oil prices, the subsequent decline in state revenues, the increase in US interest rates, and rising indebtedness. As growth stagnated, unemployment increased to very high rates, worsened in some countries (e.g. Egypt, Jordan, Yemen) by the return of expatriate labor from Kuwait and Saudi Arabia following the 1990–1 Gulf War. In order to balance budgets, increase productivity, and raise competitiveness, structural adjustment policies under World Bank and IMF auspices were adopted by most countries (e.g. Morocco, Tunisia, Egypt, Turkey, Jordan, Yemen), while other countries (e.g. Syria and Iran) began to administer their own form of restructuring. While the pace and timing of the restructuring varies, all countries have adopted measures to contract the public sector, encourage growth of the private sector, liberalize prices, eliminate barriers to imports and exports, and attract foreign investments. The overstaffing of government agencies is a constant theme in World Bank policy papers (see, for example, World Bank 1994a, 1994b), but it is still controversial and sensitive in the Middle Eastern countries themselves, where governments have preferred the strategy of wage deterioration and slower recruitment to outright layoffs. Thus, one outcome of both crisis and restructuring has been the lowering of salaries in the public sector. Privatization is being undertaken throughout the region, albeit at a slow pace, partly due to concern about the political ramifications of layoffs. Stock markets have been rejuvenated in several countries, including Egypt, Jordan, Syria, and Iran.

Jordan is not among the oil-producing and oil-exporting Middle Eastern countries, but as a labor-exporting country it has participated in the regional oil economy. As a country with few natural resources, it has depended upon remittances of its emigrant labor, along with foreign assistance. Unlike other labor-exporting countries, however, Jordan has also been a labor-importing country. During the oil-boom era, Jordan opened its doors to workers from Egypt and Syria for jobs in construction and low-skill services (e.g. doormen, waiters, gardeners, janitors); professionals from these countries and from Iraq were also given work and residence permits. Establishments requiring waitresses, such as hotels and restaurants, and well-to-do households requiring maids were allowed to import women workers from the Philippines and Sri Lanka. Jordan's labor-importation policies were in part the result of pre-existing cultural attitudes toward women, service work, and foreigners; but they also reinforced notions of the inappropriateness of certain types of work for Jordanian women (and for Jordanian men). Consequently, Jordan has had very limited involvement by women in the modern labor force. In the early 1990s, women aged 15–64 constituted just 10 per cent of the formal labor force.[2]

During the 1980s Jordan began to experience the recession other countries in the region were undergoing; it also saw the growth of an Islamist movement demanding political recognition and participation. In 1989, Jordan implemented a program of stabilization and adjustment with World Bank and IMF support; at the same time King Hussein initiated a process of political liberalization, including elections that resulted in parliamentary seats for members of Islamist parties (Brand 1992). Although much has been written about both the economic reforms and the political liberalization process (e.g. Brynen *et al.* 1995), very little attention has been directed to the gender implications of economic restructuring and the likely impact on women, whether in Jordan or in the region as a whole.

Gender relations and the patriarchal gender contract

When considering the gender aspects of economic restructuring, it is necessary to examine the relationship between gender and political economy, including the implicit or explicit rules governing the relationship between men and women, women and the state, and women and employers. These rules, which may be formal and codified or unwritten and assumed, govern the position of women and the prerogatives of men within the family and household, in the sphere of production or the labor market, in the political system, and in cultural institutions. The rules reflect the existing social relations of gender as well as reinforce them, and are influenced by prevailing cultural understandings and religious practices. These rules may be referred to as the "gender contract." In the Middle East, where the prerogatives of men are greater than those of women, the term "patriarchal gender contract" is appropriate. In connection with employment and the economy, I use the term to refer to the non-agricultural, urban-based sexual division of labor predicated upon the male-breadwinner/female-home-maker roles, in which the male has direct access to wage employment or control over the means of production, and the female is largely economically dependent upon the male members of her family.

Strictly speaking, patriarchal gender relations are kin-based and often strongest in rural areas (Kandiyoti 1985), and elsewhere I have discussed the evolving nature of gender relations in the Middle East, as well as its elaboration by social class and level of development (Moghadam 1993b). The patriarchal gender contract is not exclusive to the Muslim countries of the Middle East and was indeed present in the United States and Europe at an earlier stage of capitalist development. In her study of Latin America and the Caribbean, Helen Safa (1995) discusses the persistence of the gender ideology of the male breadwinner, although she notes that given women's increasing labor force participation, this is now largely a myth. In the Middle East the persistence of patriarchy is partly a function of the stage of development and of the social structure, and partly the result of the continuing power of religious institutions, the demands of Islamist movements, and the political agendas of states and regimes.

During the oil-boom era, the patriarchal gender contract was made possible and indeed financed by the regional oil economy, the wealth of the oil-producing states, and the high wages that obtained for male workers. This limited both the supply of female labor and the demand for women workers in industry and in services. Due to oil wealth, and also due to cultural notions that precluded certain occupations for native women, waitresses, as well as maids and nannies, were imported, largely from Southeast and South Asia. In the richest oil economies, even nurses were imported. Factory work was a predominantly male occupation. As a result, the female labor force was comprised largely of highly educated and professional women in the public sector, most of them employees of the Ministries of Education and Health.

The patriarchal gender contract assumed that women would marry young, households would be headed by men, and the men would have jobs and would provide for their families. In such a context, families invested more in the educational attainment of males than of females. This has resulted in the rather large gender gaps that exist in literacy and mean years of schooling in the region, especially among the population aged 25 and over. The patriarchal gender contract has been codified in law, especially in the region's personal status or family laws. These require women to obtain the permission of fathers or husbands for employment, seeking a loan, starting up a business, or undertaking any form of travel. Current family laws also give women a lesser share of inheritance of family wealth. It goes without saying that the patriarchal gender contract was "drawn up" by men in an "exchange" among unequal parties – men and women, and women and the state.

Today's economic realities are challenging the patriarchal gender contract in fundamental ways. In the post-oil-boom era, and in a global context of recession and restructuring, the male breadwinner role is no longer guaranteed, total unemployment has grown, wages have deteriorated, per capita incomes have fallen, inflation has soared, poverty has worsened, female-headed households

(FHHs) are increasing, and more and more women are seeking jobs out of economic need. Rising prices and deterioration of real wages have forced male wage workers to take on second jobs in all but the rich Gulf states. It is widely recognized that the demographic structure of the region, whereby 40–50 per cent of the population is under the age of 15, reflects and contributes to low labor-force participation, high dependency, low productivity, and high unemployment – a situation exacerbated by low economic growth rates and new forms of poverty. According to the World Bank, the poverty headcount index (percentage of population) in 1991 was 33 per cent for the Middle East and North Africa, compared with 25 per cent for Latin America, 48 per cent for Sub-Saharan Africa, and 49 per cent in South Asia. For the developing world as a whole, the poverty headcount figure is 30 per cent. Clearly, the stereotype of the rich Arab region should be discarded. As for FHHs, estimates vary because of definitional differences and frequent undercounting, but between 13 per cent and 17 per cent of total households in the Middle East are headed by women, according to UN estimates. In the region there are cross-national differences, and within countries, FHHs may be as high as 30 per cent in some poor urban districts (as in Cairo) or in rural districts (as in Yemen).[3] Poverty, inequality, unemployment, and challenges to the patriarchal gender contract have been singled out by Islamist movements as reasons why existing states are no longer viable and why Islamic codes need to be reintroduced or strengthened. And yet no Islamist movement or state has been able to adequately address or resolve the economic crisis, or to suggest an alternative to economic restructuring and globalization.

Globalization and feminization

In this section I situate the changing Middle Eastern political economy in global changes, in order to suggest the likely outcomes for women of the economic restructuring that is underway.

In the current global environment of open economies, new trade regimes, and competitive export industries, the process relies heavily on female labor, both waged and unwaged, in formal sectors and in the home, in manufacturing and in public and private services. Much has been written about the role of women in the industrialization of various countries and regions. Indeed, around the world there has been a surge in the numbers of women workers and women professionals, the result of rising educational attainment of women, economic need and household survival strategies, and demand for relatively cheap female labor in industries and services. Moreover, government employment has become increasingly feminized, partly because men may be seeking higher incomes in the private sector, and partly because women prefer the security and benefits of the public sector. The increasing globalization of production and the pursuit of flexible forms of labor to retain or increase competitiveness has favored the "feminization of employment" in the dual sense of an increase in the numbers of women in the labor force and a deterioration of work conditions (Standing

1989). Women have been gaining an increasing share of many kinds of jobs, but this has not been accompanied by a redistribution of domestic, household, and child-care responsibilities. Moreover, women are still disadvantaged in the new labor markets, in terms of wages, training, and occupational distribution; and they are also disproportionately involved in the non-regular forms of employment that are increasing: temporary, part-time, casual, or home-based work. Women workers are also more likely to lose their jobs during periods of enterprise restructuring or privatization – as occurred in Eastern Europe and the former Soviet Union (see Moghadam 1996b).

This pattern of accelerated female labor-force participation along with problematical work conditions and unemployment has been occurring in Europe, North America, Latin America, the Caribbean, and Southeast Asia since the 1970s (Moghadam 1995c). It is also observable in the Middle East and North Africa, especially since the 1980s. The increases are in both the female share of paid employment and in informal-sector activity. For example, in Egypt, Iran, Jordan, and Turkey, women's share of civil service employment has grown from 30 per cent to 33 per cent during the 1990s. Some of the increase in female labor-force participation is the result of better enumeration of women in the informal sector and in agriculture. In Egypt, women's share of the total labor force increased from 12.3 per cent according to the 1986 census to 28 per cent according to the 1988 Labour Force Sample Survey because the latter counted women in agriculture and in various economic activities in the urban informal sector (Moghadam 1998: Chapter 5). In Iran, homeworkers and women farmers are now being counted, with the result that the female labor force is growing statistically (Moghadam 1998: Chapter 7).

In the current context of economic crisis and restructuring, unemployment has grown and is a major social, economic, and political problem. It results from high population growth compared with the economy's low work-creation capacity (Shaban *et al.* 1995). The unemployment rates of women are especially high – 25–30 per cent, compared with about 10 per cent for men. These rates indicate that women are seeking jobs, and that they are encountering structural barriers and discrimination.

The above discussion highlights the contradictory trends within the globalization process, especially for women. Around the world, the feminization of labor has been accompanied by the feminization of unemployment, showing that the supply of job-seeking women is increasing, and that demand for women workers exists, but is limited. Economic need and household survival strategies on the part of women, as well as aspirations of women with higher education, explain the increase in the supply of job-seeking women, while changes in the economy, labor-markets, and the preferences of employers explain the increase in demand for women workers and employees. The deployment of female labor generally corresponds to the type of development or growth strategy and the imperatives of the capital accumulation process. This process involves marginalization, integration, and exploitation of female labor. But the process has not been uniformly adverse. The massive entry of women into the labor force has important implications for gender consciousness and activism, for the equality and empowerment of women, and for changes in gender relations and ideologies within the household and the larger society (Kahne and Giele 1992; Safa 1995; Tiano 1994). For example, the mobilization of women into feminist groups and women's non-governmental organizations (NGOs) has occurred on the part of women with education and work experience, and represents their response to continuing problems for women in the areas of literacy, education, employment, health, poverty, violence, human rights, and political participation.

In light of the above discussion, it is not implausible to suggest that the changing political economy in the Middle East could result in greater economic participation by women and an interrogation of patriarchal gender relations. Economic liberalization and especially the export-oriented manufacturing strategies that tend to be prescribed could favor women's employment in the Middle East for a number of reasons. First, these policies raise the demand for women in the labor-intensive, traditionally female-intensive branches that are geared for export (textiles, garments, food processing, and handicrafts, as well as more modern industries such as electronics and pharmaceuticals). Second, in the current era of globalization, countries are forced to make their industries – and their labor forces – more competitive, partly by raising skill levels. This could favor increased attention to more education, vocational training, skills-upgrading, and entrepreneurship for women. Third, economic reforms often call for fiscal changes and the mobilization of domestic resources, through such measures as expanding the tax base and making taxation more efficient. Governments may reason that in order to increase the income-tax-paying population, policies would be needed to increase the size of the female labor force. Fourth, women's numbers could rise in such expanding occupations as banking, insurance, accounting, computing, and so on, which are indeed becoming feminized internationally. Fifth, the expansion of tourism can break down cultural proscriptions against women's employment in sales and services occupations.[4] Sixth, the emphasis on private-sector development could promote women-owned or managed businesses. Finally, the changes underway could encourage feminist activism and compel women's organizations to direct their attention to economic and political issues.

Economic restructuring and women in Jordan

Since 1989 Jordan has been implementing an economic reform program through the liberalization of its commercial system, removing restrictions on licenses and imports, opening the market for internal and external competition, and adjusting economic legislation and measures in order to create and encourage a suitable climate for domestic, Arab, and international investments (World Bank 1995). This economic reform program represents a radical change from Jordan's previous development strategy, which was based on a pre-eminent role for the state and for labor migration. In October 1996 negotiations began in

Geneva between Jordan and the World Trade Organization (WTO) to discuss issues related to Jordan's membership in the world organization.

Jordan's new development strategy includes not only liberalization of its economy but normalizing relations with its closest neighbors. In 1994 Jordan signed a peace treaty with Israel, ending years of hostility and raising hopes for the establishment of economic relations that would also include the West Bank and Gaza. However, as late as 1999, Jordanian–Israeli economic relations remained stymied by continuing political uncertainties and difficulties between Israel and the Palestine Authority. Competition rather than cooperation characterizes relations, and Israeli restrictions on tourists, imports, and labor migrations have been obstacles to the implementation of the bilateral agreements which were signed following the peace treaty. Some have complained that the travel packages resulting from the bilateral agreements favor Israel over Jordan. At the same time, the increase in tourists to Jordan, many of them from Israel, has led to growth of the tourism sector, creating more job opportunities and leading to the construction of more hotels and restaurants.

During the years 1994–6, Jordan's GDP growth was 5.7 per cent, one of the highest in the Arab region (World Bank 1998). Growth of the manufacturing sector increased from 6 per cent in 1993 to 9.3 per cent in 1994, and there was a 16 per cent growth in exports (ESCWA 1995c: 16). The trade and tourism sectors contributed a higher rate of GDP than the other sectors, and also employ the largest percentage of the workforce. Growth was assisted and Jordan's debt-servicing burden reduced by external debt cancellation and debt rescheduling by the US and Europe. The construction sector boomed after the return of the Gulf expatriates, and investments in real estate soared. Jordan still receives remittances, though less than in previous years. In May 1994 Jordan introduced a new general sales tax and plans were put in place to further reform the tax system (ESCWA 1995c: 24).

In 1995, the government sector was still the largest employer in Jordan, engaging some 300,000 employees, equivalent to half of the total economically active labor force in Jordan. The liberalization and privatization program seeks to change this. Between 1987 and 1992 the total number of registered private companies increased by 118 per cent. In contrast, the number of public corporations contracted from 31 to 25, and the number of public shareholding companies declined from 115 to 113 (Khuri-Tubbeh 1995: 6). There are plans to privatize several public-sector companies, including the country's national airline (ESCWA 1995c: 25). There has been a proliferation of small-scale industry, most of it employing fewer than four workers. It is believed that private-sector growth will reduce unemployment.

Characteristics of the labor force in Jordan

The Jordanian labor market is highly segmented, mainly along lines of gender and nationality, and is highly regulated. In general, nationals are favored over non-nationals for most skilled and high-status jobs; men are favored over women;

and single women are favored over married women. High population growth rates have resulted in a very large population of young people – who are currently facing unemployment due to the economic crisis and adjustment efforts. Jordan's female labor force constitutes a very small percentage of the total workforce – a reflection of both the low participation rate for the population as a whole and the under-utilization of the female half of the human resource base. Although Jordanian women are on average more literate and better educated than other Arab women, they tend to drop out of the workforce upon marriage; furthermore, Jordan's fertility rate is quite high – 5.7 in 1994. The pattern thus far has been that the non-foreign female workforce is made up largely of young and unmarried Jordanian women, and mainly in professional positions.

This could change as a result of the economic crisis and of restructuring. Although studies carried out in the 1980s found education to be the most significant factor affecting women's decision to work in Jordan (see Shakhatreh 1995), Khuri-Tubbeh (1994) found that women from poor communities were in fact either working (in the informal sector) or were seeking work. Indeed, she found that in the three low-income communities she studied, 26.7 per cent of her sample were illiterate, and 44.6 per cent had preparatory or secondary education. The higher the family income, the less likely it was that a woman would participate in the labor force (Khuri-Tubbeh 1994: 109). Thus, although the official statistics have shown that most of the female labor force are educated women in the professions, there seems to be considerable "disguised employment" among poor and illiterate women.

That more Jordanian women are seeking employment is confirmed by labor-force statistics, which, while neglecting the informal sector and home-based work, show an increase in women's labor-force participation rates, from 9 per cent in 1987 to 11.5 per cent in 1991 to 12.7 per cent in 1993. Meanwhile, men's activity rates remained relatively stable at 69 per cent in 1987 and 1991 and 72 per cent in 1993. For women, the highest labor-force participation rates are in the age group 20–24, but there has been a noticeable increase in the activity rate of women aged 25–59 (ESCWA 1995b: Table I-8).

In recent years female participation has been rising, the female share of the labor force has been increasing (from 7 per cent in 1979 to 10–11 per cent of the labor force since 1987, and possibly as high as 22 per cent in 1996), and the rate of growth of female employment has been exceeding the rate of growth of male employment. The measured female labor force is more educated than the male labor force and consists of salaried employees in professional jobs. Jordanian women are 13.3 per cent of the total number of those working in public administration, 53.3 per cent of the total in education, 36.3 per cent of the total in the health and social work sector, 23 per cent of the total in community service activities, 7.3 per cent of the total in agriculture, and 9.3 per cent of the total in the manufacturing sector (Jordanian National Committee for Women (JNCW) 1995: 43). In terms of occupational shares, women are 46.6 per cent of the total number of professional and technical employees, but only 20.8 per cent of the total number of clerical workers, and 14.2 per cent of the total number of workers in services, sales, crafts, and commerce (JNCW 1995: 44). If my hypotheses are correct, women's numbers could rise in manufacturing and in sales and services, as a result of the growth of export manufacturing and the expansion of the tourism industry.

Liberalization and women's employment in Jordan

Will economic liberalization favor women's employment? As in other Middle Eastern countries, there has been a freeze on public-sector hiring in Jordan, and stabilization of public-sector recruitment could result in even more limited opportunities for women. On the other hand, the growth of male wages in the private sector may lure more male graduates there, resulting in additional job opportunities for women in the public sector. Certainly the expansion of the fields of education and health, including the new private schools, universities, and clinics, favor women's employment. What is unclear is whether the private sector will be able to absorb the growing number of Jordanian women university graduates, as well as working-class women seeking jobs in the industrial and services sectors.

Legal changes pertaining to importation of foreign labor could favor women's employment in a number of sectors. Because of rising unemployment, the government introduced new regulations in August 1995 to eventually phase out reliance on foreign workers, whose numbers had already been reduced by 70,000. Some 30,000–40,000 of these jobs were to be converted into employment opportunities for Jordanians. Some 100,000 of the estimated 180,000 expatriates remaining in Jordan were now formally registered "and their right to remain acknowledged" (Economist Intelligence Unit 1996: 14). The government banned the employment of foreigners in fifteen professions, while permitting expatriates to be employed in the agriculture, construction, and domestic services sectors.

The manufacturing sector has been growing and absorbing more labor; since 1988 it has absorbed about 35 per cent of female recruitment, especially in the textiles and clothing, chemical, and food industries (Khuri-Tubbeh 1995: 13). Although still a very small percentage of the industrial workforce, women workers are engaged in the production of pharmaceuticals, ready-made garments, hosiery, food and beverages, rugs, and handicrafts. However, their participation in manufacturing continues to be limited by gender attitudes that associate women with teaching and health care, by recruitment discrimination to avoid maternity leave requirements, and by the legal prohibition of "night work" for women in the industrial sector, which effectively eliminates their ability to apply for jobs in the second shift and guarantees a majority of male workers, especially in highly productive enterprises. It should be noted that several women's organizations in Jordan, most notably the Jordanian Women's Union, have focused their energies on changing the country's Labour Law to ensure equality between women and men and to address the needs of working mothers.

Will government employment be feminized in Jordan? This may occur because men's wages are higher in the private sector than in the public sector, because women prefer public-sector jobs, and because the private sector is not "friendly" to women, and especially to married women and women workers with family responsibilities. Employers who hire women workers prefer them to be unmarried, as managers told me at ATICO, a privately owned factory producing hosiery in Sahab Industrial City, and at Hikma Pharmaceuticals, a highly modern and attractive enterprise (also privately owned) in Amman, during visits to both in 1994. There remains a widespread view that married women are less reliable and committed than unmarried women, especially at the lower rungs of the occupational ladder. Two managers at Hikma Pharmaceuticals expressed the view that unmarried women professionals were more committed employees than the single or married men employees.[5] Neither ATICO nor Hikma provided an on-site nursery, although Hikma paid nursery fees for its working mothers.

A five-country study of Arab women in the manufacturing sector examining the work conditions, aspirations, and constraints faced by women workers (ESCWA 1995a) made a number of recommendations to increase women's ability to enter into and remain in the workforce, as well as to increase gender equity. One was to guarantee equal promotion opportunities for both sexes according to qualifications, skills, and years of service in the factory, and training to enable women to be promoted. Another was to provide health insurance coverage to all the family members of the female worker, as is done for her male counterpart. A third was to set up nurseries for children, or to subsidize off-site child care. A fourth was to establish shorter working days (5–6 hours) for married female workers in order to attract married women to the manufacturing sector. Finally, the study recommended that a trade union for manufacturing workers, including women, be established.

Observations and conversations in October–November 1996 confirmed a growing role for women in the informal sector, a sector that is invisible in the official statistics, but which absorbs a growing number of Jordanian women. In particular, home-based work is "very dynamic," and spans low-income subsistence-type economic activities and higher-income sophisticated services, ranging from sewing and embroidering to food preparation and catering to desk-top publishing.[6] As mentioned above, studies show that poor and illiterate women are engaging in economic activity, suggesting that economic need may surpass educational attainment as a factor behind women's economic activity. Khuri-Tubbeh's 1992 fieldwork among low-income women in Amman found that 30.4 per cent of all the women worked (N = 435). A quarter (24 per cent) of the ones who worked did so at full-time jobs, while three-quarters worked part-time. The study found that 54.3 per cent were either actually working or wished to work. There was only one group, representing 17.9 per cent of the women, who did not work and said they did not wish to work (Khuri-Tubbeh 1994: 94). "It is worth highlighting that the percentage of the women who are not working but wish to work is higher (23.9 per cent) than the women who are not working and do not wish to work" (Khuri-Tubbeh 1994: 96). In the absence of job creation in the formal sector, women from low-income households may be taking on home-based work, although data on this are not available. Almost 73 per cent of the working women in Khuri-Tubbeh's sample engaged in embroidery and sewing, activities usually carried out at home, and a smaller percentage were hair-dressers. Among the 104 women who were not working and said they wished to work, 78 per cent had not applied for a job. Fifteen per cent of the job seekers had applied at the government Civil Service office, 2 per cent had applied at the Ministry of Labour Employment Office, which provides jobs in the private sector, and 5 per cent had applied at different NGOs (Khuri-Tubbeh 1994: 99).

Will Jordanian women's involvement in sales and service work increase? In the past, women's participation in sales and private services was very limited, as has been the case in many other Middle Eastern countries, but in Jordan these occupations were usually filled by foreign workers. One rarely sees women shop-keepers, salespersons, waitresses, or hotel clerks, especially in downtown Amman. Waitresses in hotels and cafes tend to be Filipinas. However, in the more upscale districts of Amman, women employees may be seen in banks, boutiques, travel agencies, and shops selling handicrafts. The large Safeway supermarket in Amman now has young Jordanian women at the cash registers; in 1994 all of the employees were men. As previously noted, tourism is a growth industry, with hotels, restaurants, travel agencies, and handicraft centers proliferating around the country. As a result, more Jordanians are being trained for employment in hotels, replacing the Egyptians who previously were recruited for jobs in hotels. Jordan's hotel management school, which was being restructured in 1996, accepts women as well as men, and a vocational training program was in place to offer an AA degree in hotel management that includes a three-year program in secondary school followed by a two-year post-secondary course. Another three-year vocational program to which girls have been applying is in the restoration of historical sites, and especially of mosaics. In the historic town of Madaba, near Amman, the Madaba School of Mosaics trains students and assigns them to local and nearby restoration projects.

At Jordan's Arab Bank and Central Bank one sees many women employees (both veiled and unveiled), but this sector does not provide women employees with maternity-related benefits such as appropriate leaves and child-care facilities. Conversations with middle-class working women in Amman in 1996 confirmed the importance of affordable and quality "baby care," with trained staff and hours that are compatible with the length of the work day.

Women's unemployment in Jordan

Rising participation, as well as rising unemployment rates, reveal the extent to which the supply of job-seeking women has been growing. Jordan has very high unemployment rates, fluctuating between 15 and 19 per cent, and exceedingly high unemployment rates for women. In 1991 male unemployment was 13 per cent and female unemployment 35 per cent (World Bank 1994b: 23), up from 27 per cent in 1987 (JNCW 1995: 30). Most of the unemployed women are high-school graduates from low-income families; a far smaller percentage of women with higher degrees are unemployed. In Jordan, the unemployed also include returnees. The 1991 EURPS (Employment, Unemployment, Returnees and Poverty Survey) found that, "female returnees are nearly 50 per cent more likely to be unemployed than Jordanian women who stayed behind" (World Bank 1994b: 13).

Economic need is forcing more women to seek jobs, but employment opportunities in the formal sector are scarce, particularly for lower-income women aged 20–29. Thus, unemployment among poor females was 58.8 per cent in 1991, compared with 31.5 per cent among better-off women for the same year. Unemployment among illiterate women was 30.5 per cent in 1991, compared with 3.5 per cent in 1987. Levels of unemployment among females with primary or preparatory school education rose from 17.9 per cent and 30.7 per cent, respectively in 1987 to 30.5 per cent and 35 per cent, respectively in 1991. Finally, levels of unemployment among women with secondary school education also rose from 30 per cent in 1987 to 34.7 per cent in 1991 (JNCW 1995: 30). The disparity in the unemployment figures of men and women, and the greater likelihood of unemployment among educated women than among educated men, is a clear indication of discrimination against women and a preference for men. The breakdown of the unemployed women by educational attainment may be seen in Table 5.1.

On the supply side, both educational attainment and economic need will propel more women into the labor force. In particular, growing poverty can be expected to increase the supply of job-seeking women. Indeed, one sign is that whereas single women were previously predominant in the female labor force, since 1991 there has been an increase in the labor-force participation of married women.

Poverty in Jordan

According to the World Bank, Jordan's poverty incidence, at 15 per cent, is well below international and regional averages, but many Jordanian experts dispute the World Bank figures, stating that the poverty line is set artificially low, and that

Table 5.1   Distribution of job-seeking women by educational attainment, Jordan 1991

Academic qualification	Job-seeking women (% of total)
Below secondary diploma	14.8
Secondary school diploma	15.0
Community college	57.5
BA, BSc	12.5
Postgraduate studies	0.2
Total	100.0%

Source: Jordanian National Committee for Women, *The Jordanian National Report*, 1995: Table 9, p. 46.

the true poverty incidence may be closer to 25–30 per cent of the population. Characteristics of the poor are the following: they tend to be illiterate, earn low wages, work in the urban private sector or in agriculture, and live in large households. Poverty and inequality grew in Jordan because expenditures dropped, real wages fell, income inequality increased, emigration and foreign remittances declined, and the high rate of population growth exacerbated the economic contraction and the return of 270,000–300,000 Gulf workers in 1991. That same year, however, Jordan disbursed $0.4 billion, or fully 9.5 per cent of GDP, on military purchases.

One household, income, and employment survey conducted in 1992 (IES-92) found that FHHs represented 4 per cent of all households in Jordan, and that the general poverty rate among male headed-households (MHHs) was 20 per cent while among FHHs it was 23 per cent (World Bank, 1994b: 18). The 1991 EURPS survey found the proportion of FHHs to be 8.3 per cent. It also found that FHHs constituted only 5.8 per cent of the poorest 10 per cent and 6.3 per cent of the poorest 20 per cent. Male single-person households were found to have an annual income from employment of JD806, while female single-person households had only JD66 per year (World Bank 1994b: 14). Much of the difference in the average income between these two types of households is associated with age (41 for men and 65 for women) and schooling (7.1 years for men and 1.3 years for women). One study of women's poverty concludes that a "sign of the feminization of poverty is the increase in the number of female beggars, indicative of the extent to which the traditional safety-net of kinship support has been eroded among low-income strata in Jordanian society" (El Solh 1994: 19). Female beggars were evident during my stay in Amman in October–November 1996, as were women hawking cigarettes on the sidewalks of the downtown area.

These new socioeconomic trends show why the supply of job-seeking women has been increasing in Jordan. Low wages and unemployment of men, higher prices, the end of labor migration, and growing poverty compel women to supplement the household budget through participation in formal or informal work.

Initiatives to support working women

Throughout the Middle East, women's organizations are demanding increased access of women to economic resources, employment opportunities, and political participation. Some have been very critical of structural adjustment. Others are engaging in grassroots efforts to improve the well-being of low-income women. In Jordan, initiatives exist to enhance women's economic participation and increase their access to economic resources and to income. In 1993 the JNCW agreed on a National Strategy for Women, and the strategy includes economic and employment-related objectives. A number of the women's NGOs support income-generating projects for women, such as the Jordanian YWCA-sponsored workshops in which women produce school uniforms. There are also one-year vocational training courses to provide women with secretarial and computer skills and thereby enhance their employability. The Queen Alia Fund and the Noor al-Hussein Foundation sponsor high-quality handicrafts production, mainly by skilled Palestinian embroiderers, garment makers, and craftswomen. The Development and Employment Fund disburses loans to encourage self-employment among those searching for work, 13 per cent of which went to women in 1993, mainly for industrial and service-type activities (JNCW 1995: 36).

Privatization and liberalization favor the expansion of small and medium-sized businesses, and in Jordan there has been a proliferation of establishments in the small industrial sector, which can be expected to recruit women for both formal and informal-type employment. This trend is being supported by new institutions such as the chamber of industry, the chamber of commerce, Jordan Export Development Corporation and Trade Centers (JEDCO), free-trade zones, and management schools. In addition, ESCWA developed a special "Start Your Own Business" course for small-scale entrepreneurs, with special emphasis on female entrepreneurs. Furthermore, the private voluntary sector, such as the Queen Alia Fund and the Noor al Hussein Foundation, as well as the Jordanian General Women's Federation and others, are:

> also playing a major role in supporting the small-scale enterprise sector, by encouraging diversification, providing training, credit, and infrastructural services such as workshops and the relevant equipment needed for production. They are also changing their approach from a welfare one towards more feasible self-supporting and sustainable women's enterprises.
>
> (Khuri-Tubbeh 1995: 19)

Conclusions: globalization and the gender contract

Globalization is an uneven process but it is beginning to encompass the Middle East region in a post-oil boom era. This is evidenced by various restructuring measures taken by governments to deepen their integration into the global economy: encouraging growth of the private sector, increasing competitiveness, inviting foreign investment, and earning foreign exchange through tourism and exports. At the same time, economic crisis and restructuring have led to lowered wages, unemployment, and rising prices. In this Chapter I have examined the changing political economy in Jordan in terms of its current and prospective effects on women's economic participation. Liberalization has resulted in the promotion of tourism and manufacturing, in line with the prescriptions of economic reform, while economic need may be propelling more women toward market activities, as indicated by the statistical increase in the female share of the labor force, by the high unemployment rate of women, and by observations of women's informal-sector activities.

However, in a cultural context which still favors men as breadwinners, and in the absence of foreign investment and growth of the private sector, job opportunities in the formal sector tend to be reserved for men. Thus, women remain secondary workers in the Jordanian labor market. In the 1990s, the government's development plan, while promoting human resource development, did not turn the spotlight on the impact on women or on the role of women in social and economic development in Jordan. Non-elite women have problems coping with multiple roles, and given the large average size of families, family responsibilities consume a considerable amount of time.

Changing the gender contract will depend in part on the ability of the women's organizations to realize their stated economic and social objectives. The JNCW (1995) has the following among its goals: "Increasing the participation of women in the labor force, and guaranteeing that they are not discriminated against in employment in all spheres and sectors of work." And: "Embarking on media campaigns to make the concept of a working woman socially acceptable, particularly in non-traditional sectors, and providing women with the necessary training to work in such fields." And: "Making available the necessary support services to working women, and in particular encouraging the establishment of nurseries and kindergartens that are to be provided with improved levels of supervision. These facilities would encourage women to opt for and continue in the job market."

At the end of the twentieth century, Jordan remains a culturally conservative country where the patriarchal gender contract continues to characterize social relations between women and men, and women and the state. Laurie Brand (1998) has argued that the Jordanian women's movement is fragmented, largely controlled by the royal family, and subject to the great influence of Islamic norms. And yet there are signs that the modernizing women of Jordan are at the forefront of a movement for change, and that this is being assisted by the economic transformation underway. For example, at a series of nation-wide women's meetings held in the run-up to the November 1997 elections in which two well-known and controversial women ran but lost, legal and social reforms were identified that would have far-reaching implications for the society.[7] The women's organizations are also challenging entrenched cultural practices such as honor killings. New patterns of women's employment, along with the activities of the burgeoning women's organizations, could lead to a transformation of the patriarchal gender contract wherein women are minors and economic dependents while men are the breadwinners with special prerogatives, to a more equitable gender contract that acknowledges women as citizens and contributors to economic development. However, given the neoliberal capitalist environment, even if women's position as *women* improved, their position as *workers* would need to be carefully monitored.

Notes

1   A version of this chapter appears in my book, *Women, Work, and Economic Reform in the Middle East and North Africa* (Boulder, CO: Lynne Rienner Publishers, 1998). Research was conducted in Amman in October–November 1996, and was made possible by a fellowship for regional research and a grant from the Council of American Overseas

Research Centers (CAORC). I also gratefully acknowledge the cooperation of the Women and Development Unit and the Statistical Department of ESCWA, the UN Economic and Social Commission for West Asia, in Amman. Last but far from least, interviews or conversations with Nadia Takriti, Taghrid Khuri-Tubbeh, Fatma Al-Manaa, and Zohra Mrabet were of great value.

2   Female labor-force participation rates are very sensitive to measurement issues. The 10 per cent figure does not include agriculture and informal-sector labor. Other estimates have put the female labor force at 11 per cent (UN 1995: Table 11) and 18 per cent (United Nations Development Programme (UNDP) 1997: Table 16) of the total labor force in Jordan. The highest figure I have seen is 22 per cent for 1996 (see World Bank 1998: Table 2.3.) In any event, it is clear that the salaried labor force has been largely male in Jordan – as has been the case in all Middle Eastern countries.

3   For a conceptual and comparative study of the feminization of poverty, see Moghadam (1996a).

4   Tourism is a mixed blessing, for both women and the environment. It brings in foreign exchange and generates jobs and income, but it strains the environment and sometimes promotes prostitution. In the Middle East, given the absence of American military bases and considering the region's cultural features, it is unlikely that sex tourism on the scale of Southeast Asia could ever develop.

5   Interviews and site visits at ATICO and Hikma, Amman, 12 November 1994.

6   Interview with Zohreh Mrabet, Director of the UNIFEM (United Nations Development Fund for Women) office for West Asia, Amman, 18 October 1996.

7   The two women candidates were Toujan Faisal and Emily Naffa. I discuss their candidacy and the priority concerns of the women's meetings in Moghadam (1999).

6 A political explanation of the gendered division of labor in Japan

Yumiko Mikanagi

Introduction

The wave of global restructuring triggered by two oil crises and the following long-term reduced economic performance had reached the shores of Japan in the 1980s. As a result, the Japanese economy faced an increasing need to improve its efficiency in order to sustain its competitive edge in the global market. At the same time, Japan undertook another task, which some would argue conflicted with the first. As the UN Decade of Women (1976–85) unfolded, the Japanese government made promises to rectify gender inequality at home and ratify the UN Convention on the Elimination of All Forms of Discrimination by the end of the decade. Japan's willingness to conform to international rules can be in part explained by its desire to acquire global leadership.[1] To comply with these commitments, the Japanese government needed to correct its most egregious problem regarding gender: the gross inequality between male and female workers in terms of job opportunities, pay, working conditions, and benefits.[2] Eradicating gender inequality in the labor force meant a radical change in the ways the Japanese economy operated in the past, in which women were exploited as a cheap and flexible source of labor. This change, if it was implemented, could have increased the labor cost of female workers, which in turn would have offset a restructuring of the economy to sustain global competitiveness.[3]

In this chapter, I intend to demonstrate how and why this dilemma was resolved in favor of economic restructuring at the expense of attaining workplace gender equality. My argument is that the perpetuation of gender inequality in the labor force is not simply a result of decisions taken by businesses facing a need to improve global competitiveness, but is also a result of conscious public policy promulgated by the Japanese state.

Competing explanations: culture, capitalism and public policies

There are many explanations for the causes or perpetuation of a gendered division of labor, such as biological differences, culture, or economic structure. Such explanations of the gendered division of labor vary in terms of whether they speak to "its origins, its present causes, its preconditions or its perpetuating mechanisms" (Randall 1987: 43). They also vary in terms of ideological orientation, methodological approaches, and feminist perspectives. My explanation focuses on the role of the Japanese state in perpetuating a gendered division of labor despite its public pronouncements and formal commitments to end it in the wake of the UN Decade for Women.

In contrast to feminist cultural explanations (which foreground patriarchy) and feminist structural explanations (which foreground capitalism), this decidedly political explanation for the perpetuation of the gendered division of labor, at least in Japan, foregrounds the political agency of feminists and their opponents in the public policy apparatus. Such an analysis reveals what political factors and which political actors enhance or mitigate gender equality legislation. It also reveals that anti-feminist actors are not monolithic, suggesting openings for feminist interventions now and in the future. Although Japanese patriarchy and global capitalism play a significant role in creating and perpetuating the gendered division of labor in general in Japan, understanding how powerful interest groups within the Japanese state have operated to derail specific gender equality legislation is crucial to developing feminist strategies that can counter public policy that favors restructuring rather than women.

The gendered division of labor does not just refer to a simple scheme in which men work outside of their homes and women stay home and take care of the family as well as housekeeping. By 1980, 47.6 per cent of Japanese women of working age (over 15 years old) were working in the formal labor force and among these, 57.4 per cent were married (Prime Minister's Office 1994: 302, 306). Thus, the gendered division of labor in the current Japanese context is what Higuchi Keiko has called a "neo-gendered division of labor" in which "men work and women stay home but also work as mothers, part-time workers, community volunteers and/or elderly caretakers" (Higuchi *et al.* 1985: 27).

Unfortunately, extant writings do not offer much explanation for why Japanese women and men continue to have their lives defined on the basis of this gendered division of labor. As Mary Brinton states, most of the literature does not offer adequate explanations as to "why patterns of gender stratification are systematically reproduced in Japanese society" (Brinton 1993: 16). Furthermore, even when some explanation is offered, it tends to focus on cultural and/or socioeconomic factors, but political factors, such as the role of the state and the policy-making process, tend to be neglected.

The emphasis placed on cultural and socioeconomic factors can be seen in both English and Japanese writings on Japanese women. As for recent English writings, Sumiko Iwao (1993), for instance, places a heavy emphasis on the difference between American and Japanese gender relations deriving from the difference in the two cultures. She argues that women consciously choose to be part-time workers instead of full-time workers. She holds that "in Japan … part-time work is … typically a deliberate choice of women who want to work only part-time because of family obligations or other activities" (Iwao 1993: 173).

In contrast to Iwao's emphasis on culture, Mary Brinton focuses on the type of capitalism developed in Japan which systematically excludes women from "good" jobs (Brinton 1993). However, despite her reference to "conscious policy decisions in the sphere of private enterprise and in government" (Brinton 1993: 19) and her discussion of Japan's educational policies, she does not give us a comprehensive view of how the government works to sustain (or create) the gendered employment system.

Thus, writings in English on Japanese women lack extensive investigation of the role of the state and its policy making. However, among feminist scholars working on Japan and writing in Japanese, Higuchi Keiko explicitly takes political factors into account. She explains that the continuation of the gendered division of labor is in part a product of public policy. She points out that during the high-growth period of the 1950s and 1960s, the government adopted policies that were consciously designed to maintain a gendered division of labor. For instance, the Ikeda Cabinet in the 1960s adopted the so-called *hitozukuri* (Human-making) policy, which placed emphasis on the role of the family (meaning women) in reproducing people who are capable of supporting rapid economic development (Higuchi *et al.* 1985: 25). Moreover in the 1980s, several policies were adopted by the Japanese government, such as changes in taxation and the pension systems, which offered incentives for married women to stay at home or work only part-time.[4]

Despite such reference to the impact of public policies on the gendered division of labor, we are left with the questions of why and how such policies are made in the first place. What were the conditions that allowed public policies to have a gender bias? The following investigation of the process through which the Equal Employment Opportunity Law (EEOL) was made should reveal some factors that were responsible for the failure of the government to pass an effective law to rectify gender inequality in the labor force.

A case study: the making of the EEOL

In this section, I will illustrate the process through which the EEOL of 1985 (Law Respecting the Improvement of the Welfare of Woman Workers, including the Guarantee of Equal Opportunity and Treatment between Men and Women in Employment) was made. The goal is to provide background knowledge for understanding the factors which contributed to the law's ineffectiveness.

Since the mid-1960s, a number of cases of sexual discrimination have been brought into Japanese courts. After the ruling of the Tokyo District Court on the Sumitomo Cement Case of December 1966, more than twenty cases of sexual discrimination were brought into the courts over the following two decades. As a result, the courts established that the mandatory retirement of women upon pregnancy, childbirth, or marriage, the mandatory retirement of women at an age lower than men, and the exclusive lay-off of female workers in times of economic downturn are unlawful.[5]

Due to these court decisions, discriminatory retirement and/or lay-off practices had almost disappeared by 1980 (Upham 1987: 134). However, until the mid-1980s, such practices produced no statutory laws that banned discrimination against female workers. Until the mid-1980s, the only law (other than the constitution) that explicitly banned discrimination against female workers was article four of the Labor Standards Law prohibiting wage discrimination by sex. The law did not prohibit any other type of discrimination (such as discrimination in promotion).

Given the gap between legal codes and court rulings, together with the initiation of the UN Decade of Women, by the Spring of 1978, the Subcommittee on Women's Employment of the Ministry of Labor's Women and Minors' Issues Deliberation Council began a discussion on equal opportunities for male and female workers.[6] In November 1978, the Study Group on the Labor Standards Law – a private consulting group for the Labor Minister composed primarily of academics – issued a report urging the government to enact a law that guaranteed equality between male and female workers. At the same time, the study group suggested the abolition of unreasonable statutory protections of female workers, e.g. limitations on overtime, the prohibition of night work, "menstrual leave," and restrictions on employment in various dangerous and undesirable occupations. The report also suggested forging a national consensus over the issue of equality between male and female workers through a discussion among interested parties.

In response to these suggestions, the subcommittee created the *danjo byōdō mondai senmonka kaigi* (Experts Group on Equality between the Sexes) in December 1979 to continue the discussion. Unlike the Study Group, the Experts Group included fifteen (nine female and six male) representatives from labor unions, employers, and women's groups as well as lawyers and academics. Because of the inclusion of groups with diametrically opposed interests, the Experts Group could not reach any agreements. Business representatives demanded the elimination of protection for female workers while opposing strict bans on discrimination. By contrast, the representatives of women's groups and labor unions insisted that protection measures be maintained and demanded strict bans on discrimination.

In the 1980s, the Japanese government felt increasing pressure to formulate a concrete plan to promote equality between men and women. The increased sense of pressure was due to the signing of the UN Convention on the Elimination of Forms of Discrimination against Women on 17 July 1980 at the World Conference of the UN Decade of Women, held in Copenhagen. The Japanese government, having signed the convention along with fifty-two other countries, suddenly faced the urgency of adopting concrete measures necessary for the ratification of the Convention before the end of the UN Decade of Women.[7]

However, as of May 1982, even after a series of prolonged discussions, the Experts Group was not nearing any conclusions. The Experts Group issued a report entitled "Koyō ni okeru danjo byōdō no handan no kangaekata" ("Views on criteria for determining sexual equality in employment"). Reflecting the rift between the representatives of employers and labor unions, the Experts Group had to juxtapose opposing opinions in its report (Upham 1987: 148–9). The only contribution of this report to the discussion of equality was that, for the first time since the Study Group's report, the term "equality" was defined as "equal opportunity."

Because of the deadlock in the Experts Group and the rising urgency to draft laws necessary to ratify the UN Convention, the Ministry of Labor (MOL) shifted the arena for discussion from the Experts Group back to the Subcommittee on Women's Employment. As was the case with the Experts Group, the subcommittee was split between the opposing camps from beginning to end. On the one hand, the business representatives demanded that female workers' protections be removed if an equality law were to be enacted. On the other hand, labor union representatives not only insisted that protection of female workers such as "menstrual leave" be preserved,[8] but also demanded that other protections given to female workers, such as the ban on late night work, be extended to male workers (Shinoda 1986: 89).

While labor union and business representatives argued endlessly, the deadline for the subcommittee to reach a conclusion was coming closer. At the UN Copenhagen Conference, Japan promised to ratify the Convention by 1985, so it was necessary for the Japanese government to draft a law and submit it to the Diet (the Japanese parliament) before the end of its 1984 session.

In January 1984, the MOL began pressing the subcommittee to draft its proposal. On 20 February, a draft proposal was drawn up by the public interest representatives of the subcommittee (former MOL official Wada Katsumi, journalist Aoyagi Takashi, and lawyer Watanabe Michiko). However, this draft ignited further dispute between the opposing camps. The draft read that employers should "make endeavors" to eliminate discrimination in job postings and recruitment. However, the draft law also stated that there must be a ban on discrimination with regard to promotion, retirement, and layoffs. It also included a drastic revision of existing protections for female workers (Shinoda 1986: 90). Both employer and labor union representatives criticized this draft for their own reasons. The business representatives argued that the bans on discriminatory promotion, retirement, and layoffs must be relaxed. The labor union representatives claimed that this draft was too ineffective to promote equality between male and female workers.

The subsequent subcommittee discussions were focused on the content of this draft. However, because of the uncompromising attitudes of labor union and business representatives, the discussion still yielded no conclusion. Thus, by the Spring of 1984, the MOL took the initiative to draft its own version based on the draft proposal drawn up by the public interest representatives. The MOL draft aligned more with the business interests than the earlier draft drawn up by the public interest representatives. The MOL draft had the following features: (1) revision of existing laws (instead of enactment of a new law); (2) relaxation of the ban on promotion (compared to the strict ban called for in the public interest draft); and (3) elimination of the term "menstral leave" altogether, rather than elimination of menstrual leave "in principle," leaving some room for exceptions, as proposed in the public interest draft (Shinoda 1986: 91).

Thus, this draft law not only reduced the protection of female workers further, but also relaxed the strict ban on discrimination in promotion included in the earlier draft. The only bans left in the MOL draft were those regarding retirement and layoffs. However, long before the EEOL was enacted, discriminatory dismissal or retirement had already been made unconstitutional based on court decisions such as the aforementioned Sumitomo Cement case of 1963 and the Nissan Automobiles case of 1969.

Despite harsh criticism from the workers' representatives, on 14 May 1984 after the Cabinet's approval, the Ministry of Labor forced the submission of this draft law to the Diet. The House of Representatives passed this law on 27 July, which was followed by the passage of the law in the House of Councilors on 10 May 1985. The central articles of the law which came into effect on 1 April 1986, read:

> Article 7. With regard to the recruitment and hiring of workers, employers shall endeavor to provide women equal opportunity with men.

> Article 8. With regard to the assignment and promotion of workers, employers shall endeavor to treat female workers equally with male workers.

> Article 11. With regard to the compulsory retirement age and dismissal of workers, employers shall not discriminate against a female worker as compared with a man by reason of her being a woman.

> 2. Employers shall not stipulate marriage, pregnancy or childbirth as a reason for retirement of female workers.
> 3. Employers shall not dismiss a female worker by reason of marriage, pregnancy or childbirth or for taking a leave.

Why the EEOL became "toothless"

In essence, this EEOL was not designed to have much effect on gender inequality. Why, then, did the Japanese government adopt an equal employment law that was so "toothless" and a mere codification of existing legal practices? If one views the Japanese political system as some version of "Japan, Inc." in which business interests dominate government policy, the answer to this question would be rather simple. However, a closer examination of the decision-making process reveals that there were more complex factors – other than the fact that the Japanese government always represented business interests to some extent – involved that produced such weak legislation.

Labor unions vs. business

Why did labor unions lose in their confrontation with business representatives? The answer would start with labor's organizational weakness. In addition to the relatively low organization rate (under 25 per cent), labor unions in Japan are politically weak due to the decentralized manner in which individual labor unions are organized. Until the late 1980s, when a unified (at least in name) umbrella organization (*Rengō*) was created, individual labor unions, both enterprise unions and industry unions, were organized into several large national-level unions: *Sōhyō* (the General Council of Trade Unions), *Dōmei* (Japanese Confederation of Labor), *Chūritsu Rōren* (Federation of Independent Unions in Japan), and *Shinsanbetsu* (National Federation of Industrial Organizations). Furthermore, the two largest unions, *Dōmei* and *Sōhyō*, supported two different political parties, the Democratic Socialist Party and the Socialist Party, respectively. Because these political parties did not agree on the content of the new EEOL – the Democratic Socialists emphasized the importance of passing the law and the Socialists emphasized the need for making an effective law – the political power of labor unions to negotiate a stronger law was further eroded (*Asahi Shimbun* 13 July 1984).

In addition to the divisions in the labor unions, there was yet another problem. The female representatives of the labor unions in the subcommittee could not expect powerful support from labor unions. Various sources indicate that labor union leaders were not necessarily enthusiastic about promoting female workers' interests (Higuchi *et al.* 1985: 45; "Zadankai, danjo byōdō kintō hō" 1984: 7). This lukewarm support might have been due to the lower number of unionized female workers (constituting only 27.6 per cent of the organized workers) and the lower number of female union executives (an average of 1.2 female executives per union, compared to 8.2 male executives per union as of 1988) (Inoue and Ehara 1995: 169). According to *Asahi Shimbun*, which interviewed workers who were gathered for the 1984 annual *Shuntō* (Spring Offensive) – the annual union–employer wage negotiation – workers showed little interest in the EEOL. Political commentator Yoshitake Teruko stated that:

> labor unions are a man's world. It [this male domination] is represented in the way members of the Women and Young Workers' Sections of labor unions are promoted. Members from the Young Workers' Section are promoted to join the higher ranks of union elites but members of the Women's Section remain in the section forever.
>
> (*Asahi Shimbun* 2 April 1984)

Thus, labor unions were not well-organized horizontally and women's issues tended to receive a lower priority in labor union politics. As a result, female representatives of labor unions in the subcommittee could not expect strong support outside of the subcommittee. However, the organizational weakness of labor unions and the weak position of women representatives does not sufficiently account for the resounding victory for the business representatives.

Like the labor unions, the business community was also split between those who were absolutely opposed to the enactment of the EEOL and those who were in favor of the law. All business representatives did agree that protection of female workers must be removed if an equality law were to be introduced. However, despite this basic agreement, there was a rift among those who wanted to make better use of the female labor force and those who insisted that increased opportunity for women meant the destruction of the basis of Japan's employment system. For example, while the *Nikkeiren* (the Japan Federation of Employers' Associations) was an adamant opponent of the introduction of an equality law, other business organizations, such as the Japan Chamber of Commerce, realized that an equality law did not necessarily increase the costs of business. The Chambers' member business organizations, which tended to employ larger numbers of women than *Nikkeiren* members, took the approach of supporting an equality law as long as it promoted efficiency (Shinoda 1986: 96). Still, the business world appeared to be more unified than were the labor unions on certain key aspects such as reduction of protection for female workers.

Structural bias

Given the internal split of labor unions and business representatives and given the equal number of representatives from business and labor unions on the subcommittee, the relatively unified front of the business representatives and the weakness of labor unions should not have automatically translated into a triumph for the business interests. One of the immediate factors that tipped the balance of power in favor of business interests, especially that of the *Nikkeiren*, was the impact of the *public interest* representatives.

The draft produced by the public interest representatives issued on 20 February made the law virtually spineless. It read that the employers should "make endeavors" to eliminate discrimination on job posting and recruitment. Given that the public interest representatives, by definition, were supposed to represent the public interest and thus, assumed to be neutral members of the subcommittee, how could these members have drafted a law in favor of business interests?[9]

An external force influenced the public interest representatives' draft in favor of business interests: pressure from MOL officials, in particular, ones from the Women and Minors' Bureau (renamed the Women's Bureau in July 1984).[10] Three days before the public interest representatives submitted their draft, which became the foundation for the actual EEOL, the representatives were forced to change the content of the law. Originally, the draft law stipulated a ban on discrimination at every stage of employment from job posting to promotion, retirement and layoff. The only exception was recruitment. However, on 17 February, according to a public interest representative, "the administration official said that [the draft remained so restrictive that] all business representatives will boycott the Subcommittee. ... The administrators repeated the phrase 'departure of all business representatives.' It is blackmail" ("Misshitsu no kōbō" 1985: 56). Thus, the public interest representatives' draft contained no ban on discrimination against women in job postings. Furthermore, the subsequent law drafted by the MOL excluded a ban on sexual discrimination in promotions.

Thus, the law lost sanctions against discrimination at almost all stages of employment, except for retirement or layoff. That the MOL forced changes in the public interest representatives' draft and that the MOL's own draft was even further removed from that made by the public interest representatives indicate that the MOL was responsible for making the law ineffective.

Why did the MOL side with business interests (those of the *Nikkeiren* in particular) by rendering the law ineffective? One clue lies in the constraints placed on the MOL, and the Women and Minors' Bureau in particular. Certainly, the ministry officials who worked for this bureau were all personally committed to promoting gender equality. For instance, Akamatsu Ryoko, then the Director General of the Women and Minors' Bureau, a key official in making the EEOL, studied feminism and civil rights in the US when she was a delegate to the UN in New York in the late 1970s (Akamatsu *et al.* 1993: 77). Her writings and background indicate she was firmly opposed to restrictive gender roles (Akamatsu *et al.* 1986). Supported by determined officials like Akamatsu, one could argue that the Women and Minors' Bureau has in the vanguard of the promotion of women's status throughout the postwar period (Shinoda 1986: 98). However, the bureau faced a severe constraint external to it. This constraint forced the bureau to seek incremental, not radical changes. Thus, we find Akamatsu taking the position that: "[while a more effective law is desirable,] considering the reality of Japan ... it is important to start [an EEOL, regardless of its actual effectiveness]" ("Misshitsu no kōbō" 1985: 61).

The bureau's officials were constrained by the fact that they were working for the ruling conservative party, the Liberal Democratic Party (LDP). The LDP became a major obstacle to the introduction of effective EEOL for three reasons. First, the LDP maintained traditional views on the primary family roles played by women. The LDP's view of women's roles is expressed in the plan announced in June 1979 entitled "Outline of Measures Related to the Fulfillment of the Family Basis." The plan stated that care for aging parents and child rearing are all family, instead of government, responsibilities. While the plan refers to "family" responsibilities, it is quite clear that women are to be in charge of such responsibilities from such statements as "the heavy burden on housewives from the care of immobilized elders" and "the child care leave system must be established for working women because of the importance of *sukinshippu* (skin-ship, close physical contact) between mothers and babies on their growth" (Hayakawa 1979: 204–9).

The idea that women are the primary bearers of family responsibility has also been expressed by individual LDP politicians. In 1978, LDP member of the Lower House Nakajima Mamoru, for instance, stated that juvenile delinquency has much to do with the responsibility of mothers. He maintained that "as long as mothers have a contented spirit, juvenile delinquency will decline," emphasizing the primary responsibility of mothers for the care of young people (Muramatsu 1978: 55). Even Ishimoto Shigeru, one of the LDP's few advocates of women's rights, emphasized women's "double roles as mothers and workers," while failing to refer to the need of male workers to assume more responsibility as fathers (Yoneda 1977: 155). She further argued that "women have women's roles" and that a "working system is needed in which women can play the role of mothers" ("Atarashii josei no," 1975: 133, 135). In 1987, Minister of Education Shiokawa Masajuro, another member of the LDP, stated that mothers must stay home until children finish mandatory education (Kimura 1987: 40). Furthermore, an LDP member, Horinouchi Hisao, while serving as a Minister of Agriculture in 1989, argued that "women are not suitable for politics" and "women are naturally suitable for the care of family" (*Yomiuri Shimbun* 8 July 1989).

The preservation of the gendered division of labor has served two mutually related purposes for the party. First, by making women shoulder the burdens of the care of children, the elderly, disabled, and the ill, the LDP government could save on national welfare expenditure. This in turn enabled the government to use the national budget for other purposes such as industrial growth, agricultural support, or public works. Second, the LDP could continue to rely on financial support from big business in exchange for policies that preserved the current form of capitalism, including the gender-biased labor market structure. Within this market structure, Japanese firms could cut down their labor costs by hiring young women – who received lower wages under the seniority system – as full-time workers. Employers then encouraged their retirement when they reached their mid-20s, the time when their wages would begin to rise. Moreover, these corporations rehired older women (over 35 years old) as part-time workers who could be flexibly hired in times of economic boom and fired in times of recession.

This prescription for women to retire upon marriage and come back to work later is also reflected in the LDP's "New Economic and Social Seven Year Plan for Full Employment," issued in the late 1970s. This plan called for increased opportunities for women to "develop their abilities in keeping with women's life cycle," (quoted in Upham 1987: 145) meaning that women may work provided that they also continue to bear family responsibilities.

The second reason why the LDP hobbled the EEOL was that in the 1980s there was no electoral threat from the opposition and thus the LDP had little incentive to modify its conservative policy orientation. Comparative studies indicate that conservative parties may adopt progressive policy agendas when the ruling party (or parties) face serious electoral threats from the opposition. For instance, in France, by the mid-1970s, faced with the electoral challenge of the leftists led by Mitterrand, the conservative Giscard government began to adopt measures to improve gender equality. In contrast, in Japan, after a brief period in the 1970s when the LDP's rule was threatened by the rising popularity of progressive parties, the LDP faced no serious threat from opposition parties (Mazur 1996).[11]

The third reason the LDF undermined the EEOL was its inattention to the gender gap. Political leaders must be sensitive to gender gaps in voting patterns in order to become sensitive to issues peculiar to female voters. Returning to the case of France, the reason why the conservative Giscard government incorporated its rival Mitterrand's agenda for women in the mid-1970s was that at that time it became increasingly clear that previously conservative female voters began voting for Mitterrand in the 1970s.

In the case of Japan during the period in which the EEOL was drafted, there was an increasing gender gap. In the Lower House election held in June 1980, the gap was only 0.2 percentage points, with 49.8 per cent of female voters as opposed to 50.0 per cent of male voters voting for the LDP (Akarui Senkyo Suishin Kyokai 1981: 128). However, in the Lower House election held in December 1983, the gap increased to 4.0 percentage points with 45.5 per cent of female voters in contrast to 49.5 percent of male voters supporting the LDP (Akarui Senkyo Suishin Kyōkai 1984: 196). However, there is no sign that the LDP took this increasing gap as a cue to pay more attention to gender issues.

In sum, the traditional views on women's roles, the lack of an electoral threat from the opposition, and the lack of sensitivity to an increasing gender gap in voting patterns explain the LDP's lack of interest in promoting gender equality. If the Women's Bureau officials had to face the ruling party which was not enthusiastic about gender equality and was willing to support the business community, then the EEOL was destined to fail.

Conclusion

The Japanese government did adopt the EEOL because it was needed to ratify the UN Convention. However, due to the staunch resistance of the business community as well as the LDP, the law was designed so it would not cause much change and so that it would not obstruct the restructuring process of the economy.

What the case of EEOL implies is that a move toward gender equality faces major obstacles in the age of global restructuring. With the increasing need to maintain a competitive edge in the global market, business is likely to oppose anything that would increase their costs of production. However, the analysis presented in this chapter suggests that certain conditions in addition to the need for economic restructuring that existed in the 1980s were responsible for the Japanese government's failure to promote gender equality at work. Some of these conditions, the conservative view of the ruling party and the lack of an electoral threat in particular, could change in the current highly fluid state of Japanese politics. For example, opposition parties which are more sympathetic to women's issues such as the Democratic Party may become part of the ruling coalition. Thus, despite the increasing pressure of global restructuring, there is hope for a more effective policy for gender equality to be adopted in the near future as seen in the revision of EEOL in 1997.[12]

Notes

1 An explanation for the fact that Japan wanted to comply with the UN Convention needs to be provided in future studies. Not all nations cared about the Convention. For instance, the French government, while it made a law similar to the EEOL in 1983, did not pay as much attention to the UN Convention as it did to the 1976 EC directive on professional equality. One possible answer is that it is a reflection of Japan's desire to gain global leadership. Another is found in Japanese history. Since the Meiji period, Japan has made efforts to comply with (at least on the surface) international norms and rules in order to convince Western powers that Japan is a modern nation strong enough to resist colonization and other forms of influence. This urge to conform to international rules continues even today in some issue areas indicating the Japanese government is sensitive to foreign pressure.

2 For instance, in 1980, Japanese female workers in manufacturing made only 44 per cent of wages made by male workers on average; Japan ranked at the bottom of this among all the industrialized nations (Kokusai Rengō 1995: 258).

3 Note that an increase in the labor costs of female workers is only one possible consequence of increased gender equality at work. Increased gender equality in the labor force could also decrease labor costs by expanding the supply of skilled labor. Only if greater gender equality meant giving equal treatment to women who did not have comparable skills to their male counterparts would increased gender equality lead to increased labor costs. However, what mattered in the making of the Equal Employment Opportunity Law was not these "objective" economic principles. What mattered was the perceptions of business leaders in the 1980s, who generally felt that increased gender equality meant increased labor costs.

4 Since 1984, the Japanese government has introduced a series of special tax deductions for the income earned by spouses who work part-time. By setting a limit on the level of income made by spouses for tax exemption, the current tax system encourages spouses to work but discourages them from taking jobs that will pay them over 1,030,000 yen. Similarly, non-working wives of employees who did not have the right to claim a pension unless they voluntarily joined the National Pension System (NPS) gained the right to claim a pension without joining the NPS in 1985. Because these non-working wives were exempted from paying the monthly insurance premium, the new system rewards non-working wives and punishes single workers or working couples.

5 The District Court ruled that the practice of compelling female workers to resign upon marriage was a violation of Article 90 of the civil code which prohibits any private action that violated "public order and good morals" (Upham 1987: 132–3).

6 Ministries and agencies in the Japanese government organize deliberation councils with approximately five to 130 members appointed by respective ministers. Deliberation councils research and discuss issues consulted by ministers. Members of the Subcommittee on Women's Employment were: Kitamura Hiroshi (Japan Federation of Employers' Associations), Mitsuya Takao (Japan Chamber of Commerce), and Yamamoto Mitsugu (Japan Federation of Smaller Enterprises Organization) as business representatives; Yamano Kazuko (Sōhyō), Sano Miyoko (Chūritsu Rōren), and Ichikawa Kiyomi (Dōmei) as labor union representatives; Wada Katsumi (former MOL official), Aoyagi Takashi (journalist), and Watanabe Michiko (lawyer) as the public interest representatives. The composition of the members had a tremendous impact on the result of the EEOL formation. The trilateral interest representation did not necessarily represent diverse interests held by private actors. One strange fact was that women's groups were not represented directly but were represented through the labor unions. Given that women's groups and labor unions did not necessarily agree on what "women's interests" were – labor unions emphasized the importance of protection and women's groups emphasized

equality – for the reasons of fair-interest representation, women's groups should have been part of the subcommittee. How and why the subcommittee was structured with trilateral interest representation requires further investigation.

7   This sense of urgency, to some extent, was a creation of the Japanese government itself. While some countries signed the Convention without clear timelines for ratifying it, the Japanese government signed the Convention with an internal agreement to ratify the Convention before the end of the Decade of Women (Akamatsu 1985: 58; Akamatsu *et al.* 1993: 78).

8   "Menstrual leave" was provided for in the Labor Standards Law before the enactment of the EEOL. With this stipulation, women who had severe menstruation symptoms which made work difficult, or women who were engaged in types of jobs that were "detrimental to menstruation" could demand a menstrual leave (Akamatsu 1990: 221; see also *Asahi Shimbun* 25 January 1984 (evening edition) and 20 April 1984).

9   To be sure, the public interest representatives were not necessarily disinterested. For example, Aoyagi was opposed to radical changes based on strict legal sanctions. He argued "what would happen if we included penalties ignoring the state of our society which is premature on gender equality? It is clear that society will be confused" (Aoyagi 1986: 7).

10 The fact that one of the public interest representatives, Wada Katsumi, was a former MOL official may have made the public interest representatives conducive to yielding to pressure from the MOL.

11 In the early 1970s, the LDP began to face electoral threats from the opposition parties. For instance, in April 1971, the left-wing Minobe was re-elected as governor of Tokyo, and two other major cities – Kyoto and Osaka – elected left-wing governors (Ninagawa and Kuroda, respectively). In the Lower House election held in December of the following year, the number of seats held by the LDP was reduced from 288 to 271. It was during this period that the LDP tried to woo voters, urban voters in particular, back through various measures such as increased welfare programs and pollution control.

12 In 1997, the EEOL was revised and became effective on 1 April 1999. One of the major factors that facilitated the revision was the government's increased sense of urgency to add more women to the workforce. In the 1990s, the need to expand the female workforce arose from a rapid decline of birth rates (as measured by the number of children born per woman throughout her lifetime), which reached 1.39 in 1997. Among the three factors that constrained the MOL in the 1980s, one factor, the traditional view of the ruling party, seemed to have been changed by the prospect of a long-term labor shortage and rising costs of social security.

7 Beyond a reductionist analysis of female migrants in global European cities

The unskilled, deskilled, and professional

Eleonore Kofman

Introduction

The seductive thesis of the impact of economic restructuring and social change in global cities has begun to generate a debate amongst European scholars. Saskia Sassen's exposition (1991; 1994; 1996) on global cities, which she defines as prime sites of financial concentration and power, of dichotomized social structures and foci of immigration, has been particularly influential.[1] The rapid growth in financial services, expansion of high-income professional and managerial residents, and new cultural forms in everyday living, have in turn generated demand for low-skilled and flexibly provided services. Though not to the same extent as in New York, labor demand for lesser skilled and precarious work has also been filled by immigrant workers in European cities. European scholars have thus taken a cue from her analysis and raised questions about the existence of an immigrant underclass in cities with varying degrees of global command, such as London, Paris, Amsterdam, Rotterdam, Berlin, Frankfurt, and Brussels (see special issues of *Built Environment* 1994; Hamnett 1994a; *New Community* 1996).

Immigrants from low-wage countries thus play a crucial role in the new urban regime with its polarized social structures and plentiful cheap labor. Hamnett (1994a, b; 1996), however, disputes the validity of Sassen's thesis for European cities, partly on the grounds of lower rates of immigration. He maintains that professionalization, combined with a shrinkage in unskilled and semi-skilled occupational categories, typifies major European cities and suggests that her thesis is the "slave" of New York, where continuing and high levels of cheap immigrant labor have fed the expansion in absolute terms of a proletarian labor force. Whilst it is correct that immigration levels do not match those recorded for New York and Los Angeles, immigrants and refugees have nevertheless concentrated increasingly in a few major European cities.

Diversification of migratory flows

Castles and Miller (1998) have noted the increasing globalization, diversification and feminization of migratory flows. In Europe the emergence of more complex patterns in the past two decades has been largely brought about by the break-down of the old East–West divide and associated regional conflicts, the emergence of a single European market, and the unification of Germany, which more than any other country has attracted increasing flows of migrants and refugees. Other countries, too, have registered increasing levels of immigration. Even in the face of strong border controls, the net balance of immigration has been increasing in the United Kingdom in the 1990s. In 1995, a net balance of 109,000 immigrants was recorded, comprising an outflow of 26,800 British citizens in contrast to a net inflow of 22,500 European Union citizens and 113,000 other non-British citizens (Office of National Statistics 1997: 117). The numbers granted work permits, particularly for periods under 12 months, and their dependents have risen noticeably since the late 1980s (Office of National Statistics 1997: 70–1).

Global cities have also attracted disproportionate numbers of refugees and undocumented migrants in recent flows (Burgers and Enghersen 1996) who both seek support networks and work in an expanding service economy. It is estimated that about 85 per cent of refugees in the United Kingdom eventually settle in Greater London (Carey-Wood *et al.* 1995). In Germany, the opening up of Eastern Europe has led to an increased diversity of immigrants – ethnic Germans, refugees including those with temporary status, contract and rotational migrations (Morokvasic 1993). Institutional discrimination is high against non-European Union immigrants, even for those who have lived in Germany for many years, while new forms of contract migration (Rudolph 1996) are intended to limit the rights to settlement of workers from Eastern Europe.

Though almost inevitably represented negatively, international migration is not simply about the poor and unskilled of the Third World and Eastern Europe knocking on the doors of the European Union. Increasing interconnections between the key nodes of the global economy (Japan, North America, and Europe) have also resulted in the international movement of highly skilled workers and their dependents between core areas. For example, there are 90,000 Japanese resident in the United Kingdom (1991 Census of Population). They are now the largest group of work permit holders requesting extensions to the period they are allowed to remain or to settle in the country (Home Office 1997). At the same time, Europe, too, has benefited from the migration of skilled labor from less wealthy countries, even if their contribution to the labor market is being downgraded, or masked by their entry as trainees. Amongst all of these categories, women have been increasingly on the move in the past twenty to thirty years, though the long reach of feminist studies has yet to dent the hegemonic idea of women migrants either as unskilled labor (Miles 1990) or as passive dependents in family migration (Kofman 1999).

Some have argued that international migration is especially likely between colonial powers and their former colonies because of the network of cultural, administrative and economic links which, over time, have led to the formation of specific transnational markets and cultural systems (Massey *et al.* 1993: 447–8). Certainly, post-imperial cities (Amsterdam, London, Paris) have attracted intellectuals, artists, exiles, professionals, and unskilled workers from their old colonies. Many of these immigrants are citizens or retain, through family background, rights of entry (often restricted on the basis of racialized criteria) and subsequent settlement. Colonial and historical links also play a part in Spanish and Portuguese immigration. Latin Americans generally receive preferential treatment in Spain and are concentrated, as are those from the Philippines, in the major cities of Barcelona and Madrid (Escriva 1997). Brazilians are one of the largest groups of immigrants in Portugal (SOPEMI 1998).

Contemporary international migration combines sojourners and permanent settlers, for which fresh theorizations are required to capture the interplay of spatial and temporal webs. A more accurate portrait of changing social networks could be generated by combining analyses of processes of globalization and what R. Cohen (1997) calls "diasporization." Transience, settlement, and dense networks of exchanges over space and time do not only typify a migratory formation associated with so-called societies of immigration. In the European Union, globalization and European integration have encouraged the movement of skilled transients within corporate channels (Findlay 1995) between European states and from the United States and Japan (R. Cohen 1997) which, as we have seen, are also the countries sending the largest number of students. The rise in the numbers of return migrants to the UK, and an identifiable shift towards professional and managerial staff amongst this group in the 1980s (Findlay 1995: 515), also illustrate the significance of migratory circulation. Unlike the in-depth studies on business migration, there has been little research on skilled migrants who move independently, or use recruitment agencies, for example, in the sectors of health, education, and computing. Research on post-imperial cities (King 1990; 1993; 1995), global diasporas (R. Cohen 1997) and cosmopolitans (Hannerz 1996) is beginning to provide insights into the diversity of migrants and the complexity of their migratory trajectories. According to Hannerz, four kinds of migrants have shaped the transnational character of global cities: transnational business people, Third-World migrant populations, tourists, and people specializing in expressive activities. Unfortunately this analysis remains fairly general and has yet to be applied in a sustained and systematic way to particular global cities. Only King (1990: 144), commenting on London's panoply of immigrants, fully grasps the significance of the fact that "both the rich at the top and the poor at the bottom have significant effects on the institutions and culture of the city."

In Sassen's analysis of the global city, however, the focus is on immigrants from low wage Third-World countries who supply the unskilled, flexible, and cheap labor force. Skilled immigrants from both developed and Third-World countries disappear from view as immigrants (Findlay 1995: 519). One might say they are "bogus" because they fail to conform to the dominant image. Invisibility, physical and metaphorical, is conferred in particular on migrants from affluent countries. Paradoxically, in the recent flows of immigration to London, it is likely to be Europeans who supply the personnel services in the tourist-related and catering industries concentrated in the center of the city. Despite the expansion of tourism, the entitlement to work permits for unskilled and semi-skilled labor in this sector was withdrawn in 1979. European Union immigrants have the youngest age profile and, prior to immigration, were the most likely to be in clerical and manual occupational categories compared to other nationalities. Without the need for visas and work permits, which are rarely given for unskilled work, European Union citizens enjoy the greatest freedom to enter for short periods and multiple visits.

There has in fact been substantial recourse to immigrant labor in selected niches in the middle echelons, especially in sectors of social reproduction (education and health) and welfare. At present, harmonization of European Union professional qualifications is beginning to affect non-European nationals, reinforcing racial stratification in the labor force. Those without European Union qualifications are increasingly disadvantaged and may find it more difficult to remain in the European Union (Fekete 1997). In contrast, nearly all writers on the internationalized skilled labor market have privileged the rapidly expanding financial sectors to the exclusion of the more modest growth among international professions. Even feminist researchers have been overly fascinated by the robustly male financial domain (McDowell and Court 1994; McDowell 1997). Yet the expansion of middle-class female labor from the late 1960s was heavily concentrated in social reproduction and welfare. It should not be forgotten that global cities also cater to national demands and that growth in the intermediate professionals, though not spectacular in the 1980s, was nonetheless modest. For example, in the city of Paris, managerial and higher-level professional employment increased by 37.8 per cent overall but 66.7 per cent for women. For intermediate professionals, the female increase of 18.0 per cent was matched by virtual stagnation amongst men (0.4 per cent) (Hall *et al.* 1996).

Though public provision in sectors of social reproduction and welfare (employing higher-level and intermediate categories) has been under severe pressure, and subjected to frequent, and often dramatic, restructuring, there has also been expansion due to increased national and international demand. International cities attract foreigners for the quality of their educational and health services. International financial elites, too, require services, usually provided through the private sector. The expansion of commercial medicine in the United Kingdom, in particular in London, has resulted from growth in privatized medicine for nationals and non-nationals. Without the labor of immigrant professionals from affluent and poorer countries, it would have been difficult to maintain the health services of capital cities, especially in the less popular specialisms (Fekete 1997: 3). As previously mentioned, younger European doctors and nurses are now beginning, as a result of legislation implemented in 1996, to meet shortages of national personnel and training facilities.

London has become one of the dominant centers in world education, and foreign students follow courses at different levels. In 1996, 300,000 non-European Economic Area students came to study in the UK with almost 60,000 staying for at least a year (Home Office 1997). Interestingly the largest groups were from the United States and Japan. The number of foreign students in higher education institutions and language schools has mushroomed in the city since the 1970s. London has in effect become an off-shore island of American universities, which have set up numerous "branch plants" (King 1990: 129) contributing to the American presence.

Global European cities are also the centers of cultural production (publishing, media, news) within their linguistic and cultural spheres. Their hegemonic position derives not only from their economic authority and power but also their cultural status and ideological command and control (Friedmann 1995). Internationalized and post-imperial cities (King 1990, 1995) attract large numbers of students and artists (in the United Kingdom those engaged in the arts, religion, and sport do not require an employment permit). In addition, some ex-colonial populations still retain easier rights of entry and subsequent settlement.

Yet the diversity of migrants, their economic roles and cultural and educational impact have generally not been taken up in contemporary theorizations of the transformation of major European cities. It is striking that much of the literature on migrants and European cities relies on statistical information based on ethnic minorities, using categories constructed from the earlier flows of immigrants. The reliance on this kind of data does not simply arise from the poverty of information but is also due to the hegemony of the ethnic minority paradigm and the absence of a sociology of migration (Miles 1990), an intellectual configuration most strongly, though by no means exclusively, in evidence in the United Kingdom. The 1991 United Kingdom Census data, the first to include a question on ethnicity (Peach 1996), were after all not devised "to test hypotheses about a theoretical, global labor market but rather, to monitor immigration on the basis of race" (King 1990: 139).[2]

Transposing these general insights onto concrete terrains is also rendered difficult by the paucity of information available at the urban level and variations in the numerical significance, composition, and role of immigrants in different European states. In some cases I have had to draw upon studies conducted at the national level. To some extent this is less problematic than it would have been in the past since recent immigrants and refugees have tended to settle disproportionately in capital and major cities. I have paid more attention to the city with which I have greatest familiarity, namely London.[3] Whilst this may not correspond to the rigors of scientific method, London after all stands at the apex of the world cities pyramid and is unquestionably one of the most cosmopolitan cities in the world (Storkey and Lewis 1997), both in its transnational capitalist and subaltern classes (Friedmann 1995).

The failure to take account of changing migratory patterns includes the absence of a gender dimension. European migration studies have been slow to incorporate the reality of female immigration. When present, they have generally been seen as dependent family migrants whose contribution to the labor force is secondary (Kofman 1999). Furthermore this distorted view of female immigration is accompanied by a simplistic economically reductionist analysis of migratory processes (Ackers 1998).

Thus, in this chapter I shall provide an analysis of the diversified nature of immigration in European cities, which encompasses its gendered aspects. It is based on secondary sources and existing studies. This is all that can be achieved in the present chapter given the variety of national situations, the state of knowledge of many aspects of immigration, and the paucity of data. There are, however, some excellent recent studies of women migrants in European states, although the urban dimension is not necessarily uppermost. What both Ackers' (1998) and Anderson and Phizacklea's (1997) studies of intra-European female migrants and domestic workers, respectively, seek to do is go behind the statistical anonymity and delve into the life histories, aspirations, and projects of migrants. Their methodology enables them to situate individual life histories in a structural context and to capture the richness of motivations and changes in circumstances. These studies, as we shall see, call into question a number of assumptions about female migrants in particular and advance our existing knowledge of different groups.

Gender divisions and immigration

Although Sassen offered some interesting insights on gender divisions of labor and the social geography of home and work in global cities, immigrant women were slotted into the unskilled and abundant labor supply in downgraded manufacturing and low-level service sectors. A concern with demonstrating the presence of immigrant women in the labor force, and counteracting the equation of work with formal employment, was a common theme of feminist political economy analyses in the 1980s (Morokvasic 1984; Phizacklea 1983). Immigrant women have primarily filled the flexible, poorly paid, and casualized jobs, particularly where institutional discrimination against the employment of foreigners in public-sector and white-collar employment prevails (Morokvasic 1993). Despite the abundant literature on female labor migration, mainstream research and official policy still often treats female employment as an adjunct to male migration (Kofman 1998; Muus 1994), especially in northern European states. This downgrading of female work is partly due to the dominance of family reunion flows since the mid-1970s in which women were considered as passive followers of men, whose entry into the labor market was of secondary concern.

Certainly some forms of the new labor migration favor men. This is the case in the contract system introduced in the early 1990s in Germany, which allows for short-term immigration of workers in the construction industry, young skilled trainees from Eastern European countries, and commuting workers residing within close proximity to the border, for example, from the Czech Republic to Bavaria (Rudolph 1996). Yet the fastest growing form of work for immigrant women, as well as the principal means of legal employment, is domestic labor.

Official policy in states such as France and Germany has been to encourage the use of labor in the private sphere to fill the demand for care of children and the elderly through tax concessions.

There are currently an estimated one million overseas domestic workers in the European Union, a large number of whom are undocumented or do not have the right to work (Anderson 1997). In Mediterranean states the need for domestic labor has long been recognized but this is not so in northern European states. Even if domestic labor is recognized as one of the shortage categories, the numbers allowed to enter may be small, for example, in France, where domestic labor is often undertaken by French citizens of immigrant origin. Demand for domestic labor throughout Europe has risen sharply due to a number of reasons. First, there is the aging of European populations and inadequate care facilities, even in welfare states. Second, changing family structures and the employment of indigenous women has left them less time to undertake care and domestic tasks. Third, new lifestyles may lead middle-class couples to use domestic labor to free up time for leisure and consumption (Gregson and Lowe 1994). In a study of domestic work in five European cities – Athens, Barcelona, Berlin, Bologna, and Paris – Anderson and Phizacklea (1997) discuss the conditions of employment and the experiences of immigrant women, as well as the processes by which women obtain work through family, friends, social networks, churches, and recruitment agencies. Immigrant labor, of which about a quarter are thought to be men, fills the most exploitative forms of domestic work, that is live-in help which frequently requires the denial of one's own family tasks, a situation which is less likely to be accepted by working-class citizens.

Whilst wages may be low and the hours long compared to other forms of work, domestic labor has attracted immigrant women of diverse educational backgrounds and national origins. In those states with a massive deficiency of welfare provision for child care and the elderly (Italy, Spain), domestic labor is well-developed and is, though fluctuating, recognized by governments as an area of shortage. Those occupying the higher echelons in the stratification of domestic workers, such as the Filipinas in Italy and Spain and Latin Americans in Spain, are often educated (Campani 1993). Skills acquired in nursing and teaching are transferred to the private sphere (Campani 1997; Escriva 1997). Immigrant women had often been forced to leave their countries because of a surplus of qualified labor (Philippines) or as a result of the impact of structural adjustment (Peru). Some women reported that they kept silent about their qualifications (Anderson and Phizacklea 1997: 54); others commented that they might as well get paid for domestic labor as opposed to getting married and doing it unremunerated. Most have found it hard to leave the sector.

In Germany, there has been less demand for domestic labor in caring tasks, but Eastern European women have been attracted into office cleaning, live-out domestic work, and street trading. Polish women, for example, do not require visas and are hence able to move freely from one country to another. This form of pendular migration may permit them to combine work and household obligations. In the 1980s when Polish emigration gathered pace, Eastern European professionally qualified migrants to the European Union also experienced a high degree of brain waste (Morokvasic and de Tinguy 1993) or occupational skidding, i.e. loss of occupational status (Morawska and Spohn 1997: 36). Only about 30 per cent of highly skilled Poles (men and women) who left the country in the early to mid-1980s held jobs commensurate with their qualifications (Morawska and Spohn 1997: 38).

Longitudinal studies in France (Tribalat 1995) and West Germany (Seifert 1996) have noted the urban origin and substantially higher qualifications and educational levels of newer immigrants. In France women who enter through family reunification may be better educated than their marriage partners. In the German study, women have been moving out of the manufacturing sector into the service sector, probably into low-level jobs, where they were more likely to be working full-time, unlike German women, who had higher rates of part-time participation in the labor market. Significantly, for all women immigrants, whether of East German, ethnic German, or foreign origin, "integration into the labor market was more difficult than for men" (Seifert 1996: 434). Accounts of the experiences of immigrant women in the 1960s, with qualifications as teachers or nurses, but who were forced to work in manufacturing in Germany, show that deskilling was not uncommon in the earlier immigrant flows. Some women have sought better prospects through self-employment (Morokvasic 1991). In the absence of more detailed longitudinal studies and life histories, and a serious analysis of deskilling, it is not possible to gain a better idea of the degree to which different forms of brain waste and occupational skidding have been the experience of immigrant women in Europe.

If deskilling is poorly captured, the small minority of immigrant women in professional and managerial categories has also been neglected. Lost in the subsequent summaries of her thesis on global cities, but clearly picked up in the fuller version, Sassen (1991: 305) notes that women of Afro-Caribbean origin in London have a high proportion in professional and scientific categories due to their employment as nurses and teachers. Few scholars have recognized the diversity of class positions and educational levels amongst immigrants although Bhachu (1993), drawing on her own background as a member of a group with experiences of multiple migrations (East African Asian), has analyzed its implications for Asian women. The Irish-born, Black African, South East Asian and East African Asian women all have a higher proportion in professional and managerial groups than the White female population (Peach 1996). The presence of immigrant-origin women in professional and managerial strata is most common in states with ex-colonial populations (France, Netherlands, United Kingdom), where many entered as citizens. This gave them access to public sector employment. There is less ethnic segmentation in Britain than in Germany and the Netherlands (Lutz 1993a, b), where professional migrant women are frequently limited to occupations concerned with the training and welfare of other migrants.

Women's changing position in society has also to be taken into account in our understanding of international circulation, whether they be independent workers, trainees, family migrants, or students. Not only do women work in a range of occupations from the unskilled to the skilled, but they also participate as international exchange students, some of whom remain in the country in which they are pursuing their studies. They, too, are international migrants. A number of interviewees in the countries (Greece, Ireland, Portugal, Sweden, the UK) in Ackers' study of intra-European migration (1998) had moved there as single women to study or improve their linguistic skills. Just as men do, some found employment and settled. They may also marry and work, and there is no reason why they cannot do both. Only mainstream theorists continue to pigeon-hole migrants, thereby disregarding the multiple experiences of contemporary lives.

It is time that similar questions to those raised in the field of internal migration are applied to the relationship of household changes and women's career development, especially amongst professional and managerial categories. Dual career households are becoming far more common. Bruegel (1996) argues that the "trailing wife" is still with us but that amongst the higher professional and managerial levels, some of the effects of their partner's mobility may be mitigated. In Ackers' study, many women had not been able to find employment corresponding to their qualifications. In general, men derive more benefit from migration. On the international scale, it is likely that male mobility in dual career households presents severe employment problems for international and expatriate households (Hardill and MacDonald 1998). We do not know how conflicts within the household over overseas relocation are resolved. It may be that attempts are made to make international moves coincide with early parenthood when women are more likely to exit temporarily from the labor market. It would certainly help if research on migration rethought its resolute emphasis on the "principal" applicant.

For women who wish to move internationally there are also likely to be additional obstacles. Women are still being refused overseas assignments by companies (Adler 1994). Given the presence of immigrant female professionals in global cities, it is likely that they are moving and looking for work through other channels, for example using their own contacts or recruitment agencies (Gould 1988). About a fifth of work permits (virtually all in professional and skilled occupations) issued in the UK to non-European Union workers since the late 1980s have been to women (Bhabha and Shutter 1994: 172). The figures do not unfortunately indicate their marital status. Yet, the focus on skilled transients in intra-company moves, and the neglect of gender relations and household structures in determining international transfers and migration (Findlay 1995), have meant that the kinds of issues raised in studies of internal migration have not been addressed.

Conclusion

In seeking to analyse the position of immigrant women in European cities with global functions, I have combined elements of different theoretical literatures. It might seem strange that in general our understanding of immigrants in these cities is still so rudimentary. I suggested that one of the main reasons for this truncated perspective might be the emphasis on an ethnic minority paradigm, common to much of the research on migrants in European cities. Whether unwittingly or not, many researchers and policy makers have tended to equate migrants with the unskilled from less affluent countries. Though a minority, skilled transients are also actors in the development of internationalized labor markets and urban socioeconomic change. Another, and related reason for the dominant view of immigrants in European cities, is the focus on the actual occupation of the migrant rather than their original occupation, thereby missing out on the extent of deskilling that occurs, particularly among women who have "traded places" (Runyan 1996). Gender considerations are of course absent (Findlay 1995) in such research.

In feminist analyses, too, a preoccupation with unskilled female employment has prevailed with notable exceptions being studies of self-employment (Morokvasic 1991), immigrant mediators (Lutz 1993), and the diversity of class positions (Bhachu 1993). Understandably, in the pioneering research on female international migration in the 1970s in Europe, it was imperative to highlight the presence of women in the paid labor force and question the meaning of work itself. Today we need to acknowledge the diversity of female experiences in processes of international migration in European cities in relation to employment, households, and social change. I am in no way seeking to minimize the fact that the majority of recent female immigrants have been forced to seek employment in the sector of greatest shortage, that of domestic labor. Many are also lured and trapped into prostitution, where immigrant women often occupy the lower echelons of the hierarchy (Leidholdt 1996) in brothels and on the street. However, taking deskilling and brain waste more seriously would at least stop us from assuming that female immigration involves nothing but the unskilled and uneducated from poor countries. Similarly, taking account of immigrant women in professional and managerial occupations would help to bring the reality of global migration into line with the economic and social changes characteristic of women's lives today. It is highly probable that further research would reveal a polarized structure between professional and managerial women, largely from affluent countries, but with a minority from the old colonies where the educational system is still often based on the metropolitan system and those pushed into domestic labor, low-level service work, and prostitution. They are primarily from poorer countries, where structural adjustment programs (Peru), the poor remuneration and lack of opportunities for large pools of qualified labor (Philippines), and market liberalization (in Eastern Europe) have pushed many women out. These are the women, many of whom are undocumented, who have migrated in search of work. In Northern European countries, the majority of women migrants still enter as family migrants. Officially as the dependents of men, their employment histories generate scarcely any interest.

There is lamentably little research on a good number of the issues I have raised. My own attempt in this chapter at bridging disparate literatures and extracting as much as possible from existing evidence is undoubtedly partial. Much of the mainstream analysis of international migration has still to come to terms with feminist perspectives. As I have argued elsewhere (Kofman 1999), is it not time that research on processes of global migration and urban change finally engages with the reality of contemporary gender divisions and social relations?

Notes

1   Probably the main reason for its influence is the ease with which the core of her argument on earnings, income and occupations can be quantified, unlike Castells' (1994) more qualitative appreciation of the role of oppositional movements in current economic and social restructuring in European cities.
2   Ideologically, the effect is to bolster the idea that immigrants are the unskilled from the Third World, bringing with them cultural and social problems for the society of immigration. The converse is that a foreigner from another affluent country is not an immigrant.
3   I came from Australia (an Old Commonwealth country) as a postgraduate student and have lived in London for 25 years. Many women and men from these countries (Australia, Canada, New Zealand and South Africa) spend a year or two on a working holiday as a sort of rite of passage in their early adulthood. For a fascinating account of the different reasons that Australian women have left their country since the nineteenth century, see Pesman (1996).

8 Women and livelihood strategies

A case study of coping with economic crisis through household management in Paramaribo, Suriname

Mayke Kromhout

Introduction

During the 1980s Suriname was hit hard by the (regional) debt crisis. As a result, the Surinamese government has been faced ever since with a lack of foreign currency. In order to maintain control over the foreign currency supply or what was left of it, the government took – often – *ad hoc* policy measures. Among these were changes in currency exchange regulations: the Central Bank of Suriname no longer provided foreign currency against the official exchange rates. Private importers as well as manufacturers, who used to rely heavily upon government subsidies, were forced to pay market exchange rates.

By the 1990s the socioeconomic situation further deteriorated and became highly unstable. As a result, the government was forced to introduce a Structural Adjustment Program (SAP) in 1994. International pressure was being exerted by the World Bank, the IMF, and the country's main donor, The Netherlands, all of which were unwilling to carry out unconditional financing of development programs or budget support any longer. Austerity measures included the reduction of subsidies for the production sector. This measure impacted directly upon the poor, as one of the enterprises, the Melkcentrale, a state-owned enterprise, had to discontinue providing subsidized milk. Another measure attempted to reduce the number of government employees, but because of underlying (ethno) political interests, this has been put on hold.

Running inflation,[1] as well as a continuing shortage of foreign currency, were the most significant economic indicators of the crisis. However, as this chapter will show, the crisis also had important social implications, including a partial "restructuring" of gender relations at the household level. The poor, in particular, have been facing increasing problems with meeting their basic needs. To a large extent this has been due to the increasing costs of living, a lack of security with regard to household incomes,[2] and less access to housing (especially for the poor, but also for middle-income groups). Among the poor, the most "vulnerable groups" facing increasing hardship because of the economic crisis include women, young adults, and the elderly. My focus is on the strategies that low-income households use to cope with this socioeconomic situation. What kinds (or combinations) of livelihood strategies do they use and what factors influence these? How do these strategies impact women's position in the household?

Since the late 1970s, income-generating activities of the poor have caught the attention of scholars and donor agencies (e.g. ILO, World Bank). Various terms have been applied to these activities over time (e.g. informal activities, survival strategies, and livelihood strategies). "Informal" work as well as the notion of "survival" usually are used to refer to production activities of the poor, while the concept of "livelihood" stresses the multiplicity of resources and/or assets that low-income groups use to earn a living. These include household relations who can provide needed cash income, goods, and/or services.

Studies of poverty and livelihood in Paramaribo, Suriname's capital city, show that holding a multiplicity of jobs has become a necessity for low-income groups (Menke 1998, 1994; Schipper 1994). Other studies (Geerling 1998; Helleman 1995; Kromhout 1995; Schalkwijk and de Bruijne 1994) show that remittances from family and/or household members who have emigrated (primarily to The Netherlands) have become another necessary source of livelihood. These contributions can be either material – money and/or bartered goods – or non-material – information and/or services (Verrest 1998). Monetary and in-kind contributions from a resident or non-resident partner and other members of the household make up a substantial part of the household budget (Verrest 1998; Kromhout 1995; Wekker 1994). Furthermore, the poorer access of low-income groups (particularly young adults and migrants) to housing has meant that families are forced to share housing, thus increasing the average size and composition of households (Kromhout 1995). Providing housing for children constitutes another source of livelihood for low-income groups.

What all these studies about poverty and livelihood in Paramaribo show is that low-income groups do not necessarily rely on paid labor as the only means to earn a living. They also rely on resources that stem from their social networks (e.g. contributions from children, partners,[3] and others) and transfer payments (e.g. pensions, welfare, and scholarships). In this chapter I will focus on these different sources of livelihoods.

This chapter is based on an in-depth study in a low-income residential area in Paramaribo. The study focuses on forty-five women from the three main ethnic groups in the city: Creoles, Hindustanis, and Javanese.[4] They live in both male-headed and female-headed households. One of the assumptions of this study was that different ethnic groups in Paramaribo have over time developed distinct cultural practices which may affect the ways in which people are responding to the current economic crisis. Another assumption was that women from these three ethnic groups were experiencing differential personal (or life-cycle) circumstances and have had to operate within different household structures, i.e. make-up, and permission of resident (male) partner to work. These factors inform women's choices for dealing with Suriname's economic crisis at the household level, in particular their abilities to create a set of strategies to better cope with the situation.

In the remainder of this chapter I will address the livelihood strategies of Surinamese women in the face of the deteriorating economy, and I will investigate to what extent these strategies are differentiated along ethnic lines. To do so, I will first briefly provide some background information to Suriname's political and economic development since the early 1980s. Next, I will address a variety of structural factors affecting women's options and choices to cope with the economic crisis. Finally, I will discuss the findings of my study on the livelihood strategies developed by women in the residential area under study. As will be revealed, women use a certain set of strategies within the household (e.g. income pooling) and outside the household (e.g. income from relatives abroad). These are important in that they determine how well households are managing under the duress of the economic crisis.

Suriname and the crisis

Suriname is located on the northeast coast of South America, just north of the Amazon delta. It is bordered by the Atlantic Ocean in the north, by (British) Guyana in the west, by French Guyana in the east, and by Brazil in the south. Suriname' s interior is covered with rainforest, large parts of which are nearly uninhabited. The foundations for the country's multi-ethnic and multiracial population were laid in colonial times when slaves and contract laborers were shipped to the plantations, which constituted the main economic base of this Dutch colony. The estimated total population of Suriname is 440,000 with 70 per cent living in the capital city of Paramaribo. At present, Creoles (i.e. mixed descendants from African slaves), as well as Hindustanis and Javanese constitute the three largest ethnic groups in Suriname (32 per cent, 35 per cent, and 15 per cent, respectively). The Maroons, descendants of the African slaves who started a war against the Dutch slave system and who continue to live in the interior, are the fourth largest group (constituting 10 per cent). Finally, the native Amerindians,[5] the Lebanese, the Boers,[6] and the Chinese make up the remaining 8 per cent.

Economically, Suriname is heavily dependent on its main exports of bauxite and aluminum (constituting about 77 per cent of all exports), while domestic production and consumption strongly rely on imports as well as development aid. In addition, Suriname's political development has been problematic since its formal independence in 1975. Political turmoil during the early 1980s, including a bloody coup by the military under the leadership of Desi Bouterse as well as a rebellion led by the Maroon leader Ronnie Brunswijk against the military government, resulted in unstable political (intra-elite and inter-ethnic) power relations even after the return to civilian government in 1987. These political problems, in addition to the economic crisis, the temporary suspension (that was partially restored in 1987) of vital Dutch development aid and an overall rigid and outdated economic policy characterize Suriname's national development in the 1990s.

As already mentioned, the most important characteristic of the current economic crisis is the continuing shortage of foreign exchange and high levels of inflation. Therefore, the Surinamese government is barely able to maintain a minimum level of economic activity and services. In 1994 it finally adopted neo-liberal measures to stabilize the economy, reducing its public sector budget, floating the currency, and adjusting prices. However, hyper-inflation had already set in before the introduction of the SAP. In the years between 1990 and 1993, annual inflation rose from 22 per cent to 144 per cent. In the same year that the SAP was introduced, annual inflation reached its highest point ever, rising to 394 per cent. Stabilization was reached in 1996, as annual inflation was 1 per cent. But in 1997 annual inflation rose again. In the first quarter of 1999, inflation was about 30 per cent. The main reasons for the recent increase were the intro-duction and later (sudden) rise of the value-added tax for different consumption items. Furthermore, the main traders in foreign currency started manipulating exchange rates.

The purchasing power of the Surinamese guilder (sf) rapidly declined in light of the high inflation rates: by 1993 1 sf was worth the equivalent of 7 cents in 1980. In 1999, the sf was devalued by 80 per cent (*De Ware Tijd* 6 January 1999). Similarly, per capita income declined from US$2028 in 1984 to US$880 in 1997 (Schalwijk and de Bruijne 1999), a fall of over 50 per cent. The relationship between per capita income and the poverty level, however, is masked by the presumed substantial size of extra supplies of cash money and goods sent by relatives living abroad (Horowitz 1994). Remittances, in particular sent by Surinamese migrants in The Netherlands to their relatives in Suriname,[7] total approximately US$50 million annually (Entzinger 1996). This is a huge supple-ment to the US$120 million brought in annually by the main exports, bauxite and aluminum. However, these remittances are not registered and therefore real incomes of households show different patterns.

In 1996 the World Bank reported that 47 per cent of the total population of Suriname lived in absolute poverty. According to this report, Suriname ranked second among Caribbean countries with the largest number of poor people. Haiti had the highest poverty rates (65 per cent). Updates are not available because important Surinamese government agencies like the General Bureau of Statistics (GBS) and Manpower Statistics are currently forbidden to publish poverty rates and poverty lines. Research data from Schalkwijk and de Bruijne (1999) who surveyed 1000 households throughout Paramaribo show, however, that poverty rates are higher among female-headed households (FHH) (approxi-mately 85 per cent of which are in the ranks of the poor).

Some structural factors affecting women's economic options

In developing livelihood strategies Surinamese women from low-income groups are faced with various structural factors conditioning the options available to them. These factors include the structure of the labor market and employment opportunities as well as educational background. These dimensions will be discussed briefly in this section and provide the background for the discussion of my field research into how composition of the household, women's life cycle, and ethnicity further explain the variety in coping and survival strategies pursued by low-income women.

The structure of earning opportunities

Estimates of labor force participation show that the government traditionally has been the country's largest employer, providing jobs for approximately 43 per cent of the labor force in 1995 (General Bureau for Statistics (GBS) 1997). The flip side of this has been that the state's central control and intervention in labor markets has deterred the private sector from engaging in job creation and entrepreneurial activity. As a result, private sector (formal employment) shares of the primary, secondary, and remainder of the tertiary sector amount to only 15, 18, and 24 per cent, respectively (GBS 1997).

Unfortunately, a lack of detailed information on the participation of women in the Surinamese labor market makes it impossible to provide a breakdown of the (formal) sector distribution of employment by gender. The General Bureau of Statistics (1998) indicates that the share of women in the economically active population (aged 15 and over) in the period between 1994 and (the first half of) 1997 is 35 per cent.

Compared to the years before 1993 when this rate was approximately 27 per cent, this development could be regarded as positive. However, this is not so much a sign of "emancipation," but rather an indication of economic reality: the decrease in real household income has led many women to change their attitude toward working outside the home. This is particularly true for women who have a low level of education.

The degree to which women are currently engaged in paid work is difficult to assess. Because of underreporting of women's work in labor force statistics, the full extent of women's work remains invisible. This underreporting is particularly strong in areas of informal paid work, domestic production, and related tasks (Multi-Annual Development Programme (MADP) 1993). Women's organizations and researchers (Schalkwijk and de Bruijne 1997), therefore, suspect that female participation in the labor force is higher than formal statistics indicate.[8]

Women do suffer more than men from unemployment. GBS figures from the period between 1980 and 1997 show that unemployment among women is 35 per cent higher on average than among men (see Table 8.1). Also, the shift to employment is somewhat slower for women than it is for men.

Notwithstanding the fact that participation rates for women in (formal) employment are rising, men are taking the highest share of (formal) jobs. Apparently, this has to do with the ideology that men are the main providers for their families. Hence, their share in (formal) employment is higher than that of women: 65 per cent of the total economically active population (in Greater Paramaribo) consists of men.

Table 8.1 Unemployment figures for Greater Paramaribo among women and men, 1980–97 (percentages)

Year	Women	Men	Total
1980	16.0	13.0	15.0
1993	16.9	11.3	14.0
1994	14.9	11.1	12.0
1995	10.9	7.0	8.0
1996	16.4	7.9	11.0
1997	14.3	7.4	10.0

Source: General Bureau of Statistics (Suriname) 1980 and 1998.

Employment and education

Formal education is of critical importance to expand women's income earning options as well as their social mobility. Previous research studies (e.g. Schalkwijk and de Bruijne 1999; Levens and Chapman 1997) have shown that clear links exist between formal schooling and employment. At the primary level, female enrollments are nearly as high as those of males. At the secondary level, female participation is even higher. Between 1987 and 1991 and in the years thereafter, the rate of increase in overall female educational participation even surpassed that of males (GBS 1997; Ministry of Labor 1993).

Despite these overall participation rates, there continues to be traditional gender segregation at the secondary and tertiary level. Young men prefer the more technical skills while teacher-training skills are popular among young women (Levens and Chapman 1997; Ministry of Labor 1993). Unfortunately, the high rates for female educational participation do not necessarily result in a corresponding increase in female labor force participation, as adequate jobs for women are few and far between. Although there is a slight increase in jobs for women, women face sociocultural and economic barriers on the labor market that prevent them from being more flexible in their career choices (MADP 1993).

For example, women are under-represented in technical and productive jobs. Moreover, women are discriminated against because employers believe that women have more commitments to their families than men do and are more willing to quit their jobs (National Planning Office 1995; MADP 1993). These factors – in combination with the economic crisis – leave women no alternative but to find other means to earn an income, e.g. through networking or in the informal sector where their activities go unnoticed.

The research project: urban Surinamese women and family life

My study of the forty-five women from different ethnic backgrounds was conducted in the summer of 1994.[9] The objective was to explore the factors affecting the socioeconomic position of women and the functioning of these women's households. The women interviewed ranged in age from 19 to 73; 67 per cent had primary and/or secondary schooling and their average household size was 5.3. The interviews covered women's educational, employment, and migration histories, as well as a wide range of attitudinal questions. Apart from these interviews with Hindustani, Javanese, and Creole women in an urban low-income neighborhood, interviews with key informants provided useful data on the context in which to analyze the households under study.[10] Women's responsibilities in combining earning and household management have implications for the way that women are involved in livelihood activities.

The composition of households

The composition of the households under study shows a wide variety in living arrangements (see Table 8.2). Female-headed households (FHHs) exist in every ethnic group but male-headed households (MHHs) are dominant. Table 8.2 indicates that women head 29 per cent of households. The types of FHHs are *de jure* (permanent) and *de facto* (temporary). *De jure* FHHs predominate.

Javanese and Hindustani women predominantly live in nuclear family households (16 per cent and 18 per cent, respectively), while Creole women most typically live in the male extended type of household (with children and other relatives). These figures differ from research data that was collected about 30 years ago. At that time, Buschkens (1974), Speckman (1965), and de Waal Malefijt (1963) concluded that the nuclear family characterized the Javanese and Hindustani households while the single-parent family type characterized the Creole households. However, as the forty-five households in my study show, there are new developments in the types of households within each ethnic community. First, FHHs increased in all groups, particularly the Hindustani group (see Table 8.2). Reasons for these changes include divorce, men migrating abroad and leaving the family behind, widowhood, and labor market involvement of women.[11] Changes in the composition of households are also due to the migration of household members and/or family members, particularly in the case of Hindustani households. When young women and men migrate in search of better employment abroad, children who are left behind move in with grandparents (on the mother's side). Another result is that households that were headed by a male become a FHH.

Second, the male extended family-type has become important among the

Table 8.2 Women by type of household and ethnic background

	Javanese	*Hindustani*	*Creole*	*Total*
FHH	2 (13%)	6 (40%)	5 (33%)	13 (29%)
MHH	13 (87%)	9 (60%)	10 (67%)	32 (71%)
Total	N = 15	N = 15	N = 15	N = 45

(low-income) Creoles. This has much to do with the relatively poorer access of this ethnic group to housing (see Schalkwijk and de Bruijne 1999). This results in the sharing of housing. In contrast, Javanese women, when they enter the labor market, are willing to provide housing for relatives in return for the sharing of domestic tasks: the difficulties they experience in combining work for production with the management of their household make them resort to the strategy of "house-sharing." In sum, the economic crisis as well as the resulting limited access to housing is leading to the recurrence of the "multiple generation house-hold," that was once only prominent among Hindustanis. However, the new situation has "brought back" the extended family among all groups, leading to a reconsideration of this "old" concept. One positive effect of extended house-holds is, as we will see later, that they may work in favor of the bargaining power of women.

Income problems and the need for individual and networking activities

Typologies of labor, based on differences in the stability of work and income, offer a useful approach to see how women try to make ends meet. For Paramaribo such typologies provide a clear picture of the relationship between labor and income stability. Research findings direct us to the "rationality" of labor choice by human beings. In contrast to the literature, which indicates that human beings prefer wage labor because of the resulting income stability (Menke 1998; Baud 1992), the present economic situation forces women to look for alternatives. Creoles, for example, prefer a job with a secure and stable income whereas Javanese women search for jobs that provide insecure but higher incomes. Women also prefer a mix of economic alternatives, in order to spread their risks.

Of the women under study, 62 per cent are employed (see Table 8.3) and half (50 per cent) of them work in the so-called informal sector. The government employs the majority of the women who are involved in the formal sector: cleaners, teachers, nurses, cooks, and assistants in day care centers. These women are usually Creoles who are over-represented in the civil government. Their relatively early urbanization led them to take major positions in the civil service. Also, the distribution of employment by the government has always been along political-ethnic lines. The Creole political elite has favored its political

Table 8.3 Women's share in employment by type of household and ethnic background

	Employed			
	Hindustanis	*Creole*	*Javanese*	*Total*
FHH	3 (37.5%)	4 (50%)	1 (12.5%)	8 (29%)
MHH	1 (5%)	10 (40%)	9 (55%)	20 (71%)
Total	N = 4 (14%)	N = 14 (50%)	N = 10 (36%)	N = 28 (100%)

electorate by the provision of civil service jobs. Women of Creole origin have benefited from these political strategies.

The women in the informal sector are involved in secondary and tertiary production. They produce foodstuffs, flowers, mixed pickles, clothes, and crops but they also sell bread, dried fish, and natural food. Furthermore, these women perform domestically related tasks like baby-sitting, cleaning, ironing, and washing. Women who are considered to be retired also work in this sector. In most cases, jobs in the informal sector are irregular because women combine work with household production and, as a result the work location is typically the home. Of the women in this study, Javanese women constitute the majority of those engaging in informal sector activities.

Other sources of income for women are (1) the household; (2) the government; (3) friends and acquaintances; (4) family members outside the home (e.g. abroad); and (5) a non-resident partner. The household forms the internal social network, while the latter three are part of the external social network.

The internal social network consists of a resident partner, children, and sometimes other relatives (e.g. grandparent, cousin). The incomes women receive from these persons are usually spent on household items like food, rent, and transportation. Only in some cases are women able to save small amounts of money. The external social network may also consist of a partner and children. The incomes from the external social network that women receive may consist of remittances but also goods and services or information. Here it is important to stress both material and non-material incomes. Material incomes consist of money but also of goods, e.g. a box with clothes or provisions that has been sent by relatives living abroad (e.g. The Netherlands, French Guyana). Non-material incomes can be either services carried out, domestic work done, or valuable information provided. It is almost impossible to express the value of these non-material goods in financial terms.

Important alternative sources of income for Creole women include the internal social network (e.g. financial arrangements with a partner and/or children and/or other relatives) as well as part of the external social network (e.g. remittances from relatives abroad). Hindustani women generate their alternative incomes from the internal social network (largely their partners) and part from the external social network (e.g. remittances) and transfer payments (e.g. welfare). As Javanese women apparently have few relatives abroad (see Schalkwijk and de Bruijne 1994, 1999; Helleman 1995), their main alternative source of income is the internal social network. They also rely, in contrast to the Hindustanis and Creoles, less on transfer payments like welfare. The main reason for this difference is that they have adopted their own cultural standards about social and economic security: it is the children who take care of them and no one else. Only in cases where there are no children will they consider turning to government officials for needed economic security. Table 8.4 shows the ethnic distribution of remittances among households.

Despite the enormous efforts by women to generate an income, these are sometimes offset by the great difficulties women experience in holding on to their

Table 8.4   Remittances among households by ethnic background

	No remittances	*Javanese*	*Hindustanis*	*Creole*	*Total*
FHH	7 (54%)	1 (8%)	3 (23%)	2 (15%)	13 (29%)
MHH	21 (66%)	1 (3%)	3 (9%)	7 (22%)	32 (71%)
Total	N = 28 (62%)	N = 2 (5%)	N = 6 (13%)	N = 9 (20%)	N = 45 (100%)

formal sector jobs or casual work for production. These difficulties stem from women's often disadvantageous position on the labor market, but they should also be understood against the background of their personal circumstances. These circumstances are the result of a combination of factors, including: (1) the structure of the household; (2) the family cycle in combination with the structure of the household; (3) certain personal characteristics of women (such as education, age, marital status); and finally (4) the tolerance of the male partner. A combination of these factors is critical in determining the extent to which women are engaged in livelihood activities, e.g. work outside the home. These factors also account for a differentiation along ethnic lines. For example, of the women interviewed, Creole and Javanese women show considerably higher labor participation rates than Hindustani women (73 per cent of whom are unemployed). One of the main reasons for this discrepancy appears to lie with the traditional views within the Hindustani community concerning men's and women's roles. When interviewed, Hindustani men and women alike were concerned that a working wife would be interpreted as the man being unable to adequately provide for his family. In sum, intra-ethnic cultural standards seem to prevail over the increasing financial needs of the family or household.

Budgeting patterns and distribution mechanisms

Another area which has seen some dramatic changes since the onset of the economic crisis concerns household budgeting patterns and distribution mechanisms. In order to organize the main expenditures, households create or intensify

Table 8.5   Budgeting patterns in households

	Pooling				*Non-pooling*		*Total*
	M+F	*M+F+O*	*M+O*	*F+C*	*M*	*F*	
FHH	—	—	—	4 (30%)	—	9 (70%)	13
MHH	11 (34%)	9 (28%)	4 (13%)	—	8 (25%)	—	32
Total	N = 11 (24%)	N = 9 (20%)	N = 4 (9%)	N = 4 (9%)	N = 8 (18%)	N = 9 (20%)	N = 45 (100%)

Note:
M, Male partner; F, Female partner or Female head; C, Children; O, Other relatives.

existing budgeting patterns. These patterns depend upon the composition of households and the possibilities that household members can contribute to household budgets. Husbands and wives, as well as other members of the household (mainly relatives), are involved in establishing these patterns (see Table 8.5).

Two budgeting forms can be distinguished: (1) pooling (bringing together – part of – financial means) and (2) non-pooling (not bringing together financial means). Pooling appears to be fundamental in MHHs, but is employed in only a third of the FHHs. In MHHs financial contributions from the male partner are the determining factor in establishing the household budget. In most cases, wives identify the male partner as the head and main provider of the household. These women expect the male partner to provide an important, if not the most important, share of the household income. For these households different budgeting patterns can be distinguished. These include: (1) pooling between partners; (2) pooling between partners and resident relatives; (3) pooling between the male partner and resident relatives; and (4) non-pooling. In households resorting to the last type of budgeting, the female partner receives a (fixed) sum of money for the management of the household.

In the cases of pooling between partners in the MHHs, three groups of women can be distinguished. The first group consists of women who receive a major share of the income(s) from their male partner (e.g. the Javanese women). These women tend to be well-informed about the level of income(s) their male partners earn. As a result, they have considerable control over the incomes and expenditures of the household. Hence, they can manage their household very well. The second group of women receives a fixed amount of money from a male partner. In this group, some women only have minimal household expenses because the male partner takes direct financial responsibility for costs like rent, water, telephone, electricity. Other women, who have an income of their own, share household expenditures like rent, telephone bills, and water with their male partners.

The third group of women receive a fluctuating amount of money from their partners. This is the case where the male partner has a fluctuating income and/or a fluctuating private consumption pattern. The women in this group have great difficulty in managing their households, if they cannot rely upon other members for additional income. The more unpredictable the contribution of the male partner, the more difficulties women experience in managing their households. Among the MHHs, 22 per cent fall within this category.

These three dominant budgeting patterns in the MHHs reveal an interesting differentiation along ethnic lines. For instance, Hindustani households, where the female partner is unemployed, show a great deal of non-pooling. This implies that women in these households depend largely upon the income sources of their male partners. The Javanese and Creole households, where the female partner is unemployed, rely upon the resident partner and the children (or other relatives).

In the FHHs, contributions by the female head are very important. Compared to the budgeting patterns in the MHHs, there are fewer options available: either pooling between the female head and relatives, or non-pooling (see Table 8.6).

Table 8.6 Pooling by ethnic background and type of household

	Pooling			Non-pooling			
	Javanese	*Hindustani*	*Creole*	*Javanese*	*Hindustani*	*Creole*	*Total*
FHH	—	2 (15%)	2 (15%)	2 (15%)	4 (31%)	3 (23%)	13
MHH	12 (38%)	2 (6%)	10 (31%)	1 (3%)	7 (22%)	—	32
Total	N = 12 (27%)	N = 4 (8%)	N = 12 (27%)	N = 3 (7%)	N = 11 (24%)	N = 3 (7%)	N = 45 (100%)

Turning now to Table 8.6, Hindustani women who head households fall back upon incomes from their own labor rather than on incomes from other household members. This is because many of the other members have not reached the age to get employment. Pooling in Javanese MHHs is relatively higher than in households from other ethnic groups.

The female heads feel a great responsibility for their household and make the main contribution to the household budget. Of these women, 70 per cent contribute more than half of the household income. In the MHHs, the contribution of female partners is lower: about 20 per cent. From Table 8.5 we can conclude that the formation of the household budget is relatively difficult in the FHHs. They suffer from less pooling and fewer remittances.

The changes and differentiation in budgeting as well as pooling patterns affect the bargaining position of women. These bargaining positions are also affected by intra-household and inter-household relations as well as different sources of contributions by resident/non-resident relatives. Such contributions from members other than the resident partner (e.g. daughters and sons) do not always consist of money. Daughters, particularly when they remain in the household with their respective families feel the urge to share costs like bills for telephone, water, electricity, and cooking fuel. In contrast, sons are likely to hand over a fixed or fluctuating amount of money. This counters the implicit assumption by other scholars (Hoodfar 1988; Benería and Roldan 1987) that household budgeting patterns are only determined by incomes from paid labor.

The male head always decides the extent to which he contributes to the household. He always has control over his own share in the household budget. There is no joint decision making between him and his partner about his share. In most cases he tends to adjust his share in order to accommodate his private consumption. In contrast, women tend to contribute their total income (if they have one) to the household. Other household members contribute a lesser share – in most cases less than 50 per cent – of their income to the household budget.

The formation of the household budget does not emerge from a set of decision-making procedures. In most cases it depends upon expectations of household members toward each other and what they find they are committed to. In MHHs, women expect their male partner to contribute the most. To them, he is committed to that. They consider him as the (main) provider of the family. But, when his share in the household budget is low, women will not choose to argue over this. They will turn to other family members to bridge the financial gap by asking them for additional financial or other contributions. Sometimes they will approach non-resident relatives for such contributions. In FHHs, women, because of their greater financial insecurity, tend to be more demanding when it comes to contributions from other members.

In terms of daily decision making with respect to distribution mechanisms in the households under study, there are no differences between employed and unemployed women in MHHs. Apparently, the male expects his female partner to be able to organize the daily expenditure in a suitable manner. The household money he hands over has to cover needs like food, drinks, transportation, and sometimes costs like rent, telephone bills, water, electricity. He implicitly approves of her allocation behavior concerning these items. In particular, decision making among the Javanese is wife-dominant, which means that these women have the ultimate say in the allocation of expenditure; in 80 per cent of all cases they decide to what extent and in what ways the household money is spent even though they receive almost all earnings from their male partner. In contrast, a smaller percentage of Hindustani (50 per cent) and Creole (30 per cent) women have the final say in such decision making. In FHHs, women in all groups have total control over the expenditures.

However, the allocation of non-standard expenditures like consumer durables is a different matter. In MHHs, the allocation of the household money for this expenditure is a matter of negotiation between the partners or, in some cases, based on the decision by the male partner. Again, when a male decides to buy consumer durables without consulting his wife, there will be no conflict because she considers the items to add to the welfare of the household. In contrast, in FHHs, the female head has total control over the items to be bought.

Entitlements and the bargaining power of women

From the earlier examples, it is clear that women use different sets of livelihood strategies that enable them to contribute to the basic needs of the household. The question raised here is whether the share of women in household income leads to a greater share in decision making or bargaining power. As mentioned before, in livelihood activities labor exchange does not always take place. Exchange of services is also important. In this context, it is worth mentioning that the women under study also use social entitlements as a potential source of income.[12] Social entitlements are in fact the basis for the bargaining power of women in the household. These entitlements stem from: (1) the perception of women about the position and responsibilities of their male partner; and (2) the self-perception of women and their own capabilities to impose financial obligations on others within and outside the household. With regard to the first, women expect their male partners to use their income(s) for the welfare and well-being of their families. When the male partner does not fulfill this duty (that is assigned to him by Surinamese conceptions of manhood) he cannot expect to remain in the household.

With regard to the second, the self-perception of women, my study shows that women are able to impose financial obligations on other relatives because of the services they provide for those others. These services are: (1) their readiness to provide a home for other relatives, in particular their own adult daughters and sons and their respective families (as is particularly the case in Creole and Javanese extended households); (2) their readiness to take care of grandchildren when the parents are at work or have migrated abroad; and (3) their readiness to maintain contacts with relatives abroad. Often women will send Surinamese sweets in exchange for money or care packages.

The ways in which all these women strengthen their bargaining power depend upon the extent to which they are able to use the strategies mentioned above to generate financial and other resources with which to manage their households. One of these resources is their own income, which decreases their dependency on their male partners. In this respect it is worth mentioning that not only the different budgeting patterns but also the ways in which women try to cope with continuing financial shortages at the household level need to be taken into account. Women are likely to rely upon others – by using social entitlements – when sources of finance are in danger. These social entitlements as well as material sources provide women with a fall-back position to avoid direct conflict with their male partners. As long as women are able to turn to others, they are able to escape a direct confrontation with their male partners. Hindustani women, who generally do not have such a fall-back position, are forced to deal directly with their male partners about household budgeting. Compared to Creole and Javanese women, their bargaining power is relatively weak.

Finally, as is to be expected, FHHs offer the female head the greatest independence concerning the management of the household. If relatives are present, these women rely upon them for extra income (or goods). Despite the existence of a male partner, gender relations are also relevant here. In terms of budgeting patterns, gender relations operate not only in intimate relationships (e.g. husband–wife relations) but also in intergenerational relationships (e.g. parent–child relations).

With regard to the organization of the domestic work and child care, the maintenance of a gendered division of work in MHHs is evident. In these households, the male head considers domestic work and the care of children as the duty of his wife, especially in cases where she is not employed. However, wives do not fundamentally challenge this assumption despite their many complaints. Because of this, a more equitable division of domestic work and child care between men and women has not arisen. Therefore, the wife needs to rely on relatives who are either members of her household or live elsewhere. In FHHs, the situation is the same as female heads are particularly reliant on other live-in relatives, especially older daughters.

Conclusion

How do households, and the women in them, cope with the deteriorating macroeconomic situation in Suriname? The most marked phenomenon of the current crisis is running inflation. Macroeconomic policy has not guaranteed any means of more formal employment and housing for the population. It is women who bear the brunt of the deteriorating situation. From this case study, we have learned that a specific set of livelihood strategies offer women some ease. These strategies, however, depend upon the capabilities and possibilities of the women involved. These capabilities and possibilities emerge not only from macroeconomic context but also from the internal factors of the household (composition, type, life cycle, permission from the resident males for women to work outside the home), and the personal characteristics (education, age, ethnicity) and gender awareness of the women in the household.

Livelihood strategies among the women are diverse. The most common strategies include reliance on transfer payments by the state, remittances, sharing housing, budgeting, more (formal/informal) jobs, and having more non-resident partners. These strategies differ along ethnic lines and in terms of the type of household to which women belong.

Remittances are not as popular among Javanese women as they are among Creole and Hindustani women. Their relatives abroad are few and therefore Javanese women do not feel the need to intensify communication with them. Thus, having more jobs, and also budgeting are more important strategies for Javanese women. Creole women, too, rely on these strategies. Although the circumstances differ somewhat, the opportunity for Javanese and Creole women to work outside the home is typically not restricted by their male partners. Nevertheless, Javanese women look for flexible jobs that enable them to spend time with their children and carry out other types of domestic work. Hence, they dominate in income-generating activities that are located inside the home.

Budgeting takes place mainly in Javanese and Creole households where adult members have an income. Women in these households are able to provide other relatives with services that can serve as a basic means for bargaining. For some women, having an income of their own is crucial in bargaining for other resources in the home. But the possession/provision of other goods and services like a house and baby-sitting as well as having strong self-confidence also create a good bargaining position in the household. Because of their contribution to the household, women tend to solve potential conflicts by the involvement of, for example, resident adult daughters. This happens to be the case when money supplies are in danger. In this situation, it is not the husband–wife relationship that counts but the mother–daughter relationship, which is an underexplored gender relation in the analysis of budgeting and household decision making in Suriname.

The question can be raised whether there are differences in the management of crisis situations between different economic groups. Lower income groups, for example, have always been forced to develop strategies intended to protect them from continuous financial shortages. The present-day crisis forces these groups, therefore, to engage in greater inventiveness and more disciplined forms of pooling with various household members. The actual socioeconomic position of women in the household depends on their capabilities to tap financial resources. These capabilities are determined by a number of factors such as the level of education, age, household structure in combination with the family cycle, and the (in)tolerance of the male partner. Finally, ethnocultural factors also have an impact on the kinds of livelihood strategies poor women employ to cope with the deteriorating macro-economic situation in Suriname.

Notes

1   The introduction of a unification of the exchange rate with a floating character came into force in July 1994. The objective was to stabilize the exchange rates and thus bridge the gaps between the different exchange rates that were used by the Central Bank of Suriname. The commercial banks and the legal *cambios* could not stop inflation.
2   Because of fluctuating prices, between 1986 and 1991 there was a decrease of real income in all sectors of the economy. The exception was for 1989 in which there was an increase in real income. This problem could not be solved by a continuous adjustment of real incomes. Real incomes in Suriname are not being indexed. Employees began to feel insecure about the net value of their income. Civil servants felt that their income was lagging behind price developments. For example, between July 1993 and July 1994 inflation rose 394 per cent. Adjustments to the incomes of the civil servants in the same period were only 200 per cent (Ministry of Labor 1996).
3   Economic considerations have entered the marriage/partnership market: men who have emigrated to The Netherlands and as a result have more access to foreign currency are preferred over those who have not.
4   Creoles are descendants of Black slaves from Africa, while the Hindustanis and Javanese are immigrants from India and Java, respectively, who first arrived in Suriname in the late nineteenth and early twentieth centuries.
5   The Maroons and native Amerindians usually live in the interior of Suriname. However, during the war in the 1980s, a division of the Maroons migrated to the outskirts of the capital city. These migrants experienced many problems with access to housing, sanitation, and formal employment.
6   These are the descendants of the Dutch farmers who settled in Suriname in 1845.
7   Approximately 200,000 Surinamese migrants live in The Netherlands. That is nearly half the population in Suriname.
8   The few available statistics about formal employment generally only apply to the urban area of Paramaribo. Information about women in rural areas is even more scarce, in part because of formal government regulations preventing women from achieving high production rates (Defares and Khoesial 1994).
9   A repeat study followed in 1998 as part of my PhD dissertation (forthcoming, late 1999/early 2000).
10 Teachers, principals, physicians, political leaders, direct personal contacts with inhabitants and other informants as well as observation provided informative and insightful data. Access to the setting did not require a process of formal negotiation or permission.
11 This last factor leads females to make relatives part of their household who take over (some of) the reproductive tasks in the household.
12 An entitlement is a legal concept that deals with rules that govern who can have the use of what (Sen 1990). The distribution of resources within households is not always

controlled by law (like property ownership and market transactions). Therefore, there are obvious difficulties in extending the analysis of entitlement to the problem of intrahousehold distribution. Nevertheless, because distribution of income determines each person's command over necessities, it is often a source of inequality that can be mitigated through "social" entitlements.

Part III

Resistances

In Part III, our attention is drawn most directly to the politics of gender resistance in the context of global restructuring. As was argued in the introduction, dominant accounts tend to present globalization as an inevitable and overwhelming force, often leaving people feeling disempowered. Yet, we also know that periods of profound changes are prone to engender protest and mobilization. We know, too, from the previous sections that the changes represented by global restructuring create new openings for women's resistance to old and new oppressions. This raises the following questions addressed in this section. How should resistance be reconceptualized in light of women's agency in the context of global restructuring? What forms of resistance arise in what contexts? What are the connections and contradictions among various forms of women's resistance? How do women's resistances connect the local and global, the private and public, and other supposed oppositions?

In the contributions by Amy Lind (Chapter 9), Julie Beck (Chapter 10), Azza Karam (Chapter 11), and Deborah Stienstra (Chapter 12), various forms and dimensions of women's resistance are highlighted and contextualized through case studies. Together these four chapters reflect a wide range of resistance practices in terms of strategies, objectives, sites, forms, etc. However, these same contributions also suggest that we need to go beyond a mere typology of resistance to further our understanding of gender and global restructuring and to formulate an inclusive politics of resistance.

As all four demonstrate, resistance needs to be (re)conceptualized as involving attempts to intervene in and renegotiate various boundaries between the public and private, global and local, market and state, state and society, and so on. Although these interventions and renegotiations may take "local" forms, they can affect the efforts and activities of dominant or hegemonic actors representing GI to establish, maintain, or reinforce certain boundaries. For example, if the state is introducing certain structural adjustment measures, such as the lifting of food and transport subsidies (and thus reformulating the boundary between the market and the state), resistance activities and strategies will tend to be directed at this boundary. They may range from local or community organizing (including survival strategies and self-help efforts) to mobilizing in the national political arena via food riots, demonstrations, political parties, and social movements, and challenging the IMF directly by launching an international campaign. In short, conceptualizing resistance in this way allows us to capture the diverse activities which people employ to counteract the negative effects of neoliberal global restructuring. Moreover, such understanding of resistance makes women's roles and activities more visible by explicitly including those spheres and sites (the community, the private realm) in which many women tend to spend much of their lives. It also allows us to circumvent the IPE literature's existing bias toward large-scale and highly politicized mobilizations.

Lind's chapter on the resistances of Ecuadorian neighborhood women's organizations to the introduction of successive structural adjustment packages since the 1980s illustrates these points particularly well. She finds that these women's protests in response to eroding economic conditions and reduced funding for their community-based organizations are simultaneously directed at global capital (in the form of protests against Citibank), the neoliberal state (in the form of organizing against the government's modernization plan), and gender ideologies (which deny them full citizenship and position them to always be responsible for social reproduction without sufficient means). In the process, they are renegotiating market–state, state–society, and gender relations, as well as their own cultural and political identities.

Beck's chapter on an emergent form of "feminist" analysis and identity among urban professional women activists in the Czech Republic also shows an attempt to renegotiate the boundaries which typically separate and set up oppositions among liberalism, state socialism, and feminism. In her interviews with these women, Beck detects the development of an ideology which seeks to combine the positive aspects of liberalism (e.g. democratic freedoms, occupational and geographical mobility, and availability of consumer goods) with the positive aspects of state socialism (e.g. social egalitarianism, public services, and full employment). Moreover, although these women do not identify themselves as feminists, they subscribe to a kind of feminist egalitarianism, which resists gender discrimination but insists that women should not be made into men as was attempted under state socialism. Thus, they reject neoliberalism, state socialism, and Western feminism even as they embrace aspects of liberalism and socialist and feminist egalitarianism.

Karam's interviews with Egyptian women activists in Cairo presented and analyzed in her chapter also reveal boundary renegotiations going on among another set of separations and oppositions – globalization, Islamism, and feminism. She identifies at least three forms of feminism that have emerged at the interstices of globalization and Islamism: secular feminism, Muslim feminism, and Islamic feminism. These multiple and contradictory feminist voices point to the reappropriation of dominant discourses of globalization, Islam, and Western feminism as a resistance strategy.

No examination of women's resistances in the context of global restructuring would be complete without attention to the increasing internationalization or transnationalization of resistance practices. Stienstra's chapter speaks directly to this issue with her discussion of transnational women's organizing in the context of recent UN conferences. This organizing has little in common with 1970s feminist notions of global sisterhood for it is arising from diverse women's local resistances to global restructuring. On the one hand, improved means of communication (such as the fax, e-mail, and cheaper travel) have in part stimulated this transnational organizing. On the other hand, this transnational activism is a response to the diminished role of the state, as the pre-eminent site for political and economic decision making, and emerging global governance structures. Yet as Stienstra points out, there are dangers connected to transnational organizing. Getting too much involved in lobbying activities at the UN, the WTO, the IMF and the World Bank may lead to co-optation. Also, it may increasingly create a gap between professional feminist lobbyists and grassroots activists. Thus, those women who are in a position to engage in what Stienstra refers to as "dancing resistance" at the global level must be careful not to get caught up in the dance of dominant restructuring agents.

In sum, all the contributions in this section demonstrate how forces of global restructuring are creating and structuring the ways that resistances are articulated. In other words, global restructuring, to a certain extent, creates the responses to it. At the same time, responses and resistances to it affect the directions of global restructuring. These chapters also reveal that resisting and redirecting global restructuring involves a reappropriation of meanings of social processes and movements and a rearticulation of subjectivities and identities. When this occurs, resistance practices can become pro-active rather than reactive.

9 Negotiating boundaries

Women's organizations and the politics of restructuring in Ecuador[1]

Amy Lind

> The gendered dimensions of restructuring extend far beyond the economic. Instead, the current round of restructuring entails a fundamental redrawing of the familiar boundaries between the international and national, the state and the economy, and the so-called "public" and "private." This realignment, in turn, undermines both the assumptions and sites of contemporary feminist politics and invites new strategic thinking about the boundaries of the political.
>
> (Brodie 1994: 46)

> Perhaps feminism's most notable contribution to the critique of [Latin American] modernity has been to make evident in it the continuity of one of the central contradictions of a social system structured by polarities: the contradiction of gender.
>
> (Olea 1995: 193)

Introduction

In the past three decades, a range of women's organizations and movements have emerged throughout Latin America. Many urban neighborhood women's organizations have developed political strategies which are derived in part from their gendered roles in, and identification with, processes of local reproduction and consumption. Some have argued that these types of organizations position themselves as "clients," "recipients," or "consumers" vis-à-vis the state – and increasingly, vis-à-vis the international development apparatus – in order to demand state services, push for legal reforms, collectivize consumption (as in the well-documented case of Lima's communal kitchens), and protest the economic changes which affect their daily lives and households (Barrig 1994, 1996; Alvarez 1996; Schild 1998). In so doing, these movements are constructing new consumer-based political identities which, most concretely, address the daily impacts of economic crisis and political reform, and symbolically, reflect their gendered subject positions in processes of modernity and modernization in Latin America (Olea 1995; Lind 1995).

In the 1980s and 1990s, with the advent of structural adjustment policies (SAPs) and the general emphasis on neoliberal development strategies – in which the public and private boundaries of the state, the economy, and civil society are being "restructured" – women's organizations have been among the first to challenge the effects of this process. Gender-based protest against foreign banks, the IMF, or national governments often has been analyzed in terms of how and why specific sectors of women mobilize to confront the daily impacts of economic crisis and restructuring as it affects their triple roles in reproduction, production, and sometimes, in "community management" (Benería and Feldman 1992; Moser 1993; Daines and Seddon 1994). Much of the literature focuses on the gender/class dimensions of struggle which, while important, does not explain entirely how and why otherwise heterogeneous groups of women mobilize on the basis of gender, at the community level, to confront what they perceive as the negative effects of "development."[2] Often struggling in and politicizing their roles as mothers of families and/or as community caretakers, neighborhood women's organizations, which collectivize reproductive activities such as food provision and struggles for housing and infrastructure, have been called "traditional" by some and "transgressive" by others (see Barrig 1994, 1996; Alvarez 1996).

As interesting, contradictory, and complex as these processes may be, little research has been conducted to analyze the relationship between women's organizations, which are increasingly responsible for managing community development initiatives, and the neoliberal projects of Latin American states, which rely upon private (including informal, household-level, and community-level) strategies for development and survival. Much debate has taken place about the extent to which local organizations can sustain themselves and affect social change, particularly when they are placed with heavier burdens under restructuring measures, neoliberal state reform, and associated decentralization initiatives (see Lind 1997). Implicit to this debate is an analysis of whether or not women's organizations accept the premises of "modernization." On the one hand, it has been argued that women's organizations of this type are fighting merely for further access to the benefits of modernization. On the other hand, scholars of "new social movements" often herald these movements for the ways in which they pose a challenge to the dominant development order, often typifying "anti-development" struggles such as those described by Arturo Escobar (1995) and some scholars of subaltern studies.

This chapter addresses how Ecuadorian neighborhood women's organizations construct political strategies, position themselves vis-à-vis the state and development apparatus, and work simultaneously within and against the boundaries of "development." This has important concrete effects for people's lives, as well as important implications for our understandings of women's political practices, development, and modernity. First, I address some conceptual issues related to gender, women's movements, and economic restructuring in Ecuador and throughout Latin America. Second, I discuss the current context of development in Ecuador and the responses of neighborhood women's organizations to adjustment policies. Third, I discuss the political positioning of women's organizations and the changing Ecuadorian state, focusing specifically on the new institutional arrangements of neoliberalism within which neighborhood women's organizations struggle.

A key aspect of this approach is my argument that Ecuadorian neighborhood women's organizations are not merely passive recipients of state development policies, but rather contribute proactively to re-articulating the economic and political effects of "development" in their daily lives. To paraphrase Inderpal Grewal and Caren Kaplan (1994), I argue that women's organizations have brought into critical consideration categories such as gender, race, and nationality, put into question some basic assumptions of history and subjectivity upon which political practices are based, and have challenged the cultural center of development (Grewal and Kaplan 1994: 5). At the same time, the political strategies of Ecuadorian women's organizations are limited by how they have constructed their relationships with the state and development apparatus (e.g. international development organizations and non-governmental organizations (NGOs). Thus we tend to see a combination of forces at work to produce "postmodern" gendered subjects which embrace and reject different aspects of the modernization process – similar to Raquel Olea's observation of the "contradictions of gender" in Latin American modernities, and similar to Grewal and Kaplan's (1994) analysis of anti-colonial political movements as a challenge to, yet derived from within, the premises and practices of modernity and modernization. The chapter takes into account the ways in which neoliberal state projects have contributed to defining and institutionalizing the boundaries within which social actors identify their needs and expectations, construct their political identities, and understand what the scope of their options are in the current context of global restructuring.[3] In general, these movements rarely struggle for their mere incorporation into the already existing development or political process, nor do they accept entirely the premises of "modernization." At the same time, they are not simply "anti-development" struggles.

Restructured spaces: neighborhood-based women's movements

The emergence of contemporary women's movements in Latin America has been explored extensively, from various points of departure (see, for example, Jaquette 1994; Jelin 1990; Alvarez 1990; Schild 1991; Radcliffe and Westwood 1993; León de Leal 1994). Original research focused primarily on women's struggles against military authoritarianism, their participation in processes of redemocratization, and the consolidation of women's movements in post-transition societies. Most recently, scholarship has focused on the effectiveness (or lack thereof) of women's political practices in the context of formal democracy, in which women's organizations must contend with ever-changing relations of power between the state and civil society, and within civil society. One example is the struggle for representation among NGOs, the so-called "NGOization" of social movement organizations (in which some organizations have gained interpretative power in negotiating development policies while others have been further marginalized (see Alvarez 1998; Tarrés 1997). At the center of this restructuring process is a reconfiguration of power relations between nation-states and the global economy, and a discursive struggle over the meaning of the "economy," typically constructed as formal and market-oriented, and its fragmented "others," such as non-market forms of production and women's work, which defy traditional categories of "reproduction" and "production" (see Gibson-Graham 1996). Likewise, there is struggle over the meaning of the state's role in providing for its citizens, and its converse: "private" forms of development. Neighborhood women's organizations' emphasis on making "women's work" more valuable to society raises issues about all three of these aspects of restructuring – particularly the invisible, gendered aspects, as they play out and shape the physical and social environments within which people work and live.

This resonates with Janine Brodie's (1994) observation that the gender dimensions of structural adjustment measures and the broader process of restructuring "extend far beyond the economic." In addition, they serve to restructure the public and private boundaries within which people live their daily lives and shape their expectations about work, family, and sometimes, politics. Neighborhood women's organizations thus serve as an important example of how women have actively engaged with "development" as it unfolds in specific cultural, spatial contexts. Furthermore, they shed light on the very assumptions of history and subjectivity upon which frameworks of "development" – as well as political practices – are based.

Ecuadorian neighborhood women's organizations and the politics of restructuring

In May 1992, several neighborhood women's organizations participated in a protest outside the Citibank office in Quito. Within a twenty-four hour period, over 100 women mobilized to protest against Citibank's freeze on US$80 million from the Ecuadorian Central Bank's account.[4] Their participation in this protest was an important public response to the economic crisis that the country faced. It was a public statement against what they viewed as Ecuador's dependency on foreign aid, especially from the United States, and it represented a challenge to the "development establishment" as the women involved in the protest saw it. Acting in their roles as mothers of families, they felt compelled to protest the role of foreign aid – in this case, Citibank – in exerting power over the Ecuadorian government. But while critical of what they perceive as economic and cultural imperialism in their nation, they also challenged the Ecuadorian government to redistribute wealth and socialize state-led welfare activities. Thus, on one level they acted as mothers of families, and by extension, as mothers of the "under-developed" Ecuadorian nation vis-à-vis First-World states. On another level, they positioned themselves in opposition to the Ecuadorian state and placed demands upon it for further access to their rights as consumers, that is, to their social and economic rights. In this sense, this type of protest was unprecedented in Ecuadorian history.[5] Participants in the protest publicly invoked a politicized notion of reproduction based on women's roles as consumers, as those most affected by the changes in consumer prices which accompany adjustment measures.

Since the early 1980s, women's organizations have emerged throughout Ecuador to address issues of economic survival, political and cultural rights, and gender-specific issues related to their roles in reproduction and community development. A conservative estimate of women's organizations with legal status, or *personería jurídica*, may be 80–100 at a national level (Centro María Quilla/CEAAL, 1990). If one includes all types of grassroots women's organizations, both those with *personería jurídica* and those without, in rural and urban areas, there may be as many as 500 to 800 groups (Rosero, interview, 21 November 1993). In Quito, over eighty neighborhood women's organizations exist, all of which have distinct relationships with other women's and feminist organizations, traditional (male-based) neighborhood associations or cooperatives, the Municipality of Quito, political parties, the church, the state, and NGOs.

Since 1981, the Ecuadorian state had negotiated over fifteen structural adjustment packages with the World Bank and the IMF. While there have been significant ideological and political differences among the past six governments,[6] all have generally embraced World Bank and IMF models of stabilization, adjustment, economic liberalization, and state modernization. The administration of Sixto Durán-Ballén (1992–6) serves as an example of how these policies have affected local communities and women's organizations. Through its "modernization plan," the Durán administration facilitated a number of structural changes at an unprecedented rate, with the primary goals of liberalizing the economy and dismantling the welfare state. Many of Durán's policies reversed the earlier Borja administration's "gradualist" adjustment policies and state-centered approach to economic development and political participation – with important consequences for neighborhood women's organizations. This restructuring process has been continued by populist President Abdalá Bucaram (August 1996–February 1997), and most recently by the administration of Jamil Mahuad (August 1998–present), culminating in the March 1999 financial crisis which immobilized the country, forced major bank closures, and led to a new round of national protests.[7]

The Durán administration's economic policy included the reduction of trade barriers, the promotion of export-led development, a series of privatizations of key national industries, and general support for the "free market." In addition, the administration restructured and downsized social and economic ministries, laid off 20,000+ state employees, centralized social policy concerns in the President's Office, and implemented a World Bank/IMF-designed Emergency Social Investment Fund (FISE, or Fondo de Inversión Social de Emergencia (Emergency Social Investment Fund)) to address the "social costs" of structural adjustment.[8] In this approach, social policy is viewed exclusively as a response to the negative effects of structural adjustment measures.

To strengthen the private sector's role in development, Durán's 1993–6

National Development Plan emphasized the "strengthening of community service networks, through actions promoted by the State, that bring together the participation of community based organizations and of groups from civil society and local governments such as NGOs and Municipalities" (quoted in Ojeda Segovia 1993: 215). Prior to this plan, the Borja administration (1988–92) had given considerable attention to local development and "popular participation" schemes – one result being the Community Network for Child Development, a project which provided funding to over 300 neighborhood women's organizations to manage community day care centers. Upon entering office, Durán sought to dismantle Borja's policies and establish his own set of plans, including his strategy to "decentralize the [Community Network for Child Development's] administrative activities and program execution, through processes of subcontracting with entities and organizations from civil society and local government that are accredited for such activities" (quoted in Ojeda Segovia 1993: 214). In practice, this meant eliminating funding for the Community Network and establishing a new, decentralized system in which private agencies were subcontracted to take over different aspects of conventional state responsibilities. For organizations supported by the Community Network, this meant a freeze on state funding and institutional support for the management of the daycare centers.

The administration's plan to induce economic "shock treatment" made it politically imperative to develop a structure for absorbing "social unrest" (Segarra 1997). The FISE was, therefore, rapidly inaugurated to pre-empt further unrest[9] and to shift responsibilities from the welfare state to the private sector – most notably to the increasingly organized NGO sector and their constituents: local grassroots organizations and poor communities. While some professionally oriented NGOs played active roles in the FISE negotiations, local organizations, which were often informal and without NGO status, typically did not. In this context, neighborhood women's organizations have been placed in an increasingly difficult situation, due both to the impacts they feel (individually and collectively) from the new social and economic policies, and to their lack of influence in political and planning arenas.

The state budget cuts have directly affected hundreds of women's organizations. In the FISE framework, funding has been given to newly formed organizations which politically support the Durán administration; already existing organizations that received funding from the Borja administration's Community Network of Child Development have lost out.[10] In this context, neighborhood women's organizations must compete with each other for increasingly limited funds, sometimes individually, and sometimes through coalitions with other civil organizations: middle-class NGOs, labor organizations, cooperatives, neighborhood associations, etc. Despite political discourse which claims that NGOs represent popular sectors (see, for example, Rodríguez 1994), they have relatively little institutional or interpretative power in the state/NGO decision-making process. Seeking access to the public, decision-making arena by placing collective demands on the state and through direct protest has, therefore, become an essential strategy for social change.

Two neighborhood women's organizations in Quito's southernmost district of Chillogallo serve as examples. Centro Femenino 8 de Marzo, located in the central neighborhood of Chillogallo, was established in 1985. Beginning in 1987, Centro Femenino 8 de Marzo began to organize women in the surrounding neighborhoods, and it was in this context that the second organization, Centro Femenino Nuevos Horizontes, came into being. Both of these organizations have *personería jurídica*, or legal status.

The two organizations combined have an active membership of approximately seventy-five women. The larger and more established – Centro Femenino 8 de Marzo – consists of fifty members; Centro Femenino Nuevos Horizontes has approximately twenty-five active members. Members range in age from 16 to 72 years old; most are in their thirties or forties. The organizations consist primarily of *mestiza* and some indigenous women, the majority having migrated to Quito from rural areas in the past five to twenty-five years, from households which represent the "structural poor," or the "new poor" (the growing number of people living at or below the poverty line that have emerged through measures of modernization).[11] The original members of Centro Femenino 8 de Marzo organized around three principal issues: (1) to strengthen their representation in community decision-making; (2) to learn practical skills and collectivize costs; and (3) to form a group in which they could talk about themselves and discuss themes relating to their lives as women.[12] The general meetings consist of two primary activities: *concientización* (consciousness raising) and practical training workshops. Often these activities are woven throughout the meetings so that, one week, the group dedicates itself to *concientización* and, the following week, it concentrates on training workshops. The consciousness-raising sessions include: (1) discussions about particular issues they face in their neighborhood (for example, a need for water on a particular grid of streets, a disagreement with local political leaders, or the need to establish a police station in their district); and (2) workshops led by organizations in Quito which focus on an array of issues: defining community needs, sexuality, alternative health and nutrition practices, violence, and the impacts of specific government measures and policies. The training workshops focus primarily on small-scale production (e.g. clothes, shoes, arts and crafts). The Center also buys food in bulk and distributes it on a credit basis to families associated with the Center.

Centro Femenino 8 de Marzo has placed demands on the Municipality for specific services, such as the establishment of a police station in Chillogallo in 1991, and has participated in several protests over the years. The organization maintains strong links with groups and political processes outside Chillogallo. As well, the Center dedicates itself to organizing women from adjoining neighborhoods in Chillogallo and in other southern districts of Quito. A portion of the organization's funds, which have been provided by international organizations such as Oxfam and Fundación CIPIE (a small Spanish foundation), provides small salaries for three or four women who act as *promotoras*, or organizers, in adjacent neighborhoods. It was in this way that the other organization was initiated.

Centro Femenino Nuevos Horizontes was formed when a group of women from Centro Femenino 8 de Marzo announced a meeting at the local market in Cuidadela Ibarra. Since its inception in 1987, more than twenty members have participated on a regular basis, the organization has established its *personería jurídica*, and the local church lends a room to the organization for its weekly meetings. In 1993 the organization was donated a plot of land in Ciudadela Ibarra, where its members eventually plan to build their own center. The Center's most important role has been in managing a community day care center, funded by the Borja administration's Community Network for Child Development. This day care center was launched collectively by a group of parents and by members of Centro Femenino Nuevos Horizontes.[13]

Like Centro Femenino 8 de Marzo, Centro Femenino Nuevos Horizontes has placed demands on the neighborhood cooperative, on the Municipality of Quito, and on state agencies for further access to social services and/or for stronger representation in community and city political processes. One goal of theirs has been to educate community members about women's organizations; to demonstrate that women's struggles are not necessarily separate from or divisive of broad community concerns.

Between 1992 and 1996, these organizations and several others in Quito and throughout Ecuador targeted the Durán administration's modernization plan. It was generally perceived to affect disproportionately poor urban and rural sectors, and specifically, because the Durán administration terminated the Community Network's funding for Centro Femenino Nuevos Horizontes' day care center as well as other important funding for community support networks. At the first International Women's Day march following Durán's entry into office (8 March 1993),[14] the central theme was the Durán administration's modernization plan. In organization workshops and meetings, and in Centro Femenino 8 de Marzo's newsletters, emphasis has been placed almost exclusively on restructuring measures.

Negotiating boundaries: women's political responses to restructuring

The political strategies that these neighborhood women's organizations have developed operate simultaneously within and against dominant, neoliberal development strategies. They are both a response to, and themselves have implications for, the restructuring of institutions and of daily life. While the political identity of the members of these organizations is derived from their socially ascribed traditional gender roles as mothers of poor families, and by extension, as caretakers of communities, they have made public and politicized their gender roles, thus challenging the existing social order through a number of means and at various levels.

First, they challenge traditional gender relations within their households and communities in their everyday encounters with family and community members, state officials, party and/or cooperative representatives, and movement activists.

In doing so, they challenge the social boundaries of reproduction and production. Likewise, they provide a critique of the state and its lack of "dependability" in, and commitment to, providing social welfare (Alvarez 1996). Perhaps this political strategy asserts their position as "clients" of the state and reproduces the notion of the state as paternal provider; none the less, they challenge its exclusionary citizen practices – specifically, its historical exclusion of indigenous, illiterate, and poor people. Thus, they invoke traditional gender roles to call into question male leadership in their communities and in the state; although in so doing they challenge public/private relations.

Second, their strategies reveal some of the contradictory aspects of neoliberal reform. On the one hand, local women's organizations are "targeted" as community service providers, thereby becoming more visible in policy and political arenas, and perhaps gaining some political "power" in their communities. On the other hand, they are expected to participate largely on a volunteer basis, and while they may be personally transformed from their participation, they none the less are working more than before. Thus they are more visible constituents of development, yet carry heavier burdens.

Third, by addressing both the Ecuadorian state's complicity in, and victimization by, the foreign debt crisis, they pose a challenge to national as well as international interests, thus revealing the contradictory transnational dimensions of Ecuadorian state reform. In this way, their strategies pose new strategic thinking about the boundaries of the political, which suggests new political openings despite the fact that, in an important sense, they position themselves on a nationalist political terrain and are addressing long-standing historical inequalities such as neocolonialism and poverty. Below I address these three points.

Negotiating public/private boundaries

In the context of neoliberal reform, in which responsibilities are transferred to local communities both "publicly" (e.g. to local municipalities) and "privately" (e.g. to households, and therefore to the realm of women's reproductive work), these women's organizations have made important connections among different spheres of institutional power (local, national, and international) and the effects of broad structural change on their daily lives. At the core of these organizations' economic and political strategies – including collectivizing food provision, defining their communities' needs, and protesting specific institutions – is the common argument that women's roles in social reproduction and domestic work are undervalued, largely due to the ways in which the public and private spheres of society structure women's and men's lives. By bringing traditionally viewed private concerns into the public arena, their strategies reveal a fundamental contradiction in any process of "modernization": the contradiction which arises through women's struggles to incorporate themselves into a system which presupposes a universal referent ("man"), but which in reality is based on exclusionary, gendered, and racialized practices. Particularly in a neocolonial context, in which race and nation as analytic categories serve powerfully to order modern society, theirs clearly is not only a struggle for access to material resources, but also a cultural struggle, in which they question the gendered, racialized, and nationalist foundations of the "modern" political and economic system.[15] In this way, their struggle both affirms their oppositional identity and reaffirms the dominant relations of power within which they are situated, thus illuminating what some have considered the contradictoriness of a postmodern political practice (Mercer, cited in Grewal and Kaplan 1994: 5).

As organized groups of women, they critique the ways in which gender serves to structure their daily work and family lives, yet they utilize their learned, "traditional" gender roles to confront the very institutional system and set of ideologies which has historically helped to normalize the gender division of labor in the modern economy. Their participation in the Citibank protest and in more recent citywide and nationwide protests against neoliberal reform have contributed, on one level, to strengthening their collective political identity as neighborhood women's organizations. This is something which cannot be taken away, even while their material base may be eroding. Furthermore, their actions have served to make public the "invisible" aspects of restructuring processes, such as how women share an "unequal burden" in reproductive-based survival strategies (see Benería and Feldman 1992), and in how the informal aspects of women's work in households and in "community management" are not accounted for in planning and development frameworks (see Arboleda 1993; Lind 1997). The impacts that women feel in their daily lives undoubtedly have led to their visible expressions of discontent with structural adjustment measures and decreases in social spending related to neoliberal development strategies. Based on their gendered identifications with processes of local reproduction and consumption, they have mobilized to address a wide range of issues which, while centrally related to their gender roles, must also be situated in terms of their national, ethnic, racial, and class identities.

For example, they are responding to the unequal burden that they perceive to have, as women, in their households, although they politicize their experiences in social reproduction not only in terms of gender but also in terms of class oppression, neocolonialism, and Ecuador's position as an "underdeveloped" country in crisis. That is, they are struggling for their rights as a gender-based class, but also as a marginalized economic class within Ecuador, and as Ecuadorian "citizens" within an international context, vis-à-vis the United States and other industrialized countries. Thus, their struggle crosses the boundaries of gender/class/race/nation and suggests that these aspects of identity are hardly separable in political practice. They are actively reconstituting gender relations in ways which intersect, fundamentally, with their positions as members of economic, ethnic, racial and national classes.

The contradictions of neoliberalism

The current shifts in the public and private dimensions of social welfare provision and economic restructuring further complicate interpretations of women's activism. This is especially true of neoliberal development strategies, which include decentralization measures and "popular participation" laws designed to integrate people into local development and planning processes with the aim of increasing local power, particularly for urban poor and indigenous/rural communities that have benefited little from the formal planning and political structures. On the one hand, it can be argued that this emphasis on decentralizing state power and enhancing local development helps to strengthen local organizations. In the process, many participants may gain a broader awareness of their locations in political and development processes and may become more active participants in them. On the other hand, women's organizations rely upon state, as well as private, funding to continue their day care centers, educational campaigns, and community development projects, and they are increasingly "targeted" to manage and/or participate as volunteers in community-level development projects, although not always with adequate funding. Thus, women's organizations are caught in a bind: they want to maintain their organizations, yet are forced to do so under increasingly adverse economic and political conditions. Centro Femenino Nuevos Horizontes, for example – and hundreds of others like it which lost state funding – are in the complicated position of struggling for political visibility and power at a time when their economic strategies for survival are hardly sufficient. Yet, they continue to provide the service for their communities, even without remuneration. This resonates with Sonia Alvarez's (1996) concern about neoliberal development strategies and the increasing "undependability" of states, as well as with Lourdes Benería's (1992) observation, based on her research in Mexico City, that women's struggles are increasingly "privatized" along with the broader privatizations taking place. But while Benería observes women relying almost exclusively upon households for survival (as opposed to seeking support from/within community organizations), significant sectors of poor women in Quito continue to work collectively to combat the economic crisis.

A related issue concerns their symbolic positioning vis-à-vis the Ecuadorian state. Politically speaking, these organizations place demands on the state and international development apparatus for further access to material resources. That is, their struggle is derived from their self-defined sets of needs, and the demands for rights that they make are based on these sets of needs. It is precisely this relationship between needs and rights that has led researchers such as Maruja Barrig (1996) to argue that so-called needs-based women's movements position themselves as "clients," or as a political class of "recipients," of state welfare policy. According to Barrig, this political positioning is based on a narrow definition of social rights, rather than on a more inclusive concept of citizen rights. Social rights, in her analysis, include those which are derived from collective articulations of needs, and are constituted through women's locations in the process of collective consumption, vis-à-vis state provisioning for its citizens. This characterizes poor women's organizations that compete with each other to struggle for state support. Citizen rights, Barrig argues, include social, economic, cultural, and political rights, and invoke a more inclusive notion of identity which, rather than provoking competition among marginalized groups, works to coalesce around differences of identity and community. Citizen rights, however, have been practiced in highly unorthodox and uneven ways in Latin American democracies.[16]

Considering this line of thought, when neighborhood women's organizations in Chillogallo, like other groups organized around collective consumption, struggle for "equality," in practice what they are struggling for is further access, for themselves and for their families and communities, to state resources which are defined and distributed through development agencies such as those of the current FISE and of the Dirección Nacional de la Mujer (DINAMU, or the National Women's Bureau). As they position themselves vis-à-vis the state, as an articulated (consumer) class with specific needs, they are also reinforcing their positions as marginalized groups in society. Hence, their political practice, and the implicit notion of political citizenship within it, is based on their direct needs rather than on a more universal notion of citizenship – one which, if used strategically by women's organizations, according to Barrig and others, might provide a stronger basis from which to build political coalitions (Barrig 1996; also see Lechner 1982).

Yet, I ask, what would a "universal" notion of citizenship entail? Women's organizations' derived sets of needs arise from their particular experiences in Ecuador's history of modernization and modernity (based on gender, ethnicity, race, geographic location, nationality, etc.). Through their political struggles, however, they provide a critique of the very process in which they have come to identify themselves, their needs and rights. In many ways, their struggles challenge fundamental aspects of these processes and reveal their contradictions; namely, social and economic ideologies which provide order in the "modern" household, nation, and economy, and which give meaning to the process in which they, as marginalized groups of women, have been "gradually and unevenly" incorporated into the modern labor force, into post-World War II development, and into ideologies of progress in Ecuador (see Olea 1995). This is contradictory, yet it has served significantly to reshape and widen the boundaries within which women's organizations, along with other marginalized groups in Ecuadorian society, have imagined the possibilities for social change. Undoubtedly, without the participation of women's organizations and other so-called new social movements in the recent series of strikes and protests, Bucarám's administration would not have been overturned. Therefore, while they emphasize access to material needs – what Barrig might refer to as struggling for social rights – they are also questioning other issues of power in society. The question remains, however, as to how much influence they might have in policy arenas. Indeed, their participation in the mass mobilization leading to the impeachment of President Abdalá Bucarám in February 1997 and their participation in the recent protests against the Mahuad administration are two examples of how local organizations have gained a stronger political presence, even if through spontaneous protest outside the "official" political system.

Rethinking national and international boundaries

Women's organizations which contest structural adjustment policies and neoliberal reform are best understood in terms of their impacts on institutional change and in terms of the new cultural spaces they have opened. National boundaries, and the boundaries between civil society and the state, have never been as unclear, nor as contested, as they currently are. Yet the Citibank protest, the neighborhood women's organizations' strategies to collectivize social reproduction, and the mobilizations against the Bucarám administration all bear witness to the fact that women's organizations (like other local organizations and social movements) are situating themselves strategically in these institutional relations of power in a very defined way. On one hand, Centro Femenino 8 de Marzo, Centro Femenino Nuevos Horizontes and other local women's organizations challenge the role of the Ecuadorian state as it guides the development process: the state is masculine, and must provide to its citizens (and some citizens are favored over others). On another level, the state is an oppressed, feminized embodiment of underdevelopment and neocolonialism, vis-à-vis the First World. Thus women have acted out, against Citibank, the IMF, and the international financial community, in order to defend their country against First-World interests. In both cases, the nation is the symbolic terrain upon which they have mobilized to combat the economic crisis, question the meaning of gender and women's work, and seek alternative forms of community provisioning and political structures. Yet they challenge the state's role in building a "nation" on the basis of exclusionary practices, thus "remaking the nation" from their oppositional locations within it (Radcliffe and Westwood 1996).

In this sense, neighborhood women's organizations' strategies are best understood in terms of how they locate themselves in specific struggles, rather than in terms of whether or not they embody "anti-development" struggles. They are not entirely rejecting the premises of Western development models, although they are, in fact, seriously challenging the premises and effects of neoliberal development strategies and the local, national and international boundaries within which "development" is deployed. At the heart of their struggle is a set of old issues: the meaning of the modern nation-state, citizenship, and economic survival. This is deeply intertwined with an ongoing struggle to affirm their identities as subjects *in* – rather than subjects *of* – dominant political and economic practices. Thus their subjective transformation is also a matter of "survival" – an idea observed, as well, in other studies of identity-based social movements in Latin America and elsewhere (see Alvarez 1998). As they construct local political and economic strategies in the midst of adjustment measures, they are contributing to an ongoing renegotiation of the social contract between states and citizens, to challenging the cultural center of development, and to inventing new urban cultural and political identities – thus responding proactively, rather than merely reactively, to the broader process of economic restructuring.

Notes

1 Many thanks to Lourdes Benería and Susana Wappenstein for comments on earlier versions of this chapter. Fieldwork for this chapter was conducted in Quito from June–August 1989 and from September 1992–December 1993, with support from the Inter-American Foundation and Fulbright-Hayes.

2 I define "development" as a set of discourses and practices and as a contested process, operating in various contexts of power, at multiple levels of political, economic and cultural life. I develop the argument on gender as a catalyst for women's mobilization in Lind 1992.

3 Put slightly differently, I examine how women's political practices are struggles for access to material resources as well as "struggles over interpretative power" within political and development arenas, drawing from Jean Franco's (1989) original work on historical narratives of gender and national identity in Mexico, and similar as well to research conducted on the Chilean women's movement by Teresa Valdés (1994) and Verónica Schild (1991 and 1998).

4 This protest was held outside the Citibank office in Quito. Citibank – New York, as the bank leading the group of foreign lenders to the Ecuadorian government, froze the Central Bank's assets because it claimed that the Ecuadorian government had defaulted on its loan payments. This act followed a dispute between the Ecuadorian government and Citibank regarding some specific guidelines of the loan repayment schedule. The following day, a group of approximately 100 women gathered outside Citibank's office to protest (see Lind 1992).

5 Other protests of this kind, led by women, have occurred throughout Latin America, such as the so-called "IMF riots" in Venezuela and Argentina, and the food riots in Brazil. See Daines and Seddon 1994 for a comparative analysis of women's roles in food riots and protests against the IMF and World Bank.

6 These governments include the transition of government of Jaime Roldós (1980–1, killed in a plane accident) and Osvaldo Hurtado (1981–4), the goverments of León Febres-Cordero (1984–8), Rodrigo Borja (1988–92), Sixto Durán-Ballén (1992–6), and Abdalá Bucarám (August 1996–February 1997), the interim government of Fabian Alarcón (April 1997–August 1998), and the government of Jamil Mahuad (August 1998–present).

7 For an analysis of the Abdalá Bucarám administration's economic policies, see Muñoz Jaramillo (1998) and Báez (1997). The recent financial crisis in March 1999 was catalyzed most immediately by the Mahuad administration's decision to lift the fixed exchange rate, thus placing the sucre at market value and leading to its devaluation from about 5,000 sucres/US\$1.00 in early February 1999 to over 12,000 sucres/US\$1.00 in late March. The multiple facets of this financial crisis will certainly have widespread impacts on most social sectors and on women's and other community-based organizations dependent upon state funding and/or limited incomes for their survival.

8 Ecuador is one of twenty-two Latin American countries that have implemented an Emergency Social Investment Fund, based largely on the original Bolivian model (see Benería and Mendoza 1995; Segarra 1997).

9 The Durán administration was responding most directly to the highly successful 1990 indigenous rebellion, and subsequent indigenous protests and labor strikes. It also anticipated further protest to its modernization plan by labor and indigenous groups. In this context, the FISE was launched under the political rhetoric that it would enhance NGO participation, and therefore citizen participation of indigenous and other marginalized sectors, in the national development process.

10 This form of clientelism, in which local communities are given access to funding and resources in exchange for political support, resonates with historical patterns of national development and political participation. In this sense, both the Borja admin-

istration and the Durán administration sought to gain political support through their policy agendas. In the case of the Durán administration, the government sought to gain political support for its collaborative state–NGO project design – a central component of the FISE. This, like Borja's policies, had both positive and negative effects, depending on where funding was provided, for which groups, and in which region of the country. However, the Durán administration's overall social spending was less than the Borja administration's, and while it is difficult to estimate the extent to which private (for-profit and non-profit) organizations compensated for this, it is clear that women's organizations and poor sectors in general have suffered disproportionately from Durán's relatively harsh adjustment measures.

11 According to my study of thirty-five members, average monthly household income is S/144,000, or US$80.00, and each household spends an average of S/125,480, or almost US$70.00, per month on "household purchases." In contrast, the national minimum wage at this time was S/66,000 (US$37.00), and despite Durán's policy to increase wages, the percentage increase in consumer prices continues to rise comparatively faster than the real minimum wage. In general, these figures place the Chillogallo households just slightly above the national poverty line. They therefore do not represent the poorest sectors, but rather the growing sector of the urban lower classes.

12 I provide a more in-depth description of the organization's history and activities in Lind 1992.

13 For an account of this process see "Historia de la creación de la guardería" in *Nuestra Voz*, no. 5, March 1993: 12–13.

14 The annual march on International Women's Day is both a celebration and a protest, and is one of the most important events for women's organizations in Ecuador and throughout Latin America. As such, the march in Quito every year, like those in other Latin American cities where similar marches are held, is an important strategic and symbolic move to publicize and challenge specific processes, institutions, events, and/or concepts. It is also for this day that women in Chillogallo named their center "Centro Femenino 8 de Marzo."

15 For an excellent overview of theories of national identity and nation-building in Ecuador, see Radcliffe and Westwood 1996.

16 When one considers, for example, that literate women in Ecuador gained the right to vote in 1918, while illiterate men and women (the subtext being indigenous people, who speak Spanish as a second language) only gained the right to vote in 1979 and were not massively integrated into the voting process until 1984 (see Menéndez-Carrión 1994), it is not surprising that the formal concept of citizen rights has been highly contested on a cultural basis.

10 (Re)negotiating selfhood and citizenship in the post-communist Czech Republic

Five women activists speak about transition and feminism

Julie A. Beck

Introduction

The Czech transition from socialism to capitalism provides an opportunity to examine key contradictions that exist between socialism and a capitalist market system and their corresponding ideologies. The aim of this chapter is to show how individual women attempt to reconcile these contradictions by looking at how they experience the transition to a market system. In the summer of 1995, I had the opportunity to conduct in-depth interviews in Prague with five prominent Czech women activists, intellectuals, and founders of non-governmental organizations (NGOs). All of these women currently live in Prague, range in age from 20 to 55, and are actively involved in civic work in the non-governmental sector.[1] The interviewees' professions include sociology, political science, law, and public administration. Their civic initiatives in the last five years encompass the founding and directing of civic organizations which address civic education, Roma (Gypsy) rights, AIDS prevention for prostitutes, and include a women's center, and a magazine for lesbian and bisexual women and a small legal information centre.[2] Intellectuals and professionals, these women make up part of a yet small Czech middle-class, and in this sense, they belong to a privileged elite. While they by no means represent the experiences, positions or sentiments of all Czech women, these women offer particularly dynamic interpretations of the post-communist transition precisely because of their civic and political activism, the analysis they bring to the transition, and their access to the new market.

These women's accounts reflect key oppositions between capitalist and socialist systems during the transition to a market economy and reveal their tenuous identities at the intersection of the various competing discourses of liberal capitalism, socialist egalitarianism, consumerism, Western feminism, and Czech feminist egalitarianism. As they grapple with self-definition and gender questions, they strive to reconcile such opposing ethics as individual self-fashioning/state dependence; uncertainty/predictability; fluidity/stability; availability/shortage; exposure/isolation; and personal responsibility/collective provision. This chapter attempts to illuminate how the confluence of the socialist past and the rapid entrance of a neoliberal market economy into the Czech Republic directly informs these women's sense of agency. I claim that these women's embrace of Western market culture and their feminist ideas are strongly tempered by the socialist legacy. That is, while they welcome the transition to a market economy and actively appropriate aspects of liberal individualism in the process of gaining a sense of self and public agency, they remain committed to a kind of feminist egalitarianism grounded in Czech traditions and certain aspects of their gender experience under state socialism.[3] In analyzing these women's accounts, I identify an ideological commitment to what I call "gender humanism,"[4] which, in part, reflects their effort to embrace that which is enabling, and resist that which is corrupting about capitalism. I construe gender humanism as a specific form of feminism committed to self-realization, political participation, citizenship, democracy, and egalitarianism; one which remains remarkably committed to certain egalitarian ideals of the socialist (and pre-socialist) past. Essentially, then, these women's emerging sense of agency and feminism must be viewed within the context of the socialist past. It is from their vantage point on the bridge between communist and capitalist societies and through waging a critique of materialistic values, Western gender constructs, and Western feminism, that these women endeavor to reconstruct their identities. In exploring the transition-in-progress as it is personally experienced and reconciled, then, I also aim to illuminate how feminism itself emerges from specific economic and political contexts, means decidedly different things in different settings, and serves quite different needs for women internationally.

The first section examines the quest for public agency and self-realization as it is waged from these women's location at the intersection of state repression (which discouraged individuality and demanded conformity) and a liberal democratic market economy (which promises a certain degree of independence and possibility for individual expression). I claim that while these women's participation in the market culture provides a central arena for the exercise of personal agency, it does not signify an embrace of liberal individualism or of materialistic values per se, but rather is indicative of their struggle for individual and personal development as free political subjects and citizens of the newly democratizing Czech Republic. Analysis of their accounts, in the second section, aims to provide insights that raise new questions and complicate existing debates within feminism. Western feminists, in addition to pointing out the contradictions in state socialism for women's equality (see Corrin 1992), have critiqued the transition for reproducing Western forms of women's subordination in Eastern Europe (see Einhorn 1993; Mische 1993; Watson 1993a). Taking these important analyses into account, this case study attempts to illuminate some of the intricacies of the transition by showing how particular actors experience the pressures of transition. It reveals that Czech women's interaction with Western market ideologies yields) more complex scenarios than, for example, simply the ascent of "masculinism" in East-Central Europe with the advent of free market thinking and institutions (Watson 1993a). I argue that the transition to a market system is in fact generating a critical reaction by certain Czech women that is characterized by an ideology of feminist egalitarianism, which both differentiates itself from Western feminism and critically contests capitalism's materialistic values and commodification of ethical life. From the vibrant dualism of these women's position at the crossroads between state socialism and neoliberal capitalism emerges an ideology of gender humanism that accompanies their struggle both to shape their identities and futures as women and to become free political subjects and citizens within the new Czech society.

Personal agency: at the crossroads of socialism and liberal capitalism

> One aspect of the communist regime was that everybody was sure that there was no possibility to win in a conflict with the bureaucracy, or with the power ... the people were apathetic.
>
> (Jaroslava)

All of the women interviewed fundamentally accept the transition to a market economy and more democratic governance, and see it as a long-awaited and welcome change from state socialism.[5] The risks and opportunities that the transition presents, such as career options, avenues for free speech, products for consumption, a greater variety of everyday choices, and greater control over one's life options, are confidently embraced by these women as personal challenges which they approach head-on with feelings of excitement, energy and promise. Eva, for example, describes the current feeling in Czech society as an exciting mixture of flexibility, consumerism, and creative possibility:

> you go into a shoe shop – and you can pick! It's the same with your clothes – everybody can have their own style, they can choose and combine things to create it. ... I think this is the general mood on the planet, this post-modern lifestyle, where no one idea or way of being dominates – *everything* is in style!

In all of the interviewees' descriptions of the transition, what is striking is the degree to which their discussion of personal development, freedom, and self-discovery is embedded within the neoliberal discourse of opportunity, consumption, individuality, and market exchange. Flexibility and choice, and descriptions of individual autonomy and freedom, are iterated in conjunction with market freedoms. For example, when asked what has most changed since the fall of the former regime, Vlasta says:

> How can I explain it? It has to do with money ... before, you would go to buy something, butter, for example, but it wasn't there. We didn't know a situation where if you wanted to travel to, say, Geneva, you just go – not first get approval to go and then tomorrow you cannot go, no – you just go!

And indeed, in addition to availability of consumer products, and with more free time, which this convenience affords, the transition is providing these particular women with the opportunity to make great strides in their careers. This includes the possibility to travel, to write and speak openly, or to pursue entrepreneurial jobs, as well as opportunities to organize politically, all of which have immensely boosted their self-confidence. Thus, despite their critiques of the West and material values, reviewed later on, none of them disagrees that the liberal democratic revolution and a competitive market economy are a needed and desirable change from the repressive inertia of the former system. Vlasta points out that for a woman today to have access to money means she has possibilities and vastly augmented life options: "just making money for managing – we didn't know it before ... to have money allows the simple *possibility* for all of these things!" After reiterating the problem of unpredictable consumer goods, shortages, and patronizing travel restrictions that dictated one's time and curtailed autonomy under state socialism,[6] she continues, "you can imagine how it looked before, yes? ... We didn't know the power of money – and this is what put society into motion." In the aftermath of the restrictive socialist economy, rapid exchanges of goods and services and cash flow, thus, are seen not only to empower the individual, but also to stimulate and move the entire society.

The question becomes how to interpret these women's clearly exuberant reception of the market system. To what extent does it indicate agreement with the neoliberal discourses of privatization and individual responsibility that accompany this system, and signify an acceptance of the basic tenets of liberalism, individualism, and consumerism? What in fact is money expected to buy in the wake of the "command economy?" A hint lies in the problem of agency as it is related to these women's recent experience of harshly curtailed personal and political subjectivity under state socialism. Agency and volition are central themes that surface in these women's discussion – the challenge of being personally accountable for one's life, which from their perspective entails not being "dependent on the state." It is through the centrality of their struggle for agency that we can begin to comprehend the meaning they assign to the privatization and commodification processes of neoliberalism, and to see how personal agency becomes a necessary precondition for any future Czech feminism. I suggest that money and the market system, beyond its practical benefits, is invested in these women's estimation, with a particular power and potential for self-discovery and individuation. On the one hand, we see that money represents the freedom to participate in such basic tacks as "managing" one's daily affairs, making personal choices such as which doctor to go to (before decided by the state), and the simple possibility to access services and forms of social mobility. But significantly, on the other hand, in the women's conversation market liberalism and the surge of commodities are continually invested with hopes for change from the former restrictive culture of the centralized socialist economy. In this sense, money and the opportunity for material gain appear to be largely symbolic of the dream under state socialism for freedom and the hope for a better life today.

It would appear that these women currently envision the market as a tool in their process of gaining individual agency and a sense of subjectivity as citizens in the wake of the repressive state socialist regime. But what is interesting is that, at the same time, they reject the specifically materialistic values it has imported, as we shall see. This contradiction, such that these women appropriate aspects of market freedoms yet simultaneously reject neoliberal ideology, can only be more fully understood in historical context. Their "market discourse" must be understood in the context of recent experience of the tightly closed society and repressive state regime in which the chance to actively make even the smallest daily choices let alone life decisions, or to express individuality, was quite literally impossible.[7] For Eva, the transition to a market economy means the celebration of activity and initiative in the wake of imposed passivity. She says:

> Socialist realism was in the past, where everybody was under this pressure of being conformed, being the same, being average. No one was supposed to be something else, or even *themselves*, because it was dangerous.

Acquiring monetary goods and functioning within the new market-based society are associated with personal daring, risk taking, and a kind of courageous heroism. When situated in historical context, then, these women's enterprising activities mean far more than a desire for wealth, social status, or consumption. Alena illuminates the relevance of material goods to the desire for non-conformist modes of expression and uniqueness:

> There's a sort of courage and heroism of the people now, because they did not know how to "enterprise," and it is a risk compared to the very secure situation before, under communism. ... I interpret [the proliferation of materialistic values] as a very natural stage when you can *confirm your subjectivity* through your efficiency to earn money, which at the same time is not to be dependent on the state. (My emphasis.)

Interestingly, then, Alena views the current near-obsession with material gain as a necessary stage of the transition, which for the moment, she claims, appears to be the most appropriate path towards self-realization.

Thus, the themes of earning money and "enterprising" are directly associated with independence from the state, which surfaces as a central theme in the interviews. "Enterprising" is accompanied by direct references to "confirming subjectivity" and to the possibility to be autonomous, active, public citizens, not possible during communism. These women's particular relationship to the market economy, to money and the material goods and services that have entered the country, then, is largely abstract; the economic transition speaks to their desire for individuation and the sense of being a proactive citizen of the new Czech society. Opportunities for material gain with the liberalization of the economy and society, at this stage of the transition, appear to symbolize all of the freedoms lacking under state socialism. In this sense, these educated, professional, and publicly active women find themselves at the intersection of the exigencies of the former socialist regime's repressive, conformist agenda, and a wide-open field of opportunity for self-discovery and self-enactment that they attribute to the free market, and which the transition affords elite women.

Aesthetic gains of the revolution

In addition to affording certain pragmatic freedoms, I have suggested that money, material goods, and services are interchangeable with certain aesthetic values; they signify motion, risk, independence, and self-affirmation. But the transition is also fostering other outlets for individual agency and personal discovery besides access to money and commodities. Alena, stressing the central importance of new-found individual freedoms, acknowledges that although "enterprising" is the current popular pastime, the sense of personal agency and volition that it affords can in fact be found in a wide variety of activities: "It need not be through enterprise only, it can be through acting in other ways – but it is really so important, this possibility to act freely!" These women are experiencing the revolution on a personal level as much as on a political level. They see in the relative democratization brought on by the transition the chance for self-discovery and gaining personal agency through which to broaden their careers and life options, and for taking political and civic initiative, which fosters a sense of citizenship and individual sovereignty not experienced before. For example, in reference to the magazine for lesbian and bi-sexual women she started, Eva exclaims emphatically:

> We see [the transition] as a very important thing by which to find out that you can be creative, and you can work towards your goals, you can create you own life – as you want, as you wish! You don't have to be passive – it's the end of passivity!

Alena suggests that freedom to act publicly of one's own volition provides a necessary self-test of one's abilities and allows for a "realistic" self-concept. In reference to her work at the women's center, she states,

> you learn who you are through your efforts, you actually try something, you either succeed or you fail, and through that you confirm or find out what are your abilities. I know people who only just now discovered what they are talented for – now they can really find their identities through *acting*.

Her words reveal newfound agency and pro-active self-discovery – being able to do something, to exert one's will finally and definitively after decades of collective passivity and conformity. It is precisely this ability to act of one's own volition that constitutes the most cherished "good" of the revolution, and surfaces as a principal theme in these interviews.

The aesthetic values the transition yields are perhaps most directly found in the possibility to pursue new career paths and in the opportunities for grass-roots political organizing that have opened up. Careers have grown tremendously for

these and other similarly positioned women (see Š'tatsná 1995). Both the practicing of taking responsibility for oneself and the desire for personal growth, for
women who do not have to struggle to fulfill their fundamental survival needs,
can be seen as responses to past restrictions and enforced dependency on the
state. As Alena explains:

> It's a huge difference. I'm traveling, I have twenty times as many contacts as
> I had before, and it seems I just started living another way. And this is the
> case for many women. So they just want to use this chance, benefit from the
> chances, the freedom, the many possibilities – new jobs, more opportunities.

She claims that the revolution provided the chance to do meaningful work as a
researcher and sociologist, to make career choices rather than having a somewhat limited and planned life.

> Women here, as well as men, also see their chance now, so of course many
> women are very eager ... now they have the time and chance to realize
> themselves. This is true in my case as well, because before my work did not
> make much sense. But now it is much better.

In addition to career opportunities and material goods and services that allow
for self-discovery and "managing" one's life, the women speak of the newly felt
possibility for political agency in the form of grass-roots political and civic organizing. Eva describes the process of decision making in running her organization
and magazine for lesbian and bi-sexual women with the same exuberance and in
much the same terms in which economic freedoms are described:

> We discuss things that are new to us, for example, how to raise money. This is
> something that two years ago we just didn't know, or how to communicate
> with institutions, this is something was just learned also – or the trade laws of
> this country. We are organized, an organization, and this is something that
> every organization needs to know – law, including our human and civil rights.

Eva further acknowledges the liberating aspects of such tasks as fund raising for
her organization, public discussion, making links with other organizations and
institutions, and learning about human and civil rights. Similarly, just as Vlasta
found "simple possibility" in what money could buy, she also finds purpose and self-
discovery in the possibility to go out into the streets to perform her AIDS education
work with prostitutes, make international contacts, and attend conferences, rather
than being restricted to the academic sphere under state socialism, where she wrote
text books and conducted sociological studies for the socialist government.

> [the revolution] was the possibility to do something really useful, yes? You
> can describe all the time-tables, data, and one day you realize that you have
> had enough. I wanted to prove to myself that I was able to do something

with reality. Because, also, at a certain age, you would like to have something behind you, not only articles in the pigeon hole!

In this stage of the transition, the newness of relative democratic freedom is experienced as an avenue to creative expression. In addition, then, material gain is not solely representative of greed, or consumer avarice; it also serves for these women as a metaphor for self-discovery and civic initiative. The market economy and liberalism are equated with the mere opportunity to exert one's will and exercise citizenship and subjectivity in fundamental ways.

A socialist egalitarian critique of materialistic values

In actualizing personal career gains and participation in civil society within the arena of the emerging market system, I suggest that these women appropriate liberal market freedoms and liberal individualist ideology selectively, rather than uncritically accept the new market culture. They grapple with and struggle to reconcile two opposing ethics, one associated with socialism and the other with neoliberal, consumer capitalism. We find perhaps the strongest evidence of their location at the intersection of consumption-oriented market liberalism and socialist egalitarianism in their directed critique of capitalist cultural values. Here, profound feelings of ambivalence toward mass privatization and liberalism as an ideology can be detected in these activists' explicit criticisms of materialistic values and commodification of ethical life in Czech society. For instance, Jiřina confides that she feels the necessity to earn money in order to protect herself from "the very aggressive life" that market competition and the collapse of the socialist regime have ushered in. She expresses reluctance toward the society's changing values, stating that "before 1989, what was valued was intellectual power; today it is money ... so it was very difficult for me to change my thinking." Expressing doubt about the new societal ethic developing within the neoliberal revolution, she continues:

> My career has benefited from the revolution because in the previous times I would never have been able to be a lawyer because I wasn't a member of the Communist Party. But frankly, I do not feel that I am free – rather, freedom, I think, depends upon the system of *values* in the society.

Here, she throws into question the new "system of values" Czechs are faced with during the mass marketization of their society. Alena expresses similar ambivalence, making nostalgic reference to socialist egalitarianism in light of the new hierarchical relationships between workers and employees in the newly privatized corporations,

> It was a caricature, these "comrade relations," but on the other hand, it has been also internalized, you know? ... Czechs were used to very equal

relationships between the chiefs and the employees – maybe even between men and women.

In addition, Jiřina expresses concern about the direction of Czech society as a whole. She notes the lack of "broadmindedness" and the "low feeling for global issues," or intolerance, by Czechs, who have been catapulted from extreme isolation under communism, particularly since the 1968 Soviet invasion, into a fast-paced commodity culture. She warns, "we are going to be a pretty strong consuming society, I would say, much more than in America even, because it is something new here, and everybody is trying to catch up." In addition, Vlasta states cynically:

> We have a society which is full of gold-diggers, and we have a lack of, how do you say, a genteel bourgeoisie. We don't have a certain refined ethic, everybody likes fast money, yeah? They have no patience. For the future, I think it brings problems. … The people, they would like to be immediately rich. The social philosophy seems to be "easy money," "easy money." This I find very dangerous.

Jaroslava is highly critical of what appears to her to be an excessive government privatization plan, acknowledging that a free market is necessary for civil society, but that plans to privatize the highways, hospitals, the postal service, and medical care is "stupidity." We hear a strong critique of the entrance of material values into the Czech Republic, which is accompanied by a critique of the West, particularly the United States. Finally, in Alena's reluctance to simply discard the past, we can observe the ideological contradictions that arise from the uncomfortable clash of the socialist past and the capitalist future:

> That is what is so funny about this whole story, this socialism. People critique it but they in a sense also internalized it. They took something from it, they adopted it for the psyche … it cannot be seen as just white or black, it's very, very complex.

Thus, embedded in these women's critiques are constant, at times nostalgic, references to the socialist past. The interviewees position themselves between socialistic principles of equality and liberal notions of freedom, not entirely rejecting but drawing from certain of socialism's egalitarian principles. The past is viewed equally as something to be rejected and yet, as a grounding resource to be incorporated into the future. Their ambivalent relationship to the past (and the present), which are alternately and selectively eschewed or embraced (in Eva's words, "chosen and combined") provides the thread that runs through their discussion. In their discussion of their relationships to Western feminism, as the next section reveals, these women yet again place themselves at the interstices of two competing discourses – socialist egalitarianism and feminist egalitarianism.

Czech gender humanism as a reaction to "Western feminism"

> The term "feminism" – look, that is a difficult question. First, to call herself a feminist, to be a feminist here in the Czech Republic, means to diminish or liquidate herself. It's unacceptable, so every feminist here says, "Oh, I am anti-feminist."
>
> (Jiřina)

As I have suggested, while individual and political agency begin to surface in the post-communist era and are intricately intertwined with participation in the burgeoning market and consumer society, these women embrace neither materialistic values nor liberal individualism. Rather, their appropriation of consumerism and a market discourse can be viewed as a celebration of newly felt freedoms, especially that of personal volition. One could even claim that in their assuming of agency and initiative in pursuing careers and individual and political forms of self-expression, these women are participating in liberal feminism. However, their position in relation to feminist discourse is complex and equivocal (for example, the rejection of ideology *per se*, including feminism, is common among women from formerly communist countries). My conversations with these women illuminate several insights into the complexity of gender questions in the Czech Republic. First, perhaps more so than individual agency, *political* agency and freedom are still repressed and constrained by the yet underdeveloped public sphere. That is, within the Czech Republic's young democracy, the concept of exercising individual and collective public democratic rights in general, let alone women's rights, is quite new.[8] In addition, their particular historical experience informs a feminist outlook that is very different from those found in Western feminism. The possibility of a women's "movement" at present appears to be supplanted by the nascent struggle for political subjectivity and citizenship in general.

We cannot begin to speak of feminist agency in the Czech Republic, then, without attempting to understand the post-communist challenge of trying to habituate oneself after forty years of Soviet occupation to a new identity not only as individuals who exercise personal agency, but as active political, citizen subjects. These women are only just now tasting the basic democratic freedoms taken for granted in the West. The first requisite of exercising democratic freedoms appears to be the regaining of national (versus Soviet) identity as Czech citizens. As a political scientist, Jaroslava, insisting that "human rights" in general is the most important problem, explains that citizens feel a sense of fractured national identity as a result of the Soviet occupation and the split of Czechoslovakia in 1993 into the Czech and Slovak republics.[9]

> Why the women's movement is not so strong here is because I think first, you need to have the feeling of citizenship, and then you can depend on

other rights – gender, minority, and so on. … In the women's movement in the US, it is taken for granted that the participants feel themselves to be citizens of the United States, yeah?

In addition, to a general political apathy the women describe, the current lack of public discussion of gender issues might be understood as a particular reaction to the socialist past. The women repeatedly cite the infamous Czechoslovakian Communist Women's Union as the main reason why women in general do not want to organize politically or belong to formal feminist organizations. Vlasta speaks of the widespread distrust by Czech women toward politicizing women's issues. Thus, concerning political agency, these women are located in the middle zone between possession of a strong sense of citizenship and political subjectivity and enacting a positive feminist agenda.

This dilemma is most clearly manifested in a second problem concerning national identity: the women's relationship to the concept of rights. In the nascent democracy, the prospect of women (and men) taking civic initiative, and conceptualizing rights in general, is quite new. For example, Eva explains that women are still often found in "second-class work" in factories, as cleaning ladies, or as vendors in food and clothes shops; that discrimination in job advertisements seeking men exclusively persists; and even that forced gynecological exams are still sometimes performed on women before they are hired to insure that they are not pregnant. But she is pessimistic about her organization's ability to address these problems:

> I don't think we can influence these kind of things because women often do not even *recognize* discrimination against them as women, they hardly would think that they have to stand up for women's rights.

Eva's magazine and information center are trying to educate Czech women about their legal rights, but this is not an easy task. For example, concerning the common practice in Prague of lesbian women being denied entrance into bars where gay men generally congregate, she states, "A very serious problem is that lesbians do not *feel* discriminated against. There is a persistent passivity among them. There really is no level of consciousness about rights, basic human rights, and civil rights." Thus, despite the success these women report in terms of developing their own personal agency and initiative, largely expressed through a language of and practices afforded by economic liberalization, democratization has not automatically meant enactment of political agency for most women. Indeed, inertia persists at the level of grass-roots organizing, partly because of democratic inexperience and partly because of continued state centralization of power and control.

In addition to the problems of citizenship and rights, a third issue arises concerning the conceptualization of gender oppression. Despite the fact that state socialism left a legacy of political and public passivity, its institutional efforts to address gender, especially in the early years, have emboldened these women in important ways which directly influence their approach to women's issues.

Despite certain forced efforts towards gender equality employed by the socialist regime in large part to facilitate rapid industrialization (see Heitlinger 1979), their discussion nevertheless reveals deeply embedded notions of social and gender equality which they believe separates them from Western women's experience of patriarchy. Drawing on her experience as a worker during the socialist regime, Vlasta proudly differentiates herself from Western women:

> I think that in comparison with women in Western countries, [Czech women] are used to working much more, because we had a big employment of women. And we still have a big employment of women, and we have, well – equality – the feeling of keeping my power, yes? And it also provided a *chance* for women … socialism kept equality by force.

Clearly, the relative gender equality achieved during socialism is a major source of female power and confidence which has carried over into the post-communist period. What is ironic is that while these women acknowledge that state-mandated full incorporation of women into public paid employment provided them with crucial education, skills and self-confidence, they simultaneously implicate the state as the root of their oppression. (The state, not men or patriarchy *per se*, was seen to be the "enemy" and principal source of oppression during socialism. Women's central position in the "safe" and esteemed refuge of the family prevented them from seeing their situation as oppressive (Šiklová 1992; Havelková 1992).) Alena acknowledges the fundamental difference between eastern and Western concepts of the public and the private. Concerning the domestic realm of the home, she explains that due to women's work outside the home, the private sphere and motherhood take on a unique meaning:

> The private is not perceived as a prison for women. It's *not* a prison because women share authority with men. And also, although the value of the family is very high, the woman is not even much present in the family [due to working outside of the home].[10]

Thus, women's status and position under state socialism was complex, for they attained a certain status from employment and maintained a central position in the non-state-controlled sphere of the family and the secondary economy.

Despite state socialism's failure to fully eradicate gender inequality and women's "double burden" (see Corrin 1992; Heitlinger 1979), highly valued principles of egalitarianism surface in these women's discourse. Somewhat ironically, they identify gender egalitarianism as an integral part of their socialist and also their cultural past.[11] Alena explains that a general ethic of egalitarianism in fact preceded socialism, "This country was extremely egalitarian in tradition when in the pubs you have the worker sitting beside the university professor, and nobody is aware of any difference."

In a somewhat similar vein, some of these women distinguish themselves from Western feminists through reference to a "European cultural tradition" of egalitarianism, which they trace to European cultural ethics concerning gender norms such as male "chivalry." Jiřina sternly warns against emulating Western feminism's focus on patriarchy, and even its involvement in formal politics:

> I wouldn't be happy if it would go the way of the United States, like *legislated* action [for sexual equality], because I think that it would go against our very deeply rooted European tradition, and I am afraid it would ruin this society.

"European tradition," they claim, is also associated with a "softer," more aesthetically inclined culture than America's that values female sensuality and reveres femininity. Western feminist critiques are seen as antithetical and threatening to this tradition (which Jiřina notes ironically is itself often as incompatible with women's experiences under socialism as rural and factory workers). According to several of the interviewees, a woman's power and strength lie in her femininity, her sexuality and her ability for motherhood. Alena claims that Western feminists from Protestant countries in particular tend to view a woman's wish to "be beautiful … and wanting to be sexy … as something really incompatible with emancipation." Jaroslava suggests, "Maybe this is the reason why Western feminism is very difficult to be accepted, due to those radical (feminist) wings." In addition, these women deny the seriousness of the threat of "reversion back to traditionalism" in Eastern and Central Europe since the 1989 revolution, which has worried Western feminists.[12] In a similar vein, Jaroslava, although she does not agree that gender relations are ideal in the Czech Republic, points out that gender inequality is a large-scale social problem and should not be reduced to a question of gender roles – of who does which tasks – but ought to be expanded to include "how women are valued within the society on the whole."

Finally, these women's attitudes towards Western mass media, which in Alena's words permeate Czech society with representations of a sexualized "empty femininity," are intricately interwoven with their anti-Western-feminist position and the way they situate their own feminist ideas within the rapidly Westernizing Czech culture. For example, Alena refers to television and advertising images of Western women as "dependent, stupid beings … interested only in fashion – just empty, very empty." She claims that such depictions are so foreign to Czech women's understanding of gender that they distance themselves from these images.[13] In addition, these blatantly sexist images only confirm their idea that Czech women do not need feminism like Western women do.

Thus, in light of the problems of national identity, citizens' rights, and the complexities of gender concepts in the transitioning Czech Republic, I suggest that these women's "feminism" is currently less characterized by a positive political agenda than by an ethic of feminist egalitarianism that is informed by the socialist past and certain Czech traditions. In addition, the positive aspects of their gender experience under state socialism and the egalitarian ethic of certain

Czech traditions influence these women's reception of the market economy; it appears that ultimately they only conditionally embrace economic liberalism. Similarly, their past knowledge and experience both of opportunities in public-sector jobs and government, and of state repression under state socialism, leads them to wage a critique of Western feminism and to construct their own feminist paradigms.

A spirit of feminist resistance

Not only then are these women's concepts of feminism constructed both in concert with their socialist past and in contrast to their interpretation of Western feminism, but their particular strain of feminist egalitarianism, which I refer to as gender humanism, is undergirded by a foundation of resistance. Perhaps most indicative of the undercurrent of feminist egalitarianism is the way in which this resistance surfaces in these women's wariness towards the challenges to gender equality that are beginning to surface in the Czech Republic within the free-market system. As Vlasta points out, there are signs that capitalism is having a negative effect on the employment opportunities of many women at the lower end of the skill and education ladder.[14] She elaborates on how the schism between men and women's incomes is widening. "The general conditions of the state factories are the worst ones, yeah? And who stayed in the state enterprises on the whole – women." In addition, she draws a connection between the market economy and the growth of prostitution and sex tourism since the Velvet Revolution and the opening of the borders, which has become a very real problem. Vlasta claims that unemployment is affecting many young women, even those just out of middle school.

> They don't want to go to high school, they want to make money. But many young girls out of school are unemployed now. This is one of the biggest problems – nobody [no employer] wants them. ... And also, we don't have hard currency [which prostitution procures].

Referring to prostitution, she adds, sardonically invoking the law of free market economies, "When you have more demand, you also have more supply!"

And Jiřina contradicts her own anti-Western-feminist stance in saying that today she feels that social expectations pressure women to put family needs first and business second such that "it is seen as okay to ruin your career." (She explains that even women who can afford to hire help with domestic chores and child care are expected to manage their own households and children.) She concludes, "I feel that this is the main thing that keeps women down." Eva also expresses awareness of discrimination and the necessity to wage a gender-based resistance against the current modes of employment discrimination against women, stating, "I personally think that if I were to refuse the fact that I am a women, I would lose myself – I would lose my identity." In addition, Alena relates the results of a comprehensive survey of Czech women: "The women said that they do not feel any gender discrimination, but that in the case that they should experience any, they would protest right away...." Finally, in the vein of resistance, Jiřina takes a pro-woman stance, expressing willingness to take direct action against sexism: "God forbid if anybody would treat me differently or underestimate me. This is something that I absolutely cannot bear – I am very aggressive about the question of women's equality!"

Conclusion

This chapter has examined how specific elite women experience the contradictions between shifting political and economic systems, and how these women are positioning themselves within the competing discourses that accompany the massive transition from state socialism to capitalism in the post-communist period. In publicly enacting their own agency, a possibility which the influx of the market and democratic freedoms have offered them, they appropriate aspects of liberal individualism and reject internalized passivity. But in simultaneously drawing upon positive aspects of socialist egalitarianism and waging a sustained critique of materialistic values, these women essentially refuse to embrace liberal individualism, liberal feminism, and many aspects of the new market culture. Rather, their exuberant manifestations of public agency and personal initiative are more accurately interpreted as reflective of a struggle for self-realization, individual identity, political subjectivity, and democratic citizenship in the aftermath of state repression. The socialist legacy, then, is Janus-faced, for at the same time that it incites in these women to escape from its repressive constraints on personality, its egalitarian principles and achievement of mass education, training, and full employment for women sustain a strain of resistance against new signs of gender discrimination, as well as provide the foundation from which these women differentiate their feminist egalitarianism from Western liberal feminism. This legacy, coupled with pre-socialist Czech forms of gender equality and "European traditions," which boast of complementarity between the sexes, may provide yet another point from which Western market values are contested even as certain aspects of the market system are embraced.

How the transition will play out is another question, one this research raises but cannot answer. At this point in the transition, I have argued that we can, however, identify in these women's discourse a stance in favor of gender humanism, characterized by the combination of their struggle for personal identity and public agency. Furthermore, gender humanism, I claim, is indeed feminist, for although devoid of a critique of patriarchy, it is firmly grounded in these women's positive experience of relative gender equality in socialism; and it is humanist both in its reaction to state repression and in its quest for individual expression. Perhaps, most promising, as the capitalist transition wages on, these women do not hesitate to express strong resistances to creeping schisms in the actual and ideological premises of egalitarianism, premises they experienced in significant ways under state socialism and claim to have inherited from even earlier. If we in the West can learn anything from these women's stance at the crossroads of the historical passage from socialism to capitalism, perhaps it would be that resistant mentalities and struggles against neoliberalism will continue to engage questions of citizenship, agency and feminist egalitarianism in their various configurations.

Notes

1   Women constitute approximately 70 per cent of grass-roots organizations in the Czech Republic. Whereas women's influence in "formal" politics since 1989 has declined substantially, their participation in the "informal" sphere of civil society outnumbers that of men. For an analysis of this phenomenon, see Einhorn 1991; Mische 1993; Šiklová 1992; Lovenduski 1994.

2   I employ pseudonyms in the text, for my purpose, rather than to focus on specific personalities, is to reveal how these women's positionality and perspectives influence their present struggles as women and shape their ideas about feminism.

3   The positive aspects of these women's gender experience under state socialism include the gains in self-confidence they report due to the socialist policy of providing women's higher education and technical training, and requiring women's full employment in the public sphere. In addition, women inadvertently derived status from their role in the domestic sphere, which, under socialism, provided a refuge from the state (Havelkova 1993). My reference to the interviewee's reported gains from socialist egalitarianism, however, is not meant in any way to neglect or deny the vast gender inequalities that prevailed under state socialism, which have been well documented (see Heitlinger 1979; Corrin, 1992).

4   The phrase "gender humanism" embodies contradictions. Humanism connotes individualism, which is generally at odds with feminist principles. But in its more broad reference to personal sovereignty and self-realization it becomes a useful concept; I claim that these women combine a renewed quest for self-realization with a form of feminist egalitarianism. In the text, I use gender humanism interchangeably with feminist egalitarianism (which includes socialist egalitarianism). And I distinguish feminist egalitarianism from liberal feminism. I refrain from employing the term "feminism" *per se*, for East-Central European feminists have argued extensively against applying Western feminist concepts to Eastern Europe. Claiming that both men and women were oppressed by the state under state-socialism, they contest simple exportation of Western feminist concepts of patriarchy, the gendered separation between the public and private spheres, and the desirability of a women's identity politics (see Havelkova 1992; Šiklová 1992; Funk and Mueller 1993; Snitow 1993; Šmejkalová-Strictland 1993). Rather, somewhat similar to the struggle for a redefinition of feminism engaged in today by women of color in the United States, these Czech women reject what they see to be limitations of mainstream, middle-class American feminism. Hence, in seeking new ways of understanding differently situated women's struggles, I employ the term "gender humanism" in an attempt to capture, if not completely, these women's clearly woman-focused concerns and strong commitment to sexual equality combined with their hopes for self-realization and dignity in the transition from communism.

5   The Soviet-implanted regime in Czechoslovakia after the 1968 invasion was particularly repressive. In response to the famed "Prague Spring," a social movement led by Dubček and Czech intellectuals to reform the Communist Party, a period of intense repression known as the "Normalization" period followed which lasted up until the Velvet Revolution of 1989. "Normalization" included occupation by the Soviet army, repression of freedom of speech and travel, political trials, and the persecution and "proletarianization" of vast numbers of citizens, and in particular, political dissidents.

6   For example Jaroslava explains the difficult and time-consuming chore of cleaning for women, due not only to shortages of consumer goods, but to a lack of basic services in the heavily production-geared Soviet economy, such as window, carpet, and other heavy-cleaning services. Even such basic items as freezers and telephones were unavailable to most households.

7   The absence of agency and citizen subjectivity within the public sphere under socialism is partly rooted in childhood experiences. The women recall memories of learning from their parents the difficult lesson of having to hide their true feelings from public expression, and recall the indignant feelings this general rule of silence engendered. Only at home could children and parents freely express their political views. In Jiřina's case, her parents were "punished" for their outspoken political dissent against the government, such that she was denied entrance into most grammar schools and, later, into many universities.

8   The problem of agency and feminism must be understood within the context both of Czech gender relations and against the political backdrop of the as yet still central-ized political and legal structures in the Czech Republic, which thwarts citizen initiative. Democratic structures and the very concept of citizen subjectivity are only just surfacing. This unfinished social transition, with its visions and hopes of libera-tion from state socialism, complicates, and in many ways discourages, the possibilities and impetus for an organized feminist critique. As a result, within the current context, however politically dangerous the claim, many Czech women and men argue that "human rights" must precede "women's rights."

9   This raises the question, however, of the extent to which civic initiative is focused on building democratic citizenship rather than on forwarding a specifically "Czech" national citizenship and identity.

10 It would appear that several of the interviewees hold views of Western feminism and ideas of Western women's social roles that are somewhat outdated. The Western female subject they refer to does not exemplify the diversity of US women's experi-ence. There is an implicit assumption that "women" are middle-class and White, and that Western feminism is limited to liberal feminism. However, US women of color, working-class, and immigrant women, for example, have traditionally worked outside the home. More recent feminist writings in the West have radically critiqued and ruptured such limited accounts of feminism and narrow notions of women's oppres-sion.

11 Alena traces this "egalitarian tradition" to the foundation and first Constitution of the democratic Czechoslovakia in 1918, which allowed and encouraged women to be active and "present" in the public sphere. This constitution was based on the ideals of equality and social justice and formally guaranteed equal rights and voting rights for women (Šmejkalová-Strictland 1993). She explains that although patriarchal struc-tures existed, they were tempered by a degree of liberty in relationships between the sexes, by women's active participation in the Czech national independence move-ment, and by widespread social egalitarian ideals in the Czech lands even before the founding of the First Republic (Havelková 1993).

12 For example, in response to the neoliberal discourse and family rhetoric by the Klaus government, Alena claims that this rhetoric has little substance. She insists that there exists no actual government program to support the notion of women's return to the home because of their past obligation to work, and that no political party has made such statements. She claims, "No party dares it. There is a common sense about these things due to the fact that women used to be so fully in the workforce in the last regime. So the neoliberal rhetoric here is not that typical. I think it is much stronger in America."

13 The wave of Czech films in the 1960s, for example, was based on realist images of human beings and society. Alena explains that contrary to Hollywood's emphasis on female glamour and personal beauty, Czech films depicted quite ordinary men and

women, and instead of exemplifying human perfection, explored such themes as human discomfort and embarrassment.

14 There is incomplete and contradictory data concerning women's current employment status. We know that during the transition, the unemployment rate of Czech women has been higher than that of men. In addition, women's employment patterns vary by region; women experience much higher unemployment rates outside of Prague. But despite higher relative unemployment rates and new forms of sex discrimination in employment, certain groups of women have managed well in the growing market economy, evidenced by the relatively high ratio of women-owned businesses (see Paukert 1991; Šťatsná 1994; Čermáková 1993).

11 Feminisms and Islamisms in Egypt

Between globalization and postmodernism

Azza M. Karam

The global village is no longer a dream – or a nightmare, depending on the perspective of onlookers – but a reality brought about by the leaps in communication technology and the spread of the mechanisms and rationale of international capital markets, almost in spite of any national borders. At the same time, social science is also having to come to terms with changing narratives and paradigms which no longer appear to conform to interpretations and expectations of old. Voices from the "other" part of the world are increasingly raised not only in either praise or condemnation, critique or emulation of Western norms and scientific inquiry, but in a cacophony of discourses which demand intellectual *and* political recognition, and reinstate the legitimate right to differ credibly.

This chapter, therefore, will attempt to peer into this junction of globalization and postmodernity, and present some insights into the dynamics that are both a defining as well as a responsive feature of these moments in our contemporary history. During extensive fieldwork carried out in my home country of Egypt from 1991 until 1996, activists from two of the most dynamic social and political movements (Islamism and feminism) were interviewed at length. I then realized that an explosion of narratives was taking place both around and within me. In an attempt to understand these points of connection and interaction, I set out here to explore some of the narratives I heard and situate them within the moments of the constantly changing dynamics of global restructuring. The first section of this chapter will look at some of the broad theoretical underpinnings linking globalization, postmodernities, and Islamisms, while the second section will narrow down these vast fields somewhat to the interactions among globalization, Islamisms, and feminisms in Egypt. Throughout this chapter, I deal with many voices and contesting narratives simultaneously. I should therefore warn that this is not a read for someone wishing for a neat and categorized presentation of events, but rather for someone game for a journey into territories rich with competing realities.

Globalization, postmodernity and Islamisms

Globalization has, during the second half of the 1980s, become a commonly used term in different circles (intellectual, business, the media, and so on). In each the term is employed to indicate a wide range of meanings with varying degrees of precision, e.g. the strengthening of a Westernized world culture, or the internationalization of Western economic, social, and political methods of interaction, norms and values (Robertson 1990: 19).

For Featherstone, the most important aspect of globalization is the centrality of culture, or the extension of global cultural interrelatedness (Featherstone 1990: 6). Featherstone argues that a globalized culture admits a continuous flow of ideas, information and values. These flows engender situations where cultural niches are forced to face each other and relativize themselves *vis-à-vis* each other. This process of relativization may entail what I consider to be twin oppositional processes of globalization: on the one hand, certain cultural values are incorporated; and on the other hand, a self-reflexive process takes place wherein fundamental values are restated and redesigned in the face of perceived threats of cultural "absorbtion" and/or "inauthenticity." This can be seen in the way that ideologues and practitioners of political Islam (Islamism) attempt to design their ideas according to a selective incorporation of certain cultural values, while remolding other values in the name of authenticity.

Appadurai (1990) presents other important and relevant facets of globalization when he conceptualizes five dimensions of global cultural flows which move in non-linear paths: ethnoscapes, finanscapes, technoscapes, mediascapes, and ideoscapes. The latter in particular points to the flow of images and ideologies which are associated with state or counter-state movements "explicitly oriented towards capturing state power or a piece of it" (Appadurai 1990: 296–9). Appadurai further emphasizes that the ideologies are associated with the appropriation of certain "key words" within Western Enlightenment world views (e.g. democracy, human rights). Both features accurately describe Islamist discourse as I elaborate below.

Highlighting yet another important dimension, Waters (1995) expands Appadurai's list of "-scapes" by adding what he terms a "sacriscape," or the distribution of religious ideas and practices. Waters argues that in tension with the universalistic tendencies of the major world religions, is postmodernization with its displacement of the certainties offered by modernization. Ironically this tension "accelerates the search for a single, often mythologized truth that can reference all social mores and practices" (Waters 1995: 130). Nevertheless, Robertson (1990) maintains that religious systems are obliged to relativize themselves to global postmodernizing trends. This can lead to appropriating a postmodernist abstract ecumenism, or to taking the form of a rejective search for original traditions (Waters 1995: 130).

Hence "postmodernism," in the context of global culture, is herein seen in terms of a symptom and a powerful cultural image of the move away from conceptualizations of global culture as homogenizing processes (e.g.

McDonaldization), and toward diversity and hybridity of local discourses, codes, and practices.[1] Robertson refers to this situation where particularity is a global value as the "universalization of particularism" (Robertson 1992: 130). It can be argued that postmodernities, in the plural, are both symptoms and consequences of the "glocalization" of culture: the point of conjuncture between the global with the local wherein dichotomies (e.g. unity/diversity, East/West, integration/disintegration) no longer sufficiently explain the dynamism and the plurivocality characterizing what Harvey (1989) describes as the economic and cultural overlap of space that is an aspect of globalization processes. Thus, "glocalization" can be seen as the tautology referring to the particular moment where postmodernism and global restructuring meet.

I maintain here that Appadurai's ideascapes and Water's sacriscapes converge producing the flow of counter-state movements, particularly those seeking simultaneously to undermine existing regimes and appropriate state power, e.g. ideologies of Islamisms. Such movements use sacredness as their territory to legitimize their ideology and de-legitimize Western world views. Islamisms do, however, selectively reappropriate certain Enlightenment key words (such as democracy, which is constructed as equivalent to an intrinsically Islamic ideal of *shura* or consultation) in their bids to seek state power. Islamisms then can be seen as an outgrowth of the restructuring processes of globalized cultures, which benefits from the "cultural chaos" that is also an aspect of both postmodernity and globalization. Islamism can also be seen as feature of a decentering process wherein the periphery (in this case, the Islamic world), moves away from the center (the Western world) and begins to legitimize its own theories and narratives in the context of globalized events and currents of interaction. As such, Islamism can be further understood as a narrative emerging from and representative of this moment of glocalization. Another ideascape movement, feminism, has also emerged in the Islamic world at this moment of glocalization. As will be argued, feminist narratives are at the interstices of Islamism and globalization, variously embracing, selectively appropriating, or eschewing some "Western" symbols and ideas, such as women's rights as human rights. As such they are examples of restructured discourses of globalization as well.

In the following section I elaborate on the interactions of globalization, Islamisms, and feminisms in the Egyptian context.

Globalization, Islamisms and feminisms

The Arab world is about to take off.

This is not a prophecy. It is a woman's intuition, and God, who knows everything, knows that women's intuition is rarely wrong.

It is going to take off for the simple reason that everybody, with the fundamentalists in the lead, wants change. The fact that they propose to go forward by going backward doesn't alter the fact that they ardently want

change. There is a very strong wish in this corner of the world to go elsewhere, to migrate collectively to another present.

(Mernissi 1993: 149)

Mernissi's feelings reflect those of many in the Arab world. Whether the Arab
world is about to take off or not remains debatable, but what is certain about her
statement – or her "intuition" – is that it is indeed the "fundamentalists" who are
in the lead of general social and political upheavals in Arab societies.

Mernissi's point highlights one of the latest realities and consequences of the
predominance of Islamist discourses in Arab civil society. Such discourses, with
their infinite diversity and varying attractiveness, have become determining
factors in the creation and development of competing discourses. In other
words, *Islamist ideas and actions are directly and indirectly setting the tone for much of the
agendas of their opposition.* This is especially true in the case of Egyptian feminists,
despite a rich cultural and historical feminist heritage that goes back more than a
hundred years.

In the following sections I illustrate the contention, with postmodernism and
local restructuring processes in mind, that the multiplicity of Islamisms generates, in turn, a multiplicity of feminist responses. These different responses are
conveyed through a portrayal of individual narratives on feminism and
Islamism, which I gathered through personal interviews with women activists in
Egypt across a period of a few years. As much as possible, I let the women speak
for themselves, while trying to limit myself to describing the general framework
within which they operate.

Grand narratives: Islamisms in Egypt

Al-Azmeh succinctly describes the condition of contemporary Islamisms by
saying that:

> [T]he situation clearly involves some kind of social irredentism, and one
> which is articulated in terms of opposition to a godless order (for religion is
> impossible without an antithetical relation) by what takes itself for a cultural
> minority, albeit a social "majority."
>
> (Al-Azmeh 1993: 73)

One thing the Egyptian Islamists openly and secretly (dis)agree about is their
diversity. They do hold in common the fact that Islam as a religion and Islam as
rule or state (*Din wa Dawla*) is one and the same. This is an important distinction
from other religious intellectuals and lay people, who may be fervent in their
advocacy of religious principles in their personal lives, but who have no desire to
delve into politics – as traditionally defined. Hence my insistence on distinguishing the fundamentalists from the Islamists, who, as the term itself may
indicate, have specifically political agendas to Islamize society and state.
Islamism as a political ideology has many distinct strands of thought within it.

Though they may agree on the necessity of attaining an Islamic society and state under the auspices of Islamic *shari'a* (law), their understandings of these concepts, as well as the methods they advocate, differ widely.

I find Rosenau's (1992) description of "affirmative postmodernists" particularly apt when characterizing Egyptian Islamists, in the context of new postmodernist political movements. Rosenau describes affirmative postmodernists as those who emphasize grass-roots activities and often are political activists and political advocates. Another feature of affirmative postmodernists applicable to Islamists is that the membership of the latter's movements tends to be deliberately heterogeneous and cross-cutting of social categories like class. A further characteristic relevant to moderate Islamist groups in particular, is that they are less concerned with the success of a calculated strategy than they are with ongoing political practice (Rosenau 1992: 145–7).

There are those Islamists who advocate the gradual and long term process of educating society in "real" Islamic values. The education process is to start from the grassroots and to continue for a number of years until the people themselves call for and actively set out to instate an "Islamic government." Meanwhile these Islamists actively work within the existing state institutions to mobilize cadres and organize a support base. Also, they set up and coordinate various social services which provide effective alternatives to similar government services. Advocates of this ideology are generally considered to be the "moderates" within the Islamist current, and are represented in the main by the Muslim Brotherhood group.

There are other Islamists whose main ideas are to reject both the existing state with all its institutions and contemporary society, because of the extent of their abandonment and ignorance of proper Islam. As far as they are concerned, the contemporary society is living in a form identical to pre-Islamic *jahiliyya* (ignorance), without any hope of redemption. Therefore, their tactics include withdrawing completely from both and creating their own alternative society with its own rules and regulations. Their Machiavellian tactics, which justify whatever means they deem necessary to achieve their desired end of an Islamic state, render them a minority within the larger diverse Islamist current, and limit the extent of support they receive. These Islamists are referred to as "extremists" or "radicalists," and they are accredited with most of the "terrorism" against tourists during the late 1980s and early 1990s. Their chosen political path rarely coincides with that of the government, or any state apparatus.

The "moderates" are the most common form within Egyptian civil society. Their advocates have gained many elected seats within syndicates – traditionally the mouthpieces of democracy in Egypt. The Muslim Brotherhood, in fact, has aligned itself with the Labour party and has thus gained official sanctioning for its activities, as well as a platform with which to enter parliament and become a visible and audible force on the political scene. It is not unusual when talking of Islamisms in Egypt to be referring to these particular political actors in fact. It is important to point out that since the Brotherhood allied with the Labour Party before the parliamentary elections in 1987, and won a large number of seats, the discourse of the party has gradually become increasingly Islamized. This Islamization of the political discourses has also taken place among the ruling National Democratic Party and the other main political parties. A consequence of this is a gradual Islamization of discourses also within the larger civil society. This has lead to an atmosphere in which any form of political participation has to be legitimized Islamically in one way or another.

The marginalized narratives: feminisms in Egypt

As far as women's political participation is concerned, the Muslim Brotherhood has a much vaunted female membership. Though the Brotherhood itself is in no way homogeneous, the differences of opinion among the larger groups of "moderates" are more significant. One of the issues on which they differ involves the extent of women's dress and public participation. As an example, there are those who argue that women should not "need" to work outside the home – whatever the circumstances.[2] On the other hand, there are other "moderates" who advocate that women can reach high public office positions except for "the grand office," or that of head of state (information leaflet, Muslim Brotherhood 1994: 42).

Set within this scenario, in which Islamisms mostly determine the political tone, are the issues involved in the broader framework of women's rights. The term "feminism" is, to all intents and purposes, one that has originated in the West. Thus, in post-colonial Arab Muslim societies the term is tainted, impure, and heavily impregnated with stereotypes. One of these stereotypes is that feminism basically stands for enmity between men and women, as well as a call for immorality in the form of sexual promiscuity for women. Not only is feminism loaded with negative stereotypes, but some Islamists, e.g. Muhammad Qutb (1991) and Muhammad Al-Sha'rawi (1992) among others, have associated feminism with colonialist strategies to undermine the indigenous social and religious culture. In the opinion of such thinkers, colonizers used the "woman question" as a tool with which to attack Islam and portray it as oppressive and backward. In fact, feminism is viewed by most Islamist "moderates" as an imported Western ideal which:

> in the treating of women and determining their social status as well as disdaining their modesty and chastity, and to the extent to which this ideal is built on a permissive philosophy that contradicts the principles, teachings, and values of the *Shari'a*, [feminism] is totally rejected.
>
> (Al-Sha'rawi 1992: 44)

Often, there is a near total association of "feminism" with abuse of Islam. These stereotypes and associations have proved remarkably persistent. Not so much because of the limited element of truth in them, but because such ideas appeal to pre-existing imagery and are effective tools in the attempts to discredit any means that legitimize and justify women's attempts to gain control over their own lives. Yet, despite the fact that feminism is refused as a term by many women activists, some of its meanings and agendas are nevertheless made adaptable by different actors within different historical, and culturally specific contexts. If "feminism" is rejected, this does not mean that a feminist consciousness and agenda are absent. It is maintained herein that there are different forms of feminism and different expressions for the types of activism it advocates, which correspond to the types of oppression women perceive in different parts of the world. Thus, there are different feminisms, which have different starting points and understandings (i.e. of the reasons behind women's oppression). Closest to this notion is a postmodern conceptualization of feminism, which advocates a theoretical outlook "attuned to the cultural specificity of different societies and periods and to that of different groups within societies and periods" (Fraser and Nicholson 1990: 34). One of the significant features of such postmodern feminist theorizing is a forswearing of a single feminist epistemology, thus creating the space for contemporary feminist political practices (and beliefs), which would have been previously regarded as unorthodox.

I identify three main "types" of feminist thought and praxis in contemporary Egypt: *secular feminism*, *Muslim feminism*, and *Islamist feminism*. Covering the broad political spectrum, these identifications serve to highlight the multiplicity of voices through which Egyptian women activists speak and act. Though on certain issues these feminists may converge and act together (e.g. appealing to the ruling party to lobby for the lifting of sanctions against Iraq), they remain in general, separated on many points.

In what follows I will elaborate on the interaction between Islamism and feminism[3] while also presenting some of the narratives of the women taken to represent the different streams identified. Each of the women is identified as a feminist in so far as she accepts the notion that women are in a less privileged position because of their sex and is willing to change this situation to achieve more equitable gender and social relations in the society. However, their motivations and utopias differ according to the creed that each holds to be instrumental in implementing their agendas. Each woman presented here represents a particular feminist stream, or type. They have prominent social and public roles and describe themselves as political activists. They were asked what they thought of feminism, of Islamism, and how they saw themselves in relation to these forces.

Starting with the most controversial one first, I use the term *Islamist feminists* because many of the Islamist women I interviewed are indeed aware of a particular oppression of women, *and* they actively seek to rectify this oppression by recourse to Islamic principles. Nevertheless, most of the Islamist women interviewed will shy away from the term "feminists," if not vehemently criticize it outright, as an irrelevant and inaccurate Western term. What many women Islamists uphold is difficult to separate from what feminism at base connotes. I intentionally refer to these Islamist activists as "feminists" not to homogenize them, but for the following tactical reasons: (1) to distinguish them from their male and other women counterparts, who think differently, since not all Islamists are feminists by any means; and (2) to underline the importance of seeing commonalities of struggle or aims – even if not of means.

In the opinion of Islamist feminists, women are oppressed precisely because they try to be "equal" to men and are therefore being put in unnatural settings and unfair situations, which denigrate them and take away their integrity and dignity as women. For example, women are "forced" to go out and compete in the labor market – a task which means that women may come into contact with men (as in public transport, for example) in a humiliating and unsuitable way.

In other words, for Islamist feminists, it is the demands of an alien (i.e. Western) ideology purveyed at the expense of Islamic teachings, which oppresses women. As far as many of them are concerned, Western feminism, with its emphasis on total equality of the sexes, only results in women striving to be "superhuman" and, in the process, losing much of their integrity and energy while shouldering extra burdens. For Islamist women, a just (Islamic) society is one that strives for a recognition and respect for complementarity between the sexes instead of competition.

Many of them, when directly queried, are reluctant to distinguish between women's oppression and social oppression as a whole. They uphold that what is happening to women is part of a societal process wherein proper Islamic principles are absent, or at best, misused by a morally bankrupt and corrupt state regime. They see their mission as a "structural *jihad*,"[4] that is aimed at "change towards more Islamization," which in turn occurs through "active participation in *all spheres* of life."[5] This then, is not merely a call for women to stay at home. Rather, it is a "call to arms," which enhances and reconceptualizes women's roles within the family (as mothers and wives), with an Islamist feminist nuance, that gives women a sense of value and political purpose in these gendered roles, as well as a sense of confidence: they are not less than men, but equally important in different ways. Islamist feminists see the proper application of the *shar'ia* (Islamic Laws) as the answer to their problems and those of the entire society. The following narrative illustrates to some extent, the configuration of these ideas, the main aims of Islamist feminists and their opinions of both the state and other feminists.

Abeyya (Islamist, 31 years old, journalist)

> All these secular feminists have no principle, or value for which to work. They have no program or aims. They are empty. They are headed by Al-Tagammu (leftist political party). All these groups are against Islam. They are evil movements. They speak a lot and do nothing. They cannot reach anything or anybody. The most they like to do is to make parties and have a good time. Not one of them is prepared to stand up for hours and get actively involved and sacrifice anything. These are movements which have no belief and no inner value or standing.

They have all the rights they need. These women are not oppressed. We are oppressed by the demands made on us to conform to a Western way of living, and we are subjected to so much injustices from security people and ordinary people simply because we are veiled. We have to endure much hardship simply because of the way we are dressed. We are the ones who have no rights in this society at all.

If the situation continues as it is, then things will only get worse. And I am hoping that God's law (the *shar'ia*) will be applied and that God will be feared by those who rule us. Our homes and our selves are under constant threat and discriminated against as women and as true Muslims only because we are calling to God. I hope the day will come when we will be able to live under God's laws. Instead of under these other laws which intend to break up and destroy our families. Our sisters are taken and oppressed and subjected to much torture in the prisons for no fault of their own – only because their husbands are wanted or even just under suspicion by a government which God has cursed, and which does not care for proper Islam, and does not look after us as God has ordained.

Muslim feminists also use Islamic sources, like the Qu'ran and the *Sunna* (the Prophet's actions and sayings), only their aim is to show that the discourse of equality between men and women *is* valid, Islamicly. Muslim feminists try to build bridges between interpretations of sociopolitical and cultural realities according to Islam, and a human rights discourse.

Many of them would be proud to be seen as feminists, or at least have no problems with the term. As far as this group is concerned, a feminism that does not justify itself within Islam is bound to be rejected by the rest of society, and would not be capable of mobilizing the average person. Moreover, Muslim feminists feel that to attempt to separate Islamic discourses from other discourses (whether they are accused of being Western or not) can only lead to various schisms within the society, and is thus unrealistic as an option. Such a separation, they argue, impedes a possible process of mutual enlightenment between Islamic and other discourses, and in fact, risks making the Islamic one more alienating and patriarchal, and the sole domain of the Islamists.[6] The following narrative illustrates many of the standpoints of Muslim feminists.

Tahani (43 years of age, lawyer)

Feminism is under grave danger because of the many faults it has. And until now it has not been able to unify into a movement mainly because of internal difficulties: bureaucracy, lack of inner democracy and foresight, individualism, inability to bridge the generation gap and give the younger generation the ability to participate. Also an absence of strategic capacities to enable women to participate effectively. So there is no institutional backing for women to enter leadership roles and thereby be able to enter into the political process in an effective manner. To make matters worse, these women are now faced with an ideology which misuses and misinterprets religion, calls for a virtual incarceration of women and has openly political intentions. The danger is that these movements [Islamism] have a great potential to attract people because Egyptian people are religious by nature. It must be said though, that these movements are not homogeneous. There are some among them which are very progressive and have very good interpretations. But the majority tend to twist understandings and appeal to populist concepts. Women join these movements because they lack a correct appreciation and understanding of their religion, and women have not studied their religion. These people try to obliterate reason and create a priesthood in Islam even though it is forbidden. But we cannot ask people to become more conscious and aware on the one hand, and then devote much public space – media – to the leaders of such movements on the other! These movements in Egypt are not to be seen in isolation from global happenings and pressures, nor are they to be looked at without considering the kind of tacit support they are receiving from state authorities.

I see myself as a citizen who is participating in the public space and have a role in many public institutions. I have made a point of studying my religion in depth, and I have a certain influence over people in my environment. Mine is an endeavor to use all the capacities and influence I have at my disposal to counter these inclinations and spread a wiser consciousness at every opportunity. I consider that women's issues should be seen within the overall framework of human rights – especially in view of the global interest in the whole issue of human rights. Mine is an attempt to increase and deepen popular participation and democratic practices in general.

Shari'a is misunderstood and misapplied. This must be changed in order to be able to change many issues relating to women. *Ijtihad* is very important in this respect.[7] And it is an essential tool in the process of putting an end to civil violations against women.

In fact, both Islamist and Muslim feminists argue for a form of *ijtihad*, and many Islamist feminists agree with Muslim feminists that women *are* indeed capable of taking on tasks involving the interpretation of Islamic jurisprudence and providing social and political leadership (previously thought to be the exclusive domains of men). In that sense, both these sets of feminists are arguing against existing patriarchal religious formations/hierarchies and the implications for their interpretations of gender, and both use very similar "tools" of analysis and argumentation. Both sets of feminists are therefore extensively studying, analyzing, and referring to traditional Islamic texts, in order to validate and justify their arguments. However, though both "take on" established forms of thinking, there is an important difference with respect to their political positions. Namely, Islamist feminists are part of a political movement that is, on the whole, actively attempting to raise support for itself in its ultimate quest for the capture of state power. In their bid to mobilise all possible support for their cause, Islamists, particularly the moderates, cannot afford to lose the political, social, and economic backing of these women who actively participate in some of these movements. Simultaneously, Islamist women have successfully reversed traditional value judgements about women's "place." "Women's knowledge" of the home and child-raising enjoys a higher esteem than that of women only working outside their homes. Moreover, within the boundaries supposedly imposed by their understandings of Islam, women are still able to be active in the public arena. In many respects, the Islamist movements resemble nationalist movements of old in their attempts to mobilize women for their cause. In short, for the time being, and until Islamism acquires state power, attempts to curtail the public roles of women members of Islamist movements are unlikely to be forthcoming in the short-term.

Muslim feminists on the other hand, are more likely to form part of more mainstream women's groups, but lack the comparative political backing and power that Islamist women have on the ground. Moreover, as with the secular feminists, there is little support for these groups from the state. The Egyptian state's often ambiguous role in relation to its lack of a definite standpoint on women's rights, only complicates matters more for Muslim and secular women activists.[8] Furthermore, given that many of the Muslim feminists are attempting to reconcile the discourses of Islam with human rights, they are facing the same accusations of "cultural inauthenticity" faced by promoters of secular discourses.

Secular feminists would not identify their Islamist counterparts as being even remotely feminist. In turn, as promoters of a secular discourse, they are not held in high esteem by the Islamists. They are, to be blunt, "political enemies." Secular feminists firmly believe in grounding their discourse totally outside the realm of any religion: whether Muslim or Christian, and placing it, instead, within the discourse of the International Covenant on Human Rights (ICHR). Nor do they attempt to harmonize religious discourses with the concept and declarations pertinent to human rights. To them, religion is respected as a private matter for each individual, but it is totally rejected as a basis from which to formulate any agendas on women's emancipation. By so doing, they are avoiding being caught up in endless discussions on the position and status of women in religion. Also avoided are potential accusations, leveled by religious conservatives, regarding their right to (re)interpretation of religious texts for example. None the less, against them the severest and potentially most debilitating of criticisms are directed: clones of the West and non-believers.

In the following narrative, a secular feminist clarifies, among other things, the positionality of this kind of feminism *vis-à-vis* the Egyptian state and Islamists.

Aida (45 years of age, physician)

Feminism is the way forward. A feminist discourse grounded in human rights is the only response to Islamist discourse. At the moment we have a situation where the state is trying to compete with Islamists using the same discourse. The result is that women's issues get lost in all this. We have a distinctive feminist position which is articulated, thanks to the process of preparation for the ICPD,[9] inside and outside Egypt. But we must face continuous attempts – supposedly state supported – to eradicate our influence and even our existence. Even supposedly liberal forces are politically calculative and thus excluding of us. The number of people or organizations which support us are so incredibly few. These are mostly the ones which share the same legal status as ours.[10] Non-supporters justify their attitudes with a variety of reasons: they claim that we are politically miscalculating, or that we want to scandalize the government and not everybody is prepared to scandalize the government – they never personalize this point. They just say not everybody is prepared to stand against the government.

We do not change our programs or do anything special because of the Islamists. But we do try to make sure we do not produce anything that will land us in jail. Islamism is such a political abuse of religion and democracy that it does not even try to be discreet. So-called Islamist or Muslim feminists present to the West exactly what they want to see and hear. These are the people who strengthen stereotypes of Muslim women. And in the process of doing so, they end up going against the *shari'a* they are calling for. The problem is that women join these groups because of the influence of the media, and they feel they are making something of their lives. Lay people are convinced by the ideas propagated by Islamists that the country is full of corruption and they are fighting it – even though these Islamists are not far from the corruption themselves. What is worse than political Islam, is the supposed liberals who suddenly impose themselves as the defenders of Islam and say things which are incorrect – knowingly. This only infuriates us. Islamists are already in government. They are in charge. Call me paranoid. I have no figures, but I have a whole series of indications and indelible proof based on so many daily and national incidents.

We write against these people and these ideas. ... We will write and write and write.

The people who want to hold the stick from the middle and claim that *shari'a* should be stuck to, along with human rights – these people are not prepared to do all the studying that is required for this. Maybe, maybe, from those I know, there is only one that has already spent much effort to do so ... but the rest are just talking and not realizing the implications of this.

The three narratives outlined above indicate the different ways in which Egyptian feminisms are discursively trying to position themselves amidst the grander narratives of Islamism and the state. Islamist feminists perceive secular feminism as a Westernized and universal way of thought which is inimical to Islam and as such, denies them their rights as dictated within the *shari'a*. According to Islamist feminists, only "God's laws" will enable them to escape the

persecution and oppression that are characteristic of both the present government and secular global discourses as manifested by secular feminism.

Muslim feminists are urging newer interpretations of Islam that would bridge
the gap between global human rights discourse and Islamic *shari'a*, and thus
empower Muslim women to counter Islamist discourses, some of which they see
as sanctioned by the state. Secular feminists are embracing global human rights
discourse and thereby attempting to distance themselves from arguments
alluding to cultural or religious authenticity. Their quest is to argue that women's
rights are part and parcel of human rights, as framed in the ICHR, and precisely
because of this global character, validated as the most appropriate goal of feminism. This would appear to be in contrast to Islamist feminists, who perceive
global discourses as western prototypes, and thereby invalidate such quests.

The need for "new paradigms" and localized feminist resistances

> The basic challenge of Arab social science in the 1980s can be character-
> ized as the search for a new paradigm after the fall of the ancient one. This
> is a very complicated process which needs to be objectively understood
> through the adoption of a global approach in which the particular is studied
> in light of the whole.
>
> (Yassin 1988: 303)

Yassin's point is valid, especially in view of glocalization movements of Islamisms
and feminisms which arise from restructuring and which are, more often than
not, negatively portrayed and little understood. The challenge Yassin mentions is
not only presenting itself to Arab social science, but to Western social science as
well – especially the kind which attempts to analyze and represent women in the
Muslim world.

I put forward that postmodern theory's attention to contesting interpretations
of global processes, which Yassin indirectly touches upon, constitutes one of the
most illuminating ways of understanding contemporary dynamics. In particular,
"the integration of other voices and the first person narratives of experiences
and perception ... also supply a narrow path which bypasses the cul-de-sac of a
polarized Western feminist representation of Muslim women" (Watson 1994:
155).

Further, if, as some argue, postmodern political action is generally aimed at
arousing aspirations, raising consciousness, exploring the politics of identity, and
opening up opportunities for those who are marginal (Luke 1989: 209, 235),
then both Islamisms and feminisms are avowedly postmodern. However,
Islamists, with their specific political agendas, do depart from characterizations
of postmodern movements, which assume that such movements have "less
concern with the state because they have no desire to 'seize power'" (Rosenau
1992: 147). Islamists are, however, constructions of the globalized cultural flows

of ideascapes described by Appadurai (1990) above, as well as the sacriscapes that Waters (1995) elaborates. The non-desire to seize state power accurately describes Egyptian feminists (with the possible exception of Islamist feminists by virtue of the latter's involvement with the aims of the larger Islamist movement), who concentrate on neighborhood, local, regional, and community levels as the new spaces for political action. But in a way, feminists or women activists in general have no choice but to do so because the Islamists, as Aida's narrative earlier alluded to, are already in power positions.

Hence, it can be argued that Egyptian Islamists and feminists have reacted and restructured themselves in relation to globalization in similar yet different manners. Islamists (including Islamist feminists), in the process of relativizing themselves to global cultural flows, are countering a perceived threat to authenticity by resorting to particularistic religious fundamental values. Secular and Muslim feminists have seen Islamisms as the threat and, in countering them, have also (re)appropriated more universalistic human rights arguments. In other words, both kinds of movements are restructuring their discourses in globalized ways.

The need to situate feminisms, therefore, is related to the requirement that there be a more in-depth look at the way in which portrayals of feminism have been carried out thus far, and particularly with respect to Islam. Recent studies argue that generalized theories ignore the specificities of "Muslim women's subordination" (Watson 1994: 156). It is ironic, however, that the same people who make these kinds of statements are also the ones calling for new paradigms. In other words, they are calling for new paradigms to study the same thing: Muslim women's *oppression*. The fact is that while grand theories indeed ignore specificities, it is not only and always those of subordination. By calling for newer means to study the negative aspects of different cultures only, we are falling into the age old trap of perpetuating these negative images of Muslim women. Rarely do we hear calls for newer frameworks with which to analyze the specificities of these women's *empowerment strategies*.

The women's narratives indicated above point to a diversity of reappropriations of discourses and resistances to global processes, generating and interacting with Islamisms and feminisms. Their "multiplicity of truths" can best be understood when looked at through a postmodern lens. I have presented them intentionally with the aim of highlighting precisely this diversity of feminist praxis. In doing so, I have attempted to stress that polyvocality, and multiple means of reacting and resisting, must be taken into consideration when attempting to understand the intersections of restructuring, Islamisms, and feminisms in Egypt.

The strategies of empowerment feminists have used to restructure their discourse are part and parcel of larger global dynamics, not isolated ones. Egyptian feminisms, in their diversity, indicate that globalization is not "out there," in the same way that specificities are not confined to one domain. The interaction between feminisms and Islamisms in Egypt are part of the dynamic field of ideascapes and sacriscapes which are constantly changing and producing a multiplicity of voices. We need to hear the cacophony.

Notes

1   It can be argued that what is being described here as postmodernism is similar to post-colonialism. However, two significant differences are maintained here. First, the "modern" and the "colonial" discourses are not identical – despite the fact that many colonialists have claimed otherwise. Second, post-colonial discourse tend to be posited against some form of colonial discourse, whereas postmodernism, while featuring this aspect to some extent, also moves beyond this towards a *condition*, which is almost anti-everything, including post-colonial discourses themselves.

2   Al-Sha'rawi maintains that it is the society's responsibility, in case of absence or inability of any male relative, to see that women in need are cared for. So they would be forced to go out in public to work and disrupt the social fabric (Al-Sha'rawi 1992: 71–85).

3   Here I am "borrowing" from my earlier work (Karam 1998).

4   *Jihad* means effort. It is usually linked with *fi sabil allah* (for the sake of God), i.e. for a religiously commendable aim. This has various meanings. It is often understood as war with society or others, in order to enhance the Islamic character. In other instances, *Jihad* also refers to struggle with one's "self," in order to overcome one's evil inclinations. Islamists often use the word as synonymous with revolutionary struggle for Islamist ideals.

5   Islamist Heba Ra'uf in a personal interview, May 1993, Cairo.

6   Prominent and internationally known writers and theorists who advocate this stance, include Fatima Mernissi (Moroccan), Riffat Hassan (Pakistani-American), and Azizah Al-Hibri (Arab-American).

7   *Ijtihad* means independent interpretation in light of the changing/modern circumstances.

8   The role of the Egyptian state in debates about and between feminists and Islamists can best be described as that of sitting on the fence and jumping in whenever politically expedient. On the one hand, much media time and space is given to conservative Muslim preachers who advocate women's return to the home as a cure for a host of social and economic ills. On the other hand, the official party line condemns Islamists as a whole, as nothing short of terrorists.

9   The International Conference on Population and Development (ICPD), which was held in Cairo, September 3–13, 1994.

10 Aida is a member of the New Woman Association (NWA). In order to avoid suffocating government controls, NWA refrained from registering itself with the Ministry of Social Affairs – which most Egyptian NGOs are required to do – and instead registered as a non-profit organization under commercial laws. This maneuver is slowly becoming increasingly popular among other organizations hoping to operate in a democratic environment, but has now been rendered less probable after the passing of the new NGO laws in 1999.

12 Dancing resistance from Rio to Beijing

Transnational women's organizing and United Nations conferences, 1992–6

Deborah Stienstra

Introduction

Global restructuring is changing the face of the world. As others in this volume and elsewhere have argued, it is restructuring with a gendered face. Yet the processes of restructuring pursued and implemented by states and international organizations and supported by transnational corporations and world business leaders are not static. They are not simply actions that have an impact on women and men in their various localities, they are actions, policies, and discourses which shape and respond to the resistances that women and men undertake. This chapter will explore one of those sites of resistance: women's transnational organizing,[1] especially in relation to the five United Nations conferences between 1992 and 1996. These included the 1992 United Nations Conference on Environment and Development (UNCED, also known as the Rio Earth Summit); the 1993 Vienna World Conference on Human Rights; the 1994 International Conference on Population and Development in Cairo; the 1995 World Social Summit in Copenhagen; the Fourth World Conference on Women in Beijing; and the 1996 Conference on Human Settlement (Habitat II) in Istanbul.

The women's caucuses that formed to act at these conferences brought together women active in community-based, national, regional, and international networks and organizations. They denounced governmental restructuring frameworks and practices. They contested the discourses and assumptions upon which restructuring was established. They shared strategies for resisting restructuring at the local and international levels.

The metaphor of dance is one way to illustrate some of the complexities that are at work in women's resistances to restructuring. Dance can be formal or informal, choreographed within the rules of a discipline or free-form, and alone, with a single partner or with many. Yet dance is always a response to sound and music. The music changes and the dance changes. The dancers respond to the diverse rhythms and sounds and use their movements to express these responses.

In some forms of dance, the dancers create the music with their body movements and rhythms. Using this metaphor, women's movements can be seen as similar to dancers and the global political economy or world order to the music. At times women's movements dance by themselves to the music and at other times they respond to other dancers. States, TNCs, other social movements, and international financial institutions are also dancing to the same music, although their interpretation and style of dance often differs greatly from those of women's movements.

Women's responses to global restructuring bear many resemblances to dance. As I will argue in the following pages, the resistance women's movements have developed is responsive primarily to changes in women's lives across the world as a result of changes in the global political economy. Those responses reflect cultural and religious diversities, a growing sophistication and sense of cohesion around strategies and actions at the global level. They are responses to the actions of states, TNCs, international financial institutions, and other forces at work in the world order. Women's groups are not dancing by themselves. Their actions, campaigns, networks, lobbying, and strategies are changed by and provoke responses from states, international financial institutions, corporations, and others. The dance continues as the music changes, and the dancers contribute to how the music changes.

But the metaphor is not entirely analogous to the situation within the global political economy. For example, the metaphor suggests that the music usually exists independently of the dancers. In the global political economy, however, the form of the global political economy is constructed by those involved in it and does not have a separate entity apart from those forces at work within it. It also does not reflect whether there are disparities of power between the dancers in the dance or in making the music. "Dancing to someone else's tune" illustrates some of the disparities in the existing global political economy, but fails to illuminate its complexities. Keeping in mind these difficulties, dance provides a useful metaphor for reflecting how women have resisted global restructuring through transnational organizing.

Women's transnational organizing in relation to restructuring can be partially understood by framing it in the context of several important questions which arise from more general social movement literature. Why do movements arise? What causes them to act? and In what ways will they act?

Sidney Tarrow argues that social movements arise in response to what he calls political opportunity structures. "Social movements form when ordinary citizens, sometimes encouraged by leaders, respond to changes in opportunities that lower the costs of collective action, reveal potential allies and show where elites and authorities are vulnerable" (Tarrow 1994: 18). This assessment is especially applicable to the domestic or national level where there are clearly identifiable elites and, in many states, cohesive structures. Yet, as Tarrow even admits, his analysis may be less applicable when we consider transnational social movements largely because they go beyond national state structures and act in response to states other than their own or in relation to international institutions like the

World Bank or the International Monetary Fund (IMF). "If movements are becoming transnational, they may be freeing themselves of state structures and thence of the constraining influence of state-mediated contention" (Tarrow 1994: 196).

Social movements may also arise in response to changes or dislocation in the structures around them. For some at the national level it could be a response to state action, or the opportunity structures that Tarrow describes. But there are also social movements which arise in response to changes in the systems of production or other global dislocations (Stienstra 1994: 24). The level of change will likely be reflected in the level of action or response. Changes in the neighborhood or community, such as changes to transit systems, will produce movements at the local level. Changes that are more global, such as human rights concerns in countries across the world, will give impetus to more transnational forms of organizing. There are some changes which may foster movements at all levels, such as environmental degradation, which mobilizes groups at the local, national, and international level.

Women's movements have organized transnationally especially over the past twenty years in response to critical changes in women's lives. As I argue elsewhere (Stienstra 1994), these women's movements have taken their strength from the organizing done locally and nationally and translated it into transnational networks. Biomedical and reproductive technologies, security issues broadly defined, prostitution, and the gendered international division of labor have mobilized women around the world since the early 1980s to work together for action to bring about positive change in women's lives. The organizing efforts have taken a more global character than earlier women's organizing at the international level. The recent women's movements have included strong representation of and leadership from women of the South and one of the leading networks, Development Alternatives with Women for a New Era (DAWN), is made up of women of the South.

What causes social movements to act? This question suggests that we examine the relationships between the social movement and the structures of the world order to see what type of change is proposed and the response by states and other actors. Many would argue that social movements can only be motivated by emancipatory or liberation goals. They want to bring about substantial positive change in response to the negative changes that have been brought on by the changes in the world order. The civil rights movements, anti-apartheid movement, and many others can be categorized as emancipatory. While emancipatory groups are a considerable force for change within global society, there are also reactionary or status quo groups which are motivated by the desire to keep the existing world order in place or to move to an earlier status quo. Some current examples of reactionary movements are the fundamentalist Christian and Islamic movements across the world.

Women's movements have been primarily understood as emancipatory movements, but this description fails to illustrate the complexities within the movements. Women's movements are usually organized in order to bring positive change to women's lives, promote equality, or ensure the advancement of women. Yet, as we will see in the following sections, during the 1990s there have arisen at both the national and international levels organizations that are reactionary and work to maintain unequal gender relations. As well, even within those groups that would consider themselves emancipatory, there is considerable variation about what their goals are, whether they consider themselves feminist, and how their own cultures, class, and ethnicities shape their activities. There are also considerable tensions between those "professional" and more grass-roots based organizations. Transnational organizing reflects these complexities and some of the compromises that are part of working at the international level.

Finally, in what ways will the movement act? Given the nature of transnational women's movements, we can assume that women will organize in diffuse rather than unitary ways, with flexible structures, many alliances, little violence, and transnationally coordinated strategies for action. Yet, to limit ourselves to exploring these manifestations of action prevents us from recognizing the dynamic relationships between movements and other parts of world order. Some might call this relationship a dialectic, where the response of one actor is shaped by the actions of the others. I prefer the metaphor of dance which helps to foreground changing movements, responses, and creativities.

One of the theoretical questions which will frame the descriptions of these dances is to what extent do states, corporations, and international financial institutions need women's movements in their move towards global restructuring and how are they attempting to get women's compliance or approval? Has this changed over time? How are women's movements responding to these actions?

With all these questions in mind, I will outline briefly the historical developments that led to the establishment of the women's caucuses in the early 1990s as well as their structures, processes, issues, and agendas in response to the five United Nations conferences between 1992 and 1996. I will explore how the caucuses have responded to definitions, effects, and processes of global restructuring in their lobbying efforts and their presentation of alternative visions and actions. In my conclusions, I will reconsider some of the theoretical questions addressed above in the light of the case presented.

The early years of women's transnational organizing

While there was an increasing amount of transnational organizing related to women following the United Nations' International Women's Year in 1975, it was led almost exclusively by women of the North and economic or development issues remain a marginal part of their work. It was not until the late 1980s with the increased participation and leadership by women of the South that these areas received significant transnational attention by women's organizations.

Throughout the United Nations Decade for Women (1976–85) with its intergovernmental conferences and non-governmental fora,[2] women from the North took the leadership in transnational organizing. They were more often interested in changing attitudes, increasing employment and wages, and focusing on women's health and education. The global economy remained invisible in their analyses of the problems for women, reflecting in large part, the privileged position of many of those active during this period.

During the 1970s, only a few women of the South were able to participate in international events, and these women were usually academics or from the middle and upper classes within their own countries. Yet, they understood feminism differently from many women of the North, and their definitions of what changes were needed in women's lives reflected their unequal locations within the global economy. One specific incident in the 1970s illustrated these disparities very well. In 1976, 500 women and men came together at Wellesley College in the United States for a Seminar on Women and Development, a follow-up conference to the International Women's Year. It was one of the first attempts to bring women of the South and North together to discuss the specific issues related to women in the South. Most of the participants were academics and their work illustrated a very Northern definition of feminism. In an open letter, three women from the South rejected the attempts by those within the conference to separate the global political economy from the situation of women. They explained that their efforts to include discussions on the impact of economics, multinational corporations, and trade on women's lives as well as exposing the links between women's oppression and these aspects of the global political economy were seen by the others at the conference as diverting attention from women's issues ("Women and Development: The Wellesley Conference" 1977).

Little was done to address these concerns, and few women in the North made these linkages. One group of women in the North sought to explore the impacts on women of global corporations especially in the areas of electronics and textiles ("Women's Network on Global Corporations Forms" 1980).

Women of the South, however, continued to organize around the impact of the economic crises on their lives. In 1984, women from different regions of the South came together in Bangalore, India to explore the economic and environmental crises from the vantage point of poor women in the South. Their work later became the network, DAWN (Development Alternatives with Women for a New Era) (Sen and Grown 1987).

These transnational responses to the global political economy and the inequalities that preceded formal restructuring policies by governments remained isolated and primarily led by women of the South. By 1990, however, there was greater recognition that structural adjustment, with its restructuring policies, affected women in the North as well as in the South.

DAWN has continued to provide analysis of the consequences of structural adjustment policies on women's lives in the South (Vickers 1991: 112, 114). As well, in 1990, a transnational network, "Gender-focused Alternatives to Structural Adjustment," was formed to provide research and solidarity based on women's experiences as a response to government structural adjustment programs (*Beyond the Debt Crisis* 1990). More recently, Canadian, US and Mexican women organized transnationally in response to the restructuring of their societies as a result of the North American Free Trade Agreement

(NAFTA) (Gabriel and Macdonald 1994). These dispersed efforts, more like scattered students in a dance class struggling with new steps, became more coordinated in the 1990s with the women's caucuses at the United Nations conferences held between 1992 and 1996.

Women's caucuses and United Nations conferences, 1992–6

One of the primary ways that women have organized transnationally in the recent years has been through women's caucuses at United Nations conferences held between 1992 and 1996 on the environment, human rights, population, social development, women, and habitat. These conferences were called by then Secretary-General, Boutros Boutros-Ghali, to develop a map for the global community following the end of the Cold War. Each conference had an inter-governmental meeting and a non-governmental forum. However, an increasing number of non-governmental organizations (NGOs) were given access to these conferences and thus were increasingly part of the negotiations processes. The women's caucuses at each meeting encouraged governments to pay greater attention to the inclusion of gender analysis. These caucuses have been widely recognized as one of the most successful interventions made by NGOs in the United Nations processes.

The work of these caucuses on global restructuring provides a useful illustration of the ways in which the dance of the global political economy shapes and shifts in response to a variety of forces. We will first examine briefly who the caucuses are, outline what specific accomplishments they have made in response to global restructuring, and finally, analyze the movements between and among the dancers.

The dancers of transnational women's movements: the choreography of women's caucuses

Our vantage point for this dance are the women's caucuses, one set of dancers in the global political economy. What and who are they? For each of the conferences, the caucuses have involved different entities, although there have been at least two groups, the Women's Environment and Development Organization (WEDO) and the Center for Women's Global Leadership, which have taken consistent leadership roles. WEDO was born through the efforts of the Women's Foreign Policy council which organized a Women's Environment and Development Program to work in preparation for the Rio Conference in 1989–90. This program later became WEDO and its goal is to make women more visible as equal participants, experts, and leaders in policy making from the community to the international level. The Center for Women's Global Leadership was begun in 1989 to promote women's global leadership, is based at Douglass College in Rutgers University, and has Charlotte Bunch as its Executive Director. Its mandate is to develop an understanding of the ways in which gender affects the use of power and public policy at the international level.

Beginning with the preparations for the Rio Conference in 1992, WEDO played an increasingly important role in coordinating and mobilizing the women's caucuses at most of the international conferences in the 1990s. The Rio Conference was the first opportunity where WEDO initiated a women's caucus. Women's caucuses had existed at other international meetings (Lerner, interview, December 4, 1995), but they did not make the impact with NGOs, government delegations, United Nations officials, and the media that the more recent ones have. As one participant noted, "The United Nations comes to the women's caucus to find out what is going on, to do an analysis" (Kyte, interview, December 6, 1995). The recent women's caucuses have been characterized as different because they moved from a "get acquainted" session to one which mobilized participants for political action, especially around lobbying (Kyte, interview, December 6, 1995).

At the Rio Conference, the model was set for the women's caucus process, although it was fine-tuned over the following years. Preparations for a United Nations conference often began with a pre-conference event such as the 1991 World Women's Congress for a Healthy Planet, the 1992 meeting of women's health advocates from across the world or the 1994 Women's Global Strategies meeting, where women would gather to assess what had been accomplished in a particular area and where further action was needed. Using this type of research and analysis, a small number of women, coordinated by the WEDO staff, developed a line-by-line analysis of the documents being considered at the conference and provided alternative wording with rationales that women's groups could use in lobbying. Working groups were organized in several conferences around specific themes and worked over the Internet and through regular channels to ensure the participation of as many women as possible. These groups also worked at the conferences to monitor and lobby around their issues. At many of the preparatory committees and during the final conferences, the women's caucus held daily briefings, usually one hour long, where the previous day's activities were highlighted, the items under discussion by the states were outlined, and strategies were discussed. Anyone was welcome to attend these briefings, including government representatives. Representatives of women's groups took the line-by-line analyses, suggested draft texts and the information from the daily briefings, and lobbied government delegations or regional groups. As the documents changed in response to negotiations between states, representatives from the different working groups rewrote the text proposals and shared their proposed changes at the daily briefings. Following the conference, WEDO or other key organizations involved in the conference provided an analysis of what was gained in the final documents through the work of the women's caucus.

Several of the conferences diverged significantly from this model. At the Vienna Human Rights Conference, the women's caucus was organized through the work of the Center for Women's Global Leadership. The Center had organized a global campaign highlighting the violence against women and culminating in the Global Tribunal on Violations of Women's Human Rights which was held during the NGO Forum (Bunch and Reilly 1994). As well, the Vienna meetings had two parallel meetings of women's caucuses, one for non-governmental women many who were not able to have access to the official conference, and one for women who were on governmental delegations organized by United Nations Development Fund for Women (UNIFEM) (Chen 1996: 146).

The work of the women's caucus at the Beijing World Conference on Women was also different largely because it was a conference on women. Some argued that a women's conference did not need a women's caucus. There was also considerable conflict and tension, especially between Bella Abzug of WEDO and Irene Santiago, Convener of the NGO Forum, over who would organize the non-governmental presence at the conference. In the end it was agreed that a group called Équipo, made up of representatives of all twenty-eight caucuses and some from the organizing committee of the NGO forum, would facilitate the daily briefing session. WEDO organized the Women's Linkage Caucus which dealt with the four substantive issues of environment, health, human rights, and economic justice, and reported to the daily briefings. The role of the Linkage Caucus was to assist with the monitoring and lobbying of the governmental work to ensure that at a minimum the gains made at these conferences would be protected in the Beijing document and hopefully even more gains would be made.

The women's caucuses provided easy access for many people. While some of the caucuses were small with only several hundred accredited NGOs in attendance, many were very large – in Cairo the women's caucus had roughly 1,000 participants and in Beijing there were well over 1,300 groups involved. There was considerable turnover among those who participated in the women's caucus, even among those at the preparatory meetings and the final conference. The format provided a good training ground for all participants, especially those who had never attended a United Nations meeting. Much information was provided in a short period of time and it was a place where anyone in attendance could get an up-to-date account of the activities of the conference.

The caucuses enabled an effective and informed presence to promote a feminist agenda at these meetings and has helped to create a more cohesive women's presence at the international level. Yet the organizing around restructuring has also highlighted and exacerbated significant tensions within the movement. While these tensions were not created by restructuring policies, restructuring shaped and exacerbated the tensions.

The most obvious tension within the caucus has been that between women of the South and those of the North. While there has been increased leadership by women of the South, especially through DAWN, the leadership of the caucuses has remained with organizations in the North, primarily, although not exclusively, by women of the North. Both WEDO and the Center have worked diligently to include women of the South in their advisory boards or decision-making bodies. As well, both have attempted to provide training opportunities for young women, especially from the South. Yet the leadership and the "face" of the caucuses remains with the high-profile women of the North – Bella Abzug and Charlotte Bunch.

The North/South tension is more than who is perceived as leaders. It is also about who is able to participate. There is easier access for women of the North to the on-going work of the caucuses than for women of the South and this has been exacerbated through restructuring. It is also easier for women of upper and middle classes across the world to participate since most of the work is volunteer, unless they are part of "professional" lobbying women's organizations. The caucus work has been centered primarily in New York as many of the headquarters of the leading groups are there. Consultations and discussions are held via e-mail and fax, both of which are much less available to women of the South. This more limited access for women of the South could also help to explain the less prominent focus on economics within the caucuses than on human rights.

The hub of work in New York has added an extra tension to the caucuses – that between those organizations which lobby the United Nations as their regular work and more community-based organizations, for whom this is an extension of the local and service work. Often at meetings leadership is taken by feminist economists and little space is left for grass-roots activists. The choreography of the dance steps of women's movements is often set in New York with little input from those outside that hub.

In spite of these tensions, the caucuses have presented their collective message to states calling for specific measures to address the consequences of global restructuring for women.

The dance steps: women's caucuses resisting global restructuring

Women's movements are dancing resistance to global restructuring across the globe. In their communities and countries they are taking action to oppose the effects of restructuring policies. Regionally they are joining together to question and challenge the ways in which restructuring is implemented. Transnationally they have chosen to join together to work to bring their analysis and options into government deliberations. Global restructuring has primarily been addressed in the women's caucuses under the mantle of economic justice. While much of the work related to this was accomplished at the Copenhagen Social Summit and the Beijing Women's Conference, restructuring has been addressed to some extent at all conferences.

Economic justice remains the poor sister of women's transnational organizing. Economic justice does not have a tradition of strong international law like human rights does. There has also been less successful coalition building for action on economic justice issues than for environmental issues. And it has received much less recognition as an issue and much less support for action from women's groups around the world than health has. Its relatively low status reflects in part the complexity of the issues involved, the powerful actors who dominate the global economy, the mystification of economics which prevents many from understanding it, and the relative invisibility of women in analyses and practices of the global economy. The significance of economic justice within the women's caucuses also reflects disparities between and among women around the world, based on class, the international division of labor, ethnicity, and colonization.

Women have joined together through the women's caucuses to reframe the participants and definitions of restructuring; to call for accountability and transparency by those who are implementing it; to illustrate the effects of these practices especially on women; and to provide alternative visions.

Specifically, the women's caucuses have challenged a very limited definition of the actors and content of restructuring. Restructuring has often been framed as state policies which are intended to address the "realities" of an increasingly global market. Therefore many of the changes required have been addressed to states. Yet, the women's caucuses have recognized that restructuring is also facilitated by international financial institutions like the International Monetary Fund (IMF) and the World Bank, as well as TNCs. These institutions have promoted a particular form of restructuring in their policies and practices and thus must be part of who is called upon to make changes. For example, at the Beijing Conference, the women's linkage caucus called on governments to ensure greater accountability by the international financial institutions within the United Nations system.

> Their programs of stabilization and structural adjustment must be characterized by transparency, accountability, and participation by civil society, in their inception, development, implementation, and evaluation. Nation states should instruct their Executive Directors at the World Bank and IMF to ensure that all programs are designed to enhance social development, gender, race/ethnicity, equality and equity, and ecological sustainability.
>
> (WEDO 1995b: 3)

Building on the work done at the World Summit on Social Development, the caucus was successful in obtaining language, albeit fairly weak, on having the World Trade Organization (WTO) (Platform for Action para. 343) and international financial institutions be more accountable in their programs specifically for their effects on women (Platform for Action para. 342). The caucus was also successful in getting a commitment by governments to ensure that transnational corporations comply with national laws, regulatory codes, and applicable international agreements (Platform for Action para. 165(l), 177(c)). These first steps in obtaining accountability from international financial institutions and transnational corporations are morally compelling, but there can be only modest hope for their implementation. The dance of restructuring, as we shall see in the following section, involves considerable resistance and a willingness to ignore these commitments by governments on the part of transnational corporations and international financial institutions.

Women's groups across the world have also been arguing, at least since the 1985 World Conference on women, that restructuring policies have had negative effects on women and, specifically, have increased the feminization of poverty. "Women's poverty and marginalization results not only from structures of gender subordination but also from macro-economic structures which often depend on the subordination of women for their implementation" (WEDO 1995a: 2). As a result of restructuring policies, many women employed in the public sector have lost their jobs and the social safety net that may have cushioned their fall has been eroded. New jobs that have been developed as a part of the globalized economy are usually short-term, casual, and/or home-based. Women are the primary workers in these areas and thus have less secure jobs with fewer benefits and greater possibility of exploitation. With these type of changes, women's human rights, especially labor and economic rights, are under attack. Labor standards are undermined and measures to address inequalities in the workplace are often removed or weakened.

The women's caucuses have called on governments and multilateral institutions to recognize the specific effects restructuring has had on women and integrate women's concerns and perspectives in all restructuring policies. The Beijing Platform for Action (*Platform for Action and Beijing Declaration* (1996)), building on Commitment 8 of the World Social Summit Declaration, calls specifically on governments to recognize the links between women's poverty and restructuring (para. 16); analyze and adjust their policies to ensure a more equitable distribution of wealth (para. 58(b)); complement adjustment lending with enhanced, targeted social development lending (para. 59(f)); recognize and address the effects of restructuring on health, especially women's health (para. 91); integrate women's concerns, especially women in the informal sector, and a gender perspective in restructuring programs (para. 151, 175(b)); and develop employment programs for those negatively affected by structural adjustment policies (para. 178(e)).

Women's groups have also argued that global restructuring is much broader in scope than economic policies. The women's caucuses have brought forward at the various United Nations conferences their analyses of how global restructuring is implicated in the areas of human rights, health and population and the environment. For example, while most feminists and many government officials recognize that restructuring policies have had negative effects on women's access to health (because of the cuts to health funding), following the Cairo conference more argued that workers in restructured environments need stronger and better financed primary and public health programs to ensure that they could meet the demands for increased productivity and efficiency (Sen 1995). Thus, the women's caucuses challenged the logic of restructuring as inconsistent and redefined the focus of global restructuring in the area of health.

As early as the Rio Earth Summit, women's groups pushed for a recognition that "free market" restructuring policies and practices were inconsistent with measures promoting sustainable development and that restructuring had to be "redesigned and redirected to insure appropriate growth within the context of sustainable ecological policies and directed at social development" (WEDO 1995a: 2). Women's groups, through the caucuses at the Rio Earth Summit, the World Social Summit and the Beijing Women's Conference, argued that poverty is directly linked to overconsumption of resources and environmental degradation. They were successful in getting references in each of the conference documents to this link. For example, in the Beijing Platform for Action they were able to get recognition that the eradication of poverty is essential to the attainment of sustainable development (para. 247). It will be even more challenging to have states and corporations take this link seriously in their practices.

Uniquely women's caucuses have also brought forward the link between violence against women and global restructuring. Not only does violence within the household increase in times of economic crisis, but, as a result of restructuring, many support services for survivors of violence have been eliminated. At the Vienna Tribunal for Women's Human Rights, stories were told of how violence in response to global restructuring was seen by indigenous women in the Philippines and the United States, women who organized for unions in Bangladesh, migrant domestic workers in Europe, and women resisting structural adjustment programs (SAPs) in the Caribbean (Bunch and Reilly 1994: 65–72). These stories gave a face to the calls for ending SAPs and protecting the economic and social rights of women in the face of these policies.

While women's movements, especially through the women's caucuses, have argued for recognition that global restructuring has far-reaching consequences, one of the most important contributions they have made has been advocating for the participation of civil society in all restructuring decision making and practices. The caucuses have successfully lobbied to have language incorporated in conference documents which promotes the involvement of women in all policy making related to restructuring as well as to ensure that governments undertake gender analysis and impact assessment when they implement their restructuring policies. Their increased presence as non-governmental representatives to these international conferences has illustrated their firm commitment to participate in discussions about these significant changes in their lives. Since the Rio Earth Summit, NGOs have had easier access to United Nations conferences, although they must remain as observers or lobbyists unless governments invite them on delegations. The women's caucuses have spearheaded many of these efforts to include NGOs.

The work of women's caucuses has yielded a strong and clear voice advocating a cohesive feminist agenda at the United Nations conferences. States have begun to rely on their analysis and see them as important contributors to the work of these conferences. The seemingly unified (or seamless dance) caucuses presented to states, however, masks some of the diversities and tensions within the caucuses. The "mask" of a global feminist critique of restructuring, worn by the dancers of the women's caucuses, hides the complexities of these women's lives as a result of their ethnicities, class, colonization, abilities, language, and other inequalities. Many women have become impatient with the masked dance and the dance steps dictated by states. They have begun to create their own dance steps and alternative vision of the world.

In Beijing, after much of the lobbying around governmental texts had been done, non-governmental representatives still felt that more needed to be said about what their alternative vision of the world was. A significant number joined together to draft the NGO Beijing Declaration. It includes an analysis of the critical problems in the world and offers specific steps for governments, international institutions, transnational corporations, and peoples of the world to take to address these problems. The declaration boldly states that:

> the globalization of the world's so-called 'market economies' is a root cause of the increasing feminization of poverty everywhere. This violates human rights and dignity, the integrity of our eco-systems and the environment, and poses serious threats to our health.
>
> (Christiansen-Ruffman 1996: 39)

One response to this is the call for "accountable, transparent, and participatory institutions. They must be created in all spheres of life, especially to control powerful economic institutions such as the World Trade Organization and other international financial institutions as well as transnational corporations" (Christiansen-Ruffman 1996: 40). This alternative vision continues to mobilize women to resist global restructuring.

The dance steps of the women's caucuses have provided concrete and increasingly sophisticated contributions to discussions at the international level related to restructuring. At the United Nations conferences between 1992 and 1996, the caucuses analyzed and lobbied for specific commitments by governments to recognize and address the poverty, decreased health, employment shifts of, and violence against women that results from restructuring policies. They called on the governments to recognize the numerous institutions which participate and shape restructuring without being held accountable for it. They called for the inclusion of civil society actors in all discussions which affect their lives and they provided an alternative vision of what the world could look like when women's voices and concerns are incorporated.

Yet, as I argued earlier, these steps are part of a larger dance, one that includes states, international financial institutions and transnational corporations. Their responses to the steps of women's movements are also part of the dance of restructuring.

The dance of restructuring: partnering, coopting, pushing away, and side-stepping

Other dancers are part of the dance of restructuring. States, international financial institutions, and TNCs have, in many ways, set the parameters of the dance steps, leaving women's movements in a position only to resist. States and other actors have developed and implemented restructuring policies; they have decided who will lose their jobs and which measures will be introduced when. Some would argue they are the only dancers on the floor. Women's movements, however, have emphasized that states receive their legitimacy from their citizens in most parts of the world, that international financial institutions are comprised of representatives of states, and that TNCs rely on consumers to use their products and services. This gives citizens and consumers some power and it is this power that the caucuses are working to mobilize.

The caucuses have chosen to work first on getting governments to make commitments and then holding them accountable for these commitments. The inclusion of phrases or statements proposed by the women's caucuses in conference documents is in many ways starting within the confines of the government agenda. This concession is what has made the women's caucuses legitimate players in the eyes of government representatives. It has limited what could be said and confined the parameters for action. But the hope is that the results will be more promising, since governments have made these commitments themselves.

Governments have had various responses to the steps of women's movements in the dance. Some have embraced the work of the women's caucuses and used it for their own analysis, speeches, and positions. This has primarily been true of countries in the South, which often do not have the resources to send large numbers of delegates to the conferences. The women's caucuses have provided much needed assistance to these governments, in effect acting as dance partners. Other governments, especially those within North America and Europe, have worked with the caucuses on issues where their positions have been similar, but as argued in the conclusion, this partnering can take the form of coopting. Still others, primarily those which were part of the coalition of fundamentalist Christian and Islamic states, have actively worked to end the dance of the women's caucuses. They have challenged proposals to include gender and gender analysis in the Bejing Platform for Action. They have opposed what they view as "anti-family values," the use of the term "gender," and the inclusion of references to feminist movements in texts prepared for the Beijing conference. While most of the attacks have been focused on reproductive rights, the wider attacks on gender have also been directed to the inclusion of gender analysis in economic areas. Conservative and reactionary forces were successful in weakening some language in the Beijing Platform for Action with respect to reproductive rights, although not that related to gender analysis of economic processes.

Many of the significant forces in global restructuring such as TNCs and international financial institutions have remained silent in response to the work of the women's caucuses. This is a well-worn strategy. For years, they have ignored movements in resistance to restructuring and gone about their "business." The IMF and the WTO have done little to incorporate gender in their mandates and work despite the coordinated efforts towards these ends within the United Nations (Stienstra 1994: 136, 138). They have also worked through the United Nations to limit access for non-governmental actors to their areas. In effect, since they are neither accountable to nor require approval from women's movements (WEDO 1995), they can side-step the dance of women's caucuses at present.

Conclusions

Women's movements have taken their resistance to global restructuring to the international level through the work of women's caucuses at the United Nations conferences between 1992 and 1996. Their strategy has been to work within the confines of the existing government agenda to push for a more effective and feminist voice. They have been able to have greater access to the negotiations and successfully lobbied for commitments to the inclusion of gender and gender analysis in the documents of these conferences.

Accepting women's caucuses as legitimate and important actors in inter-governmental discussions is, however, a risky strategy for governments, international financial institutions, and TNCs, but may be even riskier for women's movements. While it allows women's groups to have a say and leads governments to make commitments, it does not require any action by governments. In fact, governments can begin to use the language of women's movements without implementing the significant actions that are attached to them. This process of cooptation has the effect of undermining women's dances of resistance. It appeals to women's movements because it indicates governments are listening. But governments can fail to act on these commitments without any significant effects, thus appealing to the corporate and financial forces who want to keep the status quo. Should governments begin to act on some of these commitments related to global restructuring, there will be significant pressure from the corporate sector to stop.

Women's movements need to become more aware of the complexities of the dance of restructuring. Until the music of the global political economy, written and performed by TNCs and primarily Northern states, is rewritten or removed, women's groups will be unable to lead or direct the dance. Faced with that, some groups may choose to add discordant tones to the music and try to make it impossible to dance. This could involve direct action, strikes, or other bits of cacophony. Other groups may continue to dance to a different tune – creating feminist economic alternatives including community-based economic development or self-sufficient communities. For those groups who continue in the dance of restructuring politics at intergovernmental levels, the challenge is to remain "resistant" partners, who do not allow themselves to be coopted, pushed away, or side-stepped. Such dancers need to take the lead with a strong sure step: one which unmasks and celebrates the diversities within their movements; one which is strategic, seeking to use opportunities to their greatest advantage; and one which is always listening and challenging the music with its own internal tensions and its external effects. With these steps, the dancers can recreate the music and the dance.

Notes

1   "Transnational" is a contested term. Many consider transnational to be defined by that which happens between states, within the context of interstate organizations or in a global political economy dominated by TNCs. In this article, I am using it to refer to those sites of resistance where women cross territorial borders to do their work and where they organize across and challenge other boundaries including identities like "nationalities" or "ethnicities." Transnational organizing also includes how women organize to address the ways in which women's lives and identities are shaped by transnational forces like "globalization." Runyan (1996) refers to this as "internationalized" while Grewal and Kaplan (1994) call it "transnational."

2   See Stienstra 1994 for a detailed discussion of the non-governmental and intergovernmental conferences throughout this period.

Conclusion

Feminist approaches to global restructuring

Anne Sisson Runyan and Marianne H. Marchand

It has been the contention of this volume that global restructuring cannot be understood in all its complexity without attention to gender as a significant power relation and (re)ordering system at local and global levels. A gender lens not only makes women and men visible as actors in global restructuring, thereby revealing that it is not an autonomous or inexorable process, but also leads us to take seriously, as Cynthia Enloe argues: "the amount and varieties of power at work" in the process (Enloe 1989: 197). Although much critical work on globalization has emphasized the power of transnational corporations (TNCs), intergovernmental organizations (IGOs), and wealthy states, such structural accounts of markets and states barely scratch the surface of the power relations embedded in civil society that enable the process of restructuring. Because they privilege top-down constructions of power, structural accounts tend to require either large-scale movements to counter TNCs and IGOs or, alternatively, produce political paralysis.

In contrast, feminist accounts, such as the ones in this volume, although often partaking of structural analysis, reveal more clearly the broad range of power sources at work in global restructuring by examining cultural and social forces. They also stress multiple forms of human agency in terms of both the construction of and resistance to global restructuring. Moreover, they highlight how constructions of masculinity and femininity are implicated in naturalizing "old" inequalities sustained and often deepened by global restructuring as well as how these gender constructions are reworked to produce "new" inequalities. Finally, they raise crucial questions about what new forms of subjectivities, identities, and social relations are arising out of the disruptions of and resistances to global restructuring that offer openings for redirecting restructuring toward greater equality and social justice.

Although feminist accounts of global restructuring in general can offer such insights, there is no one single feminist approach to global restructuring. Instead there are multiple feminist approaches which vary in terms of the mix of feminist perspectives, epistemologies, ontologies, and methodologies they employ. What the feminist contributors to this volume have in common is the stress on relational thinking which brings together theorizing about and analysis of meaning systems and ideologies, institutions and practices, as well as subjectivities and agencies.

By generally employing relational feminist perspectives, the contributions also reflect some similar epistemological commitments. While all are grounded in empirical investigations of various kinds, they reflect the position that knowledge is always "socially situated and, thus, productive, at best, of only partial accounts of reality" (Peterson and Runyan 1999: 24). Since none of us is "outside" global restructuring in that it represents continual shifts in subject(ivitie)s (what we understand ourselves to be) and objects (what we identify as material reality) as well as the meaning systems (produced through language and thought) that are derived from this relationship, it is impossible to have a single, definitive account of this process. However, multiple accounts from and about various social locations (especially those that are least privileged) within this process are more likely to lead to less partial accounts of global restructuring.

Such multiple accounts as those in this volume reveal that the ontology or nature of global restructuring is far more complicated than economistic accounts of this phenomenon suggest. These interdisciplinary contributions draw our attention to cultural, social, and political dimensions that are both created by and undergird the process. As has been argued explicitly and implicitly throughout the volume, the market, the state, and civil society (including the "private realm" of families/households) are being simultaneously restructured as are the previously assumed boundaries among them. At the same time, these restructurings are being enabled by reconstitutions of gender and racial ideologies which serve to justify as well as naturalize the "new" and "old" inequalities produced through restructuring. But as we have also seen, global restructuring is not a seamless or neat process, but rather produces disjunctures that cannot be fully resolved by (re)invoking ideologies of inequality.

In order to detect and document such disjunctures, a variety of methodologies are needed. What all feminist investigations of gender and global restructuring have in common is taking as their starting points the questions, "Where are the women?" and/or "Where are the men?" These questions enable us, first, to determine how global restructuring is gendered in terms of its differential impacts on women and men. As indicated in the Introduction to this volume, the bulk of feminist scholarship on gender and the more commonly used term, "globalization," has focused on the negative economic impacts on women in a globalized capitalist economy. This work stresses the marginalization and exploitation of women's productive and reproductive labor under globalization by pointing to the rise of unregulated, benefit-less, and casualized service and industrial production work for women with corresponding cuts in social welfare and public provisioning more generally. The contributions to this volume do not so much take issue with this general understanding, but rather complicate it by further asking "which women" and "which men" in what contexts experience global restructuring in what ways?

By highlighting women in varying social locations who speak to their own experiences, understandings, and actions, these contributions privilege women's subjectivity and agency in relation to global restructuring, thereby avoiding presenting them as only "victims" They also reveal that different women experience and interpret the processes associated with global restructuring in varying ways. As a result, their actions in response to these processes also vary in terms of their experiences, interpretations, and social/national locations. Thus, we not only see how uneven and non-homogeneous the process global restructuring is, but also a myriad of promising strategies to redirect various aspects of it. We also see that the "local" spaces, such as households, communities, and workplaces, from where the majority of women act, are the ones fraught with the most contradictions through which resistance strategies of the most varying types emerge.

Perhaps the most significant aspect of resistance that many of the treatments in this book reveal is the way that women in different contexts are themselves restructuring feminism. In the majority of cases, there is little political space for women to identify themselves as feminists, due to the association of feminism variously with Westernization, secularism, liberalism, state socialism, and/or sexual/social license. While this has long been the case in much of the world, restructuring, to the degree that it intensifies gender-based oppression even as it creates new circumstances for many women (such as engaging in formal production, migrating across borders, participating in market economies and liberal democracies, organizing transnationally, etc.), may further reduce the political space for identifications with feminism. At the same time, global restructuring increases the needs of and opportunities for women to struggle against the economic, social, cultural, and political oppressions that arise from it or in reaction to it. Thus, we see the emergence of new forms of feminism, which do not necessarily use the label "feminism" or terms and categories associated with Western feminism, but nevertheless entail self-conscious analyses of women's oppression in relation to particular experiences of global restructuring. Furthermore, although the sources of and remedies for women's (and others') oppression identified by "new" women activists are wide-ranging and even contradictory at times, these new forms of women's resistance, some of which are still quite nascent and inchoate, do show that connections among the local, national, and global are being made by women activists, who have become activists as a result of making these connections. As we have also seen in these chapters, there are other forms of women's resistance that are not based on an analysis of systems of oppression, but rather on an analysis of their immediate conditions. But even the "coping strategies" that arise from this more limited analysis provide clues as how women's identities and practices are shifting not just to accommodate restructuring, but also to improve or (momentarily, at least) escape their conditions. For example, when women migrate or enter the labor force out of economic necessity, they are challenging gender roles by leaving home and renegotiating gender relations at the household level where they can no longer be (solely) responsible for reproductive labor.

One could argue that this fragmentation of feminism is a healthy one for it calls our attention to the fact that women are not reduced to a single subject position under global restructuring. Instead, there is a multiplicity of subject positions that women are occupying as they negotiate within and resist restructuring. This is also the case for men. Although there appears to be a new hegemonic masculinity emerging that privileges the exploits of (White, Western, male) global managers, it is arising from the destablizations of other forms of masculinity. Although these destabilizations have had dire consequences in particular for working-class men in the West and East, the fact that masculinity is fragmenting suggests that this new form of hegemonic masculinity is vulnerable to destabilization as well. Analyses of how hegemonic masculinity is constructed by cultural "texts" remind us that it can never be fully achieved, but rather must always be "performed" (see, for example, Brown 1988; Jeffords 1989; Butler 1990; Zalewski and Parpart 1998). If hegemonic masculinity were assured, there would be no need for the constant invocation of what the "new man" needs to be and have. Nor would there be any need for images of greater and greater feats of power and control to prove one's hegemonic masculinity. And since hegemonic masculinities never replace, but only subordinate other masculinities they are always in danger of being challenged "from below" or subordinated themselves by some new form of hegemonic masculinity. Thus, they are inherently unstable and far from omnipotent. Although the fragmentation of masculinity has not been healthy for those men who have been (newly) subordinated, understanding masculinity as fragmented is vital in order to see that men, too, occupy multiple subject positions under global restructuring. Some of those positions produce efforts to further control and oppress women, but others can lead to alliances with those women who are resisting inequalities of all sorts.

In short, interdisciplinary ontologies and methodologies informed by relational feminist perspectives and epistemologies move us from looking at the gendered effects of global restructuring to examining the effects of gender on global restructuring and the effects of global restructuring on gender. The latter inquiry causes us to rethink gender, revealing it as a highly unstable category and thereby enabling us to disrupt the scripts of globalization that rely on gender to dichotomize thought and action as well as naturalize and legitimize inequality. As the contributions to this volume show, women are not powerless nor are men all-powerful in the global arena. As femininity and masculinity are rearticulated through restructuring, possibilities are opened for women and many men to challenge their subordinated positionings. Similarly, choices are not reduced to either embracing or completely rejecting all aspects of neoliberal restructuring. The women activists highlighted in this volume are reappropriating the meanings of democracy, human rights, equality, and freedom, which have been circumscribed by and subsumed under global capitalist market relations, through their agency in resistance to market imperatives and their insistence that access to goods and services must be accompanied by economic, political, and social justice at all levels. In this sense, women's resistance to global restructuring is challenging the separation between the economic and the political, social, and cultural. It is also countering the separation between the local and global. Women's struggles at both the local and global level confront the interconnected, but seemingly "scattered hegemonies" of "global economic structures, patriarchal nationalisms, 'authentic' forms of tradition, local structures of domination [including patriarchal gender contracts at the household level], and legal–juridical oppression on multiple levels" (Grewal and Kaplan 1994: 17). Thus, the question is not should resistance strategies be directed at the market or the state or civil society, but rather what strategies impact upon all three in ways that destabilize the hegemonies within and across them?

This volume only begins to offer some possible answers to this question. Much more work remains to further track trends in global restructuring and its relationship to gender in a variety of national and local contexts. We offer here a way to organize that work by encouraging attention to at least three dimensions of that relationship: sightings (the symbolic, discursive, and ideological realm); sites (the material, structural, and contextual realm); and resistances (the realm of identity, subjectivity, and agency). Without addressing all three, neither global restructuring nor gender as highly complex (re)organizing systems can be adequately understood. Indeed, as this collection shows, gender analysis enables us to see that global restructuring is not a homogeneous process nor does it produce a homogenized world. Within it, postmodern, latemodern, and pre-modern ideologies, practices, and identities co-exist in various degrees of tension, collusion, and hybridity. This means that we must simultaneously apply structural and post-structural insights in our analyses, which is what relational feminist thinking seeks to do. McDowell 1997; Moreover, such approaches, which foreground and oppose interacting forms of domination, seek to avoid the political paralysis, which can attend non-feminist structural and post-structural analyses, by stressing human, but particularly women's, emancipatory agency. They also problematize civil society, parts of which can often serve as agents of globalization and reactionary forces in response to it. In doing so, they help us identify which aspects of the state and civil society should be strengthened to advance emancipatory goals.

We realize that this volume does not centrally address a host of topics more typically covered by conventional treatments of globalization, such as global finance, information technology, international trade, and new regionalisms. While there is growing feminist literature on all these topics (see, for example, Kofman and Youngs 1996; Haraway 1997; Gabriel and MacDonald 1994; Haxton and Olsson 1997; McDowell 1997; Meyer and Prugl 1999), that reveals the gendered nature of these formations and practices, this collection focuses on looking for evidence of global restructuring in less familiar spaces and places in order to emphasize women's agency in resisting and redirecting the process. Documenting this agency in all geographical and organizational contexts is beyond the scope of a single collection, but these contributions provide the basis for expanding such inquiry.[1] We have also been more concerned with providing multiple feminist interpretive frames for thinking about global restructuring than with offering an exhaustive feminist account of every possible feature of it.

What all of us, who understand the need to take feminist approaches to global restructuring seriously, must do is to remain attentive to what sectors, institutions, actors, practices, and issues are rendered either masculinized or feminized by restructuring over time and in varying contexts. This will enable us to better determine where to look for and how to support/engage in multiple resistances to restructuring which seek to redirect it toward greater social justice, non-violence, and environmental sustainablity.

Notes

1 Other excellent sources for this kind of inquiry include Grewal and Kaplan 1994; Alexander and Mohanty 1997; Lowe and Lloyd 1997; Keck and Sikkink 1998, and Scott *et al.* 1997.

Bibliography

Abu-Lughod, L. (1990) "The romance of resistance: tracing transformations of power through Bedouin women," *American Ethnologist* 17: 41–55.

Ackers, L. (1998) *Shifting Spaces: Women, Citizenship and Migration within the European Union,* Bristol: Policy Press.

Adams, G. (1993) *The Great Hong Kong Sex Novel,* Hong Kong: AIP Publications.

Adler, N. (1994) "Competitive frontiers: women managing across borders," *Journal of Management Development* 13 (2): 24–41.

Agnew, J. and Corbridge, S. (1995) *Mastering Space: Hegemony, Territory and International Political Economy,* London: Routledge.

Akamatsu, R. (1985) "Danjo koyō kikai kintō hō no seiritsu ni tsuite," *Keizai Jin* 39 (9), September.

—— (1990) *Danjo Koyō Kikai Kintō Hō oyobi Rōdō Kijun Ho,* Tokyo: Josei Shokugyo Zaidan.

Akamatsu, R., Nuida, H., and Miura, S. (1986), "Josei no nōryoku ya yakuwari nitsuiteno koteitekina kangaekata o minaosō," *Fujin to Nenshosha,* no. 228, March.

Akamatsu, R., Higuchi, K., and Komano, Y. (1993) "Josei mondai 30-nen: kawatta mono kawaranai mono," *Nihon Fujin Mondai Konwakai Kaihō,* no. 53.

Akarui Senkyo Suishin Kyōkai (1980) *1979 December Shūgiin Giin Sōsenkyo no Jittai* (The Result of Lower House Election).

—— (1981) *1980 June Shūgiin Giin Sōsenkyo no Jittai.*

—— (1984) *1983 December Shūgiin Giin Sōsenkyo no Jittai.*

Al-Azmeh, A. (1993) *Islams and Modernities,* London and New York: Verso.

Alexander, M.J. and Mohanty, C.T. (eds.) (1997) *Feminist Genealogies, Colonial Legacies, Democratic Futures,* New York: Routledge.

Al-Sha'rawi, M.M. (1992) (in Arabic) *The Muslim Woman,* Cairo: Maktabet Al-Zahran.

Alvarez, S. (1990) *Engendering Democracy in Brazil,* Princeton, NJ: Princeton University Press.

—— (1996) "Concluding reflections: 'redrawing' the parameters of gender struggle," in J. Friedmann, R. Abers, and L. Autler (eds.) *Emergences: Women's Struggles for Livelihood in Latin America,* Los Angeles: UCLA Latin American Studies Center.

—— (1998) "Latin American feminisms 'Go Global': trends of the 1990s and challenges of the new millenium," in S. Alvarez, E. Dagnino, and A. Escobar (eds.) *Cultures of Politics/Politics of Culture: Re-visioning Latin American Social Movements,* Boulder, Colorado: Westview Press.

Anderson, B. (1997) Servants and Slaves: Europe's Domestic Workers, *Race and Class,* 39 (1): 1–37.

Anderson, B. and Phizacklea, A. (1997) *Migrant Domestic Workers: A European Perspective*, Brussels: Equal Opportunities Unit, European Commission.

Aoyagi Takeshi (1986) "Danjo koyō kikai kintō hō no genjō to shōrai," *Josei Bunka Kenkyujo Kiyo*, no. 1, January.

Appadurai, A. (1990) "Disjunction and difference in the global cultural economy," in M. Featherstone (ed.) *Global Culture: Nationalism, Globalization and Modernity*, London: Sage.

Arboleda, M. (1993) "Mujeres en el poder local en Ecuador," Proyecto "Mujer y desarrollo local," unpublished paper, IULA/CELCADEL, Quito.

Ascoly, N. (1994) "Abroad with Iron Jan," *Z Magazine*, November: 21–2.

Asian Domestic Workers Union (1995) *May Day Leaflet*.

Ashley, R.K. (1984) "The poverty of neorealism," *International Organization* 38: 225–86.

—— (1987) "The geopolitics of geopolitical space: toward a critical social theory of international politics," *Alternatives* 12: 403–34.

—— (1988) "Untying the sovereign state: a double reading of the anarchy problematique," *Millennium: Journal of International Studies* 17: 227–62.

Ashley, R.K. and Walker, R.B.J. (1990) "Reading dissidence/writing the discipline: crisis and the question of sovereignty in international studies," *International Studies Quarterly* 34: 367–416.

Ashworth, G. (ed.) (1995) *A Diplomacy of the Oppressed: New Directions in International Feminism*, London: Zed Books.

Aslanbeigui, N., Pressman, S. and Summerfield, G. (eds.) (1994) *Women in the Age of Economic Transformation: Gender Impact of Reforms in Post Socialist and Developing Countries*, London: Routledge.

"Atarashii josei no 'shinro' o saguru" (1975) (Roundtable), *Gekkan Jiyu Minshu*, no. 239, December.

Báez, R. (1997) *A ahora qué ... ? Una contribución al análisrs político-histórico actual*, Quito: Eskeletra Edutorial.

Bakker, I. (ed.) (1994) *The Strategic Silence: Gender and Economic Policy*, London: Zed Books.

—— (1997) "Identity, interests, and ideology: the gendered terrain of global restructuring," in Stephen Gill (ed.) *Globalisation and Democratisation: Structural Change and the New Multilateralism*, New York: United Nations University Press.

Barber, B. (1996) *Jihad vs. Mcworld*, New York: Ballantine Books.

Barnet, R.S. and Cavanagh, J. (1994) *Global Dreams: Imperial Corporations and the New World Order*, New York: Simon and Schuster.

Barrig, M. (1994) "The difficult equilibrium between bread and roses: women's organizations and democracy in Peru," in J. Jaquette (ed.) *The Women's Movement in Latin America: Participation and Democracy*, Boulder, Colorado: Westview Press.

—— (1996) "Women, collective kitchens and the crisis of the state in Peru," in J. Friedmann, R. Abers, and L. Autler (eds.) *Emergences: Women's Struggles for Livelihood in Latin America*, Los Angeles: UCLA Latin American Studies Center.

Baud, I. (1992) *Forms of Production and Women's Labour: Gender Aspects of Industrialization in India and Mexico*, N. Delhi: Sage Publications.

Bednáček, V. and Zemplínerová, A. (1997) "Foreign direct investment in the Czech manufacturing sector," *Prague Economic Papers* 2: 141–55.

Benería, L. (1992) "The Mexican debt crisis: restructuring the household and the economy," in L. Benería and S. Feldman (eds.) *Unequal Burden: Economic Crisis, Persistent Poverty, and Women's Work*, Boulder, Colorado: Westview Press.

Benería, L. and Feldman, S. (eds.) (1992) *Unequal Burden: Economic Crisis, Persistent Poverty and Women's Work*, Boulder, Colorado: Westview Press.

Benería, L. and Mendoza, B. (1995) "Structural adjustment and social emergency funds: the cases of Honduras, Mexico and Nicaragua," *European Journal of Development Research* Spring.

Benería, L. and Roldan, M. (1987) *The Crossroads of Class and Gender. Industrial Homework, Subcontracting, and Household Dynamics in Mexico City*, Chicago and London: University of Chicago Press.

Berger, M. (1996) "Yellow mythologies: the East Asian miracle and post-Cold War capitalism," *Positions* 4 (1): 90–126.

"Beyond the Debt Crisis: Structural Transformations. Final Report of the International Women's Seminar" (1990) New York: United Nations Non-governmental Liaison Service, 23–25 April.

Bhabba, J. and Shutter, S. (1994) *Women's Movement: Women under Immigration, Nationality and Refugee Law*, London: Joint Council for the Welfare of Immigrants.

Bhachu, P. (1993) "New European women and new cultural forms: culture, class and consumption among British Asian women," in H. Rudolph and M. Morokvasic (eds.) *Bridging States and Markets*, Berlin: Sigma.

Bhattacharjee, A. (1997) "The public/private mirage: mapping homes and undomesticating violence work in the South Asian immigrant community," in M.J. Alexander and C.T. Mohanty (eds.) *Feminist Genealogies, Colonial Legacies, Democratic Futures*, New York: Routledge.

Bird, J., Curtis, B., and Putnam, T. *et al.* (1993) *Mapping the Futures: Local Cultures, Global Change*, London: Routledge.

Bondi, L. (1994) "Gentrification, work, and gender identity," in A. Kobayashi (ed.) *Women, Work and Place*, Montreal: McGill-Queen's University Press.

Boose, E. (1993) "Techno-muscularity and the 'Boy-Eternal': from the quagmire to the Gulf," in M. Cook and A Woollacott (eds) *Gendering War Talk*, Princeton, NJ: Princeton University Press.

Bordo, S. (1990) "Feminism, postmodernism and gender-scepticism," in L.J. Nicholson (ed.) *Feminism/Postmodernism*, London: Routledge.

Boris, E. and Prugl, E. (eds.) (1996) *Homeworkers in Global Perspective: Invisible No More*, New York: Routledge.

Boserup, E. (1970) *Women's Role in Economic Development*, New York: St. Martin's Press.

Brand, L.A. (1992) "Economic and political liberalization in a rentier economy: the case of the Hashemite Kingdom of Jordan," in I. Harik and D.J. Sullivan (eds.) *Privatization and Liberalization in the Middle East*, Bloomington: Indiana University Press.

—— (1998) *Women, the State and Political Liberalization: Middle Eastern and North African Experiences*, New York: Columbia University Press.

Brdečková, T. (1994) "Cekani Na Libusi: Pristich sto let by mely svetu vladnout zeny" *Respekt* 41: 7–9.

Brecher, J. and Costello, T. (1994) *Global Village or Global Pillage*, Boston: South End Press.

Brinton, M.C. (1993) *Women and the Economic Miracle: Gender and Work in Postwar Japan*, Berkeley: University of California Press.

Brittan, A. (1989) *Masculinity and Power*, Oxford: Blackwell.

Brod, H. (1987) "A case for men's studies," in M.S. Kimmel (ed.) *Changing Men: New Directions in Research on Men and Masculinities*, London: Sage Focus.

Brodie, J. (1994) "Shifting the boundaries: gender and the politics of restructuring," in I. Bakker (ed.) *The Strategic Silence: Gender and Economic Policy*, London: Zed Books.

Brown, W. (1988) *Manhood and Politics*, Totowa, NJ: Rowman and Littlefield.

Bruegel I. (1996) "The trailing wife: a declining breed? Careers, geographical mobility and household conflict 1970–89," in R. Crompton, D. Gallie and K. Purcell (eds.) *Changing Forms of Employment: Organisations, Skills and Gender*, London: Routledge.

Brynen, R., Bahgat K., and Noble, P. (eds.) (1995) *Political Liberalization and Democratization in the Arab World, Vol. I: Theoretical Perspectives*, Boulder, Colorado: Lynne Rienner Publishers.

Built Environment (1994) A Rising European Underclass? 20, 3.

Bullock, S. (1994) *Women And Work*, London: Zed Books.

Bunch, C. and Reilly, N. (1994) *Demanding Accountability: The Global Campaign and Vienna Tribunal for Women's Human Rights*, New Jersey/New York: Center for Women's Global Leadership and United Nations Development Fund for Women.

Burawoy, M. and Krotov, P. (1992) "The Soviet transition from socialism to capitalism," *American Sociological Review* 57 (1): 16–38.

Burgers, J. and Enghersen, G. (1996) "Globalisation, migration and undocumented immigrants," *New Community* 22 (4): 619–36.

Burris, B.H. (1989) "Technocratic organisation and gender," *Women's Studies International Forum*, 12, 4.

Buschkens, W.F.L. (1974) *The Family System of the Paramaribo Creoles*, 's Gravenhage: Martinus Nijhoff.

Butler, J. (1990) "Gender trouble, feminist theory, and psychoanalytic discourse," in L.J. Nicholson (ed.) *Feminism/Postmodernism*, New York: Routledge.

Campani, G. (1993) "Labour markets and family networks: Filipino women in Italy," in H. Rudolph and M. Morokvasic (eds.) *Bridging States and Markets*, Berlin: Sigma.

—— (1997) "Women and social exclusion: the case of migrant women." Inclusion and Exclusion: International Migrants and Refugees in Europe and North America, paper presented at the International Sociological Association, New York.

Campbell, D. (1992) *Writing Security: United States Foreign Policy and the Politics of Identity*, Manchester: Manchester University Press.

Carey-Wood, J., Duke, K., Karn, V., and Marshall, T. (1995) *The Settlement of Refugees in Britain*, London: HMSO.

Castells, M. (1994) "European cities, the information society, and the global economy," *New Left Review* 204: 18–32.

—— (1996) *The Rise of the Network Society. The Information Age: Economy, Society and Culture, Volume I*, Oxford: Blackwell Publishers.

—— (1997) *The Power of Identity. The Information Age: Economy, Society and Culture, Volume II*, Oxford: Blackwell Publishers.

—— (1998) *End of Millennium. The Information Age: Economy, Society and Culture, Volume III*, Oxford: Blackwell Publishers.

Castle, M. (1990) "Our woman in Prague," *Catalyst* 4, July–September.

Castles, S. and Miller, M. (1998) *Age of Migration*, 2nd edn, London: Macmillan.

Centro Femenino 8 de Marzo (1993) *Nuestra Voz*, no. 5, March.

Centro María Quilla/CEAAL (1990) *Mujeres, educación y conciencia de género en Ecuador*, Quito: Centro María Quilla.

Čermáková, M. (1993) "The state and perspectives of research on the economic and social status of women in the Czech Republic," unpublished research paper given at the International Seminar on Gender Studies: "Towards the Year 2000," Athens.

—— (1996) "Processes of developing pro-women policies in the Czech Republic," paper presented at "Women, Gender and the Transition," Lucca, Italy, 19–24 June.

Cerny, P.G. (1995) "Globalization and the changing logic of collective action," *International Organization* 49 (4): 595–625.

Český statistický úřad (1995) *Statistická ročenka České Republiky 1995*, Praha.

Chang, K. and Groves, J. (forthcoming) " 'Saints' and 'Prostitutes': sexual discourse in the Filipina domestic worker community in Hong Kong," *Women's Studies International Forum.*

Chapman, R. and Rutherford, J. (eds.) (1988) *Male Order: Unwrapping Masculinity*, London: Lawrence and Wishart.

Charlton, S.E.M. (1984) *Women in Third World Development*, Boulder, Colorado: Westview Press.

Chase, R.S. (1997a) "Baby boom or bust? Changing fertility in the post-Communist Czech and Slovak Republic," *Yale Economic Growth Center Papers*, no. 768.

—— (1997b) "Women's labor force participation during and after communism: a case study of the Czech Republic and Slovakia," *Yale Economic Growth Center Papers*, no. 769.

—— (1997c) "Markets for communist human capital: returns to education and experience in the Czech Republic and Slovakia," paper presented at the Labor Markets in Transition Economies Conference at the William Davidson Institute, University of Michigan Business School, Ann Arbor, Michigan, October.

Chen, M.A. (1996) "Engendering world conferences: The International Women's Movement and the United Nations," in T.G. Weiss and L. Gordenker (eds.) *NGOs, the UN and Global Governance*, Boulder, Colorado: Lynne Rienner Publishers.

Chin, C.B.N. and Mittelman, J.H. (1997) "Conceptualising resistance to globalisation," *New Political Economy* 2 (1): 25–38.

Christiansen-Ruffman, L. (1996) "Pages from Beijing: A woman's creed and the NGO Declaration," *Canadian Woman Studies* 16 (3): 35–41.

Cocks, J. (1989) *The Oppositional Imagination: Feminism, Critique and Political Theory*, London: Routledge.

Cohen, K. (1997) "Needle and thread: Kanafas find a niche in the dying textile industry," *The Prague Business Journal* 21–8, November.

Cohen, R. (1997) *Global Diasporas: An Introduction*, London: University College Press.

Connell, R.W. (1987) *Gender and Power*, Cambridge: Polity Press.

—— (1993) "The big picture: masculinities in recent world history," *Theory and Society* 22: 579–623.

—— (1995) *Masculinities*, Cambridge: Polity Press.

Constable, N. (1996) "Jealousy, chasitity, and abuse: Chinese maids and foreign helpers in Hong Kong," *Modern China* 22 (4): 448–79.

—— (1997) *Maid to Order in Hong Kong: Stories of Filipina Workers*, Ithaca, NY: Cornell University Press.

Cook, J. (1996) "The Czech Republic," *Business Central Europe*, July/August.

Cook, T. (1993) "Remember nothing's impossible: an outsider's look at access to abortion in the Czech Republic," *Jednim Okem/One Eye Open* 1 (2): 65–71.

Coole, D. (1993) *Women in Political Theory*, 2nd edn., New York: Harvester Wheatsheaf.

Corrin, C. (ed.) (1992) *Superwomen and the Double Burden: Women's Experience of Change in Central and Eastern Europe*, Toronto: Second Story Press.

Court, M. (1994) "Removing macho management: lessons from the field of education," *Gender, Work and Organisation* 1, 1.

Cox, R. (1987) *Production, Power, and World Order*, New York: Columbia University Press.

—— (1993) "Structural issues of global governance: implications for Europe," in S. Gill (ed.) *Gramsci, Historical Materialism and International Relations*, Cambridge, UK: Cambridge University Press.

—— (1994) "Global restructuring: making sense of the changing international political economy," in R. Stubbs and G. Underhill (eds.) *Political Economy and the Changing Global Order*, Toronto: McClelland & Stewart Inc.

Czech Business and Trade Journal (1998) "The glass and ceramic industry in the Czech Republic," no. 3.

Dahlelrup, D. (1994) "Learning to live with the state – state, market, and civil society: women's need for state intervention in East and West," *Women's Studies International Forum* 17: 117–27.

Daines, V. and Seddon, D. (1994) "Fighting for survival: women's responses to austerity measures," in J. Walton and D. Seddon (eds.) *Free Markets and Food Riots: The Politics of Global Adjustment*, Cambridge, UK: Blackwell Publishers.

Defares, R.S. and Khoesial, S. (1994) "Programma voor de analyse van agrarisch beleid met betrekking tot vrouwelijke voedselproducenten in het Andesgebied, de Zuidkegel en het Caribisch gebied," Eeen IICA–IDB Project, Nationale Samenvatting, Paramaribo.

De Waal Malefijt, A. (1963) *The Javanese of Surinam: Segment of a Plural Society*, Assen: Van Gorcum.

Dicken, P. (1992) *Global Shift*, London: The Guilford Press.

—— (1994) "Global–Local tensions: firms and states in the global space-economy," *Economic Geography* 70 (2): 101–27.

Drainville, A.C. (1994) "International political economy in the age of open Marxism," *Review of International Political Economy* 1 (1): 105–32.

Dunning, J.H. (1988) *Multinationals, Technology and Competitiveness*, London: Unwin Hyman.

Dvořák, J. and Solčová, I. (1998) *Vadernecûm: moderní manažerky*, Praha: Management Press.

Economist Intelligence Unit (1996) *Jordan: Country Report*, First quarter.

Economic and Social Commission for West Asia (ESCWA) (1995a) "Arab women in the manufacturing industries," *Studies on Women in Development*, no. 19, New York: United Nations.

—— (1995b) *Statistical Abstract of the ESCWA Region 1984–93*, New York: United Nations.

—— (1995c) *Survey of Economic and Social Developments in the ESCWA Region 1994*, New York: United Nations.

Ehrenreich, B. (1983) *The Hearts of Men: American Dreams and the Flight from Commitment*, London: Pluto Press.

Eichengreen, B. and Kohl, R. (1998) "The external sector, the state and development in Eastern Europe," *Working Paper 125*, The Berkeley Roundtable on the International Economy, March.

Einhorn, B. (1991) "Where have all the women gone? Women and the Women's Movement in East Central Europe," *Feminist Review* 30, Winter: 17–35.

—— (1993) *Cinderella Goes to Market: Women's Movements in East-Central Europe*, London: Verso.

—— (1995) "Ironies of history: citizenship issues in the new market economies of East-Central Europe," in B. Einhorn and E. Janes (eds.) *Women and Market Societies: Crisis and Opportunity*, Aldershot: Edward Elgar.

Eisenstein, Z. (1979) *Capitalist Patriarchy and the Case for Socialist Feminism*, New York: Monthly Review Press.

—— (1994) *The Color of Gender: Re-imaging Democracy*, Berkeley: University of California Press.

—— (1996) "Stop stomping on the rest of us: retrieving publicness from the privatization of the globe," *Journal of Global Legal Studies* 4: 59–95.

Ekonom (1998) "Jsou cest zamestnánci v zahranicních firmach diskriminovani?" no. 35: 34.

El-Solh, C. (1994) "Women and poverty in the ESCWA region: issues and concerns," paper prepared for the Arab Regional Preparatory Meeting for the Fourth World Conference on Women (Amman, Jordan, November), ESCWA, Amman.

Elshtain, J.B. (1981) *Public Man, Private Woman: Women in Social and Political Thought*, Princeton, NJ: Princeton University Press.

Elson, D. (ed.) (1995) *Male Bias in the Development Process*, 2nd edn., Manchester: Manchester University Press.

Engels, F. (1992) *The Origin of the Family, Private Property, and the State*, New York: International Publishers.

Enloe, C. (1989) *Bananas, Beaches, and Bases: Making Feminist Sense of International Relations*, Berkeley: University of California Press.

—— (1993) *The Morning After: Sexual Politics at the End of the Cold War*, Berkeley: University of California Press.

Entzinger, H.B. (1996) "De kracht nvan openheid: Nieuwe sociale en culturele relaties tussen Suriname en Nederland," in L. Kloof-Monsels (ed.) *Suriname en Nederland: de volgende 20 jaar*, Verslag seminar, November 22–23, 1995, Paramaribo: IMWO, pp. 59–70.

Escobar, A. (1995) *Encountering Development*, Princeton, NJ: Princeton University Press.

Escriva A. (1997) "Control, composition and character of new migration to South-West Europe: the case of Peruvian women in Barcelona," *New Community* 23 (1): 43–58.

Espin, M. (1994) "Crossing borders and boundaries: the life narratives of immigrant lesbians," paper presented at the 102nd annual convention of the American Psychological Association, Los Angeles, CA.

Eviota, E.U. (1992) *The Political Economy of Gender: Women and the Sexual Division of Labour in the Philippines*, London: Zed Books.

Featherstone, M. (1990) "Global culture: an introduction," in M. Featherstone (ed.) *Global Culture: Nationalism, Globilization, and Modernity*, London: Sage.

—— (ed.) (1990) *Global Culture: Nationalism, Globalization, and Modernity*, London: Sage.

Featherstone, M. and Lash, S. (1995) "Globalization, modernity and the spatialization of social theory: an introduction," in M. Featherstone, S. Lash, and R. Robertson (eds.) *Global Modernities*, London: Sage Publications.

Featherstone, M., Lash, S., and Robertson, R. (eds.) (1995) *Global Modernities*, London: Sage.

Fekete, L. (1997) "Blacking the economy," *Race and Class* 39: 1–17.

Fernandez-Kelly, M.P. (1983) *For We are Sold, I and My People: Women and Industry in Mexico's Frontier*, Albany, NY: State University of New York Press.

Findlay, A. (1995) "Skilled transient: the invisible phenomenon," in R. Cohen (ed.) *Cambridge Survey of World Migration*, Cambridge: Cambridge University Press.

Fodor, E. (forthcoming) "Gender in transition: unemployment in Hungary, Poland and Slovakia," *East European Politics and Societies*.

Fong, M. and Paull, G. (1993) "Women's economic status in the restructuring of Eastern Europe," in V. Moghadam (ed.) *Democratic Reform and the Position of Women in Transitional Economies*, Oxford: Clarendon Press.

Franco, J. (1989) *Plotting Women: Gender and Representation in Mexico*, New York: Columbia University Press.

Fraser, N. and Nicholson, L.J. (1990) "Social criticism without philosophy: an encounter between feminism and postmodernism," in L.J. Nicholson (ed.) *Feminism/Postmodernism*, New York: Routledge.

Friedmann, J. (1995) "Where we stand: a decade of world city research," in P. Knox and P.J. Taylor (eds.) *World Cities in a World-System*, Cambridge: Cambridge University Press.

—— (1997) "Global crisis, the struggle for cultural identity and intellectual porkbarrelling: cosmopolitans versus locals, ethnics and nationals in an era of de-hegemonisation," in P. Werbner and T. Modood (eds.) *Debating Cultural Hybridity: Multi-Cultural Identities and the Politics of Anti-Racism*, London: Zed Books.

Fukuyama, F. (1989) "The end of history?" *The National Interest* 3–18.

Funk, N. and Mueller, M. (eds.) (1993) *Gender Politics and Post-Communism*, New York: Routledge.

Gabriel, C. and Macdonald, L. (1994) "NAFTA, women and organising in Canada and Mexico: forging a 'feminist internationality,'" *Millennium* 23 (3): 535–62.

Gal, S. (1997) "Feminism and civil society," in J.W. Scott, C. Kaplan, and D. Keates (eds.) *Transitions, Environments, Translations: Feminisms in International Politics*, New York: Routledge.

Geerling, I. (1998) "Betrekkingen tussen Nederland en Suriname op huishoudniveau. Een onderzoek onder Hindostanen in Den Haag naar hun contacten en ondersteuningsrelaties met familie en bekenden in Suriname," Doctoraal scriptie (Master's thesis), Universiteit van Amsterdam.

General Bureau for Statistics (GBS) (1996) *National Accounts Statistics, 1980, 1985, 1990–1994 of the Republic of Suriname*, Paramaribo.

—— (1997) *Statistical Yearbook 1996 of the Republic of Suriname*, Paramaribo.

—— (1998) *Households in Suriname, 1993–1997*, Paramaribo

Germain, R.D. (1997) *The International Organization of Credit: States and Global Finance in the World-Economy*, Cambridge: Cambridge University Press.

Gibson-Graham, J.K. (1996) *The End of Capitalism (as we knew it): A Feminist Critique of Political Economy*, Cambridge, UK: Blackwell.

Giddens, A. (1990) *The Consequences of Modernity*, Cambridge, UK: Polity Press.

—— (1991) *Modernity and Self-Identity: Self and Society in the Late Modern Age*, Cambridge: Polity Press.

Gill, S. (1992) "Economic globalization and the internationalization of authority: limits and contradictions," *Geoforum* 23 (3): 269–83.

—— (ed.) (1993) *Gramsci, Historical Materialism and International Relations*, Cambridge, UK: Cambridge University Press.

—— (1994) "Knowledge, politics, and neo-liberal political economy," in R. Stubbs and G. Underhill (eds.) *Political Economy and the Changing Global Order*, Toronto: McClelland & Stewart Inc.

—— (1995a) "Globalisation, market civilisation, and disciplinary neoliberalism," *Millennium* 24 (3): 399–423.

—— (1995b) "Theorizing the interregnum: the double movement and global politics in the 1990s," in B. Hettne (ed.) *International Political Economy: Understanding Global Disorder*, London: Zed Books.

—— (1995c) "The global panopticon? The neoliberal state, economic life, and demo-cratic surveillance," *Alternatives* 2: 1–49.

—— (1996) "Globalization, democratization and the politics of indifference," in S. Gill and J. Mittleman (eds.) *Globalization: Critical Perspectives*, Boulder, Colorado and London: Lynne Rienner Publishers.

Gill, S. and Law, D. (1988) *The Global Political Economy: Perspectives, Problems and Policies*, Baltimore: John Hopkins University Press.

—— (1989) "Global hegemony and the structural power of capital," *International Studies Quarterly* 33: 475–99.

Gill, S. and True, J. (1997) "Europe and the former East Bloc: structural change and democratic potentials," paper presented at Seminar for European Left Alternatives to Neo-liberalism, University of Amsterdam, The Netherlands, 4–8 February.

Gilpin, R. (1987) *The Political Economy of International Relations*, Princeton: Princeton University Press.

"Globalisation and the politics of resistance" (1997) (special issue, special editor B.K. Gills), *New Political Economy* 2 (1): 25–38.

Gould W. (1988) "Skilled international migration," *Geoforum* 19: 381–6.

Goven, J. (1993) "Gender politics in Hungary: autonomy and anti-feminism," in N. Funk and M. Mueller (eds.) *Gender Politics and Post-Communism*, New York: Routledge.

Gregson N. and Lowe M. (1994) *Servicing the Middle Classes: Class, Gender and Waged Domestic Labour in Contemporary Britain*, London: Routledge

Grewal, I. and Kaplan, C. (1994) *Scattered Hegemonies: Postmodernity and Transnational Feminist Practices*, Minneapolis: University of Minnesota Press.

Hall, R., Ogden, P., and Hill, C. (1996) "Household changes in London and Paris 1981–1991 with particular reference to the lone-person household," paper presented at the Royal Geographical Society Annual Conference, Strathclyde.

Hamnett, C. (1994a) "Social polarisation in global cities: theory and evidence," *Urban Studies* 31 (3): 401–24.

—— (1994b) "Socio-economic change in London: professionalization not polarization," *Built Environment* 20 (3): 192–203.

—— (1996) "Social polarisation, economic restructuring and welfare state regimes," *Urban Studies* 33 (8): 11407–30.

Hannerz, U. (1990) "Cosmopolitans and locals in world culture," in M. Featherstone (ed.) *Global Culture: Nationalism, Globalization, and Modernity*, London: Sage.

—— (1996) *Transnational Connections: Culture, People, Places*, London: Routledge.

Haraway, D. (1991) *Simians, Cyborgs and Women: The Reinvention of Nature*, London: Free Association Books.

—— (1997) *Modest_Witness@Second_Millennium.FemaleMan©_Meets_OncoMouse™: Feminism and Technoscience*, New York and London: Routledge.

Harcourt, W. (ed.) (1994) *Feminist Perspectives on Sustainable Development*, London: Zed Books (in association with Society for International Development, Rome).

Hardill, I. and MacDonald S. (1998) "Choosing to relocate: an examination of the impact of expatriate work on dual career households," *Women's Studies International Forum* 21 (1): 21–9.

Harding, S. (1986) *The Science Question in Feminism*, Milton Keynes: Open University Press.

Harrington, M. (1992) "What exactly's wrong with the liberal state as an agent of change?" in V.S. Peterson (ed.) *Gendered States: Feminist (Re)Visions of International Relations Theory*, Boulder, Colorado: Lynne Reiner.

Hartsock, N. (1985) *Money, Sex, and Power*, Boston: Northeastern University Press.

Harvey, D. (1989) *The Condition of Postmodernity: An Enquiry into the Orgins of Cultural Change*, Oxford: Blackwell.

"Hataraku josei ni totte 'byōdō' towa" (Roundtable) (1984) *Ekonomisuto* 62: 41, October.

Havelková, H. (1992) "A few pre-feminist thoughts," in N. Funk and M. Muller (eds) *Gender and the Politics of PostCommunism*, New York, London: Routledge.

—— (1993) "Patriarchy in Czech society," *Hypatia* 8 (4): 89–96.

—— (1997) "Transitory and persistent difference: feminisms East and West," in J.W. Scott, C. Kaplan, and D. Keates (eds.) *Transitions, Translations, Environments: Feminism in International Politics*, New York: Routledge.

Haxton, E. and Olsson, C. (eds.) (1997) *Women and Sustainability in International Trade*, Uppsala, Sweden: Global Publications Foundation.

Hayakawa, T. (1979) "Katei kiban no jūjitu ni kansuru taisaku yōkō," *Gekkan Jiyu Minshu* no. 318, September.

Heinen, J. (1990) "Inequalities at work: the gender division of labour in the Soviet Union and Eastern Europe," *Studies of Political Economy* 33 (Autumn).

—— (1992) "Polish democracy is a masculine democracy?" *Women's Studies International Forum* 15, 1.

Heitlinger, A. (1979) *Women and State Socialism: Sex Inequality in the Soviet Union and Czechoslovakia*, Catham: W&J Makey, Ltd.

—— (1993) "The impact of the transition from communism on the status of women in the Czech and Slovak Republics" in N. Funk and M. Mueller (eds.) *Gender Politics and Post-Communism*, New York: Routledge.

Held, D. and McGrew, A. (1993) "Globalization and the liberal democratic state," *Government and Opposition* 28: 261–88.

Helleiner, E. (1994) "From Bretton Woods to global finance: a world turned upside down," in R. Stubbs and G. Underhill (eds.) *Political Economy and the Changing Global Order*, Toronto: McClelland & Stewart Inc.

Helleman, L. (1995) "Een onderzoek naar de ondersteuningsrelatie op huishoudniveau tussen Nederland en Suriname," unpublished Master's thesis, University of Amsterdam.

Heyzer, N. (1989) "Asian women wage-earners: their situation and possibilities for donor intervention," *World Development* 17 (7): 1109–23.

Higuchi K., Nakajima, M., Teruoka, I., and Masuda, R. (1985) "Onna tachi no ima soshite mirai wa?" *Sekai*, no. 478.

Hirst, P. and Thompson, G. (1996) *Globalization in Question*, Cambridge, UK: Polity Press.

Home Office (1997) *Control of Immigration: Statistics United Kingdom 1996*, London: Government Statistical Service.

Hondagneau-Sotelo, P. and Messner, M.A. (1994) "Gender displays and men's power: the 'new man' and the Mexican immigrant man," in H. Brod and M. Kaufman (eds.) *Theorizing Masculinities*, London: Sage.

Hoodfar, H. (1988) "Household budgeting and financial management in a lower-income Cairo neighborhood," in D. Dwyer and J. Bruce (eds.) *A Home Divided: Women and Income in the Third World*, Stanford, CA: Stanford University Press.

Hooper, C. (1998) "Masculinist practices and gender politics: the operation of multiple masculinities in international relations," in M. Zalewski and J. Parpart (eds.) *The "Man" Question in International Relations*, Boulder, Colorado: Westview Press.

Horowitz, D. (1994) *Socioeconomic Report: Surinam, the Social Sectors*, Vanderbilt University.

Hunt, S. (1997) "Women's vital voices: the costs of exclusion in Eastern Europe," *Foreign Affairs* 76 (4): 2–9.

Hutton, W. (1996) *The State We're In*, rev. edn., London: Vintage.

Inoue, T. and Ehara, Y. (eds.) (1995) *Women's Data Book*, Tokyo: Yuhikaku.

International Labor Organization (ILO) (1997) *Maternity Protection at Work: Revision of the Maternity Protection Convention (Revised), 1952 (No. 103) and Recommendation, 1952 (No. 95)*, Geneva: ILO Publications.

—— Central European Team (forthcoming) *Women in the World of Work: Women Workers' Rights in Hungary*, Budapest: ILO Publications.

Iwao, S. (1993) *The Japanese Woman: Traditional Image and Changing Reality*, New York: Free Press.

Jaquette, J. (ed.) (1994) *The Women's Movement in Latin America: Participation and Democracy*, Boulder, Colorado: Westview Press.

Jedličková, P. (1996) "Hledáme ataktivni asistenku ředitelé do 25-ti let: Discriminace podle věku a pohlaví v inžeratěch naších zaměstnávatelu," *Zen Sen* 1, 2.

Jeffords, S. (1989) *The Remasculinization of America*, Bloomington, IN: Indiana University Press.

Jelin, E. (ed.) (1990) *Women and Social Change in Latin America*, London: Zed Books.

Joekes, S. (1987) *Women in the World Economy*, New York: Oxford University Press.

Joekes, S. and Weston, A. (1994) *Women and the New Trade Agenda*, New York: UNIFEM.

Jordanian National Committee for Women (JNCW) (1995) *The Jordanian Woman: Reality and Future Aspirations: The Jordanian National Report*, report prepared for the Fourth World Conference on Women, Beijing, September, 1995.

Jose, V. (1991) "Philippine external debt problem: the Marcos years," *Journal of Contemporary Asia* 21 (2): 222–45.

Jung, N. (1994) "Eastern European women with Western eyes," in G. Griffin *et al.* (eds.) *Stirring It: Challenges for Feminism*, London: Taylor & Francis.

Kabeer, N. (1991) "Cultural dopes or rational fools? Women and labour supply in the Bangladesh garment industry," *European Journal of Development Research* 133–59.

—— (1994) *Reversed Realities: Gender Hierarchies in Development Thought*, London and New York: Verso.

Kahne, H. and Giele, J.Z. (eds.) (1992) *Women's Work and Women's Lives: The Continuing Struggle Worldwide*, Boulder, Colorado: Westview Press.

Kandiyoti, D. (1985) *Women in Rural Production Systems*, Paris: UNESCO.

—— (1991) "Identity and its discontents: women and the nation," *Millenium: Journal of International Studies* 20 (3): 429–43.

Kapoor, M. with Lyons, R. (1996/7) "Labour pains," *Business Central Europe*, December/January.

Kapstein, E.B. (1996) "Workers and the world economy," *Foreign Affairs* 75 (May/June): 16–37.

Karam, A. (1998) *Women, Islamisms and State: Contemporary Feminisms in Egypt*, Basingstoke: Macmillan.

Karat Coalition (1999) "Regional report on institutional mechanisms for the advancement of women in the countries of Central and Eastern Europe," Report of the

Regional Network of Women's NGOS in Central and Eastern Europe prepared for the 43rd session of the Committee on the Status of Women, United Nations, Warsaw.

Keck, M.E. and Sikkink, K. (1998) *Activists Beyond Borders*, Ithaca, NY: Cornell University Press.

Kennedy, M.L. (ed.) (1994) *Envisioning Eastern Europe: Postcommunist Cultural Studies*, Ann Arbor: University of Michigan Press.

Khuri-Tubbeh, T. (1994) "The determinants of women's work: a case study from three urban low-income communities in Amman, Jordan," unpublished PhD dissertation, Portland State University.

—— (1995) "Liberalization, privatization and women's employment in Jordan," paper prepared for the Seminar on Economic Liberalization and Women's Employment in the Middle East, Nicosia, November 10.

Kimura, H. (1987) "Hataraku onna no koe naki koe," *Gekkan Jiyu Minshu*, no. 412, July.

King, A. (1990) *Global Cities: Post-imperialism and the Internationalization of London*, London: Routledge.

—— (1993) "Identity and difference: the internationalization of capital and the globalization of culture," in P. Knox (ed.) *The Restless Urban Landscape*, New Jersey: Prentice-Hall, pp. 83–110.

—— (1995) "Re-presenting world cities: cultural theory/social practice," in P. Knox and P.J. Taylor (eds.) *World Cities in a World-System*, Cambridge: Cambridge University Press.

Klaus, V. (1991) *Cesta k tržní ekonomice (výber z článku, projevu a přednášek v zahraničí)/A Road to Market Economy (selected articles, speeches and lectures held abroad)*, Praha: Top Agency.

Knight, R. (1994) "Sewing up Central Europe's work force: Western companies hire cheap labor in former communist countries," *U.S. News & World Report* 24 August: 46.

Kobayashi, A. (ed.) (1994) *Women, Work, and Place*, Montreal: McGill-Queen's University Press.

Kofman, E. (1998) "Whose city? Gender, class and immigration," in R. Fincher and J. Jacobs (eds.) *Cities of Difference*, New York: Guildford.

—— (1999) "Female birds of passage a decade later: immigration and gender in the European Union," *International Migration Review*, 33 (2): 269–99.

Kofman, E. and Youngs, G. (eds.) (1996) *Globalization: Theory and Practice*, London: Pinter.

Kokusai Rengo (United Nations) (1995) *Sekai no Josei 1995: sono jittai to tokei*, Tokyo: Nihon Tokei Kyokai.

Kollonay, C. (forthcoming) "What's good is wrong? Women's rights in labour legislation," in ILO-Central and Eastern European Team (eds.) *Women in the World of Work: Women Workers' Rights in Hungary*, Budapest: ILO Publications.

Koser, K. and Salt, J. (1997) "The geography of highly skilled international migration," *International Journal of Population Geography* 3: 285–323.

"Koyō ni okeru danjo byōdō" (Roundtable) (1984) *Rōdō Jihō* 37, 5, May.

Krasner, S. (1994) "International political economy: abiding discord," *Review of International Political Economy* 1 (1): 13–20.

Kromhout, M. (1995) *Vrouwen en economische crisis: Een exploratief onderzoek naar genderverhoudingen in huishoudens in een arme woonwijk*, Paramaribo: Leo Victor.

Lampland, M. (1995) *Objects of Labor*, Chicago: University of Chicago Press.

Lapid, Y. and Kratochwil, F. (eds.) (1997) *The Return of Culture and Identity in IR Theory*, Boulder, Colorado: Lynne Rienner

Lash, S. and Urry, J. (1994) *Economies of Signs and Spaces*, London: Sage Publications.

Lechner, N. (ed.) (1982) *Qué significa hacer política?* Lima: DESCO.

Leidholdt D. (1996) "Sexual trafficking of women in Europe: a human rights crisis for the European Union," in R.A. Elman (ed.) *Sexual Politics and the European Union: The New Feminist Challenge*, Oxford: Bergahn.

León de Leal, M. (ed.) (1994) *Mujeres y participación política: avances y desafíos en America Latina*, Bogotá, Colombia: Tercer Mundo Editores.

Leslie, D.A. (1995) "Global scan: the globalization of advertising agencies, concepts, and campaigns," *Economic Geography* October: 402–26.

Leung, B.K.P. (1995) "Women and social change: the impact of industrialization on women in Hong Kong," in V. Pearson and B.K.P. Leung (eds.) *Women in Hong Kong*, Hong Kong: Oxford University Press.

Levens, M. and Chapman, D. (1997) "Suriname Education Sector Study," draft version. Prepared for the Inter American Development Bank. Academy for Educational Development.

Lidové Noviny (1998) "Zeny v Ceské Republice berou stale o čtvrtinu méne penéz než muži," 14 April: 1.

Lind, A. (1992) "Gender, power and development: popular women's organizations and the politics of needs in Ecuador," in A. Escobar and S. Alvarez (eds.) *The Making of Social Movements in Latin America*, Boulder, Colorado: Westview Press.

—— (1995) "Gender, development and women's political practices in Ecuador," unpublished PhD dissertation, Cornell University.

—— (1997) "Gender, development and urban social change: women's community action in global cities," *World Development* 25 (8) (August): 1205–23.

Ling, L.H.M. (1996a) "Democratization under internationalization: media reconstructions of gender identity in Shanghai," *Democratization* 3 (2): 140–57.

—— (1996b) "Hegemony and the internationalizing state: a postcolonial analysis of China's integration into Asian corporatism," *Review of International Political Economy* 3 (1): 1–26, Spring.

—— (1997) "The other side of globalization: hypermasculine developmentalism and media constructions of gender identity in East Asia," paper presented at the International Studies Association meeting, March 18–22 1997, Toronto, Canada.

Linz, J. and Stepan, A. (1996) *Problems of Democratic Transition and Consolidation: Southern Europe, South America and Post-communist Europe*, Baltimore: Johns Hopkins Press.

Lovenduski, J. (1994) "The political status of European Women," address to the seminar on Women's Participation in Political and Public Life, sponsored by the Council of Europe, Budapest, Hungary, November.

Lowe, L. and Lloyd, D. (1997) *The Politics of Culture in the Shadow of Capital*, Durham, NC and London: Duke University Press.

Luke, T. (1989) *Screens of Power*, Urbana: University of Illinois Press.

Lutz, H. (1993a) "Migrant women, racism and the Dutch labour market," in J. Wrench and J. Solomos (eds) *Racism and Migration in Western Europe in the 1990s*, London: Berg.

—— (1993b) "In between or bridging cultural gaps? Migrant women from Turkey as mediators," *New Community* 19 (3): 485–94.

Lyons, R. (1996) "Economic focus: labour costs," *Business Central Europe*, November.

McClintock, A. (1993) "Family feuds: gender, nationalism and the family," *Feminist Review* 44: 61–80.

McClune, E. (1998) "So how far have you come baby?," *Prague Tribune*, March.

McDowell, L. (1991) "Life without Father and Ford: the new gender order of post-Fordism," *Transactions of the Institute of British Geographers*, 16.

—— (1997) *Capital Cultures*, Oxford: Blackwells.

McDowell, L. and Court, G. (1994) "Gender divisions of labour in the post-Fordist economy: maintenance of occupational sex segregation in the financial services sector," *Environment and Planning* 26 (9): 1397–418.

Mangan, J.A. and Walvin, J. (eds.) (1987) *Manliness and Morality: Middle Class Masculinity in Britain and America 1800–1940*, Manchester: Manchester University Press.

Marchand, M.H. (1996) "Reconceptualizing 'gender and development' in an era of 'globalization,'" *Millennium* 25 (3): 577–604.

—— (1997) "Globalization versus global restructuring," *Connections* 7: 25–28.

—— (2000a) "Gendered representations of the 'global'; reading/writing globalization," in R. Stubbs and G. Underhill (eds.) *Political Economy and the Changing Global Order*, 2nd edn, Don Mills, Ontario: Oxford University Press Canada.

—— (2000b) "Some theoretical 'musings' about gender and resistance," in R. Teske and M. A. Tetreault (eds.) *Feminist Approaches to Social Movements, Community, and Power (Volume I)*, Columbia, SC: University of South Carolina Press.

Marchand, M.H. and Parpart, J.L. (eds.) (1995) *Feminism/Postmodernism/Development*, London: Routledge.

Marshall, D.D. (1996) "Understanding late-twentieth-century capitalism: reassessing the globalization theme," *Government and Opposition* 31 (Spring): 193–215.

Massey, D. (1994) *Space, Place and Gender*, Cambridge: Polity.

—— (1995) *Spatial Divisions of Labour: Social Structures and the Geography of Production*, 2nd edn., London: Macmillan.

Massey, D. *et al.* (1993) "Theories of international migration: a review and appraisal," *Population and Development Review* 19 (3): 432–66.

Matynia, E. (1995) "Finding a voice: women in Central Europe," in A. Basu (ed.) *The Challenge of Local Feminisms: Women' Movements in Global Perspective*, Boulder, Colorado: Westview Press.

Mazur, A.G. (1996) *Gender Bias and the State: Symbolic Reform at Work in Fifth Republic France*, Pittsburgh, PA: University of Pittsburgh Press.

Melucci, A. (1997) "Identity and difference in a globalized world," in P. Werbner and T. Modood (eds.) *Debating Cultural Hybridity: Multi-Cultural Identities and the Politics of Anti-Racism*, London: Zed Books.

Menéndez-Carrión, A. (1994) "Ciudadanía," in A. Acosta (ed.) *Lexico Político Ecuatoriano*, Quito: ILDIS.

Menke, J. (1994) "Survey van de armoedesituatie in Suriname. Onderzoeksrapport voor de Caribbean Conference of Churches (CCC)," Paramaribo.

—— (1998) *Restructuring urban employment and poverty. The case of Suriname* (PhD thesis), Acadeisch proefschrift, Paramaribo: SWI Press.

Menon, R. (1996) "Beijing's lessons," book review of "The challenge of local feminisms: women's movements in global perspective," *The Women's Review of Books* 13 (12): 15–16.

Mercer, K. and Julien, I. (1988) "Race, sexual politics and black masculinity: a dossier," in R. Chapman and J. Rutherford (eds.) *Male Order: Unwrapping Masculinity*, London: Lawrence and Wishart.

Mernissi, F. (1993) *Islam and Democracy: Fear of the Modern World*, London: Virago Press.

Meyer, M.K. and Prugl, E. (eds.) (1999) *Gender Politics and Global Governance*, Lanham, MD: Rowman and Littlefield Publishers.

Mies, M. (1986) *Patriarchy and Accumulation on a World Scale: Women in the International Division of Labour*, London: Zed Books.

Mies, M. and Shiva, V. (1993) *Ecofeminism*, London: Zed Books.

Miles, R. (1990) "Whatever happened to the sociology of migration?" *Work, Employment and Society* 4 (2): 281–98.

Millett, K. (1977) *Sexual Politics*, London: Virago.

Ministry of Labor (1993) "Arbeidsmarkt Informatie," Paramaribo, Suriname.

—— (1996) "Arbeidsmarkt Informatie," Paramaribo, Suriname.

Mische, A. (1993) "Post-communism's 'lost treasure': subjectivity and gender in a shifting public sphere," *Praxis International* 13 (3) (October): 243–67.

"Misshitsu no kōbō" (1985) *Agora*, no. 100.

Mittelman, J.H. (1996) "The dynamics of globalization," in J.H. Mittelman (ed.) *Globalization: Critical Reflections*, Boulder, Colorado: Lynne Rienner Publishers.

Mitter, S. (1986) *Common Fate, Common Bond: Women in the Global Economy*, London: Pluto Press.

Moghadam, V.M. (1990) "Gender and restructuring: Perestroika, the 1989 revolutions and women," Helsinki: UNU/WIDER working paper no. 87.

—— (ed.) (1992) *Privatization and Democratization in Central and Eastern Europe and the Soviet Union: The Gender Dimension*, World Institute for Development. Economics Research of the United Nations University.

—— (ed.) (1993a) *Democratic Reform and the Position of Women in Transitional Economies*, Oxford: Clarendon Press.

—— (1993b) *Modernizing Women: Gender and Social Change in the Middle East*, Boulder, Colorado: Lynne Rienner Publishers.

—— (1995b) "Gender dynamics of restructuring in the semiperiphery," in R. Lesser Blumberg *et al.* (eds.) *EnGendering Wealth and Well-being*, Boulder, Colorado: Westview Press.

—— (1995c) "Market reforms and women's economic status: Eastern Europe, Russia, Vietnam and China," *Development* (Special Issue prepared for the Fourth World Conference on Women), no. 1: 61–6.

—— (1996a) "The feminization of poverty? Notes on a concept and trends," paper prepared for the Human Development Report Office, UNDP (September).

—— (1996b) "Patriarchy and post-communism: Eastern Europe and the former Soviet Union," in V.M. Moghadam (ed.) *Patriarchy and Development: Women's Positions at the End of the Twentieth Century*, Oxford: Clarendon Press.

—— (1998) *Women, Work, and Economic Reform in the Middle East and North Africa*, Boulder, Colorado: Lynne Rienner Publishers.

—— (1999) "Women and citizenship: reflections on the Middle East and North Africa," *Civil Society* 8 (88) (April): 9–15.

Mohanty, C.T. (1991a) "Under Western eyes: feminist scholarship and colonial discourses," in C.T. Mohanty, A. Russo, and L. Torres (eds.) *Third World Women and the Politics of Feminism*, Bloomington: Indiana University Press.

—— (1991b) "Introduction," in C.T. Mohanty, A. Russo and L. Torres (eds.) *Third World Women and the Politics of Feminism*, Bloomington: Indiana University Press.

Mohanty, C.T., Russo, A, and Torres, L. (eds.) (1991) *Third World Women and the Politics of Feminism*, Bloomington: Indiana University Press.

Molyneux, M. (1994) "Women's rights and the international context: some reflections on the post-Communist states," *Millennium* 23 (2): 287–313.

—— (1995) "Review essay: 'gendered transitions in Eastern Europe,'" *Feminist Studies* 21 (3) (Fall): 639–46.

Morawska E. and Spohn W. (1997) "Moving European in the globalizing world: contemporary migrations in a historical-comparative perspective (1955–94 v. 1870–1914)," in W. Gungwu (ed.) *Global History and Migrations*, Oxford: Westview Press.

Morgan, D.H.J. (1992) *Discovering Men*, London: Routledge.

Morokvasic, M. (1984) "Birds of passage are also women," *International Migration Review* 18 (4): 886–907.

—— (1991) "Roads to independence: self-employed immigrants and minority women in five European States," *International Migration* 29 (3): 407–20.

—— (1993) "'In and out' of the labour market: immigrant and minority women in Europe," *New Community* 19 (3): 459–84.

Morokvasic, M. and de Tinguy, A. (1993) "Between East and West: a new migratory space," in H. Rudolph and M. Morokvasic (eds.) *Bridging States and Markets: International Migration in the Early 1990s*, Berlin: Sigma.

Moser, C. (1993) *Gender Planning and Development*, Routledge, London.

Možný, I. (1991) *Proč tak snado – některé rodinné důvody sametové revoluce* (Why so easy – some family reasons for the velvet revolution), Praha: Slon.

—— (1994) "The Czech family in transition: from social to economic capital," in S. Ringen and C. Wallace (eds.) *Social Reform in the Czech Republic, Prague Papers on Social Responses to Transformation*, vol. II, Praha.

Multi-Annual Development Programme (MADP) (1994–1998) *Suriname op een keerpunt*, Paramaribo.

Muñoz Jaramillo, F. (ed.) (1998) *Asamblea … análisis y proprestas*, Quito: Tramasocial Edutorial.

Muramatsu, T. (1978) "Ichi ni sekininkan, ni ni 'shikōryoku,'" *Gekkan Jiyu Minshu* no. 268, May.

Murphy, C.N. and Rojas de Ferro, C. (1995) "The power of representation in international political economy," *Review of International Political Economy* 2 (1): 63–183.

Murphy, C.N. and Tooze, R. (1991a) "Getting beyond the 'common sense' of the IPE orthodoxy," in C.N. Murphy and R. Tooze (eds.) *The New International Political Economy*, Boulder, Colorado: Lynne Reinner Publishers.

Muslim Brotherhood (1994) *The Muslim Brotherhood*, Cairo.

Muus, P. (1994) "South to north migration," *Proceedings of the Experts Meeting on Population Distribution and Migration*, Cairo: UN Conference.

Nash, J. and Fernandez-Kelly, M.P. (eds.) (1983) *Women, Men, and the International Division of Labor*, Albany: State University of New York Press.

National Planning Office (1995) *Social and Economic Development of Suriname*, Paramaribo, Suriname.

New Community (1996) "Globalisation and ethnic divisions in European cities," 22, 4.

Ng, C.H. (1995) "Bringing women back in: family change in Hong Kong," in V. Pearson and B.K.P. Leung (eds.) *Women in Hong Kong*, Hong Kong: Oxford University Press.

Nicholls, A. (1999) "Welcome to Silicon Valley," *Business Central Europe*, February.

Nicholson, L.J. (ed.) (1990) *Feminism/Postmodernism*, London: Routledge.

O'Donnell, G, Schmitter, P.C., and Whitehead, L. (eds.) (1986) *Transition from Authoritarianism: Prospects for Democracy*, Baltimore: Johns Hopkins Press.

Office of National Statistics (1997) *International Passenger Survey*, London: HMSO.

Ofreneo, R.E. (1993) "Structural adjustment and labour market responses in the Philippines," in M. Muqtada and A. Hildiman (eds.) *Labour Markets and Human Resource Planning in Asia: Perspectives and Evidence*, Geneva: International Labour Organization.

Ojeda Segovia, L. (1993) *El descrédito de lo social: las políticas sociales en el Ecuador*, Quito: Centro para el Desarrollo Social (CDS).

Ohmae, K. (1990) *Borderless World*, New York: Harper Collins.

Okin, S.M. (1979) *Women in Western Political Thought*, Princeton, NJ: Princeton University Press.

Olea, R. (1995) "Feminism: modern or postmodern?" in J. Beverley *et al.* (eds.) *The Postmodernism Debate in Latin America*, Durham, NC: Duke University Press.

Ong, A. (1987) *Spirits of Resistance and Capitalist Discipline: Factory Workers in Malaysia*, Albany: State University of New York Press.

—— (1991) "The gender and labor politics of postmodernity," *Annual Review of Anthropology* 20: 279–309.

Open Media Research Institute (1997) "Report on Eastern Europe," 6 August.

Orenstein, M. (1996) "Out of the red: building capitalism and democracy in postcommunist Europe," PhD dissertation, Yale University.

—— (1998) "Václav Klaus: revolutionary and parliamentarian," *East European Constitutional Review* 7 (1): 46–55.

Pateman, C. (1988) *The Sexual Contract*, Stanford: Stanford University Press; Cambridge: Polity.

—— (1989) *The Disorder of Women: Democracy, Feminism and Politcal Theory*, Stanford: Stanford University Press.

Paukert, L. (1991) "The economic status of women in the transition to a market system: the case of Czechoslovakia," *International Labor Review* 130 (5/6): 613–33.

—— (1995) "Economic transition and women's employment in four Central European countries, 1989–1994," *Labour Market Papers No. 7*, Geneva: International Labour Organization.

—— (1995) "Privatization and employment: labour transfer policies and practices in the Czech Republic," *Labour Market Papers No. 4*, Geneva: International Labour Organization.

Peach, C. (1996) *Ethnicity in the 1991 Census*, vol. 2, London: HMSO.

Pearson, R. (1997) "Renegotiating the reproductive bargain: gender analysis of economic transition in Cuba in the 1990s," *Development and Change* 28: 671–705.

Pearson, V. and Leung, B.K.P. (1995a) "Introduction: perspectives on women's issues in Hong Kong," in V. Pearson and B.K.P. Leung (eds.) *Women in Hong Kong*, Hong Kong: Oxford University Press.

—— (eds.) (1995b) *Women in Hong Kong*, Hong Kong: Oxford University Press.

Pehe, Jirí (1997) "Czech government braces itself for vote of confidence," *Open Media Research Institute News, 10* June.

Pellerin, H. (1996) "Global restructuring and international migration: consequences for the globalization of politics," in E. Kofman and G. Youngs (eds.) *Globalization: Theory and Practice*, London: Pinter.

Pesman, R. (1996) *Duty Free*, Melbourne: Oxford University Press.

Peterson, V.S. (ed.) (1992a) *Gendered States: (Re)Visions of International Relations Theory*, Boulder, Colorado: Lynne Rienner Publishers.

—— (1992b) "Transgressing boundaries: theories of knowledge, gender, and international relations," *Millennium: Journal of International Studies* 21: 183–206.

—— (1995) "Reframing the politics of identity: democracy, globalization and gender," *Political Expressions* 1 (1): 1–16.

—— (1996) "Shifting ground(s): epistemological and territorial remapping in the context of globalization(s)," in E. Kofman and G. Youngs (eds.) *Globalization: Theory and Practice*, London: Pinter.

—— (1997) "Whose crisis? early and post-modern masculinism," in S. Gill and J.H. Mittelman (eds.) *Innovation and Transformation in International Studies*, Cambridge: Cambridge University Press.

Peterson, V.S. and Runyan, A.S. (1993 and 1999) *Global Gender Issues*, 1st and 2nd edns., Boulder, Colorado: Westview Press.

Pettman, J.J. (1996a) "An international political economy of sex?" in E. Kofman and G. Youngs (eds.) *Globalization: Theory and Practice*, London: Pinter.

—— (1996b) *Worlding Women: A Feminist International Politics*, London: Routledge.

—— (1998) "Women on the move: globalisation and labour migration from South and Southeast Asian States," *Global Society* 12 (3): 389–404.

Phillips, A. (1991) *Engendering Democracy*, Cambridge: Polity.

Phizacklea, A. (1983) *One Way Ticket*, London: Routledge and Kegan Paul.

Platform for Action and Beijing Declaration (1996) New York: United Nations Department of Public Information.

Poznanski, K.Z. (1998) "Rethinking comparative economics: from organizational simplicity to institutional complexity," *East European Politics and Societies* 12 (1): 171–99.

Prime Minister's Office (1994) *Josei no Genjō to Shisaku*.

Qutb, M. (1991) *Tahrir al-Mar'a* (The Liberation of Woman) (in Arabic), Cairo: Maktabet Al-Sunna.

Radcliffe, S. and Westwood, S. (eds.) (1993) *'Viva': Women and Popular Protest in Latin America*, London: Routledge.

—— (1996) *Remaking the Nation: Place, Identity and Politics in Latin America*, London: Routledge.

Randall, V. (1987) *Women and Politics: An International Perspective*, London: Macmillan Education.

Reich, R. (1992) *The Work of Nations*, New York: Vintage Books.

Research Institute for Labour and Social Affairs (1998) *Main Economic and Social Indicators of the Czech Republic, 1990–98*, no. 11, Praha.

Robertson, R. (1990) "Mapping the global condition: globalization as the central concept," in M. Featherstone (ed.) *Global Culture: Nationalism, Globalization and Modernity*, London: Sage.

—— (1992) *Globalization: Social Theory and Global Culture*, London: Sage.

Rodríguez, L. (1994) "Barrio women: between the urban and the feminist movement," *Latin American Perspectives* 21 (3) (Summer): 32–48.

Rona-Tas, A. (1998) "Path-dependence and capital theory: sociology of the post-communist economic transformation," *East European Politics and Societies* 12 (1): 107–25.

Roper, M. and Tosh, J. (eds.) (1991) *Masculinities in Britain since 1800*, London: Routledge.

Rosca, N. (1995) "'The Philippines' shameful export," *The Nation*, 17 April: 522–7.

Rosen, R. (1990) "Male democracies, female dissidents," *Tikkun* 5 (6): 11–12, 100–1.

Rosenau, J. (1990) *Turbulence in World Politics*, Brighton: Harvester Wheatsheaf.

Rosenau, P.M. (1992) *Postmodernism and Social Sciences: Insights, Inroads, and Intrusions*, Princeton, New Jersey: Princeton University Press.

Rosow, S.J., Inayatullah, N., and Rupert, M. (eds.) (1994) *The Global Economy of Political Space*, Boulder, Colorado: Lynne Rienner Publishers.

Rowbotham, S. (1974) *Women, Resistance, and Revolution*, New York: Vintage Books.

Rowbotham, S. and Mitter, S. (1994) *Dignity and Daily Bread*, London: Routledge.

Rudolph, H. (1996) "The new Gastarbeiter system in Germany," *New Community* 22 (2): 287–300.

Rueschemeyer, M. (ed.) (1998) *Women in the Politics of Post-Communist Eastern Europe*, 2nd edn., London: M.E. Sharpe Inc.

Runyan, A.S. (1996) "The places of women in trading places: gendered global/regional regimes and internationalized feminist resistance," in E. Kofman and G. Youngs (eds.) *Globalization: Theory and Practice*, London: Pinter.

—— (1997) "Gender and gendered regimes: systems to revise," in E. Haxton and C. Olsson (eds.) *Women and Sustainability in International Trade*, Uppsala, Sweden: Global Publications Foundation.

Rutland, P. (1993) "Thatcherism Czech-style: transition to capitalism in the Czech Republic," *Telos* 94: 103–31.

Sachs, Jeffrey (1994) *Poland's Jump to a Market Economy*, Cambridge, Mass.: MIT Press.

Safa, H. (1981) "Runaway shops and female employment: the search for cheap labor," *Signs* 7: 418–33.

—— (1995) *The myth of the male breadwinner: women and industrialization in the Caribbean*, Boulder, Colorado: Westview Press.

Sassen, S. (1991) *The Global City: New York, London, Tokyo*, Princeton, NJ: Princeton University Press.

—— (1994) *Cities in a World Economy*, Thousand Oaks, California: Pine Forge Press.

—— (1995) "Analytic borderlands: race, gender and representation in the new city," in A. King (ed.) *Re-presenting the City: Ethnicity, Capital and Culture in the 21st Century Metropolis*, London: Macmillan.

—— (1996) "New employment regimes in cities: the impact on immigrant workers," *New Community* 22 (4): 579–94.

—— (1998) *Globalization and its Discontents*, New York: The New Press.

Sassen-Koob, S. (1984) "Notes on the incorporation of Third World women into wage-labor through immigration and off-shore production," *International Migration Review* 13: 1144–67.

Schalkwijk, A. and de Bruijne, A. (1994) *Kondreman en P'tata: Nederland als referentiekader voor Surinamers*, Paramaribo: Leo Victor.

—— (1997 and 1999) *Van Mon Plaisir tot Ephraïmszegen. Welstand, etniciteit en woonpatronen in Paramaribo*, 1st and 2nd edns, Paramaribo: Leo Victor.

Schild, V. (1991) "Gender, class and politics: poor neighborhood organizing in authoritarian Chile," PhD dissertation, University of Toronto.

—— (1998) "New subjects of rights? Women's movements and the construction of citizenship in the 'new democracies'", in S. Alvarez, E. Dagnino, and A. Escobar (eds.) *Cultures of Politics/Politics of Cultures: Revisioning Latin American Social Movements*, Boulder, Colorado: Westview Press.

Schmitter, P.C. and Karl, T.L. (1991) "Modes of transition in Latin America, Southern Europe and Eastern Europe," *International Social Science Journal* 43: 269–84.

Schipper, W. (1994) *Je komt niet uit maar je moet. Hoe schoonmaaksters op scholen in Paramaribo hun bestaansverwerving organiseren*, Paramaribo: Leo Victor.

Scholte, J.A. (1996) "Beyond the buzzword: towards a critical theory of globalization," in E. Kofman and G. Youngs (eds.) *Globalization: Theory and Practice*, London: Pinter.

Scott, J.W., Kaplan, C., and Keates, D. (eds.) (1997) *Transitions, Environments, Translations: Feminism in International Politics*, New York and London: Routledge.

Segal, L. (1990) *Slow Motion: Changing Masculinities, Changing Men*, London: Virago.

Segarra, M. (1997) "Redefining the public/private mix: NGOs and the Emergency Social Investment Fund in Ecuador," in Douglas Chalmers *et al.* (eds.) *The New Politics of Inequality in Latin America*, Oxford: Oxford University Press.

Seidler J. (1989) *Rediscovering Masculinity: Reason, Language and Sexuality*, London: Routledge.

Seifert, W. (1996) "Occupational and social integration of immigrant groups in Germany," *New Community* 22 (3): 417–36.

Sen, A. (1990) "Gender and cooperative conflicts," in I. Tinker (ed.) *Persistent Inequalities: Women and World Development*, New York and Oxford: Oxford University Press.

Sen, G. (1995) "The lessons of Cairo," in *Reproductive Health Matters*.

—— (1996) "Gender, markets and states: a selective review and research agenda," *World Development* 24 (5): 821–9.

—— (1997) "Globalization in the 21st Century: Challenges for Civil Society," University of Amsterdam Development Lecture, University of Amsterdam, The Netherlands, June 20.

Sen, G. and Grown, C. (1987) *Development, Crises and Alternative Visions: Third World Women's Perspectives*, New York: Monthly Review Press.

Shaban, R., Assaad, R., and Al-Qudsi, S.S. (1995), "The challenge of unemployment in the Arab region," *International Labour Review* 135 (1): 65–81.

Shakhatreh, H. (1995) "Determinants of female labor force participation in Jordan," in N. Khoury and V.M. Moghadam (eds.) *Gender and Development in the Arab World*, London: Zed Books, pp. 125–47.

Shen, J. (1994) "Czech women face gender gap in banking," *Journal of Commerce and Commercial* 8 February, 399, 28: 8A1.

Shinoda, T. (1986) "Danjo kōyō kikai kintō hō o meguru ishikettei" (Decisionmaking over the EEOL), in N. Minoru (ed.) *Nihon gata Seisaku Kettei no Hen'yō*, Tokyo: Keizai Shinpō-sha.

Šiklová, J. (1992) "Are women in Central and Eastern Europe Conservative?," in N. Funk and M. Mueller (eds.) *Gender Politics and Post-Communism*, New York and London: Routledge.

Simpson, M. (1994) *Male Impersonators*, London: Cassell.

Smejkalova-Strictland, J. (1993) "Do Czech women need feminism? Perspectives of feminist theories," in S. Trinka and L. Bushkin (eds.) *Bodies of Bread and Butter: Reconfiguring Women's Lives in the PostCommunist Czech Republic*, Prague: Centre for Gender Studies.

Snitow, A. (1993) "Feminist futures in the former Eastern Bloc," *Peace and Democracy News*, VII (1) (Summer): 39–44.

SOPEMI (1998) *Trends in International Migration: Annual Report 1997*, Paris: OECD.

"Sovereignty at Bay: An Agenda for the 1990s" (1991) (Special Section), *Millennium* 20 (2): 189–307.

Spain, D. (1992) *Gendered Spaces*, Chapel Hill and London: University of North Carolina Press.

Speckman, J.D. (1965) *Marriage and Kinship among the Indians in Surinam*, PhD dissertation, Assen: Van Gorcum.

Spivak, G.C. (1988) "Can the subaltern speak?," in C. Nelson and L. Grossberg (eds.) *Marxism and the Interpretation of Culture*, Chicago: University of Illinois Press.

Spurr, D. (1993) *The Rhetoric of Empire*, Durham, North Carolina: Duke University Press.

Standing, G. (1989) "Global feminization through flexible labour," *World Development* 17 (7): 1077–95.

—— (1998a) "Societal impoverishment: the challenge for Russian social policy," *Journal of European Social Policy* 8 (1): 23–43.

—— (1998b) "The babble of euphemisms: re-embedding social protection in 'transformed' labour markets," draft paper, ILO: Geneva.

Stark, D. and Bruszt, L. (1997) *Postsocialist Pathways: Transforming Politics and Property in East Central Europe*, Cambridge: Cambridge University Press.

Št'atsná, J. (1994) "Female entrepreneurs in the Czech Republic," unpublished research, Central European University, Prague.

—— (1995) "New opportunities in the Czech Republic," *Transitions* 1, 16 (8 September).

Steans, J. (1998) *Gender and International Relations*, Cambridge, UK: Polity Press.

Stearns, P.N. (1979) *Be a Man: Males in Modern Society*, London: Holmes and Meier.

Stienstra, D. (1994) *Women's Movements and International Organizations*, Basingstoke: Macmillan.

Storkey, M. and Lewis, R. (1997) "London a true cosmopolis," in P. Ratcliffe (ed.) *Ethnicity in the 1991 Census. Social Geography and Ethnicity in Britain: Geographical Spread, Spatial Concentration and Internal Migration*, vol. 3, London: HMSO.

Strange, S. (1986) *Casino Capitalism*, Oxford: Blackwell.

—— (1990) "Finance, information and power," *Review of International Studies* 16 (3): 259–74.

—— (1994) "Wake up, Krasner! The world *has* changed," *Review of International Political Economy* 2: 209–20.

—— (1996) *The Retreat of the State*, Cambridge, UK: Cambridge University Press.

—— (1998) *Mad Money*, Manchester: Manchester University Press.

Szalai, J. (1995) "Women and democratization: some notes on recent changes in hungary," unpublished paper.

—— (1997) "Two studies on changing gender relations in post-1989 Hungary," Discussion Paper No. 30, Collegium Budapest/Institute for Advanced Study, Budapest, Hungary.

Tarrés, M.L. (1997) "Movimiento e institucionalización: La difícil integración de los proyectos y las estrategias políticas de las ONG's feministas en los sistemas políticos," paper presented at the XX Congress of the Latin American Studies Association (LASA), Guadalajara, Mexico, April.

Tarrow, S. (1994) *Power in Movement: Social Movements, Collective Action and Politics*, Cambridge, UK: Cambridge University Press.

Taylor, D. (1997) *Disappearing Acts: Spectacles of Gender and Nationalism in Argentina's "Dirty War,"* Durham, North Carolina: Duke University Press.

Thrift, N. (1992) "Muddling through: world orders and globalization," *The Professional Geographer* 44: 3–7.

—— (1994) "On the social and cultural determinants of international financial centres: the case of the City of London," in S. Corbridge, N. Thrift, and R. Martin (eds.) *Money, Power and Space*, Oxford: Blackwell.

Tiano, S. (1994) *Patriarchy on the Line: Labor, Gender, and Ideology in the Mexican Maquila Industry*, Philadelphia: Temple University Press.

Tickner, J.A. (1991) "On the fringes of the world economy: a feminist perspective," in C.N. Murphy and R. Tooze (eds.) *The New International Political Economy*, Boulder, Colorado: Lynne Rienner Publishers.

—— (1992) *Gender in International Relations: Feminist Perspectives on Achieving Global Security*, New York: Columbia University Press.

Tierney, M. (1995) "Negotiating a software career: informal work practices and 'The Lads' in a software installation," in K. Grint and R. Gill (eds.) *The Gender–Technology Relation: Contemporary Theory and Research*, London: Taylor & Francis.

Tong, R. (1989) *Feminist Thought*, Boulder, Colorado: Westview Press.

Tribalat, M. (1995) *Faire France*, Paris: LaDcouverte.

Tripp, A.M. (1997) *Changing the Rules: The Politics of Liberalization and the Urban Informal Economy in Tanzania*, Berkeley: University of California Press.

True, J. (1999) "Expanding markets and marketing gender: The integration of the post-socialist Czech Republic," *Review of International Political Economy* 6, 3.

United Nations (UN) (1995) *The World's Women 1995: Trends and Statistics*, New York: United Nations Publications.

United Nations Conference on Trade and Development (UNCTAD) (1996) *World Investment Report: Investment, Trade and International Policy Arrangments*, New York: United Nations.

United Nations Development Programme (UNDP) (1996) *Human Development Report*, Oxford and New York: Oxford University Press.

—— (1997) *Human Development Report*, Oxford and New York: Oxford University Press.

Upham, F.K. (1987) *Law and Social Change in Postwar Japan*, Cambridge, Mass.: Harvard University Press.

Valdés, T. (1994) "Movimiento de mujeres y producción de conocimientos de género: Chile, 1978–1989," in M. Léon (ed.) *Mujeres y participación: avances y desafíos en America Latina*, Bogotá, Colombia: Tercer Mundo Editores.

van der Pijl, K. (1998) *Transnational Classes and International Relations*, London: Routledge.

Večerník, J., Hraba, J., and McCutcheon, A.L. (1997) Zivotni šance mužu a žen v odobí transformace: Srovnáni Ceské a Slovenské republiky," *Sociologický časopis* 33 (4): 405–21.

Verrest, H. (1998) "Je Diploma is Je Eerste Man. Takenpakketten en sociale netwerken van dochters als bestaansverwervingsstrategieën van huishoudens in Paramaribo, Suriname," Doctoral scriptie (Master's thesis), Universiteit van Amsterdam.

Vickers, J. (1991) *Women and the World Economic Crisis*, London: Zed Books.

Walby, S. (1990) *Theorizing Patriarchy*, Oxford: Blackwell.

Walker, R.B.J. (1993) *Inside/Outside: International Relations as Political Theory*, Cambridge: Cambridge University Press.

Ward, K. (ed.) (1990) *Women Workers and Global Restructuring*, Ithaca: Cornell University ILR Press.

Waters, M. (1995) *Globalization*, London and New York: Routledge.

Watson, H. (1994) "Women and the veil: personal responses to global process," in A. Ahmed and H. Donnan (eds.) *Islam, Globalization and Postmodernity*, London: Routledge.

Watson, P. (1993a) "Eastern Europe's silent revolution: gender," *Sociology* 27, 3, (August).

—— (1993b) "The rise of masculinism in Eastern Europe," *New Left Review* 198 (March/April).

—— (1994) "Explaining rising mortality rates among men in Eastern Europe," paper presented at ESRC Seminar on "Gender, Class and Ethnicity in Eastern Europe", University of London.

Waylen, G. (1994) "Women and democratisation: conceptualising gender relations in transition politics," *World Politics* 46: 327–54.

Weedon, C. (1987) *Feminist Practice and Poststructuralist Theory*, Oxford: Blackwell.

Wekker, G. (1994) *Ik ben een gouden munt. Ik ga door vele handen maar verlies mijn waarde niet Subjectiviteit en seksualiteit van Creoolse volkslasse vrouwen in Paramaribo*, Amsterdam: Vita.

Welfens, P.J.J. (1989) "The globalization of markets and regional integration," *Intereconomics* November/December: 273–81.

Whitworth, S. (1994a) *Feminism and International Relations: Towards a Political Economy of Gender in Interstate and Non-Governmental Institutions*, London: Macmillan.

—— (1994b) "Theory as exclusion: gender and international political economy," in R. Stubbs and G.R.D. Underhill (eds.) *Political Economy and the Changing Global Order*, London: Macmillan.

WIDE (Women and Development Europe), (NAC) National Action Committee – Canada, Alt-WID (Alternatives for Women in Development), CRIAW (Canadian Research Institute for the Advancement of Women) (1994) "Wealth of nations – poverty of women," framework paper prepared for "Globalization of the Economy and Economic Justice for Women" workshop, NGO Forum of the ECE Regional Preparatory Meeting for the Fourth World Conference for Women, Vienna, Austria, 13–15 October.

Williamson, J. (1986) "Woman on an island: femininity and colonisation," in T. Modelski (ed.) *Studies in Entertainment: Critical Approaches to Mass Culture*, Bloomington: Indiana University Press.

Wolchik, S. (1994) "Women and the politics of transition in the Czech and Slovak Republics," in M. Rueschemeyer (ed.) *Women in the Politics of Post-Communist Eastern Europe*, London: M.E. Sharpe Inc.

Wollstonecraft, M. (1985) (first published 1792) *Vindication of the Rights of Woman*, Harmondsworth: Penguin.

"Women and Development: The Wellesley Conference" (1997) *ISIS International Bulletin* 3 (April): 17–19.

Women's Environment and Development Organization (WEDO) (1995a) "Take the brackets off women's lives: Women's Linkage Caucus Advisory Chart," New York: WEDO.

—— (1995b) "Transnational corporations at the UN: using or abusing their access?" New York: WEDO.

"Women's Network on Global Corporations Forums" (1980) *AFSC Women's Newsletter* (Summer): 9–14.

Wong, T.W.P. (1995) "Women and work: opportunities and experiences," in V. Pearson and B.K.P. Leung (eds.) *Women in Hong Kong*, Hong Kong: Oxford University Press.

World Bank (1994a) "Egypt: labor reform and structural adjustment," October.

—— (1994b) *Hashemite Kingdom of Jordan Poverty Assessment. Volume II: Labor Market*, Washington, DC: The World Bank, 28 October.

—— (1995) *Jordan, Trends in Developing Economies 1995*, Washington, DC: The World Bank.

—— (1998) *World Development Indicators 1998*, Washington, DC: The World Bank.

Yassin, A. (1988) "In search of a new identity of the social sciences in the Arab world: discourse, paradigm, and strategy," in H. Sharabi (ed.) *The Next Arab Decade: Alternative Futures*, Boulder, Colorado: Westview Press and London: Mansell Publishing Limited.

Yoneda, T. (1977) "Kinro fujin fukushiho no zensen o yuku," *Gekkan Jiyu Minshu* no. 253, February.

Youngs, G. (1996a) "Beyond the 'inside/outside' divide," in J. Krause and N. Renwick (eds.) *Identities in International Relations*, London: Macmillan.

—— (1996b) "Political economy of spatiality: gender, power and conceptualizing globalization," paper presented at International Studies Association Annual Conference, San Diego, 16–20 April.

—— (1999) *International Relations in a Global Age: A Conceptual Challenge*, Cambridge, UK: Polity.

"Zadankai, danjo byōdō kintō hō" (Roundtable) (1984) *Fujin to Nenshōsha* no. 222, September.

Zalewski, M. and Parpart, J. (eds.) (1998) *The "Man" Question in International Relations*, Boulder, Colorado: Westview Press.

Zemplínerová, A. (1997) "The role of foreign enterprises in the privatization and restructuring of the Czech economy," WIW Research Report No. 238, The Vienna Institute for Comparative Economic Studies.

Index